OTHER BOOKS BY GEORGE F. WILL

THE LEVELING WIND:
POLITICS, CULTURE AND OTHER NEWS, 1990–1994

RESTORATION:
CONGRESS, TERM LIMITS AND THE RECOVERY OF DELIBERATIVE DEMOCRACY

SUDDENLY:
THE AMERICAN IDEA ABROAD AND AT HOME, 1986–1990

MEN AT WORK:
THE CRAFT OF BASEBALL

THE NEW SEASON:
A SPECTATOR'S GUIDE TO THE 1988 ELECTION

THE MORNING AFTER:
AMERICAN SUCCESSES AND EXCESSES, 1981–1986

STATECRAFT AS SOULCRAFT:
WHAT GOVERNMENT DOES

THE PURSUIT OF VIRTUE AND OTHER TORY NOTIONS

THE PURSUIT OF HAPPINESS, AND OTHER SOBERING THOUGHTS

The Woven Figure

CONSERVATISM AND
AMERICA'S FABRIC, 1994–1997

GEORGE F. WILL

SCRIBNER

SCRIBNER
1230 Avenue of the Americas
New York, NY 10020

Copyright © 1997 George F. Will

SCRIBNER and design are trademarks of Simon & Schuster, Inc.

DESIGNED BY ERICH HOBBING

Set in Caledonia

Manufactured in the United States of America

1   3   5   7   9   10   8   6   4   2

Library of Congress Cataloging-in-Publication Data is available.

ISBN 0-684-82562-7

Permissions are on page 384.

"But I cannot deny my past to which myself is wed
The woven figure cannot undo its thread."

—Louis MacNeice,
Valediction

ACKNOWLEDGMENTS

This is the sixth collection of my columns and other writings, and the pleasure of the process increases with the proficiency of those who participate. They include Bill Rosen of Scribner, a fine editor but not otherwise vicious; Alan Shearer and Anna Karavangelos, two reasons for the high reputation of the Washington Post Writers Group; Maynard Parker who edits *Newsweek* and Olwen Clarke of *Newsweek* who edits me, both of whom improve my work. In a world in flux, my office isn't, because Dusa Gyllensvard and Mary Longnecker cannot be improved upon. The functioning of the office has recently been better than ever because of the work of three of Georgetown University's finest—Jed Donahue, Christopher Cillizza, and Seth Meehan.

Contents

Introduction 17

CHAPTER ONE

From the Whirring Loom

The Tyranny of Nonchalance 25

With Friends Like These 27

The Food and Drug Administration vs. "Family Discord" 29

Sheldon Hackney Teaches Talking 31

Neo-Paternalism and the Battered Woman Syndrome 33

Sex in Sacramento 35

Tears and Chinese Take-Out Food at Tufts 37

The Sensitivity Sweepstakes at Chico 39

Anti-Americanism at the Smithsonian 41

Of Metal Dollars and Males Bonding with Strippers 43

Baby Boomers, So Elevated in Every Way . . . 45

A Heartbreak Hunk and a Nice Prom 47

At Melissa Drexler's Prom 49

Choice 51

Fanatics for "Choice" 54

Eventful 1965 56

"Sixties Idealism" and "Psychedelic Optimism" 65

Understanding the Sixties: Begin with Barry 67

1994: Tacky Royalty and Tonya Harding 72

1995: Oh, a Revolution 74

1996: In Our Wee Galaxy 76

CONTENTS

CHAPTER TWO
CONSERVATISM'S SEVERAL THREADS

An Epithet No More   79
Contra Croly   84
The Fourth Awakening   86
The Politics of Soulcraft   89
1828 and 1971   91
The Agrarian Movement Against Modernity   93
A Course Correction in the Capital of Liberalism   95
Big Government in the Black Canyon   98
The Cultural Contradictions of Conservatism   100

CHAPTER THREE
SOCIETY FRAYED AND MENDED

Oklahoma City: From the Fevered Minds of Marginal Men   113
Anti-Fascism in Phoenix   115
The Abstract Compassion of "Gladiators for Liberation"   117
Law and the Making of a Scofflaw Nation   119
Connoisseurs of Conflict   121
"Extreme Fighting" and the Morals of the Marketplace   123
The Crisis of Character Development   124
Prepare the Wee Harnesses   127
Eloise Anderson: Off the Plantation   129
The Chambers Brothers' Career Choices   131
Replaceable Product, Fungible People   132
A Colombia Within America's Borders   134
At the Border: Arduous Lives of Honorable Frustration   136
The "Growth Model" and the Growth of Illiteracy   138
Multiculturalism as Compulsory Chapel   140
The Paradox of History Standards   142
Intellectual Cotton Candy   144
Intellectual Segregation   146
The Abuse of Excuses   149
Coney Island and the Guiding Arithmetic of Delusion   151

CONTENTS

The "Decent" Against the "Street"   152

Ambiguities of Assimilation   154

Our Towns   156

The Great Divide   159

Ignition in Sandtown   161

Harlem's Pink Hallways   163

"Tipping the Forty": Growing Up in Jersey City   165

Atoms to Molecules in Dorchester   167

CHAPTER FOUR
POLICY

The First Amendment and the Speech-Rationers   171

The Outlaws at KTOZ-AM   175

How Bad Law Begets Bad Law   177

"Wacko" Hurley Gets His Way   179

VMI R.I.P.   181

And Now, a Right to Be Obnoxious   183

Judges and the Definition of Marriage   185

Animosity and the Constitution   187

Dead End: From Topeka to Kansas City   189

The Dangerous Cult of Cultural Diversity   192

Arizona, a Conquered Province   194

The Case Against Categorical Representation   196

Dismaying Good News About Race   198

Gotham Gets "Reality Therapy"   200

New York, Between Singapore and Dodge City   202

Shaming   204

Corrections Cocktails and Supermax   206

1937: Leviathan's Birth   207

The Equity of Inequality   210

Here We Go Again: Is Economic Dynamism Desirable?   212

Malthus Reversed   214

First, Sell the Prison to Yourself   216

The Case for a Supermajority   218

CONTENTS

The Case Against 219

Bilingual Ballots: A Seriously Bad Idea 221

Voting by Mail: Another Improvement That Isn't 223

Artistic Dependency 225

A Case Study of Contemporary Government: "Rent Seeking"
with the "Perimeter Rule" 227

Moralism and Cynicism in Rhode Island 229

Sheep and Supply-Side Government 231

Maryland Sacks Itself 233

AIDS: The Evolution of an Epidemic 236

The Real Opiate of the Masses 238

Gambling: "The Pathology of Hope" 240

CHAPTER FIVE

(EPI)PHENOMENAL POLITICS

1994: 1938 Redux 243

Thermidor 245

Bob Dole: The Ledger of His Daily Work 247

Taking Conservatism Slumming 250

A Weird Sincerity 252

Clinton the Inconsequential 254

It's Over? 256

Entitlement and Disappointment 258

Fast Ride, No Driver 260

Sweeney Sends a *Frisson* 262

Incivility and Senator Byrd 264

Astronomy Cures Zealotry 267

CHAPTER SIX

A WORLD STILL MUCH WITH US

America's Lost Sense of the Tragic 269

"What Have We Gone Through the Twentieth Century For?" 271

A Tale of Two Cities: Madrid and Belgrade 273

Contents

Sabbatical from Seriousness   275
A Distinctively Human Activity   277
Fascism's Second Spring   279
History Revs Its Engine   281
America: Rome or Venice?   284
Safety and Sanguine Predictions   285
A Marvel of Naval Architecture   287
The Counterculture at Quantico   289
Russia's Memory   291
NATO and Russia's National DNA   293
China and Curzon's Law   295
The Brothers Netanyahu   297
The Spectacle of Suffering   299

CHAPTER SEVEN:

WEAVERS OF THEIR TIMES

Thomas Jefferson: Clay, but Uncommon Clay   303
The Passionate Life of William Gladstone   305
TR: "Steam Engine in Trousers"   310
FDR's Heroic Ebullience   312
The Greatest American of the Century?   314
Lenin: Man of the Century   316
Richard Nixon's Life of Resentment and Tenacity   318
Frederick Taylor: Busy, Busy, Busy   320
Alger Hiss's Grotesque Fidelity   324
Justice for "Engine Charlie"   325
Zora Arkus-Duntov: Zooooooooooom   328
Vance Packard's Self-Refutation   330
Al Capone and Huey Newton: Two Styles of Upward—
    For a While—Mobility   332
Allen Ginsberg, Symptom   336
Philadelphia's Deliverance   337
Strom Thurmond, Bringing Pleasure to the Beacon   339
Paul Wellstone's Political Unitarianism   341
Erwin A. Glikes 1937–1994   343

CONTENTS

CHAPTER EIGHT
SWATCHES FROM THE CENTURY'S END

Hurrying to the Next Traffic Jam 347
Learning to Worry at a Higher Level 349
The Ladies in the Tub in the Rotunda 351
Chief Illiniwek: In a Hostile Environment 353
Pennsylvania Excitements 355
Huck in a Ford Explorer 357
The Problem with Cats: Their Catness 359
"Counting Sheep" 361
Disney Sounds Retreat 363
ESPN Dependency 365
Strange Doings in the Living Room 366

Index 369
Permissions 384

The Woven Figure

INTRODUCTION

The University of Michigan scholars who are preparing a dictionary of Middle English have extracted from the mists of the past a word for what many Americans feel describes the current condition of their country's politics: "spaciosite." It means a hollowness. Certainly in the century's tenth decade American politics has taken on a pastel cast. The bold colors of unfurled banners are but faded memories. Well, fine. The tumult and the shouting dies, the captains and the kings depart, and perhaps the banality of contemporary politics should be a national boast. The deflation of politics is not a bad coda to a blood-soaked century.

Indeed, the miniaturization of American politics has its own fascination, especially given the fact that government, although currently disparaged, has a recent record of substantial successes. Far from producing "uncontrollable" deficits, by the mid-1990s its revenues matched outlays for programs. Which is to say, the budget would have been in balance, but for debt service. As a result of a lot of social learning, inflation, which twenty years ago seemed like a disease endemic to, and perhaps destructive of, democracy, is controlled. So are business cycles, which within living memory produced surges of unemployment huge enough to threaten social stability. Granted, there have been other, less happy dimensions of social learning. In 1966, when Sargent Shriver, head of President Johnson's "war on poverty," was asked how long it would take to win the war, he replied "about ten years." Still, we have largely eliminated one kind of poverty—financial distress among that portion of the population that possesses the accumulated social capital of good habits.

Not a bad record. And not one calculated to make Americans ripe for revolution, as some Republicans should have considered.

Around A.D. 982, Eric the Red, explorer and pioneer of the public relations business, named one of his discoveries Greenland because it wasn't. He hoped the name would lure colonists. He soon learned the limits of creative labeling. So have those practitioners of American politics who, in the years covered by the columns collected in this volume, have bandied the

17

word revolution. They have learned the limits of politics as an engine of abrupt change in a free and complex society that is neither able nor inclined to divorce itself from its past.

The aspiring revolutionaries have called themselves conservatives, so they should have known those limits. A cardinal tenet of conservatism is that social inertia is—and ought to be—strong. It discourages and, if necessary, defeats the political grandiosity of those who would attempt to engineer the future by rupturing connections with the past. The Republic is a woven figure disinclined to unravel the threads that connect it to its antecedents. Here, then, is a paradox: The recent disappointments of some conservatives actually vindicate conservatism's critique of extravagant aspirations.

However, these years have not been, on balance, disappointing for conservatives, or uninteresting or uninstructive to anyone mindful of the conversation of this continental nation. These years have featured a particularly intense recrudescence of the familiar American argument about what government is and is not good for. It is an argument about whether many of our discontents are caused by, or can be cured by, government. As a result of these years, some conservatives are wiser than they were. They should not be sadder, because they have acquired a virtue—a quickened appreciation of politics as epiphenomena.

That is a word formerly used by Marxists when they were insisting that politics is, always and everywhere, just the "reflection" of deeper, meaning economic, dynamisms. It has been said that what was original in Marxism was false and what was true was derivative. Marxism's doctrine of the limits on the autonomy of politics was a characteristically unnuanced recasting of a fundamental assumption of conservatism. As the Democratic senator from New York Daniel Patrick Moynihan says, "The central conservative truth is that it is culture, not politics, that determines the success of a society."

"The central liberal truth," Moynihan continues, "is that politics can change a culture and save it from itself." However, the political debate of the 1990s has been driven by the worry that politics is damaging the culture. To see how the debate got to this point, stand back and look back.

Different eras are defined by different problems. James Q. Wilson of UCLA, past president of the American Political Science Association, notes that from the Founding until the Civil War the defining problem was that of firmly grounding the federal government's legitimacy. From the Civil War until the New Deal the problem was power: Under what limits did the federal government operate? From the New Deal until recently, the problem was representation: Were all groups appropriately involved in

Washington's increasing importance? Today, Wilson says, the defining problem concerns collective choice: Can a federal government which acknowledges no limits to its scope, and which responds assiduously to the multiplying appetites of proliferating factions, make choices that serve the society's long-term interests?

Think about it. Is there now *any* human want or difficulty that is not considered a federal policy problem? Policy making, says Wilson, has been thoroughly nationalized, in this sense: There are virtually no arguments about whether the Constitution bars federal action in particular spheres of life. The last barriers to action were swept aside in the twelve-month period, 1964–65, with the passage of the Civil Rights Act, the Elementary and Secondary Education Act and Medicare.

Still, at the century's end, conservatives can take considerable satisfaction from the contagion of their ideas in the second half of the second half of the century. "In the United States at this time," wrote Lionel Trilling in 1950, "liberalism is not only the dominant but even the sole intellectual tradition. For it is the plain fact that nowadays there are no conservative or reactionary ideas in general circulation." Trilling worried that "it is not conducive to the real strength of liberalism that it should occupy the intellectual field alone." Well, that is one worry that liberalism is now spared.

Today, as usual, conservatism is less a creed than a climate of opinion. And in the years covered by the essays in this volume, conservatives have learned the limits that politics places on their aspirations, particularly on their aspiration to revive the pre–New Deal tradition of American politics.

The New Deal made, and was made possible by, something novel in American history—a sanguine estimation of the competence and trustworthiness of the central government. The New Deal frame of mind was presaged by this change: Eleven of the Constitution's first twelve amendments added more restrictions to the federal government than those written into the unamended document in Philadelphia in 1787. But six of the next seven amendments enlarged federal powers. Still, from the Founding until the 1930s, the American premise was itself a formidable inhibition of the central government. That premise was that the function of government was to provide the conditions in which happiness can be pursued—ordered liberty—but not to provide happiness itself.

Since the New Deal, the government has been steadily more ambitious. But Americans have not become steadily more content with their government. In the 1990s they have been forced to face the ambiguities in their feelings about government. They talk a fierce game of Slay the Federal Dragon, making lists of programs and even whole departments that must perish for the public good. In this mood, their spirit is that expressed by the bumper sticker on a New York taxi: SO MANY PEDESTRIANS, SO LITTLE TIME.

However, it turns out that Americans are more comfortable while entangled in the tentacles of "big government" than their rhetoric suggests.

Addressing a labor audience during his first Senate campaign, in 1976, Pat Moynihan said, "Look, there's this particular fringe, and their one fundamental problem is they simply never accepted the New Deal." Moynihan added: "Didn't Franklin Roosevelt settle this issue once and for all? I mean, do we really *have* to go over it *again*?" Yes, and then yet again. Some arguments are never settled in this contumacious country. The American tapestry remains a work in progress.

The most remarkable institutional change of the 1990s has been the reassertion of congressional supremacy, and the corresponding marginalization of the presidency. William Allen White's autobiography tells a story of President McKinley. In the summer of 1901, at William McKinley's home in Canton, Ohio, a photographer approached to take the president's picture. McKinley laid aside his cigar, saying, "We must not let the young men of this country see their president smoking!" The camera was a harbinger of the graphic revolution in communication that would help enlarge the place of the presidency—the most photogenic piece of America's government—in the nation's consciousness.

McKinley was a transitional figure. He had presided over America's passage into imperialism in the war with Spain, and his assassination late that summer produced the first modern president, Theodore Roosevelt, who proclaimed his office a "bully pulpit" for shaping the public's mind and morals. At the end of this century the public, noting the federal government's difficulties delivering the mail, is disinclined to think that any federal official can deliver appropriate states of mind.

Along with the waning hold of the presidency on the nation's imagination, the exhaustion of the federal treasury and the evaporation of confidence in centralized problem solving all help account for the centrifugal forces that are producing the devolution of powers from the central government. This can have various consequences for the nation's political culture. Justice Charles Fried of the Massachusetts Supreme Court notes that citizens may come to be governed "less grandly and remotely" and the states may develop "more distinct characters." If so, "Although we would be more strangers to other Americans, we would be more closely tied to the smaller places where we live." However, Fried worries about a cost attached to such a transaction: "Our economy of allegiance simply is not infinitely expandable. If we become more Virginian or Georgian, surely we will also feel more remote, less responsible for the poor of Kentucky or of the ghettoes of Chicago. If we became more Virginian, we would be less American."

Conservatives demur, arguing that if we become more tied to where we live, we will become more connected to those, including the poor, who live with us. Conservatives worry that unless we multiply and strengthen attachments to society's little platoons, our fellow-feeling will become attenuated, and civic life, expressed through bureaucratized compassion, distantly organized, will be thin gruel.

Politics is always driven by competing worries. Today conservatives are more radically worried than liberals are concerning conditions in the government and the culture. And conservatives worry about the relationships they think they discern between the former and the latter. Liberals still express their worries in an essentially 1930s vocabulary of distributive justice, understood in economic, meaning material, terms. This assumes a reassuringly mundane politics of splittable differences—how much concrete to pour, how many crops to subsidize by how much, which factions shall get what.

Conservatives worry in a more contemporary vocabulary, questioning the power and ambitions of the post–New Deal state, and finding a causal connection between those ambitions and the fraying of the culture. Many of today's conservatives believe, or say they do (their actions in power often say otherwise), that government's principal functions, and perhaps its only proper functions, are the preservation of freedom and the removal of restraints on the individual. Such conservatives do not fit easily into the conservative tradition that traces its pedigree to Edmund Burke.

Liberalism's ascent in the first three-quarters of this century reflected the new belief that government could and should also confer capacities on individuals who were ill-equipped to cope with the complexities of modern life. Liberalism's decline in the final quarter has reflected doubts about whether government has that competence to deliver capacities—and doubts about whether a tutelary government that is good at such delivering would be good for the nation's character.

One count in conservatism's indictment of liberalism is that liberalism takes too much for granted. Liberalism, according to conservatism, does not understand how its programs threaten those habits—thrift, industriousness, deferral of gratification—which make free societies succeed. Conservatives worry that the severest cost of solicitous government is not monetary but moral. This cost is measured in the diminution of personal responsibility and of private forms of social provision.

This worry has a distinguished pedigree. Tocqueville warned of a soft despotism that "makes the exercise of free choice less useful and rarer, restricts the activity of free will within a narrower compass, and little by little robs each citizen of the proper use of his own faculties." In the 1990s, conservatives have argued that the foremost victims of this robbery are children of the poor. Liberals argue that those children are the foremost victims of conservatism. Be that as it may, liberals and conservatives begin by agreeing with Charles Dickens's Mr. Jarndyce in *Bleak House* that "the children of the very poor are not brought up, but dragged up."

At first blush, the 1994 election results, ending forty years of Democratic control of the House of Representatives, seemed to foreshadow a large step away from an essentially European idea of an omnipresent and omniprovident state, an idea incorporated into twentieth-century American liberalism. That blush faded quickly. However, in this last decade of the century, which is the first decade of our third century under the Constitution, we are in a particularly intense flare-up of the perennial American argument about what the Constitution permits and what it requires. That is why so many of our controversies are couched in the clanging language of clashing rights.

Napoleon said a good constitution should be short and confused. American courts certainly have augmented the latter attribute. In the process, they have become more central to civic life than courts should be in a democracy. And they have done much to unleash the spirit of aggressive, elbow-throwing individualism that some conservatives believe is shredding the culture.

There now seems to be brewing a wholesome backlash. The nation may not have rethought and rejected the New Deal era, but it has begun to get over something even more deplorable. Call it the Shelley mentality. That excitable poet's spirit bloomed here in the 1960s.

> The painted veil is . . . torn aside;
> The loathsome mask has fallen, the man remains
> Sceptreless, free, uncircumscribed, but man
> Equal, unclassed, tribeless, and nationless,
> Exempt from awe, worship, degree, the king
> Over himself. . . .

But now the condition of the culture seems to be a reason for thinking that it might not be such a bad thing if man were a bit more circumscribed by manners and mores, and had a pinch or two of awe about something other than his own splendor. America's normally sunny disposition has become somewhat clouded over with anxieties about the uses to which freedom is being put.

Samuel Beckett, the novelist and playwright, was walking with a friend on a sunny English afternoon when his friend exclaimed, "On a day like this it's good to be alive." Beckett replied, "I wouldn't go as far as that." That was a bit of his characteristically mordant humor. However, of late, Americans have been feeling, or at least have been talking as though they feel, uncharacteristically bleak about their prospects. For this, journalism deserves a portion of the blame. The problem is not that journalists consider the phrase "good news" an oxymoron. Rather, the problem has two dimensions, which are somewhat contradictory.

First, journalists, far from being the hard-bitten and world-weary sorts found in *The Front Page* and other popular fiction, may be America's last romantics. They really seem startled, even scandalized by the fact that their society always seems to have serious problems. Journalists feel that someone, or some identifiable faction, must be to blame. And the fault must be a sin of omission, because something can always be done to correct imperfections and right wrongs.

Second, and in contrast, journalists have, by the working of our trickle-down culture, absorbed from the academy a watery postmodernism that makes a dogma of skepticism. It teaches that nothing is what it seems; everything must be "unmasked"; the veil of appearances must be torn aside. That, increasingly, is how journalists understand their vocation. This is particularly the spirit of television journalism which, being enslaved to an inherently superficial news-gathering instrument, a camera, deals with pictures, meaning the surfaces of things. (Librarian of Congress Emeritus Daniel J. Boorstin's *The Image: A Guide to Pseudo-Events in America* tells a joke of a proud mother with a pram. The mother says to a woman who is admiring the baby in the pram, "Oh, that's nothing—you should see his photograph.")

These two journalistic tendencies partially explain a puzzle: This is a successful nation that is constantly susceptible to melancholy because things are not perfect. Americans are increasingly susceptible to the suspicion that no one is telling the truth—or there is no truth to tell. So this is a good time to say what I hope some of the essays in this volume clearly say: It is good to be alive in America at the end of the first (but not the last) American century.

"Man," says the comedienne Lily Tomlin, "invented language to satisfy his deep need to complain." Which is, of course, where columnists come in, to "grutchen." (That is Middle English for "to complain.") However, readers will find in what follows ample evidence to convict this columnist of violating the code of his craft by having a wonderful time out in the contiguous country.

CHAPTER ONE

FROM THE WHIRRING LOOM

The Tyranny of Nonchalance

Pursuant to the Motion Picture Production Code's mandate that "no picture shall be produced which will lower the moral standards of those who see it," the script of *Casablanca* (1942) was changed, the word "like" replacing "enjoy" in what was originally this line for Captain Renault (Claude Rains): "You enjoy war. I enjoy women." The Hays Office, enforcer of the code, issued this edict after reviewing the script of *The African Queen* (1951): "There must be no unacceptable exposure of Rose's (Katharine Hepburn's) person as she 'tucks her skirt up into her underclothes.' We assume the intention here is to tuck the skirt under the knees of her bloomers."

America has liberated itself from not only such pettifoggery but also from what is now considered the tyranny of taste. So, is everyone happy?

Not exactly. There is a certain troubling lack of refinement in Dennis Rodman's America, a lack linked to three peculiar ideas: distinguishing between liberty and license is incipient fascism; manners are servants of hypocrisy; concern for appearances and respectability is a craven treason against self-expression, hence not respectable.

The eclipse of civility is a fact fraught with depressing significance, as explained in the Autumn 1996 *Wilson Quarterly,* in essays by Richard Bushman, a Columbia historian, and James Morris of the Woodrow Wilson International Center for Scholars. The gravamen of their arguments is: A coarse and slatternly society—boom boxes borne through crowded streets by young men wearing pornographic T-shirts and baseball caps backwards; young women using, in what formerly was called polite society, language that formerly caused stevedores to blush—jeopardizes all respect, including self-respect.

Bushman says the young American nation had to overcome the fear that gentility, the product of an elite culture, put common people at a disadvantage, hence compromised democracy. But as American lives became less and less governed by austere material conditions and austere religious codes, rules of gentility (young George Washington was required to read *110 Rules of Civility and Decent Behavior in Company and Conversation*) supplied governance for human nature's unruly impulses.

Bushman defines gentility as "a compulsion to make the world beautiful," beginning with the individual and extending to the home—a piano on a carpet in the parlor; polished walnut furniture; ceramic dinnerware—and to parks and museums to elevate the public's taste. Gentility stimulated a market for many of capitalism's goods, and capitalism democratized gentility by making those goods affordable.

As urban density came to a formerly frontier society, Bushman writes, "The premium on simply getting along in public grew." There were uniformed ushers in theaters, sometimes distributing printed rules of decorum, such as not talking during the performance. Behavior was better when cinemas were opulent. Bring back the printed rules for the boors whose minimalist manners are suited to today's "multiplexes."

Time was, writes Morris, Americans understood that rules of civility do not just smooth surfaces, they "inscribed the soul." Today America is a nation of "voluble solipsists," chatting away on cellular phones in public, unconcerned for privacy or dignity. Or safety. A bumper sticker: HANG UP AND DRIVE. Morris warns: "In this age of 'whatever,' Americans are becoming slaves to the new tyranny of nonchalance. 'Whatever.' The word draws you in like a plumped pillow and folds 'round your brain; the progress of its syllables is a movement toward . . . a universal shrug. It's all capitulation. No one wants to make a judgment, to impose a standard, to act from authority and call conduct unacceptable."

So this nation, where traditions "have the shelf life of bread," is getting perhaps not the behavior it deserves, but that which it countenances. Why, "even the meek drive like Messala out to teach Ben Hur who's boss." The future stares blankly at us through the eyes of the "fragile young men/women" in Calvin Klein ads, "in a conga line of pointless sexuality," having opted "for a new cologne over bathing."

In the imperturbable cool of the 1990s, writes Morris, "Sights that not so long ago would have left audiences open-mouthed with wonder leave them droopy-eyed with boredom. To every age, perhaps, its proper surfeit: in old Rome, worried impresarios probably cut deals for more spears, more tigers, more Christians."

Today's is not the "honest coarseness of frontier settlers removed from society and struggling with bears and the seasons." It occurs in a land where plenitude inflames the sense of entitlement to more of almost everything, but less of manners and taste, with their irritating intimations of authority and hierarchy.

Today, Dennis Rodman. What next?

Whatever.

December 22, 1996

With Friends Like These

It is eight P.M. Do you know where your teenagers are? If it is Thursday, they probably are watching NBC's *Friends*. One recent, and representative, episode, featuring what may have been prime-time television's first premature ejaculation joke, illustrates why popular culture will be a prominent subject this presidential season.

Friends involves various twentysomethings and their "relationships." The script for the episode that aired February 8 contains several subplots. One young woman falls for an older man. Joey and Chandler, thrilled by their new television, hope never to rise from their reclining chairs.

> Chandler: "Pizza's on the way. I told you we wouldn't have to get up."
> Joey: "What if we have to pee?"
> Chandler (picking up the phone): "I'll cancel the sodas."

The central story concerns Ross and Rachel having their first and second dates. At the end of their first they kiss. She starts to giggle.

> Rachel: "I'm sorry. It's just that . . . well, when you moved your hands to my butt, it was like 'Hey, Ross's hands are on my butt!'"
> She composes herself, again they kiss, again she giggles.
> Ross: "My hands were nowhere near your butt!"
> Rachel: "I know! I was just thinking about when they were there the last time. I'm sorry. I promise I won't laugh. Now come on, put your hands back on my butt."
> Ross: "No. I can't now. I feel all self-conscious."
> Rachel: "Oh, come on, touch my butt."
> Ross: "No."

Rachel: "Just one cheek."
Ross: "The moment's gone."
Rachel: "Then hold out your hands and I'll back into them."
Ross: "Oh, that's romantic."
Rachel: "Come on, touch it."
Ross: "No."
Rachel: "Oh, come on, squeeze it."
Ross: "No."
Rachel: "Rub it?"
Ross: "No."
Rachel (her voice rising): "Oh, come on, would you just grab my ass?"

The next night, before their second date, Ross, a museum curator, is called to deal with a mistake in a display.

Ross (on the phone): "Australopithecus isn't supposed to be in that display. . . . No. No. Homo habilis was erect. Australopithecus was never fully erect."
Chandler: "Well, maybe he was nervous."

Rachel accompanies Ross to the museum, where he corrects the display of prehistoric mannequins. She sits next to a mannequin. The script says: "Her face is right at his waist. . . . (She) lifts up his loin cloth and takes a peek. With an impressed shrug, she drops it down."

Ross finishes too late to take Rachel to dinner, so grabbing some animal skins from the display of mannequins, he takes her into the museum's planetarium, where he illuminates the stars and they recline on the furs. He puts down a small carton of juice, they begin ardently undressing each other, he rolls on top of her. The script directions then are: "Passionate, they roll on the floor. After a moment, Rachel stops, pulled up short." She emits a cry of dismay.

Rachel (disappointed, but tender): "Oh, no. Oh. Oh, honey. That's okay."
Ross (looking puzzled, then recognizing her misapprehension): "What? Oh, no. You just rolled onto the juice box."
Rachel (passionately relieved, looks heavenward): "Oh. Thank God!"

Then, proving there was no premature ejaculation, he again rolls back onto her, and the scene ends. The next scene is the next morning. They are back in the mannequin display, slowly awakening, embracing naked beneath the animal skins. And a priest, a nun, and a group of schoolchildren are staring at them.

Well.

More depressing than what *Friends* considers wit, which rises only from the cretinous to the sophomoric, is the fact that the program transmits to teenagers the message that such shallow sexuality is not only acceptable, it is expected of them. Those who accept this notion of sophistication are apt to have such an impoverished sense of sensuousness, of the delights of real adult sexual electricity, that mature eroticism will be unimaginable to them.

Asked if she understood the juice box joke, Victoria Will, who is fifteen and perfect, replied in the tone of a patient duchess addressing a dimwitted footman: "Dad, I'm not four." What did she think of it? She has a flair for concision like that of the sovereign of the same name: "Uncalled for."

Indeed. America was born in a struggle to remove restraints imposed from without. Today it is struggling to achieve restraints arising from within each American. Today, as at the nation's birth, the great political question is, What kind of character is produced by American life? When parents cannot watch early-evening television with their children without wincing, their distress will take on political coloration, and the winner of the nation's premier political office is apt to be he who best exemplifies credible disgust with what distresses them.

February 25, 1996

Neither candidate exemplified it. At first base, a tie goes to the runner. In presidential politics, a tie goes to the incumbent.

The Food and Drug Administration vs. "Family Discord"

Hillary Clinton's epiphany, confided to the country during her speech to the Democratic Convention, that it takes not only a village but also a president to raise a child, does not do justice to the scope of caring in her husband's administration. Sure, it takes a president, everyone knows that, but it also takes this president's Food and Drug Administration.

Evidently the FDA thinks it has a roving commission to prevent "family discord." And it has acted to do so by issuing an edict designed to prevent parents from getting too intimately involved in raising their own children. Herewith a story melding many themes of today's political debate—drugs, families, and whether the country's contempt for Washington is sufficiently severe.

When Sunny Cloud, a Georgia mother, found her son smoking mari-

29

juana, she took him to an emergency ward for a drug screening test. She found the experience so disagreeable and expensive that she developed a kit that would enable parents to administer tests to their children. The mere possession by parents of such kits would give children a powerful reason to resist peer pressure for drug use.

Ms. Cloud's kit consists of a small plastic cup for a urine sample, a temperature-measuring strip to prevent the substitution of old urine, two saliva-sample strips, and a box and mailing label addressed to a federally licensed laboratory which tests for numerous drugs. Each sample is assigned a number, and the household that sent the sample is notified of the results associated with that number. The name of the person who gave the sample is not involved.

Ms. Cloud, a former teacher, started a business, Parent's Alert Inc., to manufacture this forty-dollar diagnostic kit. Then on June 15, 1995, she received from Washington a bellow of reproach.

The FDA's "warning letter" stated that "our investigator" has revealed that the kit is "a Class III device" and does not have the FDA approval such devices require. The FDA darkly noted that "this letter is not intended to be an all-inclusive list of deficiencies at your facility." (Imagine an all-inclusive list of deficiencies at the FDA.) The letter commanded "prompt action" to correct "deviations."

CAT scan machines are Class III devices. So are MRIs, pacemakers, and X-ray machines. And so, it seems, is Ms. Cloud's plastic cup. But only when used by parents to protect their children.

Another drug-testing kit is made for hair samples. This supposedly Class III device consists of aluminum foil for the hair and a labeled box. Such urine, saliva, and hair kits are in legal commercial distribution. They are used for drug screening by many companies and governmental units, such as General Motors and the New York City Police Department.

After a meeting of FDA officials with one of the manufacturers, the FDA's policy was reported by an attorney for the manufacturer and seemingly corroborated by the FDA's own minutes of the meeting. The policy is to allow the sales of kits "marketed exclusively for forensic purposes (e.g., law enforcement, employment)." But over-the-counter sales "indicated for teenagers" should be regulated, meaning prevented. The attorney's memorandum describes this as "a deliberate policy decision that has been made at a high level within the FDA." According to the memorandum by the manufacturer's attorney, the FDA, whose minutes refer to "ethical and social issues," has a capacious notion of its mandate and competence. It "is concerned about issues such as anonymity, confidentiality, coercion, and family discord."

Oh, so this tentacle of the nanny state really should be called the FDDA—the Food, Drug, and Discord Administration. Perhaps some of the FDA's caregivers could drop by at breakfast time, when there are three pairs of hands reaching for the newspaper's sports section. Talk about family discord. And then there is custody of the television remote control. . . .

The FDA's overreaching, overbearing busybodies merit derisive laughter. But the gargantuan presumptuousness of this federal bureaucracy elbowing its way into family matters is infuriating for many reasons, one of which is: Children on drugs often are uncommunicative and in denial until confronted with undeniable evidence, at which point they become open to rehabilitation. Parents will be more inclined to seek evidence from home tests that preserve anonymity and confidentiality than from emergency room or other procedures that generate medical records.

Of course, this assumes that if parents say "pretty please" and "mother may I," the FDA will give them permission to participate—as Washington's junior partners, naturally—in parenting.

September 29, 1996

Sheldon Hackney Teaches Talking

Have you got your kit yet? You don't want to start conversing without the government's guidance. And conversing about the topic the government has selected for us is, according to Sheldon Hackney, chairman of the National Endowment for the Humanities, something we all "have a responsibility" to do.

Hackney may sound slightly hectoring but that is just because he wants to be helpful. He believes we need help if we are to converse properly about "American Pluralism and Identity," so the NEH has produced a kit of "materials—conversation starters, book and film lists, documents, essays—to help spark the individual conversations."

This may seem like carrying coals to Newcastle because there is not and never has been a shortage of talk in America about that subject. It undoubtedly was a topic of conversation on the pitching decks of the *Mayflower,* and is, to put it mildly, not now neglected.

Furthermore, this designated topic of the Conversation, in the NEH's capacious notion of it, concerns just about everything. That conclusion is compelled by the "suggested reading and film list" included in the kit. The readings run from Aristotle to Maya Angelou, and the films, well, for example, the list includes these items:

"*Casablanca*—this World War II classic explores American values in the multinational setting of war-torn Casablanca. Pertains to question 6" (Question 6 is "Where do we as Americans belong in the world?"); "*Meet Me in St. Louis*—this musical depicts a family's experiences during the year of the St. Louis World's Fair. Pertains to question 5" (Question 5 is "What do we share as Americans?"); "*Shane*—a former gunfighter comes to the defense of homesteaders and is idolized by their son. Pertains to question 5."

In the NEH's attempt to organize "thousands of small-group discussions around the country," no detail is too small for the NEH's attention. Its advice includes:

> The meeting should not go longer than planned without the consent of all present. . . . The site should be convenient to get to and there should be sufficient parking. . . . Consider the size and the temperature (not too hot or too cold) of the room. . . . Chairs should be comfortable and placed so that participants are able to sit facing each other. . . . All participants will show respect for the views expressed by others . . . name-calling and shouting are not acceptable.

It is sweet and true to the spirit of democracy that our government, which thinks we need to be told not to have the room too hot or too cold, nevertheless thinks we can read Aristotle and converse about momentous matters. At least we can if we are given meticulous instructions, particularly pertaining to sensitivity, about which the NEH is very sensitive:

> Consider having each session at a different location, allowing each racial, ethnic, or cultural group to play host. . . . If your community has little racial or ethnic diversity, look for other kinds of diversity. You might find people of different ages, religions, political affiliations, socioeconomic levels, professions, or neighborhoods. . . . You might need to help some participants overcome lingering feelings that they were invited solely because of their race, ethnic origin, or cultural background.

Yes, you might.

In the kit's booklet of scholars' essays, there are many worth reading and one that should be read slowly and loudly to Hackney. James Q. Wilson of UCLA, noting that there actually may be less cultural diversity in America today than in the 1890s, writes:

> Most Americans have never doubted that there is or ought to be an underlying unity. The motto, *E pluribus unum*, though often violated in practice has never been challenged in principle. Except by intellectuals. . . . If a "national conversation" occurs, what will happen? The activists most likely to participate will be those most disaffected by America, and their

conversation will provide further evidence to ordinary people that the great divide in this nation is not between rich and poor or between one race and another but between two cultures, the public and the elite. . . . The "conversations" some want to foster are already happening; if they are to be made better, questions posed by a few dozen intellectuals acting with government encouragement will not help, especially when a large fraction of these folk occupy, or are seen by the common man or woman as occupying, an adversary posture vis-à-vis the common culture.

Still, there is currently a congressional conversation about the importance of the NEH relative to other recipients of scarce public resources, and the National Conversation kit is timely as evidence.

March 26, 1995

Neo-Paternalism and
the Battered Woman Syndrome

After having sex with her husband, who then fell asleep, the Denver woman, who was having an extramarital affair at the time and had recently taken out a large life insurance policy on her husband, shot him. She then disordered the house to suggest that the killer had been a burglar, and went to a disco with her sister.

Her conviction was a setback for Lenore Walker, who testified as an expert witness that the woman's behavior was consistent with the "battered woman syndrome." Walker says a battered woman is one "repeatedly subjected to any forceful physical *or psychological* behavior by a man in order to coerce her to do something he wants her to do without any concern for her rights" (emphasis added). Concerning another case, in which the woman initiated the assault, throwing a glass at the husband's head and hitting him with a chair, Walker says the husband "had been battering her by ignoring her and by working late."

In Canada, a woman was convicted only of second-degree murder after she stabbed her boyfriend to death following a quarrel. He had never abused her but she is seeking a new trial because she says her history of being abused by other men means she should be able to cite the battered woman syndrome as a defense. In another Canadian case, the syndrome served not merely to establish a mitigating circumstance to reduce the charge from murder to manslaughter, but to produce the acquittal of a woman who shot her husband in the back of the head as he was leaving the room after threatening her. Such cases overturn the traditional rule that deadly force can only be justified by an imminent threat.

Such troubling cases are cited by Michael Weiss and Cathy Young in their study "Feminist Jurisprudence: Equal Rights or Neo-Paternalism?" published by the Cato Institute, Washington's libertarian think tank. Weiss, a law professor associated with the Texas Public Policy Foundation, and Young, vice president of the Women's Freedom Network, argue that feminist jurisprudence is portraying women as perpetual victims in need of dispensations that seem to ratify some unflattering stereotypes. These include the neo-Victorian notion that women are frail creatures, easily unhinged, and perhaps having a single sensibility.

The Supreme Court has ruled that a woman can sue an employer for sexual harassment if she experienced a "hostile environment." Although Weiss and Young are uneasy about intrusive government "regulating the mental comfort level of the workplace," obviously hostile environments exist and should be actionable. But some feminists insist that harassment be defined as any behavior or "environment" that causes any woman "discomfort." Weiss and Young compare that to replacing speed limits with a law under which one could be fined for driving through a neighborhood at any speed which made any resident uncomfortable. And is there not something amiss when, as in Minnesota, sexual harassment law covers children from kindergarten on?

Regarding rape, for too long many courts considered rape complaints inherently less trustworthy than complaints pertaining to other crimes, and rape laws unjustly required proof not only of force but of resistance to force, a standard that required victims to risk additional physical harm. But now, write Weiss and Young, some states' laws have eliminated physical force as an element of the crime. Others, virtually reversing the burden of proof, require the accused to prove consent as an affirmative defense.

In Canada, "sex is rape when the man fails to 'take reasonable steps' to ensure consent." Weiss and Young worry that rape law is sliding from "no means no" to "absence of a yes means no" to a strict criminal liability regime in which "all heterosexual sex is like statutory rape unless affirmative, explicit verbal consent given in a clear and sober frame of mind can be demonstrated." They cite a dissenting feminist who says "the idea that only an explicit yes means yes" patronizes women by implying "that women, like children, have trouble communicating what they want."

However, the feminist avant-garde is thinking like this: A woman sued a moving company for damaging her household goods. She lost because she had signed a contract containing an insurance waiver without reading it. A feminist law professor says the woman should have been able to collect anyway, given that she signed hurriedly only because the house was cold and the movers were weary. The professor says the court should have considered that "women are socialized to value other people's feelings highly, so she was acting like a reasonable woman."

July 18, 1996

Sex in Sacramento

"Here's a cute one," said the professor according to one of her students. The professor was commenting on one of the slides of female genitalia that she used, together with a catalogue of sex toys, in her lecture on female masturbation. According to the professor's lawyer, she was discussing masturbation "to help women learn how to achieve more and better orgasms and to help men learn to be better sexual partners." Just another day in the life of America's institutions of higher learning.

But why does the professor, Joanne Marrow of California State University in Sacramento, need a lawyer? Because she and CSUS are being sued by a male student who says the lecture made him feel "raped." He is seeking $2.5 million, saying the lecture constituted sexual harassment of him. That amount, says the thirty-three-year-old student, Craig Rogers, is the price he puts on the lecture's consequences of "mental anguish, pain and suffering, loss of concentration to study for finals, and emotional distress." Asked to specify the "damage or injury" that resulted from the experience he said "traumatized" him, Rogers says, "I have had to seek counseling to deal with past problems stemming from pornography." His lawyer says Rogers used to like pornography, got over that, but was upset by the fact that as a result of Marrow's materials and manner he became "sexually aroused," which was "extremely upsetting in a classroom setting." According to the *Sacramento Bee*, Rogers says that when Marrow "stroked" some of the images, "I was sitting there in total disgust and yet I was stimulated."

Anyone with "problems stemming from pornography" might well have problems with Marrow's lecture, titled "The Anatomy and Function of the Clitoris," if the lecture was as Rogers remembered it in a description he recorded two days later. What he says he found "sickening" and "horrifying" and made him want to "vomit" included: "She told us about her buying dildos for her family for Christmas, and how one sister didn't really like the present she got because it wasn't the right size. . . . She was showing us all the nooks and crannies and nuances of women's genitalia. . . . All the wisecracks about masturbation, about vibrators, and about dildos, and about using a wine bottle, wrapping a wine bottle in a towel, and . . ." You get the idea.

Among the eighteen ideas that Marrow, a lesbian, hoped listeners would get from her lecture and the slides projected on a large screen (including slides of the genitals of pregnant and postpartum women, and of nine- and eleven-year-old girls) were that women can "use genital self-examination as an exercise in self-acceptance," that "the sole function of the clitoris is to provide physical pleasure to the woman" and that "women have a right to enjoy their clitoris through masturbation." The flavor of the course in which Marrow was a guest lecturer is suggested by this from a list of exam questions "taken from supplemental readings": "The traditional double standard of morality for men and women is an example of: (a) sexual democracy, (b) woman's freedom from matriarchal responsibility, (c) sexual fascism, (d) the natural superiority of men." Marrow, who has taught at CSUS since 1974, has recently written, "The policy of silence around sexuality extends into the educational system."

The taxpayers of California, which is in constant financial crisis these days, can decide whether they like their money put to this use. For the rest of us, the question is: How can Rogers say that Marrow's lecture constituted sexual harassment? Marrow's lawyer says, "[Rogers] didn't like it and therefore he wants it to be illegal." But it sort of is at CSUS. There the sensitivity enforcers have written an admonitory brochure giving examples of sexual harassment, including this: "The display of sexually explicit pictures or cartoons." The brochure begins: "If you believe you are a victim of sexual harassment, it is important that you act." Rogers acted.

Two tenets of contemporary academic life are in hilarious conflict here. One is that academic standards are incompatible with academic freedom, so academics must feel no inhibitions about doing whatever they want. The other is that everyone has a right not to be offended or have their feelings hurt or be otherwise distressed. So Marrow rhapsodizes about wine bottles; Rogers acts like an antebellum southern belle who in the presence of a cad gets the vapors and collapses in a swirl of crinkling crinolines; lawyers are summoned; rights are unsheathed. Marrow says that in the future, "I intend to be even more narrative." Marrow exemplifies the travesty that much of today's academia is; so does the theory of victimization and rights that Rogers is invoking.

So it goes on campuses, where sensitivity about rights and sensibilities is particularly advanced. A student at San Bernardino Valley College has filed suit against the college, charging that she was told by an English professor to leave his class because she is not black and the course was reserved for students who are. At the University of Pennsylvania, a female student from Jamaica was asked to leave a meeting of "White Women Against Racism" because that is a "support group" and the presence of a black person would make the white women uncomfortable as they examined their prejudices. Besides, said a representative of the group, "We believe racism is a white problem." The New York State Education Department is investigating Cornell University's policy of racial and ethnic dormitories.

Of course campuses have not cornered the market on lunacy. An African-American in Omaha is seeking $40 million compensation for the emotional distress he and his sons suffered from their CD-ROM encyclopedia, which he says contains racial slurs. He is suing the company that made it and the store that sold it because when he inadvertently typed "nigger" while looking for references to the Niger River, he found that the CD-ROM hurt his feelings by including the word "nigger." The CD-ROM references include Joseph Conrad's novel *The Nigger of the Narcissus* and a passage from a biography of Martin Luther King, Jr. So it goes in a society exquisitely sensitive to rights, including the right to be exquisitely sensitive.

April 3, 1995

Tears and Chinese Take-Out Food at Tufts

Tears and Chinese take-out food were recently on Tufts University's political menu. The episode illuminated the paradoxical condition of political passion on America's campuses, where there is an inverse relationship between the prevalence and the importance of political passions.

Almost everything on campuses has become politicized. But given the peculiar notion of "the political" that obtains on campuses, academics have little political resonance outside their cloistered settings.

Tufts's student senate includes three nonvoting "culture representatives" elected by voting within organizations of African-Americans, Hispanic-Americans, and Asian-Americans. This bit of "identity politics" expresses contemporary liberalism's principle of "categorical representation," which underlies racial gerrymandering and other practices. The principle holds that the interests of particular groups can only be understood, empathized

37

with, and represented by members of that group. Who taught the Tufts students this principle? Their teachers, no doubt.

When the Senate cut $600 from the Chinese Culture Club's budget, Kim Tran, copresident of the Asian Community at Tufts, said that although the cut was not "face-to-face racism," it reflected institutional bias against Asians. Carol Wan, the CCC treasurer, called the cut an attack on "the legitimacy" of her culture. A portion of the cut pertained to Chinese take-out food that the CCC ordered for a Chinese New Year observance, and Wan said the cut "questioned the authenticity of take-out food as part of our culture." The student newspaper reported: "Several times during her speech, Wan began crying. 'It's sad that this is happening at Tufts, where it's supposed to be intercultural,' she said."

Nothing lubricates academic decision making as effectively as liberal guilt, so the CCC's funds were restored. But a lingering question is: Who teaches young people to be so exquisitely sensitive to perceived slights, so ready to read affronts into routine events in everyday life? Their teachers, no doubt.

America's professoriate is "politicized, yet apolitical." That is the judgment of Russell Jacoby, an adjunct professor of history at UCLA, writing in *The Chronicle of Higher Education.* He means that although "the immediate domain of the academic" has been politicized—knowledge and language; what the curriculum contains, what is said in the classroom—there is little interest in real politics.

The politics of the academics is political narcissism, or perhaps it is political solipsism. Jacoby calls it the "politicization of self," whereby one can be an activist merely by presenting oneself as a political issue, as in: "As a forty-nine-year-old black, lesbian, feminist, socialist mother of two, including one boy, and a member of an interracial couple. . . ." As Jacoby says, "This person's life is her political project."

There was a time—and Jacoby, a man of the nostalgic left, regrets its passing—when academics were incandescent about things like the fate of the Spanish Republic or the Vietnam War. But ethnic cleansing in Bosnia barely registered among academics. Instead, they have busied themselves with bizarre utterances such as (Jacoby provides this example) "postcolonial studies" having "positioned itself (*sic*) as a broad antiimperialist emancipatory project."

Today the academics' political—if it can properly be called that—focus is on "interpersonal encounters" and symbolic gestures, as with the instructor at the University of California at Santa Cruz who declared his classroom a deodorant- and perfume-free zone, as an antipollution measure. 'Twas a famous victory. . . .

Jacoby is particularly impatient with the intellectuals' conceit that various academic practices constitute "subversion" of the established order. In what Jacoby calls "the micropolitics of protest" there is earnest talk of, and courses about, "the insurgency of popular culture" and "the creativity of consumption." In the jargon of the moment, almost any subject can be "a site of contestation."

What does that mean? Nothing, really, but it illustrates the comic solemnity of academics investing what they do with cosmic significance. "It is," Jacoby writes, "all too easy for professors, whose lives unfold in front of books and computer screens, to begin seeing the world as completely made up of texts and symbols, and to conclude (or at least implicitly to believe) that changing the name changes the thing itself."

Perhaps conservatives should stop complaining about the sandbox politics practiced on campus. The students will outgrow their acquired reflex to read racism into a reluctance to subsidize take-out food. And the sublimation of political passions into such microdisputes may be a small price to pay for keeping the professors out of serious politics, where their record— remember their many infatuations, from Stalin to Mao to Castro—has been, to put it mildly, mixed.

April 18, 1996

The Sensitivity Sweepstakes at Chico

When communicating, little things can mean a lot. The actress Margaret Anglin once sent the following note to another actress, Minnie Fiske: "Margaret Anglin says Mrs. Fiske is the best actress in America." Mrs. Fiske added two commas and returned the note: "Margaret Anglin, says Mrs. Fiske, is the best actress in America." Buy a television set, you can get a "universal" remote control, so called because it controls both the set and a VCR. Is it "universal" because a television set and a VCR are, for most Americans, the universe? But perhaps it is possible to subject common usage to scrutiny that is too exacting. As they now know at California State University at Chico.

There someone used the D word and in the ensuing hubbub someone else used the L word. By the time the dust settled, sensitivities had been rubbed raw and an entertaining episode had been added to the annals of political correctness—assuming, perhaps insensitively, that the enforcers of campus orthodoxies are wrong when they say political correctness is a figment of reactionaries' imaginations. Anyway, here is what happened, as reported in *The Chronicle of Higher Education* by Courtney Leatherman.

The university administration was looking for a professor of philosophy, so it ran an advertisement: "We are seeking a dynamic classroom teacher and program builder. . . ." Well, sensitive people can only take so much in silence, and two women, an associate professor of English and the university's affirmative-action director (who initially approved the ad), spoke out. In an e-mail message to an administrator at another institution the affirmative-action director explained:

> The concern over the use of the word "dynamic" in advertising was over the fact that this term might send a message that the university is only interested in a certain kind of teaching style—the kinetic, dramatic style. As many members of minority groups are not associated with this style and as many women, particularly "ladylike" women do not go in for this style, it was decided that, as what we are looking for is an excellent teacher regardless of their (*sic*) teaching styles, it would be better to stay away from the term "dynamic" to avoid confusion.

Let us not trivialize this insight by citing contrary evidence that is merely anecdotal. (Jesse Jackson and Lady Thatcher, not dynamic; Al Gore and Richard Lugar, dynamic.) The university's provost, a sensitive sort, saw the point, saying "There is no necessary connection between being dynamic and being an excellent teacher," which is true. In subsequent ads the word "excellent" was substituted for "dynamic."

The associate professor of English said dynamic teachers may not be excellent, merely "windbags." She also noted that her Asian and Hispanic students are more reticent than whites in classes. However, she gave a Darwinian explanation of why most women academics are dynamic: "We had to compete with aggressive white males to get our jobs."

A Chico professor of history who is marvelously unmarked by modern history dismissed the controversy as "an incredibly tortured abuse of the English language," and a professor of philosophy said the university had advertised for a program builder, for goodness sake, and "didn't say 'inseminator' or 'nurturer.' " And it had better not.

A dean—deans are sensitive; it is part of the job description—said future advertisements will use adjectives like "innovative and creative." Only someone as dumb as a drawer full of doorknobs would suggest that those adjectives do not fit some minorities.

But before bidding farewell to sensitivity-soaked Chico, it would be nice to know why an associate professor of English bandies the provocative word "ladylike" and yet is allowed to remain at large. Everyone knows that that locution serves to privilege the phallocentric patriarchy's gender-benders. And why would a self-respecting, dynamic woman academic, having clawed her way into academia past aggressive white males, give a hoot what happens to females so retrograde as to allow themselves to seem "ladylike"?

Such conundrums constantly vex and roil campuses. And they should. After all, this is an age in which a town has removed DEAD END signs because they cause some people to think of death, and one university's law review uses, when possible, only female pronouns (except, of course, when referring to criminal defendants) and an Eddie Bauer catalogue has offered pitch-saturated kindling wood "felled by lightning or other natural causes," lest the friends of trees have their feelings hurt. Higher education must keep pace.

January 11, 1996

Anti-Americanism at the Smithsonian

President Clinton is looking for love in all the wrong places, with fatuities like a "middle-class bill of rights" and banalities like another increase in the minimum wage. He could add ten easy points to his approval rating without spending a dime or more than five minutes of his time. But before saying how, consider how life has felt to many Americans during recent decades of in-your-face government.

Their children have been bused away from neighborhood schools. Their children have come home from school, using the condoms they got there as bookmarks in the books they got there (*Heather Has Two Mommies* and *Daddy Has a Roommate*), condoms that are facets of sex education designed to compensate for the presumed backwardness of the parents. They have seen courts concoct myriad constitutional impediments to the execution of even vicious killers, and have seen courts make it problematic for parents even to be notified when their minor children want to have abortions. They have seen their nation's electoral map smeared with congressional districts shaped like roadkill so that some government-certified victim group can enjoy an entitlement to send one of its own to Washington. They have seen the federal government weave a racial, ethnic, and sexual spoils system, the premise of which is that life in America is so dismal that about 280 percent of the population qualifies for victim status. (A Hispanic-surnamed lesbian qualifies three times over—four if she is "disabled" by the "stress"

FROM THE WHIRRING LOOM

of working.) They have been called Yahoos for objecting to their tax dollars being used to display photographs of bullwhips in rectums and crucifixes in jars of urine. They have recently seen their tax dollars finance the writing of ideologically tendentious standards for the teaching of history (nineteen references to McCarthyism, none to Edison; the founding of the Sierra Club and National Organization for Women are considered momentous; so are Prudence Crandell and Speckled Snake).

The Smithsonian Institution, like the history standards, is besotted with the cranky anti-Americanism of the campuses where the American left has gone to lick its wounds, rationalize its irrelevance, and teach the humanities as an indictment of America as a blemish on Western civilization, which itself is considered a blemish on the planet. Four years ago the Smithsonian produced an "art" exhibit, "The West as America," wherein westward expansion was portrayed as an alloy of only three elements—capitalist rapacity, genocide, and ecocide. And now the Smithsonian is hip-deep in another morass of its own making.

For the fiftieth anniversary this August of Hiroshima, the Smithsonian is planning to display the fuselage of the *Enola Gay*, the B-29 that dropped the bomb. The Smithsonian wants to portray Japan as yet another victim of racist, imperialist America. Said the Smithsonian's initial script, "For most Americans, this . . . was a war of vengeance. For most Japanese, it was a war to defend their unique culture against Western imperialism." Never mind that the Japanese used bayonets to try to pin their unique culture to Manchuria, China, Southeast Asia, and the Philippines.

Washington knows what the Smithsonian is up to, thanks to the reporting of the *Washington Post*'s Ken Ringle and the *Post*'s editorials. ("Incredibly propagandistic and intellectually shabby," said the *Post* of the Smithsonian's initial plans.) And on television last Sunday, the president's chief of staff, Leon Panetta, was asked if he understood how annoying the Smithsonian's antics are to many people.

He said: We are in a "transition period" and people are "angry about a lot of things"—government, their security, their children's future—and we need "tough decisions" and not "simplified answers." Panetta's questioner tried again, asking if Panetta can sympathize with people who say, "Can't the government in Washington even display artifacts without attacking the country?" Panetta replied that "there are legitimate views on all sides of difficult issues like that."

Until Democrats—what *is* the matter with them?—stop talking such mush about assaults on the nation's values and honor, their party will continue to wither. But suppose Panetta's boss strode into the White House press room and, with appropriate podium-pounding, declared: "Heads are going to roll and funds are going to become scarce at the Smithsonian unless the cloth-headed, condescending perpetrators of such insulting rubbish quit using our money to tell us that our nation is nasty and that we are philistines for resenting it when our betters tutor us about our nation's sinfulness." Etcetera.

Five minutes, maximum. Ten points, minimum.

January 26, 1995

Of Metal Dollars and Males Bonding with Strippers

Women on the farther shores of feminism might be right after all. Perhaps America really is a phallocentric patriarchy run for the convenience of men. Perhaps that is why Congress is so reluctant to save hundreds of millions a year by replacing the one dollar bill with a longer-lived metal coin.

Metal coins, although heavier than paper bills, are fine for women to carry in their purses, less so for men's pants pockets. So metal coins may be too great a sacrifice even for this autumn of frugality.

Still, if metal coins replaced dollar bills, men might start carrying purses, which would advance an agenda favored by many advanced thinkers, that of blurring the distinction between the sexes. And a men's purse industry would nicely nudge the economy onward. So, the metal dollar would be a triple play—an economic stimulus, a bite out of the deficit, and an affirmation of androgyny.

Every other industrial nation has replaced with metal coins those paper bills valued comparably to the dollar. Of course the Clinton administration, which praises generic "change" and opposes most specific changes, opposes the metal dollar. However, hundreds of millions of dollars in savings is not chopped liver. Think of all the chocolate-covered performance artists and homoerotic photography exhibits the National Endowment for the Arts could sponsor with that piece of change. You would rather not think of that? Then think of whatever the government does that you would like it to do more of. Take your time.

But while you tarry, interest groups are weighing in. Kelly Owen of the *Los Angeles Times* reports that the Mount Vernon Ladies Association, keeper of George Washington's memory, is appalled that their hero would lose his place of honor on the venerable greenback. Some people worry that the metal dollar would look too much like a quarter, but metal partisans say it could be colored by including copper in it. Of course that, like everything else anyone thinks of doing, alarms environmentalists, who say copper mining makes holes in the ground, pollutes water, and disturbs animals.

The American Council of the Blind favors a metal dollar for obvious reasons. But the metal dollar is opposed by a group called Save the Greenback, which Kelly Owen says represents unions from the Bureau of Printing and Engraving and companies that supply things like the ink and linen that go into dollar bills. Urban mass transit officials prefer metal to paper. The Chicago Transit Authority, for example, spends twenty-two dollars to straighten and count every thousand one dollar bills, and it counts 285,000 a day. The vending machine industry is backing the metal dollar, although vending machines are perfectly capable of ingesting a perfectly ironed paper dollar.

The metal dollar is an idea ripe for this autumn, which features the Republican Congress calling the nation's bluff. Republicans are saying to the country: You say you want a balanced budget. How much do you want it? Enough to bear the burden of metal dollars?

Apparently not, perhaps because the last two times the government tried metal dollars, it made a hash of things. The Eisenhower dollar, introduced in 1971, was a clunker, the size of the old silver dollar. Besides, paper dollars stayed in circulation, as they did in 1979 when the Susan B. Anthony dollar appeared, looking too much like a quarter. The mint stopped making the things after three years, although the mint still has many millions of them in a closet.

John F. Kelly of the *Washington Post* reports that some women artists, and men who salute their artistry, passionately want paper dollars preserved. The women are topless dancers who receive part of their compensation in the form of dollar bills tucked into their garters and G-strings by appreciative patrons. This form of positive feedback could not survive the coming of metal dollars, according to an expert that Kelly found. He is Don Waitt, publisher of the *Exotic Dancer Directory*. (Is this a prolific country, or what?)

"Girls," says Waitt, "have been dancing topless and nude since caveman days. They'll find a way to adapt, whether it's to carry a cup or something else. But it definitely destroys the whole mystique and the whole give and take of the industry. When you tip the girl a dollar, there is a brief bond there, or an imagined bond between the girl and the guy. To just drop a dollar into a cup, it's just not the same."

A balanced budget will involve pain, but evidently will not involve the cruelty of metal money that would impede such bonding.

November 2, 1995

Baby Boomers, So Elevated in Every Way . . .

What? You say you have not yet bought a Patek Philippe wristwatch? Yes, of course, no law says you have to do the right thing for your descendants. But, really, buying such a watch, even though it is a bit pricey, is not crass. Quite the contrary, it is simply the thoughtful, genteel thing to do.

That is the message of a successful advertising campaign. Patek Philippe is easily selling all the watches it allocates to the American market, where, says a Texas jewelry store owner, people "are coming in and asking for the watch in the ad." This is worth pondering because advertising generally works not when it changes society's mind but rather when it conforms to society's thinking.

The ads appear in magazines read by people who, to say no more, know where their next meal is coming from—magazines like *Forbes, Town & Country, Architectural Digest,* and *Newsweek International.* One version features a photograph from the rear of the rear—the photo is cropped just above his waist—of a man seated on a piano bench. Beneath the bench dangle the legs of a child in pajamas. The child is sitting on the man's lap, evidently playing on the keyboard. The text of the ad reads:

> Begin your *own* tradition.
> Whatever innovations Patek Philippe introduce, every watch is still crafted by hand. . . . And because of the exceptional workmanship, each one is a unique object. Which is perhaps why some people feel that you never actually own a Patek Philippe. You merely look after it for the next generation.

In another ad, three generations of blonde females are in the backseat of a car, and in ecstasy. Mother and grandmother, both looking vivacious, flank a winsome girl who is blowing bubbles, delighting the other two. The text says:

> Begin your *own* tradition.
> Every Patek Philippe watch is crafted by hand. So each one is subtly different from the next. This is what makes it uniquely personal to its owner. The ladies' Golden Ellipse ref. 4831 has 160 of the finest diamonds set in 18 karat solid gold. Any woman who owns one will treasure it, enhancing its true value for the one who wears it next.

Get it? Spending more than $8,000 for a flashy watch—the Golden Ellipse costs $15,000—may be a pleasure, but certainly not a tacky pleasure, or only a pleasure. It also is an act of altruism, of responsible stewardship regarding a tradition. In short, it is . . . family values.

This, according to a *Forbes* news story on the advertising campaign, is what a deep thinker about social trends calls "conditional hedonism." Cheryl Russell, who writes *Boomer Report*, puts it in perspective: "Family history and heirlooms become increasingly important in life, particularly when parents start dying, and that's exactly the situation a lot of boomers are in right now." ("Could become an heirloom," says the Lands' End catalogue about . . . a handmade cableknit sweater.)

Wouldn't you know that the baby-boom generation, which has pioneered new dimensions of narcissism and self-approval, would find a way to flatter itself by presenting conspicuous consumption as an activity of high-mindedness and social responsibility, like recycling soda cans or mailing a check to Planned Parenthood. And this has a political dimension, in light of the history of greed, as currently understood.

Greed, like other forms of disagreeableness, entered the world when Adam and Eve were disobedient. Still, through the centuries the human race had its moral ups as well as downs, producing, on the up side, such exemplary people as Socrates and Saint Francis and Adlai Stevenson. But at noon on January 20, 1981, there began a big down: the Reagan Era of Greed.

It was terrible. Young men started wearing red suspenders and selling one another junk bonds, and even government employees got caught up in the dark spirit of the times—became, so to speak, victims of the Reagan Era of Greed. When authorities finally caught on to the spying that Aldrich Ames had begun doing for money during the 1980s, *Newsweek* explained that "greed was a national pastime in the mid-eighties."

Because the Reagan Era of Greed was replaced by something kinder and gentler at noon on January 20, 1989, and especially because the White House has been scrubbed clean of Republicans since January 20, 1993, it is important to understand that it is theoretically impossible for coarse materialism or other wretched excess to be at work in America today. Granted, there is a brisk business in Patek Philippe watches, $1,600 Hermès handbags, $600 Gucci boots, $2,000 Chanel suits, and Porsches and Mercedes-Benzes. But only superficial people will be misled by the superficial resemblance to the bad old days, as the *Washington Post*'s Margaret Webb Pressler explains: "This market has evolved from the 'greed-is-good' era 1980s, when well-to-do consumers wanted glitzy products to show off their new wealth. Now, the emphasis is on traditional brand names that connote quality."

You do see the difference, don't you? As Pressler notes, "Glitz is out; quality is in." In the morally improved 1990s, customers want brands which, "although wildly expensive, convey extremely high quality and a sense of timelessness." For example, a Patek Philippe watch "doesn't shout a message of status; rather, it's a quiet statement to a more discerning group of people." Retailers and analysts tell Pressler that spending "is not as showy or status-conscious as it was in the 1980s. People who can afford luxury goods still want to have something that sets them apart, but they don't want or need to advertise it the way they used to."

That is, unlike in the Reagan Era of Greed, people now want to be set apart, but *tastefully*, and as custodians of heirlooms for the rising generations of altruists. You do see the difference, don't you?

March 3, 1997

A Heartbreak Hunk and a Nice Prom

"What does a woman want?" Freud famously asked, then failed to answer in a slew of books. But suppose he were still with us and asked, "What does a teenage girl want?" That's easy: Brad Pitt and a nice prom.

That conclusion is reached after deep and prolonged immersion in the fat, glossy magazines that cater to that cohort of females. The two most successful magazines are *Seventeen* and *YM* (which stands for Young and Modern). *The New York Times* recently reported that those two, each with a circulation of about two million, are in hot competition for the advertisers who are in hot competition for the loose change in the pockets of the baggy jeans of teenage girls. It is a tidy sum: $34 billion. It can buy a lot of skin cream ("Every moisturizer is soft on skin. Here's one that's tough on zits"), compact discs, prom dresses, and tickets to Brad Pitt movies.

Pitt played the younger brother in *A River Runs Through It.* In it he was a terrific fly fisherman. He is even better as a subject for magazine stories, such as "Heartbreak Hunk Brad Pitt" and "Brad Pitt's Weird Secret" (the secret is that he carries a roll of toilet paper in his car). He even creeps into advice on decoding dreams: "If you dream about Brad Pitt, you want a long-term romance with a guy you're crushing on."

About that last item, two things to remember. First, "long-term" is a phrase with elastic meaning. Witness a letter that begins, "My boyfriend and I got into a fight on the night of our one-month anniversary." And if the use of "crush" as a verb in the paragraph above gives you the willies, you will find these magazines hard sledding. Their texts are blizzards of sentences featuring words like "stressed" and "bummed" and "psyched" and "grossed." And "like," as in the title of an article, "Like, Yuk: Don't Be a Fashion Disaster." And "omigod," as in this cover headline: "Omigod! My Boyfriend Gave Me a Gross Disease."

Which brings us to the subject of sex. It does pop up. About everything:

47

"Extra: Best Bikini (Make Him Sweat)." *The New York Times* says that *YM*, somewhat the brassier of the two magazines, features "sex-on-the-surface articles about how to attract young men and then avoid sex with them." Not always.

True, *YM* reports—with a breathlessness suggesting astonishment, but with the evident intent to reassure readers that abstinence is not weird— this: "70 percent of all teenagers are still virgins by the time they turn sixteen." And a recent cover story was, "Guy Virgins: Why So Many Hunks Are Holding Out."

Evidently readers are looking for advice, and some of the advice is useful in dispelling misunderstandings, such as "You can't get pregnant the first time you have sex." Says *YM*, briskly: "Yes, you can. Sex isn't like the SATs, where the first time doesn't always count."

Much of the advice is not, well, strenuously judgmental: "Get to know what kind of person someone is before you have sex with him." But a lot of the advice concerns rather sweet worries, such as "My boyfriend is really into PDAs." (Those are public displays of affection.) And there is a remarkable amount of analysis of the mechanics and etiquette of kissing, which turns out to be more complicated for novices than you, seasoned reader, may remember.

When you come up for air after a dive into these magazines, you are decidedly not nostalgic for your teenage years, which obviously are years of high anxiety—about hair, skin, nails, breath, and every other facet of the body. For teenage girls, even more than for teenage boys, the body is a comprehensive problem, and a frequent betrayer.

A fundamental philosophic debate is between those who say "I have a body" and those who say "I am a body." There are many more of the former than of the latter, partly—largely, no doubt—because humanity's self-esteem is served by the idea that there is more to us than flesh and blood and sinew.

Is there really a "ghost in the machine"? Let's not try to settle that here and now. But regarding teenagers of all sorts—and some of my friends, including one of my best friends, my daughter, are in that cohort—let us note a thought from essayist Joseph Epstein. In his latest book, *With My Trousers Rolled,* he faults one author for "anthropomorphizing children." But it is acceptable to do that with teenagers.

July 13, 1995

At Melissa Drexler's Prom

According to a friend, eighteen-year-old Melissa Drexler paused in front of the mirror in the bathroom to touch up her makeup before rejoining her date on the dance floor at the prom. She had just tossed her six-pound, six-ounce baby boy into a trash bin next to the bloodstained stall in the restroom where she had given birth. "She seemed to be enjoying herself," said a classmate about Drexler's postpartum dancing.

Medical examiners have determined that the baby was alive during the birthing process, which occurred early in the prom. He was soon discovered by a maintenance worker who thought the trash bag was unusually heavy. Unsuccessful attempts were made to resuscitate him.

Believe it or not, much may depend on whether it can be determined that the baby died before the umbilical cord was cut. Or whether the air sacs in his lungs inflated, indicating that he breathed, however briefly, independent of his mother. Ms. Drexler may be charged with something. Maybe murder. Maybe endangering a child. (Maybe conducting a partial-birth abortion at a prom without a license?)

Who taught Ms. Drexler to think, or not think, in a way that caused her to regard her newborn baby as disposable trash? Many people and things, no doubt.

She may have come from a less than attentive home environment. An assistant prosecutor says family members did not know she was pregnant. She has grown up in a society that does not stress deferral of gratification, and it's not her fault that the baby arrived during the prom, for Pete's sake. She has come of age in a society where condom-dispensing schools teach sex education in the modern manner, which has been well-described as plumbing for hedonists. If she is like millions of other young adults, she has spent thousands of hours watching movies and television programs not designed to encourage delicacy of feelings or to suggest that sexuality has morally complex dimensions and serious consequences. If she is like millions of other young adults, she has pumped into her ears thousands of hours of the coarsening lyrics of popular music. And she certainly has grown up in a social atmosphere saturated with opinion leaders' approbation of, and collaboration with, the political program of reducing abortion—the killing of something—to a mere "choice," like choosing to smoke a cigarette, only not nearly that serious.

However, foremost among the moral tutors who prepared Ms. Drexler to act as she did is the Supreme Court. By pretending in *Roe* v. *Wade* not to know when life begins, the Court encouraged looking away from the stark fact that abortion kills something. Ignoring elementary science, the Court said, preposterously, that a fetus is "potential life." But as Walker Percy, an M.D. as well as a novelist, wrote, it is a commonplace of modern biology that a life begins "when the chromosomes of the sperm fuse with the chromosomes of the ovum to form a new DNA complex that thenceforth directs the ontogenesis of the organism." Percy continued: "The onset of individual life is not a dogma of the church but a fact of science. How much more convenient if we lived in the thirteenth century, when no one knew anything about microbiology and arguments about the onset of life were legitimate."

Biology does not allow the abortion argument to be about, or anyone to be agnostic about, when life begins. Conscientious people can disagree about the appropriate moral and legal status to be accorded the life that abortion ends. But science complicates—to say no more—the "pro-choice" movement's project of making the world safe for the likes of Ms. Drexler, the project of presenting the ending of an inconvenient young life as akin to a bowel movement.

Pregnancy is a continuum. What begins at conception will, if there is no natural misfortune or deliberate attack, become a child. If it becomes a child at a prom, it must be attacked quickly, lest the whole night be a bummer.

The barbarism at the prom is being termed a "tragedy" calling for "compassion" all around. No, an earthquake is a tragedy. This is an act of wickedness—a wicked choice—and a society incapable of anger about it is simply decadent. Perhaps the brevity of the life of Ms. Drexler's son will accelerate the transformation of the nation's vague unrest into a vivid consciousness that today's abortion culture, with its casual creation and destruction of life, is evil.

June 15, 1997

POSTSCRIPT

"Go tell the boys we'll be right out," Ms. Drexler called to a friend from the stall before returning to the dance, where she ate a salad. Authorities surmise that she may have cut the umbilical cord with the sharp edge of a sanitary napkin dispenser. Two weeks later Ms. Drexler was charged with murder and endangering the welfare of a child. An assistant county medical examiner established the cause of the baby's death as "asphyxia due to manual strangulation and obstruction of the external airway orifices." Said a county prosecutor, "The child was alive when he was born. It fits the definition of a 'knowing murder.'" Some people, conducting diagnoses from a distance, argued that Ms. Drexler's act was so aberrant as to be indicative of psychosis and without social significance derived from promptings by the culture.

However, this was the third case—the third of which there was knowledge—of alleged infanticide and baby abandonment involving New Jersey
youths within a few months. And the Washington Post story reporting Ms.
Drexler's indictment included this: "Since the prom-baby case at least two
other newborns have been found, one of them alive, after being abandoned in
northern New Jersey." This, just in one part of one state. It is a big country.

The day Ms. Drexler's indictment was reported, the lead story in the
Post's Metro section began: "Whoever discarded the baby yesterday did not
bother to wrap her. She was dumped naked amid a pile of beer cans and cigarette butts on the cold concrete floor of an apartment building storage
room at Alpine Apartments in Temple Hills, Prince George's County [Mary-
land] police reported yesterday."

Choice

RACINE, WISCONSIN—On a cold night last March, Deborah J. Zimmerman, drunk and nearly nine months pregnant, was wheeled into a
local hospital for an emergency Cesarean section. As the obstetrics
staff pleaded with her to allow attachment of a fetal monitor, Ms. Zimmerman at first refused. Insisting that she did not want to give birth,
she told a surgical aide, "I'm just going to go home and keep drinking
and drink myself to death, and I'm going to kill this thing because I
don't want it anyways." Later that night she gave birth to a girl whose
blood alcohol level was .199, nearly twice the threshold for a legal
finding of intoxication in Wisconsin. . . . Ms. Zimmerman . . . has been
charged with attempted murder.
                                        —The New York Times, August 17, 1996

CORPUS CHRISTI, TEXAS—A man who drove drunk into a pregnant
woman's car was convicted today of killing the woman's baby, who
was born a month and a half premature because of the crash. Jurors
were not required to consider whether Krystal Zuniga was a person or
a fetus at the time of the accident. . . .
                                        —Associated Press, October 17, 1996

A healthy baby girl only a few hours old was found yesterday in a
cardboard box outside an apartment building in Brooklyn. . . .
                                        —The New York Times, October 28, 1996

COMMACK, LONG ISLAND—A cleaner found the body of a newborn in a movie theater rest room this morning, and the authorities said the infant had died of asphyxiation.
—The New York Times, *November 19, 1996*

The college student accused of helping his girlfriend kill their newborn son after she gave birth in a Delaware motel room became the subject of a nationwide police search last night after he failed to surrender to face murder charges.
—The New York Times, *November 19, 1996*

Questions come to mind concerning some recent exercises of the right of "choice," the foundation of "reproductive freedom."

About the two eighteen-year-olds who are charged with having chosen to kill their seven-and-a-half-pound boy, putting his body in a trash bag in the motel's Dumpster: Don't young people read newspapers? Don't they know that, thanks to President Clinton, they could have chosen to have a doctor suck their baby's brains out, and Delaware would not have chosen to charge them with murder?

How did the person who chose the Long Island movie theater rest room as the place to discard the asphyxiated baby make that particular choice? How does one choose that venue over, say, a Starbucks? Has the mother subsequently received any, well, questioning looks from friends, family, or coworkers? Pregnant one day, not pregnant the next, when is the baby shower?

Instead of scandalously choosing to leave the baby in a box in Brooklyn, why did the woman, if it was she, not choose, a few hours earlier, to exercise her presidentially protected (by President Clinton's veto of Congress's ban on the procedure) right to a partial-birth abortion? The baby would have been pulled by its legs almost out of the birth canal, the doctor would have stuck scissors into the base of its skull, opened the scissors to make a hole for a suction tube, and sucked out its brains. No box, no scandal.

How could the Corpus Christi jurors decide that a murder had occurred without deciding whether the victim was a person or a fetus? What was murdered, "fetal material"? The logic of *Roe* v. *Wade*, as of partial-birth abortion, is that until birth, a fetus has the legal status and moral standing of hamburger in a woman's stomach. How could the Corpus Christi man, drunk or sober, be guilty of murdering Krystal when Krystal's mother has that presidentially cherished right to choose to have Krystal's brains sucked out?

For that matter, why does not Ms. Zimmerman's constitutional "privacy" right—"our bodies, our choices"—give her the right to choose to kill her fetus with alcohol? Why is a doctor's scissors and suction tube a preferable choice?

On September 26, 1996, during the Senate debate on whether to override Clinton's veto of the ban on such abortions, there occurred the following exchange between Senator Rick Santorum (R., Pa.), who favored the override, and Senator Russ Feingold (D., Wis.), who opposed it:

> Santorum: "The senator from Wisconsin says that this decision should be left up to the mother and the doctor, as if there is absolutely no limit that could be placed on what decision that they make. . . . My question is this: That if that baby were delivered breech style and everything was delivered except for the head, and for some reason that that baby's head would slip out—that the baby was completely delivered—would it then still be up to the doctor and the mother to decide whether to kill that baby?"
>
> Feingold: ". . . The standard of saying it has to be a determination, by a doctor, of health of the mother, is a sufficient standard that would apply to that situation. And that would be an adequate standard."
>
> Santorum: "That doesn't answer the question. Let's assume . . . the head is accidentally delivered. Would you allow the doctor to kill the baby?"
>
> Feingold: ". . . That is a question that should be answered by a doctor, and by the woman who receives the advice from the doctor."

There was also this exchange with Senator Frank Lautenberg (D., N.J.):

> Santorum: "If the baby was delivered accidentally—the head slipped out—would you allow the doctor to kill the baby?"
>
> Lautenberg: "I am not making the decision. If that is . . ."
>
> Santorum: "But that's what we are doing here, senator; we are making decisions."
>
> Lautenberg: "You are making decisions that say a doctor doesn't have . . ."
>
> Santorum: "So two inches make the difference as to whether you'll answer that question?"
>
> Lautenberg: "No, what makes the difference is someone who has the knowledge and intelligence and experience making the decision . . ."

That is clear enough: Neither Feingold nor Lautenberg would say "no" to treating the killing of a newborn baby as a mere *choice*. The point of contention has become, as abortion opponents have long warned that it would, not whether legally protectable life begins at conception but whether legally protectable life begins at birth.

Meanwhile, back in Delaware, the Delaware law requires prosecutors to seek the death penalty when a homicide victim is under fourteen. So the two eighteen-year-olds who are charged with choosing to kill their baby just minutes after it was no longer eligible for a partial-birth abortion are themselves eligible for capital punishment.

In Delaware, such punishment is by lethal injection. Could Delaware choose to execute the two by inserting scissors into the bases of their skulls, opening the scissors, inserting suction tubes, and sucking out their brains? Of course not. The Constitution forbids choosing cruel and unusual punishments.

November 24, 1996 and February 3, 1997

Fanatics for "Choice"

Americans are beginning to recoil against the fanaticism that has helped to produce this fact: More than a quarter of all American pregnancies are ended by abortions. Abundant media attention has been given to the extremism that has tainted the right-to-life movement. Now events are exposing the extraordinary moral evasions and callousness characteristic of fanaticism, prevalent in the abortion-rights lobby.

Begin with "partial-birth abortions." Pro-abortion extremists object to that name, preferring "intact dilation and evacuation," for the same reason the pro-abortion movement prefers to be called "pro-choice." What is "intact" is a baby. During the debate that led to House passage of a ban on partial-birth abortions, the right-to-life movement was criticized for the sensationalism of its print advertisements featuring a Dayton nurse's description of such an abortion:

> The mother was six months pregnant. The baby's heartbeat was clearly visible on the ultrasound screen. The doctor went in with forceps and grabbed the baby's legs and pulled them down into the birth canal. Then he delivered the baby's body and the arm—everything but the head. The doctor kept the baby's head just inside the uterus. The baby's little fingers were clasping and unclasping, and his feet were kicking. Then the doctor stuck the scissors through the back of his head, and the baby's arms jerked out in a flinch, a startle reaction, like a baby does when he thinks that he might fall. The doctor opened up the scissors, stuck a high-powered suction tube into the opening, and sucked the baby's brains out.

To object to this as sensationalism is to say that discomforting truths should be suppressed. But increasingly, the language of pro-abortion people betrays a flinching from facts. In a woman's story about her chemical abortion, published last year in *Mother Jones* magazine, she quotes her doctor as saying, "By Sunday you won't see on the monitor what we call the heartbeat." "What we call"? In partial-birth abortions the birth is kept (just barely) partial to preserve the legal fiction that a baby (what some pro-abortion people call "fetal material") is not being killed. An abortionist has told *The New York Times* that some mothers find such abortions comforting because after the killing, the small body can be "dressed and held" so the (if pro-abortionists will pardon the expression) mother can "say good-bye." *The New York Times* reports, "Most of the doctors interviewed said they saw no moral difference between dismembering the fetus within the uterus and partially delivering it, intact, before killing it." Yes.

Opponents of a ban on partial-birth abortions say almost all such abortions are medically necessary. However, an abortionist at the Dayton clinic is quoted as saying 80 percent are elective. Opponents of a ban on such abortions assert that the baby is killed before the procedure, by the anesthesia given to the mother. (The baby "undergoes demise," in the mincing words of Kate Michelman of the National Abortion and Reproductive Rights Action League. Does Michelman say herbicides cause the crab grass in her lawn to "undergo demise"? Such Orwellian language is a sure sign of squeamishness.) However, the president of the American Society of Anesthesiologists says this "misinformation" has "absolutely no basis in scientific fact" and might endanger pregnant women's health by deterring them from receiving treatment that is safe.

Opponents of a ban say there are only about 600 such procedures a year. Let us suppose, as not everyone does, the number 600 is accurate concerning the more than 13,000 abortions performed after twenty-one weeks of gestation. Still, 600 is a lot. Think of two crashes of jumbo airliners. Opponents of the ban darkly warn that it would be the first step toward repeal of all abortion rights. Columnist John Leo of *U.S. News & World Report* says that is akin to the gun lobby's argument that a ban on assault weapons must lead to repeal of the Second Amendment.

In a prophecy born of hope, many pundits have been predicting that the right-to-life "extremists" would drastically divide the Republican Party. But seventy-three House Democrats voted to ban partial-birth abortions; only fifteen Republicans opposed the ban. If the ban survives the Senate, President Clinton will probably veto it. The convention that nominated him refused to allow the Democratic governor of Pennsylvania, Bob Casey, who is pro-life, to speak. Pro-choice speakers addressed the 1992 Republican Convention. The two presidential candidates who hoped that a pro-choice stance would resonate among Republicans—Governor Pete

Wilson, Senator Arlen Specter—have become the first two candidates to fold their tents.

In October in *The New Republic*, Naomi Wolf, a feminist and pro-choice writer, argued that by resorting to abortion rhetoric that recognizes neither life nor death, pro-choice people "risk becoming precisely what our critics charge us with being: callous, selfish, and casually destructive men and women who share a cheapened view of human life." Other consequences of a "lexicon of dehumanization" about the unborn are "hardness of heart, lying, and political failure." Wolf said that the "fetus means nothing" stance of the pro-choice movement is refuted by common current practices of parents-to-be who have framed sonogram photos and fetal heartbeat stethoscopes in their homes. Young upscale adults of child-bearing age are a solidly pro-choice demographic group. But they enjoy watching their unborn babies on sonograms, responding to outside stimuli, and they read *The Well Baby Book*, which says: "Increasing knowledge is increasing the awe and respect we have for the unborn baby and is causing us to regard the unborn baby as a real person long before birth. . . ."

Wolf argued for keeping abortion legal but treating it as a matter of moral gravity because "grief and respect are the proper tones for all discussions about choosing to endanger or destroy a manifestation of life." This temperate judgment drew from Jane Johnson, interim president of Planned Parenthood, a denunciation of the "view that there are good and bad reasons for abortion." So, who now are the fanatics?

December 11, 1995

Eventful 1965

There never has been an uneventful year in American history. How could there be? This nation, continental in scope and creedal in nature, is congenitally restless and constantly improvising. But rarely has there been a year eventful in the way 1965 was. That year was the hinge of our postwar history. The prestige of government, and government's confidence, not to say hubris, were at apogees. They were higher than at any time since 1945, and arguably higher than at any time since government came here with the first colonists on their errand into the American wilderness. In the autumn of 1965, that year that was the incubator of so many of our current controversies, *The Public Interest* was born. In the nick of time. There was a whirlwind in the White House and whirl was about to become king.

The first issue of this journal appeared in the first week of October. The front pages of *The New York Times* that week reported Fidel Castro's revelation that Che Guevara had left Cuba earlier in the year for what Castro called "a new field of battle in the struggle against imperialism." Secretary of Defense Robert McNamara announced that U.S. forces in Vietnam—there had been no combat troops there when the year began—numbered 130,000 and might be increased. Republican leaders, still smarting from the anti-Goldwater landslide of the previous November, denied any connection between their party and the John Birch Society. At the Statue of Liberty, President Johnson signed a bill liberalizing immigration: A society assured of a future characterized by surplus could afford to be welcoming. In Crawfordville, Georgia, state troopers turned away black children as they tried to board buses bound for all-white schools.

The most popular movie was *The Sound of Music* and the most-watched television program was *Bonanza*: folk singers and cowboys practicing what would come to be called family values. One of the year's most popular songs was Frank Sinatra's ballad "It Was a Very Good Year." For those for whom the going was especially good, a six-room duplex on Fifth Avenue in the 1960s could be had for $575 a month. Even an IBM key punch operator could make as much as $90 a week. Another very popular song—decidedly no ballad—was the Rolling Stones' "(I Can't Get No) Satisfaction." But that song was about girls, not politics.

It was a year in which the 8 percent growth of GNP drove the Dow Jones average to 969, with negligible inflation (1.6 percent) and essentially full employment (the unemployment rate was 4.5 percent). It was a year of immense satisfaction to the president who bestrode Washington and was causing that city to supplant New York, where *The Public Interest* was published until 1987, as the focus of national attention. After *The Public Interest* moved to Washington, Irving Kristol, its coeditor, wrote, "New York may not be what it used to be, but we understand that Washington is not yet what it might be." If in 1965, Washington was not the nation's steering wheel and accelerator, that wasn't for want of trying by Lyndon Johnson.

In 1965 Lyndon Johnson was in a hurry. On the fourth of January, sixteen days before his inauguration, he stood at the rostrum of the House of Representatives announcing "the excitement of great expectations." Woodrow Wilson, the first president to provide a theory for the modern presidency as uniquely qualified interpreter of the public's unarticulated yearnings and unrecognized needs, had, fittingly, been the first president since Jefferson actually to go to Congress to deliver a State of the Union message. Johnson, characteristically, would do more than that. Stephen Gettinger of *Congressional Quarterly* notes that in 1965 Johnson became the first president to deliver a State of the Union address to a national prime-time television audience. There was a time when virtually all presidential communication was addressed to the legislative branch, not to the public at large. But that had changed, especially since the coming of broadcasting, and the use made of it by Franklin Roosevelt, who was president when Johnson first came to Washington as a Capitol Hill staffer. The legislative branch was no longer enough of an audience.

Besides, the legislative branch arrayed before Johnson that night was, he had every right to think, his poodle. It had been decisively shaped by the 1964 election, which presumably had forever settled the hash of a certain strand of conservatism—the southern and southwestern sort that spoke anachronistically of a federal government of limited, delegated, and enumerated powers. That conservatism had been ridden into the sunset and out of history by Barry Goldwater, the "cheerful malcontent." His was the ideology of a minority that was not at all cheerful. That minority believed that the government was becoming oppressive. But Johnson's 61 percent of the vote indicated that that minority did not much matter. Sixty-eight of 100 senators and 295 of 435 representatives were Democrats. House Democrats took away the seniority of two of their southern colleagues who had supported Goldwater. Best to nip in the bud any southern flirtation with the Republican Party. (The punishment may have fit the crime, but it was not a success as a deterrent. In the South, in every election since 1964, Republican candidates for House seats have received more votes than in the preceding election, and Democratic candidates have received fewer.)

Johnson is the only president (his successor, Richard Nixon, came close) who spent virtually his entire adult life in Washington. Marinated in the culture of government, and the first southern president elected since the Civil War, Johnson understood what the swollen ranks of Democrats meant: For the first time since 1938, the Democratic congressional party was no longer hostage to its southern contingent. In 1938, when Johnson was a Texas freshman congressman, he had seen Roosevelt rebuked in the congressional elections, partly as a reaction against his plan to "pack" the Supreme Court by enlarging it. Between 1939 and 1965, coalitions of Republicans and southern Democrats could, more often than not, prevent the ascendancy of a liberal legislating majority. Now, at last, liberalism had something elusive and evanescent—unlimited opportunity. Thirty years later, liberalism would still be struggling to recover from the use its adherents made of their opportunity.

Gettinger writes that Congress took no recesses that year as it responded to sixty-three formal presidential messages. In October, Johnson would declare it the greatest session of Congress in history. Not everyone was enthralled. Goldwater called it "the Xerox Congress" and Representative Mel Laird of Wisconsin, chairman of the House Republican Conference, said, "Unless the legislative branch stands for something more than a rubber stamp, it is not Republicans who will be a minority; it will be the entire Congress, dwarfed and dragooned by a great and overbearing executive branch." Thirty years later, the presidency is a miniaturized and marginalized office in a Washington dominated by the Republican speaker of the House—the strongest speaker since Johnson's friend Sam Rayburn. When the country decided it wanted less-energetic government, it—with a large assist from the end of the Cold War—caused energy to flow from the executive to Capitol Hill.

Actually, in spite of Congress's year of hyperkinesis in 1965, both political branches were then in the process of being somewhat marginalized by the judiciary. It is arguable that, since the 1954 school-desegregation ruling, the Supreme Court has been the most important institution shaping the evolution of American society. In 1965 the Court lit a fuse that would lead in eight years to an explosion that still rocks American politics.

In 1965, *Griswold* v. *Connecticut,* the Court ruled unconstitutional an unenforced Connecticut law banning the use of contraceptives or the giving of advice about their use. The case was ginned up with the help of several liberal organizations, perhaps to get the Court to strike a blow for advanced thinking in general. The Warren Court never had to be asked twice to do that. However, in this case, the Court did rather more than that. And in yet another demonstration of the Law of Unintended Consequences, its ruling ignited a political force that the people who liked the ruling did not consider at all advanced in its thinking.

It is reported that, when the justices met in conference to begin deliberations about *Griswold,* Chief Justice Warren said he favored striking down the law but did not—yet—have a theory of why, exactly, the law was unconstitutional. The prime movers behind the challenge to the law—the director of the Planned Parenthood League and the League's New Haven Center—said the law violated their First Amendment right of association. To Justice Black, a sturdy friend of the First Amendment, this was a bit thick: "The right of association is for me a right of assembly and the right of the husband and wife to assemble in bed is a new right of assembly for me." Not to worry. The Warren Court operated on the principle of first deciding what is right and what is wrong and then finding a constitutional pretext for doing good works. In his opinion for the majority, Justice William Douglas said the Connecticut law was unconstitutional because it offended against a "right of privacy," which, although not mentioned in the Constitution, was there anyway because "specific guarantees in the Bill of Rights have penumbras, formed by emanations from those guarantees that help give them life and substance." Armed with emanating penumbras, what could not the Court do?

What it did in 1973 with that 1965 emanation was *Roe* v. *Wade*. That struck down laws regulating abortion in all fifty states. That irritated some people who, in their irritation, rose from their church pews and became something few of them had hitherto been: politically active. The "evangelicals," a.k.a. "the Christian Right," were on the way. By the time of *Roe* v. *Wade*, states with 40 percent of the nation's population had liberalized their abortion laws. A national debate was underway, giving satisfaction to those who desired change and reconciling others to change through democratic debate and compromise. The Court short-circuited this process, leaving millions of Americans feeling disenfranchised regarding an issue of the highest moral sensitivity. Some of the seeds of the revolt against Washington, the source of such judicial thunderbolts, were sown by the 1965 "right-of-privacy" decision.

Perhaps there was among liberals a sense of the perishable nature of their 1965 ascendancy in Congress. Perhaps they sensed that this was apt to be a final flaring of their persuasion. For whatever reason, the creation in 1965 of the Legal Services Corporation (LSC) was congruent with the turn of liberalism away from legislation and toward litigation as the preferred instrument of social change. Created by a Democratic Congress, at the behest of a Democratic president, in the name of the central Democratic value, compassion, the LSC became a battering ram for reformers to use against the policies of Democratic mayors across the country. Welfare policies, housing policies, school policies—in an era when rights are trumps, the litigious idealist's work is never done. An organization like the LSC, funded by Washington and used largely to force enlightenment on "unresponsive" public officials, aimed not merely to succor the poor, but to arouse them. Against whom? Why, against those closest at hand—mayors, city councils, school boards, public-housing authorities, police departments. These good works added to the irritation quotient of people who would in time be called Reagan Democrats.

Ronald Reagan, who became a Republican pinup in 1964 by virtue of one nationally televised speech for Goldwater, spent 1965 driving himself around California, deciding whether or not to run for governor. As he went from one question-and-answer forum to another, one thing particularly puzzled him: "This university thing comes up each time I talk." That thing, which he came to call "the mess at Berkeley," was a leading indicator of the widening cultural and social distance between the intelligentsia and the country. Soon the former would adopt an adversarial stance toward the latter. But in 1965, intellectuals were not yet in their full alienation pose. They had not yet decided that President Johnson was a genocidal imperialist and, worse, vulgar. He craved their approval and was willing to give them his attention, or that of his aides, such as Joseph Califano.

In July 1965, Califano, just turned thirty-four, joined the White House staff. He joined it the week the president decided on the major escalation in Vietnam. Never mind. There would be money enough for guns and butter and *Masterpiece Theater.* On December 29, 1965, Califano led the president through a book titled *The Great Society—A Second Year Legislative Program.* It was a loose-leaf book. It had to be, with so many new ideas coming in all the time from campuses and foundations. The intelligentsia was constantly being urged to send ideas for ways the federal government could spend the dangerous fiscal surplus that, if unspent, would become a drag on the economy. The year had seen the creation of, among many other things, the National Endowment for the Arts and the National Endowment for the Humanities. The Corporation for Public Broadcasting was just two years over the horizon. The keepers of the nation's culture would surely be grateful.

Califano's loose-leaf book was a manifestation of something limned by Daniel Patrick Moynihan in the first article in the first issue of *The Public Interest,* "The Professionalization of Reform." The pressure for government-driven social change was not coming from large constituencies out in the country, "beyond the Beltway." (That is what America would come to be called in years after the Washington Beltway was opened in 1964.) Rather, the pressure was coming from elites who thought of reform as their sovereign vocation. Wrote Moynihan in that first issue:

> War on poverty was not declared at the behest of the poor. . . . The poor were not only invisible . . . they were also for the most part silent. John F. Kennedy ventured into Appalachia searching for Protestant votes, not for poverty. . . . The war on poverty began not because it was necessary (which it was), but because it was possible.

One price that would be paid for the professionalization of reform, wrote Moynihan, would be "a decline in the moral exhilaration of public affairs at the domestic level." But that would be a small price to pay for a consummation as devoutly desired as the one Moynihan thought possible:

> The prospect that the more primitive social issues of American politics are at last to be resolved need only mean that we may now turn to issues more demanding of human ingenuity than that of how to put an end to poverty in the richest nation in the world.

Well. Perhaps Moynihan was assuming that we would know what to do about the subject of something else he wrote about in 1965, in his report, published by the Department of Labor, "The Negro Family: The Case for National Action." More about that anon.

The day Califano was showing that loose-leaf book to the president, the issue of *Time* magazine that was on the newsstands had on its cover a picture of a dead white European male. An economist: Keynes. The news, so to speak, was that we had mastered the management of the modern capitalist economy. Business cycles had been, as it were, repealed. Guaranteed economic growth would guarantee a constant gusher of revenues to government at constant tax rates.

(Constant rates, yes, but there would still be surreptitious tax increases because of "bracket creep" as inflation floated people into higher taxes. At least there would be until 1981. Then, in what was arguably Ronald Reagan's most consequential fiscal act—more consequential, because less easily repealed, than his tax cuts—Reagan, as a final trump in his bidding war with a Democratic Congress that was also hot to cut taxes, endorsed indexing the tax code.)

In 1965, the guaranteed gusher of revenues in excess of existing government needs, seemed to mean that for the foreseeable future—a long time, presumably; we were getting awfully good at seeing the future—the political problem would be to allocate government surpluses equitably. Government had better look lively about putting in place programs to allocate those surpluses. Otherwise they would exert that "fiscal drag" on the economy. Government had an urgent duty to pump out money in order to pump up demand. So politics was going to be the disbursement of pleasures. What fun.

The fun was well underway in 1965. Medicare was passed. Harry Truman attended the signing ceremony for this idea of his (and of others) whose time had at long last come. There was a new Department of Housing and Urban Development to think up uses for surpluses. This would guarantee that our alabaster cities would gleam undimmed by human tears. There was the Elementary and Secondary Education Act, too. This measure completed the erasure of the last trace of a distinction between federal responsibilities and state and local responsibilities. The federal government may have begun as a government of limited, delegated, and enumerated powers, but in 1965 it put away that idea as it entered the local schoolhouse. It soon would do so regarding another (or so it had long been thought) quintessentially local responsibility: crime. In May 1965, for the first time in its experience, the Gallup polling organization found crime ranked with education as the most important national problem. Odd, such evidence of a pervasive sense of national fraying at this moment of a quick-step march toward progress on so many fronts. What could it mean? Probably regnant racism, something else for Washington to correct.

Crime figured in one picaresque political event in 1965. When New York City Republicans nominated the very liberal Congressman John Lindsay to run for mayor, William F. Buckley ran as the nominee of the Conservative Party. Asked what would be the first thing he would do if he won, Buckley said, "Demand a recount." He did not need to. But his campaign did give voice to those New Yorkers who were incensed about a proposed civilian review board to monitor the city's police. Law and order was on many minds. To other minds, the words "law and order" were "code words" for racism.

But in 1965, one hundred years after Appomattox, it was possible to believe that the American dilemma of race was being resolved, that the civil rights agenda was virtually fulfilled. From March 9 to March 25, the march from Selma (a town 42 percent black, where less than 1 percent of the voters were black) to Montgomery had held the nation's attention. The Edmund Pettis Bridge became a station of the cross for the civil rights movement when Sheriff Jim Clark led an assault on the marchers. On the evening of March 25, a Michigan woman, Viola Liuzzo, who had been driving marchers back to Selma, was riddled with bullets from a passing car. She was not the only person murdered during the march: The Reverend James Reeb, a Boston minister, had been beaten to death in Selma by five whites. All this occurred in the living rooms of a nation now wired for television. On May 26 the Senate passed the Voting Rights Act, 77–19.

That was to be one of the transforming acts of twentieth-century government. In 1964, in the eleven states of the former Confederacy, there were 1.5 million blacks registered to vote. By 1969, there were 3.1 million. In 1963, there had been fewer than 100 black elected officials in all of the South. By 1973, there were 191 in Mississippi alone. Signing the act on August 6, 1965, the president said, "Today we strike away the last major shackle of those fierce and ancient bonds [of slavery]." With access to the ballot box assured, and politics becoming a career open to talents, surely the sunlit uplands of racial harmony were at hand.

Five nights after that signing ceremony, in the Watts section of Los Angeles, a white police officer arrested an unemployed twenty-one-year-old black man he suspected of drunk driving. The suspect's mother verbally abused the officer. A crowd gathered. Rocks were thrown. The next night and for four more nights there was rioting that left thirty-four dead.

Perhaps the striking of that last major shackle would not suffice after all. In fact, the president had said as much two months earlier. On June 4, in a speech at Howard University, he had warned: "You do not take a person who, for years, has been hobbled by chains and liberate him, bring him up to the starting line of a race and then say, 'You're free to compete with others,' and justly believe that you have been fair." So: Blacks might have all the shackles struck from them and still remain "hobbled." Blacks were to be thought of as a group, a group defined by victimization. And by passivity: They were to be "taken" toward progress. The taking would be the white person's burden. From that premise a policy with many names was born. It was called "compensatory opportunity" as well as affirmative action in the 1976 Democratic platform. And it had unintended consequences. It became a facet of identity politics organized around grievance groups and an agenda for redefining America. Where Lincoln had seen a nation "dedicated to a proposition," others now saw not really a nation at all but a simmering "multicultural" stew of groups defined by ethnicity and dedicated to maneuvering for social space and ethnic entitlement.

President Johnson's Howard speech followed by two months the publication of the Moynihan report on the crisis in the black family. This was an early harbinger of the arguments of 1995. It suggested—actually, it just allowed the thought—that what the needy need most, and first, are not material things that government can give. Not housing, not jobs, not income maintenance. Maybe what is fundamental is not material. Maybe it is society's moral economy, for the explanation and regulation of which no Keynes has come forward.

The crisis of which Moynihan wrote in 1965 was a black illegitimacy rate of 26 percent. That was just four percentage points higher than the white illegitimacy rate would be in 1990, when the black illegitimacy rate would be 68 percent and that of American society as a whole would be 30 percent. By the mid-1990s, it would be predictable—knowable—that by the year 2000 the rate for minorities would be approximately 80 percent and for society as a whole 40 percent. That would be about all we did know about this. What caused it? What can be done about it? No one quite knows.

Some people think they do. They think government has got the incentives wrong. They think work is natural, meaning universally desired, and so if people drop out of the labor force, getting them back in should be a manageable problem. In 1995, many people believe that tinkering with welfare payments will decisively alter the incentives for having babies, and hence will alter the sexual behavior of welfare recipients. (As the Duke of Wellington said to the man who approached him and said, "Mr. Smith, I believe?", "If you can believe that, you can believe anything.") This faith in behavior modification by means of fine-tuning incentives may be the last remnant—the almost undiscernibly faint trace—of utopian thinking at the end of the millennium: Incentives, particularly monetary ones, make the world go 'round. They do because human beings are simple materialists making predictable, manipulable calculations. But of course people are not.

Thirty years after the Moynihan report there is an exhilarating sense of not knowing as much as we thought we did, and could. That fact, that the nation is not unnerved by not knowing, is among the encouraging results of the years that *The Public Interest* has been with us. And it is, to some extent, one of the results of *The Public Interest*. That journal's pages repeatedly have given its readers the pleasurable shock of nonrecognition—of seeing that the world is not as we have been used to seeing it. In the first issue, Daniel Bell and Irving Kristol said, "The past decade of American history is just chock full of Great Debates that never happened." Thirty years on, an insufficiency of debates about fundamentals is one problem that has been alleviated—perhaps because so few other problems have been. Is that progress? It is progress's precondition, which is a fine description of *The Public Interest* itself.

Reprinted from **The Public Interest,** *Fall 1995*

"Sixties Idealism" and "Psychedelic Optimism"

"If you're going to San Francisco," said a song of the sixties, "you're gonna meet some gentle people there." If you had gone this June you might have met Wolfgang and Lisa Von Nester. Meet them now, before immersing yourself in the hot tub of bathos about the sixties occasioned by the death of Jerry Garcia. If you are not steeped in the cult of the sixties, you may not know that he was the "rock oracle" of the Grateful Dead, "a band that epitomizes freedom" (the *Washington Post*). Garcia, a guitarist, was a "mellow icon of sixties idealism" and embodied "psychedelic optimism" (*The New York Times*).

Wolfgang, twenty-three, and Lisa, twenty-four, will be sentenced next week by a California judge who they must hope is a deadhead, as the band's astonishingly loyal and often nomadic fans like to be called. He could sentence the Maryland couple to six years in prison for abandoning their three-year-old son at a San Bernardino mall on June 2. "I figured that without food and without money and without diapers to put on his butt what else could I do," says Wolfgang, who also says, "I walked away in tears." Then he dried his tears and he and Lisa, who were not really without money, abandoned their car and took a bus north to a Grateful Dead concert in San Francisco.

Then, with the help of a driver of a strawberry truck they had met in Nevada, they headed for Maryland. There they boasted of abandoning their son, and talked of hiking the Appalachian Trail. On the trail a sheriff's investigator first detained Lisa on a 1993 warrant for failing to appear in a child support case involving her four other children. Later both were charged with endangering their child. What a bummer for two deadheads who probably only wanted to have their own version of the Summer of Love, as the summer of 1967 was known in San Francisco.

Garcia, who was rarely a martyr to the strictures of healthy behavior, died in his sleep at a drug treatment center. He had used a lot of LSD and heroin and other substances in his day, but his death at age fifty-three strikes his fans as proof that the universe as currently administered is unfair. *The New York Times* front-page obituary said that the Grateful Dead "symbolized a spirit of communal bliss, with free-wheeling, anything-can-happen music," and Garcia "had come to represent the survival of 1960s idealism."

But Wolfgang and Lisa really represent that survival. And they may well be wondering just what exactly they did that was so awfully wrong. Why are the authorities now acting so, well, so *judgmental*? After all, the sixties are incessantly praised and they were a celebration of "liberation," understood as emancipation from the oppression of social restraints and from the repression of inner restraints. Duties, responsibilities, obligations, and other notions that interfere with immediate gratifications were understood to be mere "hang-ups." Or they were considered "constructions" of bourgeois society, imposed by the "power structure" to prevent the free-flowering of a truly human counterculture. The sixties were, and the unending rhapsodizing about that decade is, a sustained exhortation to a four-word ethic: "Do your own thing." Which is precisely what Wolfgang and Lisa did.

Garcia, who was as personable as he was industrious, and the Grateful Dead cannot be held accountable for the character of all their fans. But he and the band were pleased to be thought of as keepers of the flame of the sixties. The band's music may have been grand but the band has promoted much more than music. Around it has hung an aroma of disdain for inhibitions on recreational uses of drugs and sex. During the band's nearly thirty-year life the costs of "liberation" from such inhibitions have been made manifest in millions of shattered lives and miles of devastated cities. The band has been a touring time capsule, keeping alive the myth that there is something inherently noble about adopting an adversary stance toward "bourgeois" or "middle-class" values. But it turns out that society's success depends on these values. Never mind that the band is big business (some years it has grossed more than some major league baseball teams) and that some of its fans are stockbrokers. The band has prospered as the emblem of an era and is complicit in the continuing consequences of the era.

The spirit of the sixties was, strictly speaking, infantile. For an infant, any appetite is self-legitimizing. Infantilism was the leitmotif of that decade and is the insistent theme of much of today's popular culture. In the August 21 & 28, 1995, double issue of *The New Republic*, Stanley Crouch explains why "the value of youth is hysterically championed at the expense of a mature sense of life. This exploits the insecurities of young people by telling them, over and over, that never growing up is the best defense against an oppressive world where fun isn't given its proper due." But that is only part of the story. The portion of popular culture that constantly sentimentalizes the sixties also panders to the arrested development of the sixties generation which is no longer young but wishes it were and seeks derivative vitality from graying rock stars.

However, every once in a while mortality rears its ugly head. Then the sixties generation gets terribly serious and goes to the movies. To *The Big Chill*, to be exact. You remember that one, in which popular music is the all-purpose cue for memories and some alumni of the sixties gather and act almost affronted by the fact that death can happen to someone of their generation. Speaking of a mature sense of life.

Shortly before she died of a heroin overdose, Janis Joplin sang, "Freedom's just another word for nothing left to lose." No, it is not, and it does not just mean an absence of restraints. What does it mean to say a rock band "epitomizes freedom"? Nothing, really. And what is the meaning of the phrase "psychedelic optimism"? The adjective "psychedelic" is an echo of the sixties. Webster's dictionary used it to refer, not altogether helpfully, to "a person with psychedelic social and cultural interests and orientation." It also said the adjective could mean "brightly colored" or could refer to the results of drugs that produce hallucinations, delusions, and other abnormal psychic states sometimes resembling mental illnesses. The phrase "psychedelic sixties" suitably suggests that the decade, and today's nostalgia for its "idealism," are subjects to be considered in the context of mental states and disturbances that are not benign.

August 21, 1995

Understanding the Sixties: Begin with Barry

The sixties, you may well feel, have been too much with us. Since the sixties, our national life has been a running argument about, and with, the sixties. The argument is far from running out of steam. The sixties were not a radical decade, as the term "radical" is commonly used in connection with that decade. It was not a decade of the left ascendant. Rampant, perhaps, but not ascendant. Rather, the decade was radicalizing; that, subsequent decades have shown, is different. Politically the decade invigorated the right more than the left. But of course politics is not everything. In fact three decades down the road from the sixties, the nation's political discourse may be driven by conservatives, but they, although by many measures triumphant, seem aggrieved because politics seems peripheral to, and largely impotent against, cultural forces and institutions permeated with what conservatives consider the sixties sensibilities.

Treating a decade as a discrete episode obviously makes the assumption that history during that decade had an obliging tidiness, opening with a decisive and tone-setting episode and closing with a suitably climactic event. History rarely accommodates that assumption. Such a treatment of a decade also makes the equally dubious assumption that the decade in question had a clearly dominant tone or profile. So the 1920s were the decade of jazz, flappers, the birth of sports celebrity (Babe Ruth, Red Grange, Jack Dempsey), the Lost Generation, Sacco and Vanzetti, and . . . Warren Harding, Calvin Coolidge, and Herbert Hoover.

Or consider another measurement. What would you say was the American "book of the decade" for the 1930s, the emblematic publishing event? Many, perhaps most Americans would name John Steinbeck's novel *The Grapes of Wrath*, published in 1939. Today it is thought to have expressed the general, or at least the most significant, social experience and political consciousness of the Depression decade. However, it is at least arguable that two other books, taken singly or together, constitute the publishing event of that decade. Those two would be Douglas Southall Freeman's Pulitzer Prize-winning four-volume biography *R. E. Lee*, the final two volumes of which were published in 1935, and Margaret Mitchell's novel *Gone with the Wind*, published in 1936. These widely read and remarkably durable works reflected, and helped shape, a sensibility that was, to say no more, unlike that of Steinbeck's novel.

So let us stipulate this: A decade, even one as intensely felt at the time and as hotly debated afterward as the sixties were and are, can come to seem, when recollected in tranquility, quite unlike the decade as it felt at the time and unlike the decade as it is portrayed by people with an emotional or political investment in portraying it a particular way.

It is arguable that we should think of the sixties as beginning in November 1963 and ending in October 1973. That is, the years we associate with the tumultuousness associated with the phrase "the sixties" began with the assassination of a president and ended with the Yom Kippur War and the energy crisis. The assassination shattered (or at least many people say it did) the nation's sunny postwar disposition; it supposedly "ended American innocence." It is unclear how innocent was this nation, which had been made possible by Puritans, had been founded by such innocents as Benjamin Franklin, John Adams, and James Madison, had been born in the bloodshed of what actually was not only the American Revolution but also America's first civil war, had been preserved by the worst civil war the world had until then seen . . . you get the picture. The sixties as a decade of "lost innocence"? Please. The 1973 oil embargo, which produced a sense of national vulnerability and pervasive limits, did seem to bring down a curtain on something. But on what?

Perhaps on a sense of limitlessness. In the middle of the 1960s the United States, or at least the leading members of its political class, acknowledged few limits on the nation's power or their competence. The United States could fight a war, and engage in "nation building" in the nation where the war was being fought, and build a Great Society at home, simultaneously. And the 1960s counterculture, which fancied itself at daggers drawn with the "establishment," partook of the same central assumption: that limits, sometimes known as hang-ups or repressions or bourgeois values, were to be ignored, confronted, transcended, abolished. The makers of the nation's Vietnam policy may have had more in common with their most vociferous critics than either the policy makers or critics could comfortably admit.

Of course the 1950s were pregnant with the 1960s. In the beginning there was not the word but the sound: rock and roll, the vocabulary of a self-conscious and soon self-confident youth cohort. Rock and roll was nowhere in 1950 and was here to stay in 1960. Indeed, the first crashing intimation of what was to come ten years later was the first chord of the sound track of the movie *The Blackboard Jungle* (1955), Bill Haley and the Comets playing "Rock Around the Clock." The subject of that movie was juvenile delinquency. "Delinquency." How quaint that word seems in the era of Bloods and Crips and other gangbangers. How quaint that the nation's leading musical light, Leonard Bernstein, would recast *Romeo and Juliet* as a story of delinquents on Manhattan's West Side. The 1960s took part of the 1950s and stirred in danger—sex, drugs, and rock and roll.

Another 1950s cohort, a small one, the Beats, anticipated the large cohort of adversarial intellectuals in the 1960s. Of course many of the Beats, unlike their 1960s children (if members of the 1960s "counterculture" can be so regarded), were passionate lovers of America—its cars, its beckoning spaces, and the sense of no limits that those cars and spaces intimated. But the Beats also had that sense of generational uniqueness and of being set upon by an unfeeling world that was to characterize those who were pleased to be called the sixties generation. Remember Allen Ginsberg's "Howl" from 1956:

> I saw the best minds of my generation destroyed by madness, starving hysterical naked,
> dragging themselves through the negro streets at dawn looking for an angry fix. . . .

Lots of people were to find lots of fixes soon enough. Some of those people would be trying to fix their sense of being "jailed in the prison air of other people's habits" and to express "a disbelief in the socially monolithic ideas of the single mate, the solid family, and the respectable love life." What was coming, said the author of those words, was a "psychically armed rebellion whose sexual impetus may rebound against the antisexual foundation of every organized power in America," a rebellion demanding "that every social restraint and category be removed, and the affirmation implicit in the proposal is that man would then prove to be more creative than murderous and so would not destroy himself." So said Norman Mailer in "The White Negro," a peek over the horizon into the future when we would indeed be liberated from the tyranny of the single mate and the solid family and would stay off the streets at night. Mailer's essay was published in *Dissent* magazine in 1957 and republished in pamphlet form at 1562 Grant Avenue in San Francisco, by City Lights Books.

But the 1960s as a decade of dissent did not begin where the "Beat Generation"—that word "generation" again—supposedly did, at the City Lights bookstore in San Francisco's North Beach section. (Talk about quaint. Only in America could a bookstore be the Finland Station of what fancied itself a revolutionary movement.) Neither did it begin in 1964 at Sproul Plaza on the Berkeley campus, with Mario Savio and the free speech movement. Rather, the decade of dissent began at a place not famous as a locus of tumult, the podium of a Republican National Convention.

In the beginning was Barry Goldwater. In 1960 in Chicago, the junior senator from Arizona, seething with the ancient (well, by American standards) and accumulated grievances of the American West against the American East, thundered to the convention that he was mad as hell at Nelson Rockefeller and his ilk and was not going to take it anymore: "Let's grow up, conservatives. We want to take this party back, and I think some day we can. Let's get to work." Four years later he and his people had control of the party. Eight years later the Nixon-Wallace share of the popular vote was 57 percent. In fact, the most remarkable example of "people power"—a favorite incantation of the left in the 1960s—was the achievement of George Wallace's ragtag army in getting him on the ballot in all fifty states in 1968, when laws impeding third-party candidates were much more onerous than they now are.

Understanding the Sixties: Begin with Barry

Thirty-five years after Goldwater became the first potent dissenter of the decade of dissent, it seems that the foremost fecundity of the sixties radicalism of the left, particularly on campuses, was in manufacturing a conservative movement, including a cadre of conservative intellectuals. It is an unanswerable question who was angrier in the 1960s, the Goldwater (and later the Wallace) right or the left. But there can be no argument about which one was more serious about, and successful regarding, the acquisition of power.

The radicalism of the left did not seek power; it purported to despise power. Whereas the left in the 1930s exhorted its adherents to organize, the left in the 1960s celebrated spontaneity. The left in the 1930s was produced by hard material conditions. In the 1960s social abundance and personal affluence were the prerequisites for, and contributing causes of, the campus-based radicalism. That radicalism sought a revolution in "consciousness," sometimes with chemical assistance.

Which is not to say that the radicalism of the left was otherwise sterile. By acts of bravery and skill and perseverance, acts that have not lost their power to take one's breath away, the legal edifice of racial injustice was dismantled. Whatever one thinks of the other consequences of the decade, the decade is redeemed by what was done in bus terminals, at lunch counters, in voter registration drives on ramshackle porches along dangerous back roads and by all the other mining and sapping of the old system. But a revolution interested primarily in "consciousness" is bound to be self-absorbed—each revolutionary looking inward, fascinated by the supposed malleability of his or her "self." The shaping of the "self" is apt to be a more fascinating project for the "consciousness revolutionary" than any mere social reform.

So, then, who won? That is, which of the two antagonistic tendencies activated by the radicalizing decade? It is too soon to say. Politically—or, more precisely and narrowly, in the contest for political offices—the right has won. But conservatives are not happy because they sense the primacy of cultural forces and feel that the culture is still shaped by the forces that have lost in electoral politics, by people who believe what the left believed in the sixties: that the social order is an infringement on freedom rather than freedom's foundation. Society is the crucible in which the citizen's character is formed, and conservatives in their elective offices are dismayed by the formative power of the society they're supposedly governing.

So powerful were—are—the energies let loose in the sixties there cannot now be, and may never be, anything like a final summing-up. After all, what is the "final result" of the Civil War? It is too soon to say. But regarding the unfolding consequences of the sixties, there is much that is important to say.

A foreword to **Reassessing The Sixties:
Debating the Political and Cultural Legacy,** *1997*

Each December I write an end-of-the-year column for Newsweek, *partly for the pleasure of noting how we need to be reminded of recent events that recently seemed so memorable.*

1994: Tacky Royalty and Tonya Harding

With wonderful insouciance, 1994 proved that America, in its heart, knew Goldwater was right. It just took thirty years to say so, which it did thunderously on November 8 in elections that endorsed shrinking government. In 1994 Tip O'Neill died and so did his axiom that "all politics is local." Politics isn't when Newt Gingrich nationalizes elections. On November 9, Washington was miraculously full of people confiding to each other that they always have been close to, and close to worshipful about, Newt. On November 8, Cherokee Township, Kansas, elected as clerk a woman who died September 28. Death be not proud.

For some reason, people in 1994 seemed impatient with government. Four women living in a Hampton, Virginia, public housing project were threatened with eviction because they cleaned up a playground without asking the government's permission. A California woman, unamused by the feds' administration of the Endangered Species Act, said, "The federal government owns 50 percent of the dirt in this state. My personal feeling is that if the critters can't live on 50 percent of the land, then God is calling them home."

Moffett, Oklahoma, has a population of about 300 and an annual budget of less than $20,000, and not much of a crime problem, although two people were shot last year because (according to a person in the know) they were "trying to be overbearing." Someone may have overreached a bit in asking for $106,000 as Moffett's share of the crime bill pork. National politicians threw caution to the winds and endorsed "family values." A *New York Times* headline announced: "Gay Sperm Donor Awarded; Standing As Girl's Father Enabled Lesbian Couple to Have the Child." The Surgeon General said perhaps schools should teach masturbation. (America's schools may have nothing more urgent to do, having taught everything else perfectly.)

A few hours after 100 pounds of undelivered mail was found burning under a Chicago viaduct, a quarter of a ton of mail, some of it nearly twenty years old, was found in a Chicago-area post office. Congress declined the Clintons' invitation to turn delivery of health care over to the government that delivers, sometimes, the mail. Regarding the most important act of the 103rd Congress, Senator Robert Bennett, a Utah Republican and a recklessly honest man, mused, "People in my area called and said, 'How can you support [GATT] when you haven't read it?' They assume I haven't read it. They're right, of course—but I resent a little that they assume I haven't read it."

Tonya Harding left the violent world of figure skating. Lorena Bobbitt was acquitted of "malicious wounding" in her dispute with the man who subsequently starred in the porno movie *John Wayne Bobbitt Uncut*. A judge warned Colorado prison officials to provide an inmate with a black robe, a gong, and incense to avoid violating his rights as a Satanist. Rodney King received $3.8 million in his civil rights suit arising from his videotaped beating by Los Angeles police, and also received lawyers' bills totaling $4.4 million.

A jury initially awarded $2.7 million to a woman who burned herself when, in a moving car, leaving a McDonald's with a cup of coffee between her legs, she spilled it. She said the coffee was hot. In a New Haven theater a member of the audience stormed onto the stage to demand that an actress extinguish her cigarette. An Indiana dancer, Cynthia Hess, a.k.a. Chesty Love, won a court's approval to treat her surgically enhanced breasts as business assets that can be depreciated for tax purposes. Her fees for dancing expanded dramatically when her breasts did, but there was a downside: Because of her new imbalance, she slipped and fell on ice, rupturing one of her implants.

The United States, home of the Menendez brothers, lectured Singapore about the inadequacies of its justice system. Robert Sandifer, the eleven-year-old Chicago gang member who allegedly murdered a fourteen-year-old girl and then was murdered by other gang members, was buried with his teddy bear. Citing violence, poverty, and despair, President Clinton ordered an invasion of—no, not Chicago—Haiti. North Korea succumbed to Jimmy Carter's charm, promising not to proceed with its nuclear weapons program until it is ready to do so. In Northern Ireland and South Africa old wounds began to heal. In Bosnia and Rwanda the century's tenth decade was stained by genocide. Americans were mesmerized by two murders near O. J.'s house. Malaysia banned the movie *Schindler's List* because it "incites sympathy for only one race."

Britain's Windsors pioneered a new category—tacky royalty—and America's president discussed his underwear on MTV. Paula Jones's court documents discussed the presidential penis. Hillary Clinton, scourge of those who did well in the "decade of greed" because they did not "play by the rules," turned out to have played by amazing rules, turning $1,000 into $100,000 in a one-shot fling with cattle futures. Richard Nixon's funeral was hijacked by various politicians who extolled him as emblematic of America's spirit. *De mortuis nil nisi bonum,* but that was ridiculous. Jacqueline Kennedy Onassis, a reminder of vanished dignity, died.

So did baseball's season. The owners were furious at the players because the players irresponsibly refused to stop taking the salaries the owners offered to them. To protest the players' strike, WJMP radio in Akron played nothing but "Take Me Out to the Ball Game" 57,161 times through sixty-nine days. In his seventy-eight year in professional baseball, Jimmie Reese, most recently with the California Angels, died at ninety-two. Reese roomed briefly with Babe Ruth. Actually, he roomed with Ruth's suitcase, the Bambino having been a late-night rambler while on the road. A casket company found a market niche: a deluxe model in the red and white colors of Indiana University, with the option of an embroidered basketball hoop.

The year ended with Washington reeling under the impact of radical questions, such as: What if there were no Energy Department? Why does the government run a railroad? Was there art in America before there was a National Endowment for the Arts (that is, before 1965)? The year ended with the rest of the country marveling that Washington thinks such questions are radical.

December 26, 1994–January 2, 1995

1995: Oh, a Revolution

In 1995, the nation ran a remarkable gantlet of amusements, the most gaudy of which was the Revolution. You remember. It was the Republican assault on decency, defined as a certain rate of increase of federal spending. The assault culminated when Congress passed a budget that the president then vetoed because Republicans in their callous parsimony proposed to collect only 37 percent more revenue in 2002 than in 1995. The president said principles are principles, doggone it, and the government should collect $11.4 trillion in revenue over the next seven years rather than the piddling $11.2 trillion the Republicans planned to collect.

He said, "We're working on getting rid of unnecessary regulations and making them more sensible." (Be charitable. If you talked as much as he does, you, too, would say some odd things.) Republicans, he said, would let Medicare "wither on the vine" with their plan to let it balloon to only 15 percent of the budget in 2002.

Republicans sternly said the government is doing many things it should not be doing—subsidizing the arts, running a railroad, paying for television programming—and principles are principles, doggone it, so the government must henceforth do these improper things a little less lavishly. Democrats dug in their heels against such "extremism." "It is a glorious day—if you're a fascist," said Representative George Miller, a California Democrat. "Worse than Hitler," said Representative Major Owens, a New York Democrat, of his Republican colleagues who were, he said, "practicing genocide with a smile."

In Washington's darkest hour since the secession crisis, the government was shut down, a calamity noticed by people who needed new passports. Workers deemed "nonessential," including 11,071 of HUD's 11,500, were sent home. Elsewhere, compassion and rectitude flourished. In Italy a law forbidding imprisonment of persons infected with HIV resulted in a gang of HIV-positive bank robbers passing through a revolving door in the criminal justice system. And in North Carolina a state legislator, who, when not legislating, is a funeral director, said he should not vote on a bill to legalize carrying concealed weapons: "Seems like if anyone is going to make any money on a bill, I'm going to make money on this one."

In the Trial of the Century (you remember: the Weeping Judge, the Racist Cop, and a vast supporting cast), the jury's decision left open the possibility that Nicole Simpson and Ron Goldman committed suicide. Mississippi ratified the Thirteenth Amendment that abolished slavery. The most admired man in America was an African-American who decided not to seek the presidency but to become a Republican anyway. White America seemed amazed that the Million Man March on Washington drew a mostly middle-class crowd from mostly middle-class black America, and produced no outbreaks of crime or basketball.

A doctor's book, cleverly combining two of America's favorite topics, sex and the Civil War, reported that Union troops were more sexually rambunctious because Confederates were so often on the march. The Gay and Lesbian Commission of the Los Angeles public school system reported that Abraham Lincoln had a homosexual affair with his friend Joshua Fry Speed. "You mean Cleveland High was named after a former president?" exclaimed a student at Los Angeles's Grover Cleveland High School. "I always thought it was named after that city in Canada." There was a metaphor congestion at Harvard, where a cochair of a student committee studying various injustices said, "There need to be enough women on the boat to rock the glass ceiling." Shannon Faulkner was a solider-in-training for five days.

The *Rocky Mountain News* reported that tax dollars made possible lawsuits by a Nevada inmate who claimed he suffered "cruel and unusual punishment" when he ordered two jars of chunky peanut butter but received one of chunky and one creamy, and by a New York inmate who said a "defective" prison haircut caused his chest pains, and by an Oklahoma inmate who said his religious freedoms were being violated but he was not allowed to say how, because his religion enjoins secrecy about its practices. In Düsseldorf, a new play, *Love Letters to Adolf Hitler*, based on genuine letters, depicted Hitler as causing women to swoon throughout the Third Reich.

After some of Hitler's emulators slaughtered thousands of people from the "safe area" of Srebrenica in Bosnia, the West, having said "Never again!" again and again, abandoned its policy of evenhandedness between the butchers and the butchered. From a couple of demented cowards came the carnage in Oklahoma City. Yitzhak Rabin, a warrior and leader true to a motto of Israel's officer corps—"After me!"—was shot in the back by someone fresh from conversing with God. Prince Charles and his spouse infused fresh meaning into the phrase "a royal bore."

With a few keystrokes of a computer in Singapore, Nicholas Leeson, twenty-eight, sank his employer, London's oldest investment bank. Windows 95 was born; the Smith-Corona typewriter company filed for bankruptcy. Rose Kennedy, 104, born during the presidency of Benjamin Harrison, died. So did Grover Cleveland's son Francis Grover at ninety-two. The lives of the father (born in 1837) and son spanned 158 of the 219 years since 1776. Jonas Salk, whose polio vaccine made summers safer and iron lungs scarce, was eighty. Fred Astaire, a perfectionist, once said to a new dance partner, "Don't be nervous—just don't make any mistakes." Ginger Rogers, who died at eighty-three, rarely did. Jerry Garcia, now playing guitar among the harps, made lots of mistakes, as did number 7, the switch-hitter now, as always, playing a heavenly centerfield.

Michael (if you wonder "Michael who?" you have been off the planet for a few years) returned to basketball from baseball and baseball returned to its senses, sort of. You say you want a revolution? The mighty Cleveland Indians had baseball's best winning percentage since the Indians of 1954, and the quarterback of the magnanimous Northwestern Wildcats knelt to kill the clock in order to avoid rolling up the score against Penn State. On September 6, the nation was mesmerized by the spectacle of a man going to work, as usual. He works between Second and Third in Baltimore. If anything is predictable, it is that he will do that 162 times in 1996.

December 25, 1995–January 1, 1996

1996: In Our Wee Galaxy

Ever since Copernicus came to his conclusions about the heavens, the idea has been seeping into the consciousness of our species that we are not, after all, the center of the universe. Thus few took notice of, and no one was scandalized by, the biggest news of 1996, reported in San Antonio at the meeting of the American Astronomical Society. A headline in *The New York Times,* January 16: "Suddenly, Universe Gains 40 Billion More Galaxies." Fifty billion instead of ten billion. In the Milky Way, our run-of-the-mill galaxy, the sun is just one of 50 billion to 100 billion stars.

And, it seems safe to say, nowhere out there among the 50 billion times 100 billion stars was there this year a presidential campaign as dispiriting as the one that occurred on our little portion of this itsy-bitsy planet. When the student paper at Berkeley endorsed the California Civil Rights Initiative, which bans racial preferences, indignant defenders of civil rights destroyed 23,000 copies of the paper. When a sixteen-year-old sniffed computer cleaner to get high, then drove off a road into a lake and drowned, his parents sued the store that sold him the cleaner, the builders of the road, and the engineering firm that designed the lake. A court ruled that the Constitution's proscription of "establishment of religion" was violated by a probation officer's recommendation that attendance at Alcoholics Anonymous meetings be a condition of probation for a person who had been convicted three times of drunken driving. Some students at Emory and Henry College in Emory, Virginia, protested that cheering for the college mascot, the Wasp, sounds distressingly like speaking well of the unspeakable—white Anglo-Saxon Protestants.

This year Britain's *Dictionary of National Biography* began to be available on CD-ROM, with entries like this one on King George IV: "There have been more wicked kings in English history but none so unredeemed by any signal greatness or virtue. . . . He was a dissolute and drunken fop, a spendthrift and a gamester . . . a bad son, a bad husband, a bad father, a bad subject, a bad monarch, and a bad friend . . . his word was worthless and his courage doubtful." Speaking of his sort, Fidel Castro visited Vatican City. There, in the home of the pope who lit the fuse that blew communism to smithereens, Castro proclaimed it a "miracle" that he got to meet the pope, who now will visit Cuba. (How many divisions has the pope got? Castro will find out.) Castro posed for photographers in the Sistine Chapel, in front of Michelangelo's depiction of the "Last Judgment," an event Castro will find instructive. At memorial services for the spy Alger Hiss, he was praised as "strangely without bitterness." Think about that.

This year air bags were pronounced more dangerous than Richard Jewell, and a man who lost a Bible-quoting contest shot the winner. And in addition to Di's divorce and John-John's marriage, and a Hawaiian court's decision that same-sex marriages cannot constitutionally be denied, 1996 enriched the annals of modern romance with this: A prenuptial agreement (the third marriage for him, the second for her) stipulated that the couple will have "healthy sex three to five times a week," she will do inside chores, he outside chores, and they will buy Chevron Supreme gasoline. A U.S. Postal Service ad said: "In 1940, a one-pound loaf of bread cost 8 cents, and in 1995 cost 79 cents; a half-gallon of milk went from 25 cents to $1.43 in the same period; and a first-class postage stamp went from 3 cents to 32 cents. Which, bottom line, means that first-class postage rates remained well below the rate of inflation." Not exactly. Noting that the price of the stamps rose 9 percent faster than the price of bread and 105 percent faster than the price of milk, Jeff Jacoby of the *Boston Globe* asked, "Doesn't anyone at the Postal Service have a calculator?" Not yet. It's in the mail.

"Hold Mummy's hand and be a good girl" were the last words her father said that night on the *Titanic* to seven-year-old Eva Hart, who died this year in London at ninety-one. In Connecticut, Mary Bidwell, believed to be the oldest American, died at 114 even though she said she never drank, smoked, or bobbed her hair. Dominguin, the matador who deserves some of the blame for Hemingway's celebration of bullfighting, *The Dangerous Summer* (1956), died at sixty-nine. The rapper Tupac Shakur, who celebrated violence, was shot to death. For Spiro Agnew, heaven is a place without the *Washington Post*.

Faraway places with strange-sounding names—Bosnia-Herzegovina, Rwanda, Zaire, the Bronx—continued to provide televised examples of three recurring factors in the history of this century, refugees and war criminals and the New York Yankees. Time was, faraway places really seemed far away. Seventy years ago, in 1926, one of the year's biggest news stories was Admiral Byrd's flight to the North Pole. This year, a scholarly analysis of the diary Byrd kept on the flight strongly suggests that he never got there and knew he did not. In 1996, assuming that everything we think happened did happen, and considering the possible calamities that did not happen, we had a tolerable year, given who and where we are.

This is who and where, according to Galen Strawson writing at year's end in the *London Times Literary Supplement*, about how hard the millennium has been on human hubris: "Copernicus displaced us from the centre of the universe. Darwin closed Eden, showing that we are apes with shrews for ancestors and cabbages for cousins. Freud pointed out that we are not our own masters even in our own heads. . . . Modern genetics showed that we share over 98 percent of our genes with chimpanzees." This has all been part of what Strawson calls the process of "our dispossession, the story of how we began to acquire a sense of proportion." It is a process of "disillusionment," and that is a positive term. It is fine to be without illusions. However, it is an illusion that the dignity of our species is diminished because we are at the back of the beyond of the universe.

December 30, 1996–January 6, 1997

CHAPTER TWO

CONSERVATISM'S SEVERAL THREADS

An Epithet No More

In 1950 a man was arrested for creating a public disturbance. A witness said: "He was using abusive language, calling people conservative and all that." Yes, once upon a time (and not so very long ago) conservatism in America was widely considered, at best, an eccentricity, and "conservative" was an epithet.

When Clinton Rossiter revised *Conservatism in America* in 1962, seven years after he published it, he added a subtitle: *The Thankless Persuasion.* Today, that may be the only dated aspect of what he wrote. It is as certain as anything in politics can be that for the foreseeable future, conservatism in America, and what Rossiter wrote about it, will be more interesting to more people than could reasonably have been expected when Rossiter published the book in 1955.

Conservatism should not be called an idea whose time has come, because, as Rossiter understood, conservatism is a complex constellation of ideas and dispositions whose fortunes have waxed and waned throughout American history. Clearly conservatism is a more potent political force than it was when Rossiter first wrote about it; its relative weakness was one reason he paid so much useful attention to the long history of cultural conservatism in America.

Those of us who are pleased to be called conservative are inclined to explain the improved political fortunes of conservatism by saying that the truth will always prevail, and leaving it at that. But, then, proper conservatives are skeptical about the power of mere truth to reform a naughty world. Surveying the littered landscape of America's recent social history, it is not hard to discern events that lent conservative truth a helping hand. The Great Society legislative initiatives were quickly perceived (fairly or unfairly) as having promised much more than the government was competent to deliver. The Vietnam War and Watergate deepened skepticism about the competence of government, and stimulated skepticism about the good motives of government. The turmoil of the years 1965 (the Watts riot) through 1975 (the fall of Saigon) induced in many people a conservative insight: The crust of civilization is thin, and the traditions of civility are brittle. Unrest on campuses, and the intrusion of federal "affirmative action" and other regulations into academic life, helped bring forth a conservative intellectual movement.

But history is the history of ideas—of mind—not of autonomous events shaping minds. The history of conservatism in America is at least as confused as the history of almost everything else in America and has become more confused since the ranks of conservatives have begun to grow rapidly. This country takes ideas, and the words that convey them, seriously. The ideas and vocabulary of American politics derive directly from the liberal-democratic tradition of the eighteenth century. It sometimes seems that many American conservatives are unreconstructed "classic" or "nineteenth-century" liberals who would be recognized as such in a European context. Furthermore, this country was founded by liberal gentlemen who made a conservative revolution. Many of the most revered figures of the liberal tradition, from Jefferson on, were temperamentally conservative, and conservatives are inclined to consider temperament as important as doctrine in politics.

Writing the book was for Rossiter a somewhat thankless task—he certainly got little thanks from many conservatives. He had to impose a semblance of order on a disorderly jumble of disparate but related impulses, and he had to make explicit the implicit relationships between kinds of conservatism. To do this, he adopted a latitudinarian approach to defining conservatism. This exasperated those conservatives who regarded conservatism less as a political program for winning and wielding power than as a church militant more devoted to preserving the purity of its doctrine than to converting the world.

Among those who have been placed in the conservative tradition are: Alexander Hamilton, among the architects of national power, and Albert Jay Nock, the author of a reverent biography of Hamilton's great rival, Thomas Jefferson; Jefferson, the advocate of decentralization, and his rival, John Marshall, whose jurisprudence consolidated federal power; Andrew Carnegie, industrialist, and the southern "agrarians," critics of industrial civilization; John C. Calhoun and William Fitzhugh, South Carolinians whose doctrines about states' rights and slavery helped produce the Confederacy, and Lincoln, whose thought (with not a little help from the Union Army) defeated the Confederacy; Theodore Roosevelt, an inventor of the modern presidency, and Robert Taft, who sought the office by promising that he would conduct it differently. Any definition of conservatism elastic enough to encompass Ayn Rand had better find room for the Walter Lippmann who wrote *The Public Philosophy* (1955).

The Western liberal tradition has many saints—Locke, Paine, Jefferson, Mill, to name just four—but conservatism in the modern age has one fountainhead: Edmund Burke. Among America's Founding Fathers, John Adams was the closest approximation to a Burkean. Since then, as Rossiter knew, traditional conservatism has often been in the custody of literary rather than political persons: Herman Melville, Henry Adams, Paul Elmer More, Irving Babbitt, William Faulkner, James Gould Cozzens, and, more recently, Herman Wouk, Walker Percy, and Mark Helprin.

The preeminence of Burke in the Western conservative tradition is (or should be) a bit embarrassing for those American conservatives who seem to think that conservatism is capitalism, no more, no less. Burke knew that economic thinking, although necessary, is too thin a gruel to serve as a political philosophy. He thought that economic reasoning encouraged a desiccated rationalism inappropriate to a rounded understanding of the life of society. (That is probably why in a particular denunciation he lumped "economists" with "sophisters" and "calculators.") Thus it is strange that conservatism twice (in the Gilded Age and again today) has come perilously close to disappearing into an economic doctrine. And it is passing strange that this doctrine—laissez-faire capitalism—should be most skillfully advocated by a scholar (Milton Friedman) who punctiliously notes that he is not a conservative at all but a classic "Manchester" liberal.

The natural (by which I mean Burkean) conservative dubiousness about politics controlled by abstractions is admirable, but some American conservatives added, for a while, a less wholesome suspicion of ideas, or at least ideas other than a particular economic doctrine. There were three reasons for this. First, by identifying themselves so thoroughly with the American enterprise system, and by ascribing so much good to the entrepreneurial impulse, conservatives came to distinguish too emphatically between people of thought and people of action, and to identify too much with the latter. Second, respect for free markets as rational allocators of resources became, for some conservatives, an almost irrational faith in the solution of all social problems through spontaneous, voluntary cooperation in markets. This produced disparagement of political ideas, which conservatives associated with government planning and direction. Third, conservatives thought intellectuals had a vested interest in disparaging markets because markets work so well without the supervision of intellectuals.

However, in the thirty-five years since Rossiter's revised edition appeared, the intellectual landscape has changed a lot. There are many more conservative journals, organizations, and columnists, and liberalism seems (not least to many liberals) to be intellectually tuckered out.

It would be quixotic, not to say confusing, to try to pull the American usage of the word "conservatism" into line with traditional usage in the Western political tradition. European conservatism has generally been defined in terms of historical phenomena that have little if any relevance to American experience. These phenomena include clericalism and established churches, attempts to preserve well-defined hierarchies of social classes, resistance to popular sovereignty, and disdain for commerce. The way Americans use the word "conservatism" strikes Europeans as peculiar. They see Americans packing into the idea of conservatism some ideas that are, if not flatly incompatible, at least in tension with it.

Truth be told, contemporary conservatism sometimes is as confusing as it is vigorous. Some persons say that their conservatism primarily concerns governmental due process. They emphasize judicial restraint and federalism, and contend that conservatism is as much about the correct allocation of governmental powers as it is about the advancement of particular policies. Others argue that libertarian social policies that expand commercial and personal freedom, whether by legislation or litigation, are the essence of conservatism. Still others say that the basic conservative criticism of modern society is that there is altogether too much freedom—for abortionists, for pornographers, for businesses trading with Russia, for young people exempt from mandatory national service.

A problem discerned by Rossiter (and Peter Viereck, and others who consider themselves conservatives) is an incoherence in conservatism that is closely identified with free-market economics. The severely individualistic values, and the atomizing social dynamism of a capitalistic society conflict with the traditional and principled conservative concern with traditions, among other things. Those other things include the life of society in its gentling corporate existence—in communities, churches, and other institutions that derive their usefulness and dignity from their ability to summon individuals up from individualism to concerns larger and longer-lasting than their self-interestedness.

There is a sense in which the current phase of conservatism's history opened in 1960. A Democrat was elected to follow Dwight Eisenhower, who was considered highly unsatisfactory by conservatives, many of whom now know better. And in 1960 a senator from a state with three electoral votes published *The Conscience of a Conservative*, a tract that became, for a time, the defining document of the conservative movement. In it Barry Goldwater said: "The laws of God, and of nature, have no dateline. The principles on which the conservative political position is based have been established by a process that has nothing to do with the social, economic, and political landscape that changes from decade to decade and century to century."

"Nothing"? Surely most conservatives would insist that conservatism has everything to do with prudent accommodation to perpetually changing social, economic, and political landscapes, and that the essence of unconservative approaches to politics is the attempt to apply fixed doctrine to a world forever in flux. Goldwater said that a proper conservative's overriding concern "will always be: *Are we maximizing freedom?*" But other conservatives would emphasize that the distinguishing virtue of the conservative mind is suspicion of politics organized around one single overriding concern, because too much is apt to get overridden. The late Alexander Bickel of the Yale Law School, the most subtle American interpreter of Burke, emphasized Burke's abhorrence of doctrines plucked from the air without reference to traditions and other important conditions. Rights, Burke said, are defined "in balance between differences of good, in compromises sometimes between good and evil, and sometimes between evil and evil. Political reason is a computing principle: adding, subtracting, multiplying, and dividing, morally and not metaphysically, or mathematically, true moral denominations."

Rossiter wrote his book a quarter of a century before Ronald Reagan was inaugurated. Before conservatism became interesting to a large public, Rossiter understood that conservatism in America is a rainbow of persuasions. His great service to America's understanding of itself, and conservatives' understanding of themselves, was in arguing that the conservative tradition is less sharply defined than most people think—and less exclusive than some conservatives seem to wish it were. Rossiter's inclination to count, for example, Adlai Stevenson in the conservative tradition convinced many that Rossiter was construing conservatism so broadly that "conservative" would become a classification that would not classify: it would include almost everyone. But when one considers some of the people and policies that have bubbled to the top of the Democratic Party since Stevenson's day, Rossiter's argument seems less strained than it seemed when the partisan passions of the fifties still clouded understanding. The question of whether this or that person shall be counted among America's conservatives is less important than the central point of Rossiter's book, which is that American conservatism is an older, deeper, broader, and more attractive stream than many people think. There are many currents in the conservative river, a fact that has not always pleased some who fancy themselves conservatives and who cherish the cozy purity of the "movement" (as they understand it) more than they desire influence and responsibility. But as American conservatism has grown in political strength and intellectual confidence, conservatives have become less sectarian and more comfortable with the complexity of conservatism's intellectual pedigree. Rossiter's book should now receive a less chilly reception than it met with from some conservatives in 1955.

John Dos Passos, who came to conservatism after a misspent youth, once wrote: "In time of change and danger, when there is a quicksand of fear under one's reasoning, a sense of continuity with generations before can stretch like a lifeline across the scary present." I do not know when Dos Passos expressed that impeccably conservative sentiment, but it is certainly germane to the scary present. Conservatism is a tributary that has become a powerful part of the main current of American intellectual life. Clinton Rossiter's explanation of where conservatism has come from contributes to a sense of continuity, not only for conservatives but for all Americans who understand that ideas have consequences.

A foreword written to the Harvard University Press edition
of Clinton Rossiter's Conservatism in America

Contra Croly

Few American books published in 1909 are still in print. One of them has never in eighty-seven years been out of print and its influence on American governance goes marching on. Herbert Croly's *The Promise of American Life*, a manifesto for the Progressive movement, is this century's most influential book on American politics, and now it is again newsworthy.

It is because last year Lamar Alexander coedited (with Chester Finn), and contributed to, a collection of essays published by the Hudson Institute. *The New Promise of American Life* is a rejoinder to Croly. It also is a clue to Alexander's conservative credentials, and a reason for him to insist that Pat Buchanan's conservative credentials are bogus.

A concise summation of conservatism in this century is "contra-Croly." Although few conservatives understand the pedigree of their creed this way, modern conservatism is a sustained reaction to policies engendered by Croly's arguments for "a new nationalism."

Teddy Roosevelt adopted that phrase, and adopted Croly as an adviser, after reading the book during an African safari. But it was the Democratic administrations of Woodrow Wilson (whom Croly endorsed in 1916), Franklin Roosevelt, and Lyndon Johnson that were animated by Croly's belief that "national cohesion" required the emancipation of Americans from "traditional illusions," especially the Jeffersonian tradition of "individualist and provincial democracy."

Croly spoke for a growing class of "progressive" intellectuals and politicians for whom progress meant movement away from local institutions and attachments, which they regarded as retrograde. Progress meant increased conscription of the people into a national consciousness and collective undertakings, including, in Croly's words, "increasing control over property in the public interest."

He believed that "human nature"—human nature, not just behavior—"can be raised to a higher level by an improvement in institutions and laws." But if that is so, there really is no human nature, only malleable human material taking whatever shape institutions, and the elites that command them, choose.

In 1909 progressives were full of faith in modernity, meaning, among other things, experts applying science, including political science, to society. Three years later a former professor of political science was elected president. Woodrow Wilson was the first president to criticize the Founders—because their system of separation of powers, checks and balances, and federalism prevented government, in the hands of modern elites, from acting with proper boldness and dispatch for the improvement of what Croly called "unregenerate citizens."

Croly meant most citizens. He was candid where later, more circumspect liberals would be cryptic. He said "the average American individual is morally and intellectually inadequate to a serious and consistent conception of his responsibilities as a democrat." So national life should be a "school": "The exigencies of such schooling frequently demand severe coercive measures, but what schooling does not?" And "a people are saved many costly perversions" if "the official schoolmasters are wise, and the pupils neither truant nor insubordinate."

Croly's book was a blueprint for twentieth-century liberalism's aspiration, the state as schoolmarm. Against this stood the conservatism of President William Howard Taft, his son, Senator Robert Taft, and Senator Barry Goldwater—conservatism aiming to minimize the role of government, and especially the federal government, in the lives of individuals and communities. But Alexander's coeditor Finn says that today the "cult of governmentalism" is so pervasive that it is finding followers among conservatives.

Finn says the Republicans' 1994 Contract with America, with its call for Washington action to change the behavior of welfare recipients, enforce child support, and increase parental involvement in education, reflects the attitude that Washington should try to shape people's behavior, attitudes, and values. Finn says attempts by conservatives to use Washington to alter those aspects of society that displease them mirror the hubris and central-izing impulses of liberal, Crolyesque social engineers.

Alexander largely agrees with Finn, so this is a reason for the spirited argument that occurred, briefly, among the Republican candidates. Here is another.

The crux of Pat Buchanan's "conservatism with a heart" (i.e., conser-vatism thinking with the wrong organ) is protectionism and other ingredi-ents of what liberals celebrate as "industrial policy." President Buchanan would pick the industries that should flourish even though they cannot flourish without the subsidy of protection, and to finance his picks he would tax (by tariffs) American consumers.

Never mind the mockery this makes of Buchanan's flaunting of his southern heritage. (The South's experience with protectionism was indi-cated by the name southerners gave to the 1828 Tariff of Abominations which, with the tariff of 1832, stimulated secessionism.) Buchanan's pro-tectionism is Washington-knows-best hubris married to coercion. It is a policy that disciples of Croly could salute. But no conservative can, and it will be interesting to see with what vigor Alexander will say so.

February 18, 1996

The Fourth Awakening

When controversy erupted concerning gays in the military, it was noted that many members of the media have gay friends but no friends in the military. Today the socialization of journalists may also explain the incom-prehension that colors coverage of the conservative Christian Coalition. Robert Fogel, professor of American institutions at the University of Chicago, explains that today's large political changes are "to a large extent spawned by trends in American religiosity," which is usually how change is spawned in this deeply religious country.

In "The Fourth Great Awakening and the Political Realignment of the 1990s," Fogel's Bradley Lecture at the American Enterprise Institute, he argues that today's religious activists, by their numbers and, even more, their intensity, are driving today's reconsideration of "the theory that cul-tural crises can be resolved by raising incomes," a theory thoroughly tested in this century and refuted. Today's religious awakening is related to this fact: In this century the real income of the bottom fifth of the population has increased thirteen-fold, more than twice the increase for the other four-fifths, yet the cultural crises of urbanization deepen.

The first of the three previous political-religious stirrings was the Great Awakening of 1730–1760, which emphasized "new birth" achieved at revival meetings. It produced heightened sensitivity to British moral and political corruption and helped produce the American Revolution. The second stirring, in the era of the camp meetings between 1800 and 1840, taught that anyone could acquire saving grace by inner struggle and by struggling against social sins. This prepared the ground for the abolitionist and temperance movements that believed slavery and alcohol impeded personal and national salvation.

The third quickening of religious life, between 1890 and 1930, coincided with increased urbanization, immigration, and labor strife. Its core belief, shaped by Darwinism and the new faith in science, was that human beings and society could evolve toward perfection as scientists discovered God's laws in the laws of nature. The Social Gospel movement preached that poverty is not a personal but a social failure. Embraced by the growing ranks of people running universities and mass media, this doctrine provided the intellectual predicate for the welfare state. The fourth "awakening" began, Fogel says, with the intensification of religious life that produced growing membership in all church denominations in the late 1950s. In the mid-1960s, membership in the Protestant mainline churches began what has become a 25 percent decline. However, membership in the "enthusiastic" churches nearly doubled. "By the end of the 1980s," Fogel says, "enthusiastic religion had about sixty million adherents representing about one-third of the electorate." In the 1982 congressional elections, such votes split almost evenly between the two parties. But in 1994, 74 percent voted Republican. If they vote in the same numbers and pattern in 1996, there will have been—in just one decade—an interparty shift of about 7.5 million votes. If so, then perhaps the biggest blunder of the Clinton presidency, bigger even than the health care plan, was the tactic of implying that the religiosity of religious conservatives compounds the unpleasantness of their conservatism.

As Fogel explains, the religious and political impulses are fused. Reducing taxes and government's size are aspects of an agenda for refocusing politics on cultural reform through individual responsibility and personal compassion. The "reemergence of confidence in the power of personal compassion" undergirds conservative demands for returning power to the people, beginning with power over individuals' earnings. Hence the durability of the tax revolt, concerning which Fogel is particularly acute.

The mix of households represented in the top 10 percent of income earners has changed from the day when they represented a "leisure class" deriving most of its income not from labor but from ownership of land or other assets. Today a majority of the households in the top decile are there because they have multiple income earners. A typical family in the top decile might include an accountant and a teacher, each in the third decade of his or her professional lives and each earning more than $50,000 a year. So, says Fogel, taxing the top 10 percent of earners is taxing not the idle rich but rather people near the end of their careers "who, after years of scrimping, and hours of work much longer than average," are finally comfortable.

Resistance to increased taxation of the top 10 percent is strong among those who are younger and earn less but who are on a career path to that decile. In fact, the middle ranks of income earners can identify with even the top 2 percent of earners. Says Fogel, "The mythical Huxtables, made famous by Bill Cosby, are typical of these super rich, since a fifty-five-year-old gynecologist married to a fifty-year-old lawyer would probably have a joint income quite close to the mean income of the top 1 percent of households."

Fogel says that even a long conservative ascendancy will not mean reversal of this century's egalitarian gains, because the gains were not primarily the result of redistributive fiscal policies. Rather, they resulted from economic and social changes (e.g., the change of agriculture from the largest sector of the economy to just 2 percent of GNP) that made human capital—skills— more important than land and physical capital in the productive process. Government played a large role in this, by making primary and secondary education compulsory and free, by multiplying the number of city and state universities, and by expanding scholarship programs that democratized access to higher education.

By making private contributions to colleges and universities tax deductible, government encouraged the transformation of old wealth, produced by land and physical capital, into human capital—again, skills— possessed by children from the middle and lower classes. This, says Fogel, was one of the largest acts of redistribution of wealth in history. It was the transfer, from the rich to the children of the nonrich, of capital that, in the new form of productive knowledge, "now greatly exceeds the value of all privately held land and industrial capital." Thus does Fogel—an empiricist, not an advocate—find that conservative values buttressed by religion can support—did support—egalitarian change.

October 2, 1995

The Politics of Soulcraft

American political discourse has become thin gruel because of a deliberate deflation of American ideals. So says Michael Sandel in a wonderful new book, *Democracy's Discontent: America in Search of a Public Philosophy.* Sandel, a Harvard professor of government, believes that politics has been impoverished and life coarsened by the abandonment of the idea that self-government should be—indeed, cannot help but be—a "formative" project, shaping the character of citizens.

Before it fell from favor, the "republican" strand of our public philosophy taught that liberty depends on sharing in self-government. But the "voluntarist" philosophy implicit in today's political practices teaches that freedom consists simply in the right of the individual to choose his own ends. And the citizen is understood with scant reference to the civic realm—not as a "situated self," defined by and fulfilled through a web of social relations and activities; rather, as a freely choosing individual bristling with rights but otherwise "unencumbered." Sandel's book will help produce what he desires—a quickened sense of the moral consequences of political practices and economic arrangements.

Time was when political disputants shared the premise that the success of society should be judged in terms of whether it was conducive to the cultivation of the kind of character needed for self-government and that cannot be taken for granted. Today the focus is on how government is treating the citizens, with emphasis on government recognition of proliferating rights. But in what Sandel considers healthier times, when political people thought hard about how social processes drive society's evolution, the focus was on how political and economic practices might nurture, or impede the growth of, citizens capable of the dignified independence that self-government presupposes.

Today, when society's action is neither slow nor quiet, Sandel hankers for the muscular debates of yesteryear, when government was not big but had bigger ambitions than today's bland Leviathan has. The ambition was to cultivate a virtuous people. So Hamiltonians and Jeffersonians disputed the effect of large-scale manufacturing and its concomitant, cities, on the citizenry's character; Jeffersonians defended the Louisiana Purchase (more room for sturdy yeomen), Jacksonians waged war on the Bank of the United States (engine of decadent speculation and cause of enervating luxury), Clay men advocated "internal improvements" (to harmonize the regions and nationalize sentiments). The mills of Lowell, Massachusetts, were organized to uplift the workers as part of a national debate about whether people working for a wage could avoid a degrading servitude incompatible with democracy.

As America developed what Sandel calls "an economy increasingly at odds with the civic conception of freedom," debates—such as those about antitrust policy and economic planning—concerning the civic consequences of economic arrangements raged. Then in the span of a generation, between the late thirties and early sixties, the debates disappeared. Politics lowered its aims as Americans decided to settle for what Sandel calls a "procedural republic." Government would concentrate on expanding the sphere of individual choices, respecting persons without regard for the respectability of the character they revealed in the choices they made about the lives they would lead.

Instead of concern about the formative force of various forms of production, the only concerns would be the pleasures and equities of consumption—economic growth and the distribution ("fairness") of its bounties. The moral concerns that moved earlier Americans were swept aside. The new spirit of neutrality was expressed by Keynes: "Consumption . . . is the sole end and object of all economic activity." Sandel acutely says that as the formative project was abandoned and the moral dimension was drained from public questions, political discourse became too watery to satisfy the public's moral energies, which were diverted into preoccupation with the private vices of public officials.

Some of Sandel's preoccupations are problematic. He laments the "impersonal" economic forces that shape the lives of individuals and communities. But personal forces—political forces—are not necessarily preferable. Indeed, often they are more bitterly resented. And before too heartily celebrating the organic life of small communities, one should revisit the American literary genre that gave us Sinclair Lewis's depiction of Gopher Prairie, Minnesota, and Sherwood Anderson's Winesberg, Ohio. Sandel deplores the devastation of Main Street by a Wal-Mart at the edge of town, but let us not impute nobility to the downtown merchants' attempts to keep captive customers by banning competition.

Sandel is right to regret the missing moral dimension of public discourse. Or he was until recently. Suddenly politics has reacquired a decidedly Sandelean dimension. Political debate is reconnecting with the concerns Sandel so lucidly examines.

The debate about protectionism is in part about whether communities are being forced to pay too high a price for the benefits free trade confers upon consumers. The debate about welfare is in part about the relation between the discipline of work, the entitlement mentality, and the culture of freedom. The debate about the minimum wage is in part about the propriety of burdening the small business community that is analogous to Jefferson's yeomanry. Advocates of the flat tax present it as a political reform that would combat the corruption of public life by the parasite class of lawyers and lobbyists who profit by gaming the tax code for grasping clients. Told that the Commerce Department's cooperation with big business enlarges the GDP, conservatives say: We don't care. Kill the department because such cooperation is corrupting to both government and business. From the V-chip to the national standards for teaching history to the impact of agriculture policy on family farms, our political debates are echoing traditional moral concerns. Statecraft is again soulcraft, and the citizens who will participate best, and with most zest, will be the fortunate readers of Sandel's splendid explanation of our rich political tradition.

May 13, 1996

1828 and 1971

War unleashes powerful centralizing forces in nations, and from the Civil War through the Cold War it was the principal cause of the concentration of government power in Washington. Which may partly explain why in 1942, with war freshly upon the nation, the Supreme Court ruled as it did in the case of *Wickard* v. *Filburn*. Today, with the nation at peace and uneasy about the centralizing tendencies of this war-filled century, conservatives are toiling to reverse the tide that resulted in farmer Filburn's setback. Their constitutional argument is getting a large assist from economic and scientific developments.

Filburn was an Ohioan caught in the toils of federal agriculture policy. In 1933 Congress passed an anti-Depression measure called the Agricultural Adjustment Act, which sought to stabilize commodity prices by restricting production. In 1936—the last year of constitutional government, as some conservatives see it—the Supreme Court struck down that act on the ground that the federal government was prohibited from regulating production by the Tenth Amendment, which says: "The powers not delegated to the United States by the Constitution, nor prohibited by it to the states are reserved to the states respectively, or to the people."

But the Court's composition changed, and one justice began reading the Constitution by the flickering light of election returns. So there came to be another Agricultural Adjustment Act, which authorized the setting of production quotas not only for wheat sold into interstate commerce but also for wheat that was consumed on the farm as food or seed or feed for poultry and livestock. Filburn thought that this provision, as a putative exercise by the federal government of its power to regulate interstate commerce, was a bit thick. So he produced 269 bushels of wheat in excess of his quota for use as chicken feed on his farm, and refused to pay the stipulated penalty. The case reached the Supreme Court, which used it to dismantle further the constitutional doctrine (a.k.a., the Framers' design) that the federal government is a government of limited and enumerated powers.

The Court upheld the provision, arguing that the cumulative effect of even minor and local economic activities can have interstate consequences—rather like the butterfly in Brazil, the beating of whose wings has some effect, indiscernible but supposedly real, on Detroit's weather. The Court said that even if wheat such as Filburn's bushels never goes to market, "it supplies a need of the man who grew it which would otherwise be reflected by purchases in the open market. Home-grown wheat in this sense competes with wheat in commerce." And if wheat prices rise, many farmers like Filburn might send their wheat grown for home use to market after all, upsetting the government's plans.

Clearly this was a far cry from what the Constitution's Framers had in mind when they reassured various state ratifying conventions that the new central government would be limited to powers enumerated in the document, and would be further limited by various amendments, one of which became the Tenth. What happened to cause (as Pete du Pont says) that amendment to become "to the Constitution what the Chicago Cubs are to the World Series—of only occasional appearance and little consequence"?

The Constitution's enumeration of limited powers turned out to be unconfining, particularly when construed by people eager to augment national power. In the hands of people unsympathetic to decentralization, the enumerated power to, for example, tax and spend for "the general welfare" is not very limiting. So whatever power the Tenth Amendment has in any epoch is less as a leash that enforces particular behavior on the federal government than as the Framers' endorsement of a general predilection for decentralization.

That predilection got run over by a steam locomotive. Michael Rothschild, president of The Bionomics Institute in San Francisco, locates a crucial constitutional turning point in an economic development—the founding in 1828 of America's first railroad, the Baltimore & Ohio. "Unavoidably," writes Rothschild, "the rise of the railroads undermined the decentralized vision of America's Founders." The private power of national enterprises shaping national markets caused many Americans to think nationally and to regard states' powers as feeble anachronisms. Another development with constitutional consequences was intellectual.

It was the cult of science, of modernity, of expert elites that seized the nation's imagination early in the twentieth century and favored the concentration of government power.

Rothschild suggests that the revival of the constitutional theory of decentralization was fostered by a scientific event in 1971—the Intel Corporation's introduction of the first microprocessor. Two decades later there were millions of such slivers of silicon in personal computers and millions more in fax machines, cell phones, voice-mail systems, and other devices. In 1989 fax and e-mail traffic soared. Rothschild writes that the Information Age began in earnest as the Berlin Wall, symbol of the century's centralizing tendencies gone mad, collapsed. So today people sitting in bed at midnight in Arizona shop by telephone at L. L. Bean in Maine, and suburbs and rural areas are rapidly gaining jobs and the centralizing impulse is a spent force.

Small wonder, says Rothschild, that the Clintons' health care plan, "the next logical step in the consolidation of federal power," was unappealing. Centrally designed and controlled social policies no longer imply rationality and fairness but "bureaucracy, Kafkaesque regulation, and one-size-fits-all mass production." He suggests a test: "If you had to trace a missing package, would you rather deal with the U.S. Post Office or Federal Express? If you had to correct an error on your retirement account, would you rather deal with Social Security or your mutual fund?"

Today the Framers' constitutional vision of decentralized governance, until quite recently regarded as a quaint antique, is being rejuvenated by modernity. Thus do arguments acquire momentum from events.

October 16, 1995

The Agrarian Movement Against Modernity

COLUMBIA, SOUTH CAROLINA—A chapter of America's intellectual history came to a quiet close two weeks ago with the death at age ninety-two of Andrew Lytle at his cabin in Monteagle, Tennessee. He was the last survivor of the twelve southern writers—Robert Penn Warren, John Crowe Ransom, and Allen Tate were the best known—who in 1930 contributed essays to the book *I'll Take My Stand.*

It was the manifesto of the Agrarian movement, a small but luminous band of intellectuals who initially were energized in part by resentment of northern condescension toward the South after the 1925 Scopes trial in Tennessee, concerning the teaching of evolution. However, their larger theme was a Jeffersonian defense of the distinctiveness and dignity of the southern culture of rural yeomanry, against urbanization and industrialization. A "New South"? They wanted none of it.

A new chapter, or a postscript to the old one, is now being written by people such as Professor Clyde Wilson. Talk about your angry white male: Wilson is angry at John Quincy Adams, among many other people and things. Wilson knows how to nurse a grudge.

A historian here at the University of South Carolina, and editor of the papers of the state's most famous son, John C. Calhoun, Wilson actually is too amiable to be characterized as constantly angry, but he is comprehensively disapproving of most of the modern world, which is why he is active in the Southern League. If you believe America is becoming too homogenized, that regional differences are being blurred and ancient passions are growing cold, the league should assuage your regrets.

Founded two years ago in emulation of the Lombard League, which seeks to preserve the traditions of northern Italy, the Southern League's more than 1,000 members seek "the cultural, social, economic, and political independence and well-being of the Southern people." Yes, independence.

You may think all that was settled 130 years ago in the living room of a McLean farmhouse at Appomattox. Try to tell that to the sort of league members who refer to the Revolutionary War as "the first war for independence." The second one was unavailing but some members are sharpening their swords, spoiling for a third. Others content themselves with delivering learned papers to league meetings, arguing, in Woodrow Wilson's rhetoric of "self-determination of peoples," the right of secession. They insist that the North won the secession dispute because it had better factories, not better arguments.

The papers and symposia at league meetings (the most recent was attended by the great-great-grandniece of Nathan Bedford Forrest, the Confederate cavalry general), show that most league members subscribe not only to regional chauvinism but also to variants of conservatism. However, they deeply dislike capitalism's ethos of rationalism and what its dynamism does in dissolving organic communities based on local sentiments and traditional senses of place. Furthermore, some league members give aid and comfort to leftist "multiculturalists" when they say "America is only a geographical expression."

Actually, the logic of most league members, including Wilson, is that the "northernization" of the South by economic and cultural forces has, alas, made America one nation. Wilson, who speaks with defiant disdain of "the Deep North," probably wishes New England states had acted on secessionist threats voiced at their Hartford Convention in 1814. They would have taken with them the whole Adams family, which to Wilson symbolizes the North's cultural condescension and political imperialism toward the South.

The league's bimonthly newsletter, *Southern Patriot*, bristles with quirky agitation against "Yankee hegemony." The term "Copperhead" survives in its pages as a term of endearment for northern sympathizers. Readers are urged to say loudly "divisible" instead of "indivisible" when they "absolutely must recite the 'Pledge of Allegiance' to the flag of our Yankee conquerors." Mel Gibson's movie *Braveheart* is warmly recommended for its portrayal of thirteenth-century Scottish nationalism. The disintegrations of the Soviet Union and Yugoslavia, and the near disintegration of Canada, are celebrated.

Although there is in all this a certain sophomoric delight in shocking polite society, there also is an admirable seriousness about the intellectual pedigree of a particular cultural critique of American modernity. However, if you want to know just how lost the Lost Cause is, and how much the league needs a leavening sense of irony, note the newsletter's unembarrassed announcement that the league is on the Internet, and that league information can be obtained by e-mail at NBForrest@aol.com. Andrew Lytle, who in his eighties still practiced what he preached—simplicity and subsistence agriculture—would have had none of that.

December 28, 1995

A Course Correction in the Capital of Liberalism

The case could get conservatives' danders up. A category of small businesses is being subjected to injurious regulation in New York City. That city, the capital of liberalism and hence of overbearing government, is disrupting the free market by burdening, with the intent to discourage, a form of commerce involving a legal commodity. The government is doing this because it disapproves of the practice of supplying the particular commodity for which there is a demand. Furthermore, the government wants to engage in social engineering, shaping the social climate of neighborhoods by purging this commerce from most of the places where market forces have produced it.

It is enough to make conservatives' blood boil. Or maybe not. The commodity is pornography and other "adult" entertainment. Hence the conservatives' conundrum: Can they square their advocacy of smaller, less intrusive government, with a more ambitious moral agenda for government?

New York City's government is acting against the pollution of the social atmosphere, and in the name of such conservative causes as neighborhood preservation and family values. So the city's new censoriousness provides an interesting coda to this political season. Many conservatives have been bewildered almost to the point of vertigo by the rapid reversal of their fortunes. Two years ago their blanket castigations of government seemed to be resonating with a national majority. Today the national mood about government's uses seems more ambivalent, conflicted, nuanced. Conservatives seeking a small confrontation with their own ideological tangles can take a stroll down West 39th Street in Manhattan, to Richard Kunis's store.

Large lettering on his front window announces YOUR NEIGHBORHOOD VIDEO STORE SINCE 1985. In the 1970s he sold office furniture. Then came the real estate boom of the 1980s. Property values rose and the furniture business was not profitable enough to pay the rent. Kunis switched to renting and selling videos, mainstream as well as X-rated. Now his inventory is all . . . what? "Erotic" is not the word. Watching an "adult" movie is an experience about as erotic as reading *Gray's Anatomy*. Suffice it to say that Kunis's movies are energetically pornographic. Customers can rent them, buy them, or view them in booths in the store. He is building, at the law's behest, a "handicapped-accessible" booth.

Kunis thinks his transactions with consenting adults are private enterprise without consequences that are the proper concern of public authorities. Mayor Giuliani and the city council say: Just as smoking in confined public places is not a purely private matter because second-hand smoke is objectionable to, and perhaps injurious to, other people, so, too, the activities of Kunis and the operators of about 180 other "adult" businesses, in the dense living conditions of a city, have injurious secondary effects against which government can act.

The city says those effects include decreased property values, retarded economic development, damage to neighborhood character and to children. And when such businesses are clustered, there are increased illegal sexual activities and other crime, as well as loitering and littering and other nuisances. Hence the new zoning law will disperse such businesses to manufacturing and commercial areas designated by the city, and will require buffer zones between them and places, such as homes, schools, and churches, that are particularly vulnerable to the secondary effects.

Civil liberties hysterics consider this a step down the slippery slope toward tyranny. Their hyperbole is preposterous, but not their contention that precisely proving the various secondary effects is problematic. However, precision should not be necessary. One does not need a moral micrometer to gauge the fact that the sex industry drowned Times Square in squalor. And arcane arguments are not needed to establish the principle that residential neighborhoods merit some protection from forms of commerce that abrade the spirits of the residents.

Pornography merchants argue that the new law will put most of them out of business and relegate the remainder to inaccessible locales, thereby unconstitutionally burdening the exercise of a fundamental right, freedom of expression. They say the law patently discriminates against their form of expression because of its content, and therefore violates the constitutional requirement of content-neutrality. The city replies that pornography will still be available, and many laws regulate the "time, place, and manner" of expression (e.g., no loudspeakers near hospitals).

But the larger significance of the law is this: A course correction is underway in the capital of liberalism, where for decades the tension between individual rights and community values has been too often resolved in favor of the former. In liberal social analysis, the individual is the only reality, and the community is an abstraction without claims. No more. Panhandling is no longer invested with constitutional grandeur as (in the words of a liberal judge) "informative and persuasive speech." Instead, it is seen as a form of disorder. Graffiti is no longer regarded as a "statement" by the voiceless and downtrodden, but as ominous evidence of an uncontrolled environment.

About one-third of the recent decline in the nation's crime occurred in this city, which has not increased its police force. What has increased is intolerance, which can be a virtue. The mayor understands that there simply is no such thing as a "minor crime" because all crime breeds disorder, which is an infectious social disease. It atomizes communities, increases anxiety, wariness, avoidance, and truculence, and dissolves the sense of mutual regard and obligations of civility. Note that word.

Selling pornography is not a crime, but by catering to, and inflaming, vulgarians' sensibilities, it contributes to the coarsening of the culture, which erodes civility. In its original meaning, "civility" denoted the virtues requisite for civic life—the life of citizenship in a city. For too long now, the word "civil" has appeared in American discourse almost exclusively as an adjective modifying the noun "right." New York's decision to get judgmental, to stigmatize pornography by pushing it to the fringe of city life, rests on this recognition: the words "civil," "civic," "citizen," and "city" have a common root and are related in complex ways.

November 11, 1996

Big Government in the Black Canyon

HOOVER DAM, IN NEVADA AND ARIZONA—First, the Colorado River had to be temporarily moved. And it was. Then, thousands of men working in three shifts around the clock every day except Christmas and the Fourth of July, and paid $6 a day—from which $1.60 was subtracted for food, housing, and transportation—poured 4.4 million cubic yards of concrete, enough to pave a highway sixteen feet wide from New York to San Francisco. They did this in less than four years, finishing two years ahead of schedule, sixty years ago this summer.

Let us now praise those who conceived and executed this still breathtaking marvel in the Black Canyon. And let us pause during this season of discontent with the federal government and all its works to consider what we have lost that the country had when it had a will for such great works.

The dam is named for the president who was an engineer and who encouraged the project. He was secretary of commerce in 1922 when the Colorado River Compact allocated the river among the states it serves. Today half the population of the West is to some extent dependent on the river he helped subdue.

The dam, says an inscription here, was "inspired by a vision of lonely lands made fruitful." Back then, even the Los Angeles basin was relatively lonely. Today Southern California and Arizona are the biggest users of the electric power generated here. Just down the road there is a novel form of fruitfulness—the fastest growing city in the nation: Las Vegas, population 1 million. In 1935 its population was about 7,000. (But don't blame the dam for modern Las Vegas, which gets its power elsewhere.)

Behind the dam—660 feet thick at its base—is 110 miles of Lake Mead, enough water to cover Pennsylvania a foot deep. Construction of the dam cost the lives of 110 men, some of them victims of heat prostration in temperatures that often topped 125 degrees deep in the canyon. Flood control, irrigation, power generation, water storage—the dam serves many functions. But could it be built today?

Perhaps, if it did not unduly inconvenience some cousin of the snail darter, and if all the impact statements and racial set-asides could be negotiated before everyone decided the whole thing was too much trouble. But back then, before it was considered correct to be a conscientious objector to the "conquest" of nature, America had an appetite for big conquering projects.

As the dam was being completed, trains were rolling west from Pittsburgh carrying steel beams bearing banners that proclaimed "Bound for the

Golden Gate Bridge," which was completed in 1937. The bridge, like the dam, expressed the soul of the nation as Stephen Vincent Benet had sung it:

> We made this thing, this dream,
> This land unsatisfied by little ways.

Or by slow paces. Around 1940, when the government got interested in atomic physics, it asked some leading scientists what they needed. They asked for $6,000 worth of graphite. By 1944 investment in the Manhattan Project equaled investment in the prewar automobile industry.

In the 1950s the first Republican president since Hoover produced the biggest public works project in the nation's history to that point: The Interstate Highway System had been born in the brain of young Lieutenant Colonel Eisenhower in 1919 when he was assigned to take a convoy across the country to test equipment and demonstrate the inadequacies of the nation's roads. (Later, General Eisenhower saw autobahns as instruments of Germany's national defense strategy, and he required, in the first enabling legislation, that all interstates be straight for one mile in every five, thus ensuring their utility as emergency airstrips in the event of an invasion.)

In 1969 the Apollo Project fulfilled a government vow made in 1961. In 1995 the movie *Apollo 13* is thrilling audiences for whom the exhilaration of collective achievement through government is but a rumor about long ago.

Speaker Gingrich recently called for "rethinking how we mobilize the American people." He said: "We need a series of large projects. You don't hold together the free people of the planet by small things: 'Let's get another thirty thousand cars in this year.' That's not exactly a noble battle cry. . . . We ought to be back on the moon. We ought to be on Mars. And we ought to do it with all the free nations of the planet participating, so that we build a momentum of the human race. . . ."

Many people will be surprised, and certain kinds of conservatives will be scandalized, by the speaker's belief that government is competent for, and has a duty to attempt, the peacetime mobilization of people for projects explicitly designed to elicit nobility through collective actions. His belief is incompatible with the agenda of those conservatives who are bent on instilling indiscriminate skepticism about government's utility.

But he has much modern American history on his side. It is as clear as black and white—the soaring affirmation of glistening white concrete, shimmering in the desert sun between the black canyon walls.

August 13, 1995

The Cultural Contradictions of Conservatism

A poetic episode in our national history occurred July 4, 1826. On that fiftieth anniversary of the Declaration of Independence, the author of that founding document, Thomas Jefferson, died. So did John Adams, who did as much as anyone to produce the occasion for Jefferson's document. The second president's last words referred to the third president: "Thomas Jefferson survives." The third president's last words were, "Is it the Fourth?"

Three days later, in Quincy, Massachusetts, after attending Adams's funeral some dignitaries were taken to see a prosaic force that would shape what the two Founders had helped to found. They saw something novel. They saw a railroad, one of the nation's first. It was not much of one; it was built to carry granite a few miles from Quincy to Boston for the Bunker Hill Monument. But it was huge as a harbinger.

Railroads soon would have constitutional consequences, and not just because, in the coming war against southern insurrection, they were to help the army of the central government settle a constitutional argument about the primacy of that government. Railroads also had constitutional consequences because they influenced Americans' thinking about the nature of their regime. Railroads, and the industrialism of which they were emblematic, filled our "extensive Republic" with energy. Our big country acquired a big economy, and a big government.

Today, conservatism is asking whether a big government is merely a contingent, or a necessary, outcome in a big country with a big economy. That the country was to be big was never in doubt. In the Revolutionary era, there were just four million free Americans, and 80 percent of them lived within 20 miles of Atlantic tidewater. Yet these Americans audaciously called their legislature the Continental Congress. They knew where they were headed—for California. They would get there by many means, including railroads. To promote construction of these steel sinews of national strength, the central government lent its considerable weight. For example, it gave 4.8 million acres of Nebraska—one-tenth of that state—to the Union Pacific.

By 1908, eight decades after the deaths of Adams and Jefferson, a professor of political science marveled at what industrialism had wrought: "The copper threads of the telegraph run unbroken to every nook and corner of the great continent, like the nerves of a single body. . . . Railways lie in every valley and stretch across every plain. . . . Industrial organization knows nothing of state lines, and commerce sweeps from state to state." So wrote Professor Woodrow Wilson, five years before becoming president.

He became the first president to criticize the Constitution, which he considered more ingenious than was suitable for changed conditions. The Constitution, he said, is elegantly Newtonian with its checks and balances, but it is not conducive to the energy and dispatch requisite for regulating an urban industrial society. He postulated the need for heroic presidents to marshal public opinion in order to override the government's constitutional creakiness. What the Founders would have considered an anticonstitutional infusion of direct popular will, Wilson considered necessary to enable the national government to implement the national idea. He seems not to have worried about the possibility that his ideas might encourage passivity in the public, producing a nation of mere followers. When Wilson wrote and governed, Newton was out of fashion, Darwin was in, and the Constitution was coming to be thought of in organic terms, as a "living" document. However, it was unclear, then as now, what a "living," evolving, ever-in-flux constitution is. What can a constitution constitute if, instead of shaping its times, it takes its shape from its time?

In 1893, three years after the Census Bureau declared the closing of the frontier, Wilson had pondered the changes that were challenging the old American faith that freedom is, in large measure, a function of space—that freedom consists partly of being unable to see the smoke from your neighbor's cabin or to hear the sound of his ax. In 1893 Wilson wrote, "Slowly we shall grow old, compact our people, study the delicate adjustments of an intricate society." In classical political theory, compactness was a precondition for a successful republic—a small population compacted in a small polity. The audacity of the American experiment was—is—its attempt to have a republic that is big, but in which life nevertheless is conducive to the virtues requisite for self-government, the virtues of self-reliance and self-restraint. However, in the century since Wilson brooded about the emergence of "an intricate society," our big country has acquired a big government that seems to foster dependence, and that inflames incontinent appetites, including appetites for government provision of illimitable wants.

This was written in the twelfth month of 1995's intense debate about our domestic arrangements, the most intense debate in sixty-two years, since 1933. Then, the New Deal accelerated the already-changing relationship between the individual citizen and the central government. Since then, government has become omnipresent in American society. It has increasingly aspired to be omniprovident. In the process, it has suffered a debilitating leakage of legitimacy.

This has provoked a conservative critique of the nation's political tendencies in this century and has produced this year of conservative opportunity. Unfortunately, conservatism is not yet measuring up to this moment.

Perhaps conservatism has become intoxicated by triumphalism; perhaps it has become intellectually flaccid because of the sterility of its opposition— contemporary liberalism. In any case, conservatism's critique of current conditions is not as searching as it should be, and its prescriptions raise three troubling questions. First, does conservatism have a distinctive and defensible understanding of the Constitution, or merely a different policy agenda? Second, is conservatism unaware of its own problematic tensions? Third, is conservatism capable of identifying and proclaiming the austere principle of our constitutional republican government?

Woodrow Wilson, to give him his due, once put the principle succinctly. He said that our constitutional government has not only "exalted" the individual, it has "thrown him upon his own resources, as if it honored him enough to release him from leading strings and trust him to see and seek his own rights." Our republic's premise, said Wilson, "is that no man must look to have the government take care of him, but that every man must take care of himself." Such government does not merely presuppose "intelligence and independence of spirit," it "elicits intelligence and creates independence of spirit."

Can contemporary conservatism stiffen its sinews and summon up its blood and talk in that tone of voice to the American people? If not, the incapacity may reflect what can be called the cultural contradictions of conservatism.

A few years ago there was lively debate about the "cultural contradictions of capitalism." The postulate was that capitalism is jeopardized by its success: Its prodigies of wealth-creation produce habits and character traits that subvert the very virtues—thrift, industriousness, deferral of gratification—that are capitalism's prerequisites. This was not a new worry. It had occurred to that accomplished worrier, John Adams. In 1819, he wrote to Jefferson, "Will you tell me how to prevent riches from being the effects of industry? Will you tell me how to prevent luxury from producing effeminacy, intoxication, extravagance, vice, and folly?" Today's conservatism is much in need of a John Adams as it addresses the nation's principal worry, the condition of its culture, meaning all the institutions that compose civil society.

The contradiction in today's conservatism is, happily, a contingent, not a necessary, aspect of conservatism. But it can be a crippling contingency if it is not corrected. It is this: Conservatism is advocating not just disrespect for many activities of government, but even blanket disdain for government, and hence for the political vocation. However, conservatism's vision of civic virtue depends on more than adherence to a particular policy agenda. It depends on respect, even reverence, for our political regime— for our constitutional order understood as a formative enterprise.

The Cultural Contradictions of Conservatism

Conservatism has come to power in the 1990s largely because this is the decade in which the nation has looked into the mirror and blanched. What Tocqueville called "the slow and quiet action of society upon itself" now seems neither slow nor quiet nor wholesome. The crux of the conservative diagnosis is that "big government" is to blame. There is much truth in this diagnosis, but it is by no means the whole story, and it is a diagnosis altogether too easy for conservatism's own good.

Contemporary conservatism's greatest service to society has been to refocus attention on an elemental fact that the Founders understood: Society is a crucible of character formation. Human beings are political, meaning social, beings, fulfilled in associations. Government can damage associational life, and big government can do big damage.

Our party system was born of an argument about the action of American society on itself and on the character of Americans. Hamiltonians wanted a society of high-velocity commercial energy and restless, striving individualism in order to produce national greatness. Jeffersonians aimed to promote other virtues, particularly simplicity and the serene independence of the self-sufficient yeoman. Such Americans would, Jefferson thought, avoid the degrading dependence of the urban manufacturing workers who, Jefferson said, "must live on oatmeal and potatoes" and "have no time to think."

We have been worrying and arguing about national character ever since. Sometimes the argument has taken comic turns, as when, in 1908, the Democratic candidate for president, William Jennings Bryan, said that the Republican candidate, Vice President William Howard Taft, was unfit to be president because, being a Unitarian, Taft did not believe in the virgin birth. But, more often than not, in arguments about the national bank and abolitionism and immigration and prohibition and desegregation and, today, popular entertainment, American political argument has been driven by serious concerns about character.

The Founders bequeathed us a political order founded on realism about human attributes, beginning with this truth: In human beings, interestedness is a given, virtue must be acquired. Contemporary conservatism is resoundingly right when it argues that government itself has become inimical to those virtues essential to responsible self-government. It has become inimical because it fosters both dependency on government and uncivic aggressiveness in attempting to bend public institutions to private factional advantage. But does conservatism have the steely resolve required to tell the country the hard truth about how radically it has gone wrong in its thinking about, and expectations of, government?

Conservatism is driving today's political debate because it senses, and is struggling to act on, the fact that human beings are biological facts, but citizens suited to self-government are social artifacts. However, conservatism is not yet sufficiently clear-sighted about how our constitutional order is supposed to contribute to the creation of such artifacts. And conservatism is not alert to the way its own tenets can complicate the creation of virtuous citizens.

Let us be clear about what conservatism is *not* saying about citizens as social artifacts. Conservatives do not subscribe to, indeed are implacably hostile to, the idea that human nature has a history. The hostility is implacable because that idea is utterly subversive of government based on respect for natural rights. This is so because if human nature has a history, then there really is no such thing as human nature, understood as something the essence of which is unchanging.

The idea that human nature has a history—that human beings only have a nature contingent on their time and place—is the idea that has animated modern tyrannies. It has done so because people susceptible to that idea are susceptible to the idea that self-government is a chimera—an impossibility—because the self is a fiction or, at best, a flimsy reflection of the individual's social setting. To say that human nature is utterly plastic is to open the way to governments that regard the creation of a new, improved form of humanity the highest government project. Such governments are apt to unleash "consciousness-raisers," who would use political power to extirpate "false consciousness." Such people insist that, until proper consciousness is made universal, any consent necessarily arises from false consciousness and, hence, is not worth seeking.

However, to say, as conservatives are prepared to, that individuals are not entirely autonomous and unconditioned is not to say that human nature is utterly unfixed and unformed, or utterly plastic to the manipulations of government or society. On the contrary, conservatism warns that people who believe there is no human nature must believe that no rights are natural rights. Indeed, if there is no human nature, then rights are just appetites tarted up in the aggressive language of rights talk in order to acquire momentum for respect.

Conservatism seeks equilibrium, arguing that nature has political claims and that nurturing has a political role. Nature's political claims rise from this fact: The idea of human nature involves the idea of essential human qualities or virtues that are conducive to excellence. And the task of political nurturing takes its bearings from that idea of excellence.

Wise conservatives take that task seriously. For example, John Adams, perhaps the most conservative Founder, declared that education makes a greater difference between man and man than nature has made between man and brute. The Founders understood that popular government would be—could not help but be—a formative experience, for better or worse. They thought that popular government properly constituted would be good for our souls. Today, conservatives correctly argue that our government has become a deforming force, corrupting the country's character. They say government has become a bland Leviathan, confirming Tocqueville's warning that government can "degrade men without tormenting them."

However if conservatives are to be faithful to the full philosophy of the Founders, conservatives must understand that hostility to government, especially hostility to the central government, is not sufficient. Indeed, it is not permissible. The Founders believed that the nation should be, and would be, constantly conditioned by its founding. Our constitutional government was to be both agent of, and shaper of, the citizenry. It is not true that they subscribed to the notion that government should be neutral regarding the cultivation of virtues—regarding, that is, what we today, in the thinness of our moral vocabulary, call "values." The Founders intended the Constitution to promote a way of life, and they understood that to promote a way of life is to promote a kind of person. Listen to the words of one of the Constitution's first great construers, John Marshall. In his biography of Washington he wrote:

> [The] great and visible economic improvement occurring around 1790 [was in part due to] the influence of the Constitution on habits of thinking and acting, [which] though silent, was considerable. In depriving the states of the power to impair the obligations of contracts, or to make anything but gold and silver a tender in payment of debts, the conviction was impressed on that portion of society which had looked to the government for relief from embarrassment, that personal exertion alone could free them from difficulties; and an increased degree of industry and economy was the natural consequence of this opinion.

Note this: Marshall said the Constitution was designed to encourage particular habits of thinking and acting. From visible habits we make inferences as to invisible attributes of the soul. Therefore statecraft, as the Founders understood it, is soulcraft. Hence politics has a great and stately jurisdiction, and it is an inherently dignified vocation, no matter how imperfectly practiced at any given time.

Note this, too: Marshall understood that acceptance of the Constitution was an act of self-denial in the name of self-government. The Constitution deprived the states of certain powers that they had used, under the Articles of Confederation, licentiously. The states had produced what Madison tartly called "a luxuriancy of legislation." Because the Founders understood the contagion of faction, they did not believe that the best government is always that which is closest to the people. Being unsentimental about the people, the Founders were not sentimental about state and local governments. As Marshall saw, by depriving states of some of their powers, the Constitution helped to equip citizens for the dignity of life without degrading dependence on government.

The Anti-Federalists opposed the Constitution in the name of intimate government; the Founders framed the Constitution to provide effective government and to spare citizens the discomfort and dependence that comes from being intimate with government. The Founders hoped that one effect of exalting the central government over other governments would be a diminution of the total amount of government—local, state, and national. This, the Founders thought, would encourage self-reliance in the pursuit of happiness.

This, then, was an important dimension of the rationale for a strengthened central government. But that government was supposed to be strong within the strict limits of enumerated powers—powers that Madison insisted were "few and defined." However, we have not had such a government for a long time. Indeed, it is arguable that we never really did.

From its first year, the national government has asserted powers proportional to national needs, and, from the first, it has defined national needs in ways that did not produce government precisely, or even notably, limited in sphere or methods. Of the thirty-nine members of the House of Representatives who were present when the First Congress took up its first order of business, sixteen were Framers—they had been at the Constitutional Convention. Yet their first order of business was the enactment of tariffs. And they did not regard tariffs as merely revenue-raising devices but as instruments of what today is called "industrial policy." The aim: the promotion of local or regional interests and the purchase of political advantage. Was that the exercise of an enumerated power?

The enumeration of powers in Article I, Section 8 of the Constitution includes the power to "lay and collect taxes . . . to . . . provide for . . . the general welfare" and "to make all laws which shall be necessary and proper for carrying into Execution the foregoing powers." Jefferson insisted that the word "necessary" meant more than just "useful," but, in practice, it never has meant more than that.

In 1944, with the nation more at war than ever before, and with the federal government permeating the nation's life more than ever before or since, Justice Felix Frankfurter, writing for the Court, recurred to Woodrow Wilson's theme of the effect of modern technology on federalism. Frankfurter insisted, "The interpenetrations of modern society have not wiped out state lines. It is not for us to make inroads on our federal system either by indifference to its maintenance or excessive regard for the unifying forces of modern technology. Scholastic reasoning may prove that no activity is isolated within the boundaries of a single State, but that cannot justify absorption of legislative powers by the United States over every activity."

Well. Such reasoning may be, in Frankfurter's pejorative term, scholastic, and such "absorption" may be, as Frankfurter insisted, unjustified, but Frankfurter went immediately on to say that the Court should do next to nothing about it. He said: "When the conduct of an enterprise affects commerce among the states is a matter of practical judgment. . . . The exercise of this practical judgment the Constitution entrusts primarily and very largely to the Congress, subject to the latter's control by the electorate."

Just so. The lesson of 206 years of constitutional history is clear: If the federal government is to be limited, it will not be limited primarily, or even significantly, by courts construing the Constitution, which has proven to be merely a parchment barrier to enlargements of the federal government's sphere. Never mind the Supreme Court's recent small nibbling at the far fringes of powers exercised under the Commerce Clause. Limits on government must be grounded in the character of the people. However, the good news is that the character of the people can be shaped by constitutional arrangements and arguments, if they are given proper exegesis.

Big government did not fall out of the sky, unbidden, like hail in Kansas. And it was not foisted on a reluctant public. It grew for many reasons. Daniel Webster, a champion of the national idea, championed the Delaware breakwater as an "internal improvement" by the federal government because neither Pennsylvania nor New Jersey nor Delaware would build it: They would not pay all the costs because they would not get all the benefits. One use to which the Interstate Commerce Commission was put after its creation in 1887 was to keep certain east-west freight rates low in order to encourage commerce that would strengthen the national union. Do you think large federal entitlement programs are a recent development? In 1893, 42 percent of federal expenditures were for Civil War veterans. The federal Meat Inspection Act of 1906, which initiated federal meat inspection, did not come about simply because the nation's stomach was turned by Upton Sinclair's novel *The Jungle*. The federal government began regulating the meat-packing industry because the industry wanted it to. The industry wanted it because state regulations were so unreliable that some European markets were being closed to American meat.

The nationalization of our lives has taken many forms, and the nationalization of politics has proceeded apace. However, the change that made government not merely big but also bad for the nation's soul was a change of mind. Ideas have consequences and today's government is one of them.

The Constitution's framers believed that individuals are endowed with natural rights essential to the pursuit of happiness and that governments are instituted to secure those rights, not to secure happiness. But life in this commercial republic has not been conducive to an ethos of limits, of any sort. It had been hoped that potentially disruptive passions might be tamed by being diverted from factional politics into commerce. It had been hoped that dangerous energies would be sublimated in wealth creation and acquisition. But what was to prevent acquisitive people from coming to regard government as just another arena in which they could strive for material well-being? Nothing was to prevent that, because the nation was to abandon the Constitution's underlying ideas, and because some new ideas were to encourage actively the conception of government as deliverer of material well-being.

In October 1932, the Democratic Party's presidential nominee said, "I have . . . described the spirit of my program as a 'new deal,' which is plain English for a changed *concept* of the duty and responsibility of Government toward economic life." Said Franklin Roosevelt, "Government has a final responsibility for the well-being of its citizens." Thus was the final responsibility for much of life removed from private life to the public sector—and to the banks of the Potomac. And thus was the "well-being" of the citizen defined with reference to material conditions, and without reference to the citizen's character or virtues.

In his second inaugural address, FDR spoke of government's responsibilities toward "the one-third of a nation ill-housed, ill-clad, and ill-nourished." Toward the end of his presidency, he claimed for government a responsibility that would still further enlarge its sphere. In his January 1944 State of the Union message, he avowed a government "duty" to establish "an American standard of living higher than ever before known," and he said: "We cannot be content, no matter how high that general standard of living may be, if some fraction of our people—whether it be one-third or one-fifth or one-tenth—is ill-fed, ill-clothed, ill-housed, or insecure."

This was a summons to permanent discontent on the part of citizens and government. This was the bestowing on government of a roving commission to define civic health solely in terms of the material standard of living, yet also to add to the growing list of citizens' entitlements an entitlement to a mental state—a sense of security. Roosevelt said political rights would no longer suffice to insure "equality in the pursuit of happiness," so there must be a "second Bill of Rights." It would include rights to "a useful and remunerative job," "adequate" food, clothing, and recreation, "good" education, "decent" homes, a "decent" living for farmers, "adequate" medical care, and a right to freedom from "unfair competition" and from "the economic fears of old age, sickness, accident, and unemployment."

All these rights, and myriad others that would be enumerated as the years rolled by, were necessary, Roosevelt said, because "necessitous men are not free men." Therefore, government's new task would be nothing less than the conquest of necessity. And so, twenty years later, in 1964, at the Democratic Convention, the presidential nomination was accepted by a man who had been in Washington since Roosevelt was president and who planned to complete Roosevelt's project—the elimination of necessity from Americans' lives. Lyndon Johnson said to the 1964 Convention: "This Nation—this generation—in this hour, has man's first chance to build the Great Society—a place where the meaning of man's life matches the marvels of man's labor." It was going to be hard to top that entitlement—the entitlement to meaningfulness.

But twenty years after that, the Democratic party gave its presidential nomination to Walter Mondale, perhaps the last nominee to adhere to New Deal liberalism or, at least, the last not to disguise his adherence. In his concession statement after losing forty-nine states, Mondale said his thoughts were with all those in need of caring government, including "the poor, the unemployed, the elderly, the handicapped, the helpless, and the sad." Yes, the sad. Sadness, too, like necessity, qualified as a public concern.

Now, how did it happen that liberalism annihilated all sense of limits on government's responsibilities and competence? James Q. Wilson has said that New Deal liberalism was concerned only—only!—with who gets what, when, where, and how; but liberalism in its new phase was concerned with who thinks what, who acts when, who lives where, and who feels how. Especially if you feel insecure. Or sad.

In President Johnson's 1965 speech at Howard University, which adumbrated the rationale for what has come to be called affirmative action, he said "men are shaped by their world." That is certainly true. Johnson also said people are shaped by "a hundred unseen forces." That also is true. But what was new was the idea that a government could and should master all forces, the unseen and the seen, and, for that matter, should master "the world." The planted axiom was that, because government frames society, government is complicit in, and hence morally responsible for, all social outcomes and should make them come out right.

But this notion erases the very distinction on which classical liberalism—the liberalism of Locke and the American Revolution—was founded, the distinction between the public and the private spheres of life. On this distinction, freedom depends. Never mind. Government set out to "level the playing field." That recurring phrase is revealing: Playing fields are leveled by bulldozers—which are not nice emblems of government.

The result of government's equalizing aspirations is a paradox—power wielded by elites claiming expertise in the manufacture of equality. In its attempt to equalize "well-being," liberalism exalted one virtue—compassion. And compassion is a capacious concept. It can mean the prevention or amelioration of pain, of discomfort, of insecurity, or even of sadness.

However, the frustration of desires is uncomfortable and can make people sad. So compassionate government must toil for the satisfaction of all desires. If a desire unfulfilled is painful, or even a discomfort, fulfilling that desire is a duty of compassionate government. Such government believes that the pain of unfulfilled desires makes fulfilling the desires necessary. So the desires are upgraded to necessities. People suffering disappointed desires are therefore necessitous people, and, according to Franklin Roosevelt, necessitous people are not free.

Now, what moderation, what temperance, what restraint can there be in government animated by the idea that freedom, understood as emancipation from necessity, is the gift of comprehensively compassionate government? Such government has metastasized recklessly, and conservatism has risen on the tide of reaction against such government's hubris and overreaching. But life in this target-rich environment has been a bit too easy for conservatism. With so many lurid faults to liberalism, conservatism has not had to ask itself some hard questions about what it is prepared to tell people, especially people that would rather not be told.

Again, limited government cannot be attained by getting the judiciary to put the political branches on a short leash. The judiciary will not do that, and conservatives should not incite the judiciary to an even more imperial role than it already has seized. Limited government can only be attained by shifting the shiftable sands of public opinion. So the central political problem for conservatives is to get the public to consent to government that censors their desires, refusing to fulfill many of them.

However in order for popular government to be strong enough to say "no" to popular desires, it must be respected. And if our constitutional government is to be respected, the Constitution must be regarded as something more, something grander, than a mere framework for competing forms of willfulness. The conservative agenda of governmental restraint depends on government having the strength that comes from respect. And respect is never accorded to the servile.

So conservatives must drop their populist rhetoric about making government more "responsive." And they must abandon their populist posture, which has them living with their ears to the ground. As Churchill said, it is hard to look up to someone in that position.

Now that conservatives are convinced that they are riding a wave of antigovernment opinion, it is comfortable for conservatives to think their mission is merely to remove impediments to popular opinion. However, their real mission is (in the language of *The Federalist*) to "enlarge and refine" opinion. Is that an elitist thought? Of course. But the question, now as always, is not whether elites shall rule, but which elites. Republics rely on the principle of representation, which is that the people do not decide issues . . . they decide who shall decide. And they decide by elections, not by drawing lots. Elections, unlike lotteries, are searches for certain special and scarce attributes. The attributes of worthy representatives involve more than a willingness to represent the public merely by re-presenting the public's opinions back to itself.

Representation, properly practiced, involves responsibilities entailed by this fact: Public opinion rarely really exists independent of government actions and deliberations. Conservatives may be most comfortable taking the anticonstitutional position that politics is just the task of conforming policies to a particular set of interests. But if that is what they think, then all that distinguishes them from liberals is the interests on whose behalf they want government to be "responsive."

Is there a tension between the idea of government based on consent and the idea of representation somewhat independent of opinion? Of course there is. But that tension is built into our regime; it is constitutional tension. The tension is inherent in the idea of popular government operating at a constitutional distance from the populace that legitimizes government by its consent. The tension is inherent in the idea that the deliberations of representative government will "refine and enlarge" the public mind. The tension is inherent in the idea of constitutional government as a formative experience—government as both agent and shaper of the people.

Our nation had a founding moment, which means it is founded on more than inertia. Our nation emerged not from forces obscured by the mists of the past but from a clear, public act of choosing. Of the correctness of their choice, the Founders were breathtakingly confident. Think about this: The First Amendment forbids the establishment of religion because the Founders thought that religious truth was unknowable and so must remain an open question. But the Constitution guarantees the establishment of republican governments in all the states because the Founders considered the best form of government a closed question for our open society.

One measure of a political philosophy's seriousness is what it requires of its adherents. Conservatives today are required to tell people that they should be formed by respect for the Constitution. That is, they should be formed for a life of choosing not to choose all that government can offer, because those offerings come at a cost to the virtues of independence and moderation.

Which brings us back to what may be the cultural contradiction of conservatism: Conservatism depends on eliciting from citizens a public-spirited self-denial. But that is not easily elicited in a commercial republic of the sort conservatism celebrates, where individualism enjoys maximum scope for private pursuits.

Public-spirited self-denial can only be elicited by a conservatism standing for more than the sum of the demands of the groups in its coalition; it can only be elicited by respect for the Constitution and, hence, for the virtues of self-reliance and self-restraint that our polity presupposes. As today's conservative party struggles to develop a constitutional vocabulary for infusing self-government with self-restraint, it should remember this: The party first became a national factor because of one man's refusal to accept popular sovereignty as a complete expression of the formative project of American politics. That is, the Republican Party's intellectual pedigree traces directly to Lincoln's denial that Kansans could choose to have slaves.

Lincoln's noble insistence was that a great continental nation could be, indeed had to be, a single moral community. Conservatism's task today is to demonstrate that the dignity of constitutional government depends on restraints of a sort that do not come easily to conservatives or any other Americans. And these restraints will not come automatically or spontaneously from institutional arrangements—from federalism or judicial review. The restraints requisite for limited government, and hence requisite for the citizens' virtues that republican government presupposes, will come only as expressions of a thoughtful reverence for their nation's founding, a reverence that not only honors the memory of the Founders but is thoughtful in understanding their principles.

The search for restraint is an American constant. It is a search in which liberalism is not helpful. Liberalism was born when the primary enemies of freedom were forces of order—oppressive governments and established churches. Hence liberalism's breezy faith that the good life would flourish when the last king had been strangled in the entrails of the last priest. Today, we know it is not that simple; we know that the good life is menaced by forces of disorder and that big government has become one of those forces.

Fortunately, conservatism is on the case in the 1990s. We shall see if conservatism can give constitutional dignity to its message. One thing already is clear. In the 1990s, as in the 1850s and the 1790s, America cannot be accused of living an unexamined life. The exhilaration and the essential goodness of our politics flow from the fact that we had a founding moment, presided over by thoughtful men. Their reflections resulted in documents— the Declaration of Independence and the Constitution—the construing of which will drive our national conversation as long as we are recognizably the nation they founded. And we shall long endure.

This article is based on the author's Francis Boyer Lecture, delivered at the annual dinner at the American Enterprise Institute on December 6, 1995, and which later appeared in The Public Interest.

CHAPTER THREE

SOCIETY FRAYED AND MENDED

Oklahoma City: From the Fevered Minds of Marginal Men

The Tennessee marble on the side of the Morgan bank building in lower Manhattan still bears, defiantly, scars inflicted on September 16, 1920, when a horse-drawn wagon loaded with sash weights exploded amidst a lunchtime crowd. Among those blown to the pavement was Joseph P. Kennedy. He was among the fortunate. The blast, which shattered windows over a half-mile radius, killed thirty and injured more than 100.

There were no arrests, or explanations. Someone probably had taken too seriously some socialist critique of capitalism, but the incident fed J. P. Morgan Jr.'s many phobias, which included: "The Jew is always a Jew first and an American second, and the Roman Catholic, I fear, too often a papist first and an American second."

Today, as the nation sifts and sorts the many jagged and tangled fragments of emotions and ideas in the aftermath of Oklahoma City, it should remember that this was not America's baptism of lunacy. Bleeding Oklahoma City is a few hundred miles down the road from Pottawatomie in what once was bleeding Kansas, scene of a memorable massacre. John Brown's body lies a-moldering in the grave, but his spirit—massacres in the name of God—goes marching on in the paranoia of a few.

A very few, on society's far fringes. Which is progress. After Brown killed the mayor of Harpers Ferry and seized the arsenal, he was sentenced to be hanged. Yet America's preeminent intellectual, Ralph Waldo Emerson, said of him, "The Saint, whose fate yet hangs in suspense, but whose martyrdom, if it shall be perfected, will make the gallows as glorious as the cross." Morgan wrote the words above about Jews and Catholics to A. Lawrence Lowell, president of Harvard, of which institution Morgan was an overseer. It is unthinkable that such sentiments could be expressed in such circles today.

Today when the fevered minds of marginal men produce an outrage like the Oklahoma City bombing, some people rush to explain the outrage as an effect of this or that prominent feature of the social environment. They talk as though it is a simple task to trace a straight line from some social prompting, through the labyrinth of an individual's dementia, to that individual's action.

Now, to be sure, it is wise to recognize that ideas, and hence the words that bear them, have consequences. Those who trade in political ideas should occasionally brood as William Butler Yeats did when he wrote this about the civil war in Ireland:

> Did that play of mine send out
> Certain men the English shot?
> Did words of mine put too great strain
> On that woman's reeling brain?
> Could my spoken words have checked
> That whereby a house lay wrecked?

However, an attempt to locate in society's political discourse the cause of a lunatic's action is apt to become a temptation to extract partisan advantage from spilled blood. Today there are those who are flirting with this contemptible accusation: If the Oklahoma City atrocity was perpetrated by individuals gripped by pathological hatred of government, then this somehow implicates and discredits the current questioning of the duties and capacities of government.

But if the questioners are to be indicted, the indictment must be broad indeed. It must encompass not only a large majority of Americans and their elected representatives, but also the central tradition of American political thought—political skepticism, the pedigree of which runs back to the Founders.

The modern pedigree of the fanatics' idea that America's government is a murderous conspiracy against liberty and decency—a moneymaking idea for Oliver Stone, director of the movie *JFK*—runs back to the 1960s. Those were years John Brown could have enjoyed, years when *The New York Review of Books* printed on its cover directions for making a Molotov cocktail, and a student died when some precursors of the Oklahoma City fanatics practiced the politics of symbolism by bombing a building at the University of Wisconsin.

Today, when some talk-radio paranoiacs spew forth the idea that the AIDS virus was invented by Jewish doctors for genocide against blacks, it is well to remember that the paranoid impulse was present in the first armed action by Americans against the new federal government. During the Whiskey Rebellion 200 years ago a preacher declared: "The present day is unfolding a design the most extensive, flagitious and diabolical, that human art and malice have ever invented. . . . If accomplished, the earth can be nothing better than a sink of impurities."

It is reassuring to remember that paranoiacs have always been with us, but have never defined us.

April 25, 1995

Anti-Fascism in Phoenix

PHOENIX—"Hormones," is his answer. The question put to the concise Ramon Leyba is this: What makes a school full of teenagers turbulent?

There were 1,174 of that species—falling head over heels into eternal love at 8 A.M. and falling just as emphatically out of love by noon—at Phoenix Preparatory Academy, when Leyba, who is principal, instituted, after consultation with the community, a policy requiring the wearing of a school uniform. The policy was accepted by 1,172 students and their parents.

The two who objected found, or perhaps were found by, a lawyer who may have the Southwest's most serious case of a civil liberties fetish. He decided the school uniform policy was the thin end of the wedge of fascism, or at least a rape of the First Amendment—clothes as speech—and a threat to the full blossoming of that delicate flower, the soul of the teenager.

He began litigating and fulminating, vowing "guerrilla warfare" leading to victory "by getting the media worked up, by getting the time of your administrators used up." He said "there aren't enough National Guard troops in the state" to deal with his war.

The war is over. A judge is preparing to make permanent the temporary restraining order that tells the lawyer's clients, who refuse to wear the uniform, to keep off the academy's campus and transfer to a public school that does not require uniforms. Justice sometimes prevails, even when a court is involved.

The academy, now in its fourth year, is a diamond in a lead setting. It is a sparkling, gated middle school in the shadow of downtown commercial towers, but mostly surrounded by what nowadays is called a challenging urban environment. In a less delicate age such environments were called slums. The school's name, which suggests a tony private school, was chosen to inspirit this public school, which has a mission that requires spirit. Its mission is to educate a student body that is 92 percent minorities and that is drawn from a sprawling district large enough to be enlivened by fifteen teenage gangs—guns and hormones.

Leyba wanted his school to be an island of order for his students, 80 percent of whom cite neighborhood violence as a cause of stress. He and other school officials thought uniforms would help.

They thought uniforms would improve the climate for learning by eliminating "label competition" and other peer pressure concerning clothing; by eliminating gang clothes and enabling security personnel to identify trespassers instantly; by instilling school spirit and pride; and by equalizing at least one sphere of life for children from different socioeconomic settings. (At a California school that requires uniforms, a teacher told a visitor to a classroom that one student was the child of a wealthy movie producer, another lived in a shelter for the homeless. The visitor was asked if he could tell which was which. He could not.)

Phoenix school officials knew that when uniforms were required in elementary and middle schools in Long Beach, California, in the 1994–95 school year, attendance and test scores improved, incidents of students fighting decreased 50 percent, student crimes decreased 36 percent, and student suspensions decreased 32 percent. Parents like the academy's uniforms (white tops with collars and without printed messages; blue bottoms) because they usually save clothing budgets and because they prevent seven A.M. arguments about appropriate dress.

The anti-fascist lawyer was abetted by the local American Civil Liberties Union, but was stymied by one of the academy's constitutional subtleties: Students are allowed to wear buttons bearing political, religious, and other messages. This means that not only is the uniform policy "content neutral," a student who can no longer wear America's foremost literary genre, the T-shirt, emblazoned with a message praising Jesus or Charles Barkley, cannot claim to be utterly oppressed.

The anti-fascist lawyer wanted the academy to allow parents to opt out of the uniform requirement. School officials argued that in California, which has adopted a state law requiring an opt-out procedure, the uniform policy is eroding. Besides, school officials argued, a uniform might teach students to express themselves other than through what they wear.

The day the judge issued the temporary restraining order, the lawyer filed for $2 million in damages for his clients. It cost the school district about $70,000 in legal fees to fend off the lawyer. It is a measure of the condition of contemporary America that it is considered a bargain when a victory for common sense costs only $70,000.

January 28, 1996

The Abstract Compassion of "Gladiators for Liberation"

Vague, overbroad, cruel and unusual punishment, a violation of the constitutional guarantee of equal protection of the laws, and a violation of the constitutional right to travel. Those, according to the lawyers for several of the more litigious homeless persons in Santa Ana, California, were the defects of that city's ordinance that makes it "unlawful for any person to camp, occupy camp facilities, or use camp paraphernalia" in any street, public parking lot, or public area such as parks, or to "store personal property, including camp facilities and camp paraphernalia" in such areas.

A lower court agreed with that indictment of the ordinance. But now California's Supreme Court has upheld the validity of the ordinance. This small skirmish in the nationwide struggle to maintain minimal public order illustrates how problematic that elemental task has become. It is problematic partly because of lawyers well-described as "gladiators for liberation."

The ordinance was supposedly vague because it did not give an exhaustive list of "paraphernalia" and "facilities." Overbroad? Supposedly the verb "store" could criminalize leaving a beach towel unattended at a public pool, or a wet umbrella in a library foyer. And perhaps picnickers in a park could be arrested as campers. And . . .

California's Supreme Court, which must have the patience of Job, said, in effect: Good grief, give public authorities some credit for being able to construe particular terms in reasonable contexts. The purpose of the ordinance was to rid public places of persons sleeping, cooking, drinking, removing trash from bins, destroying vegetation, blocking passageways, urinating, and defecating.

The alleged violation of equal protection was, according to lawyers for the people doing those things in public, in the fact that Santa Ana would not arrest nonhomeless persons who did those things. Really.

As for the right to travel, neither the U.S. Supreme Court nor California's has ever held that a law is constitutionally flawed if it has an incidental impact on travel but has a purpose other than restriction of the right to travel. With few exceptions, the recognition of a constitutional right does not impose on state or local governments the obligation to provide people with the means of enjoying that right.

The idea that Santa Ana's ordinance constituted cruel and unusual punishment was that it punished a particular status, homelessness. However, California's Supreme Court held that the ordinance proscribed conduct, noting that punishment for the possession or use of narcotics, even by an addict, is not punishment for a status.

The arguments against Santa Ana's ordinance were made, in part, by "public interest" lawyers who specialize in championing this or that right to act against the interest the public has expressed in maintaining at least a minimal amount of order. Karl Zinsmeister, editor of *The American Enterprise* magazine, says the lawyers he calls "gladiators for liberation" have made it impossible to clean up Lafayette Park across Pennsylvania Avenue from the White House, and have persuaded various courts to overturn sanctions against vagrancy, aggressive panhandling, and antisocial behavior by residents of public housing. He writes:

> The liberators, however, have no regular experience of actual neighborhood life as it must now be endured by lower-income city dwellers, day in and day out. Don't ask a liberator how her city's biggest public school has been affected by ACLU-induced bans on expulsion of troublemakers. Her kids don't go there. Don't inquire how inner-city grocery stores cope with rampant shoplifters. She never gets anywhere near them. Don't ask her how police officers gain control of a man rampaging down a sidewalk on PCP now that civil suits have taken away use of nightsticks and chokeholds. Scarcely a liberator has ever seen such a sight.

Abstract compassion is the business of lawyers who often are young, childless, and affluent enough to live in neighborhoods with more Starbucks coffeehouses than drug dealers. These lawyers' professional lives are devoted, as Zinsmeister says, to "cramping cops, loosing the mentally ill, probationing or acquitting criminals, suing teachers who dare to discipline and landlords who try to evict, and generally defending moral relativism and the whole poverty culture's right to reproduce itself without stricture."

More than ninety California cities and the state Association of Counties filed briefs in support of Santa Ana, arguing that cities have not only the inherent power but the duty to keep streets and other public property available for the purposes for which they are dedicated. It speaks volumes about the country's condition that this elemental proposition had to wage a last-ditch fight for affirmation in the largest state's highest court.

May 7, 1995

Law and the Making of a Scofflaw Nation

Perhaps one reason so many New Yorkers are so surly is that they have to go to the bathroom but can't, public toilets being scarce. However, at least rights are plentiful.

In 1991 the city proposed testing six sidewalk toilet kiosks small enough not to impede pedestrian traffic. However, wheelchairs would not fit in them and New York's antidiscrimination law makes it illegal to "withhold or deny" from the disabled access to any "public accommodation." The toilets, said the city government would be "discrimination in its purest form." How about providing wheelchair-accessible bathrooms in nearby buildings? "The law," said a spokesperson for the disabled, "requires that everyone go to the bathroom in exactly the same place."

Rights are nonnegotiable, so two kiosks were tried at three locations, one for the general public, and one, with a full-time attendant, for wheelchair users. The regular toilet averaged 3,000 flushes per week, the other was virtually unused. It is 1995, the sidewalk toilet proposal is stalled, the procedural mills grind on, civic rancor increases.

This vignette is from Philip Howard's book *The Death of Common Sense: How Law Is Suffocating America.* Howard, a New York lawyer, believes government looks increasingly absurd because increasingly it tries to use detailed laws as substitutes for reasonable judgments by individuals.

He says the Occupational Safety and Health Administration has more than 4,000 detailed regulations (at one point it had 140 pertaining to wood ladders), and there may not be a workplace in America that isn't in violation of at least one. One requires "poison" signs where sand is stored because sand contains silica, which some scientists think might in certain unusual situations cause cancer. That is why OSHA once classified bricks (a brick, says OSHA helpfully, is "a hard ceramic body with no odor") as poisonous because if sawed they release small amounts of silica.

Such maddening meticulousness results from the casting of every social good as a "right," as in a worker's "right" to health and safety. As rights multiply, the vocabulary and skills of accommodation fade. Says Howard,

"The rights that are the foundation of this country are rights *against* the law." Those rights are shields. The new rights are bludgeons, blunt powers to enable some people to coerce others.

Howard says, "Our hatred of government is not caused mainly by government's goals, whatever their wisdom, but by government's techniques." Actually, the techniques express two goals—compassion, meaning safety from material or mental distress, and equality, not meaning treating like cases alike but rather treating everyone the same.

As Howard recognizes, the lunatic proliferation of law expresses the urge to produce an instruction manual for living the life we have a "right" to—a life without risk of injury or injustice. So New York regulations of day care centers enjoin caregivers to "comfort a child when in distress." In states without such punctilious regulations, do children go uncomforted? It is to ensure perfect propriety that the task of getting a $50 lock fixed in a New York school involves a six-month, ten-step process reviewed by a "supervising supervisor." But one result of too much such law is a scofflaw nation. As Howard says, when law is too dense to be known and too detailed to be reasonable, why respect it?

Indeed, why not exploit it? Howard says that recently posters spotted on Manhattan's Upper West Side advertised for someone to share an apartment rent-free. The plan, detailed on the posters, was to move in, refuse to pay rent, and live free for the eighteen months it takes a landlord to get an eviction order. Such scams are one price of procedures made rococo in attempts to give maximum protection to the maximum number of "rights."

So is this: A disruptive student at a Bronx high school assaulted a guard. The assault was witnessed by another guard, a teacher, and a dean. But the student was not suspended because, under one filigree on due process, a student witness is required in a case involving such significant discipline.

Law, says Howard, no longer just facilitates society's enterprises, it is one of society's main enterprises. The *Los Angeles Times* reports that in 1992 California lawyers' fees totaled $16.3 billion, more than was spent on auto repairs, funerals, tanning salons, one-hour photo finishing, videotape rentals, detectives, armored car guards, bug exterminators, laundry, haircuts, day care, shoe repairs, and septic tank cleaning—combined.

Says a representative of the California bar, "I'll put up the social contribution of the legal profession any day against that of the motion picture industry." As a defense of the current practices that are devised by and benefit lawyers, that illustrates the death of common sense.

January 22, 1995

Connoisseurs of Conflict

"My friends," exalted Ron Brown, then Democratic Party chairman, to an American Bar Association forum in November 1992, "I'm here to tell you the lawyers won!" That was true, given the Democrats' enthusiasm for the regulatory state and their aversion—rewarded by campaign contributions from trial lawyers—for reforms such as the "loser pays" rule to inhibit litigiousness.

So, are lawyers happy? Not exactly.

Nearly a quarter of them say they would choose a different profession were they starting over. Seventy-five percent of the members of the California Bar Association do not want their children to become lawyers. Levels of job satisfaction are falling; alcoholism and clinical depression are rising. Lawyers, says Mary Ann Glendon of the Harvard Law School in her new book *A Nation Under Lawyers: How the Crisis in the Legal Profession is Transforming American Society,* are like many other Americans, only more so. Lawyers are experiencing release from traditional restraints and are experiencing high anxiety.

As society's complexity and government's regulatory role increases, so does recourse to law. This is both cause and effect of the weakening of the democratic culture of persuasion, and of habits of accommodation.

What Glendon calls "skills of associating," sometimes called manners, have atrophied and been supplanted by lawsuits over the disappointments of everyday life. "One day we complain of suffocating in a regulatory miasma," writes Glendon, "on the next we ransack the legal cupboard for nostrums to rectify every wrong, to ward off every risk, and to cure every social and economic ill." Law, rather than harnessing the passions, is increasingly pressed into their service.

Time was when much of lawyering consisted (according to the turn-of-the-century lawyer and statesman Elihu Root) in "telling would-be clients that they are damned fools and should stop." Today lawyers are "connoisseurs of conflict" maximizing billable hours.

The pressure to do that discourages preventive lawyering—accommodations to avoid time-consuming litigation. And aggressive activities, Glendon warns, have a "constitutive" effect on character: We become what we do. We are institutionalizing conflict, giving rise to "Rambo litigators" destructive of the "moral ecology of the community." As lawyers' adversarial activities crowd out their order-affirming activities, the legal profession (now nearly 800,000 strong, counting judges and teachers) is, Glendon says, "rapidly shedding the habits and restraints that once made the bench and the bar pillars of the democratic experiment."

Young people do not acquire respect for restraints at the law schools where the prevailing ideology is that "law is nothing more than concentrated politics" and there is disdain for the classical ideal of the judicial role. That ideal involves three forms of self-control: "structural restraint" (respecting limits on judicial power set by federalism and the separation of powers), "interpretive restraint" (respecting limits imposed by precedent, statute, and the Constitution's text and structure), and "personal restraint" (not allowing personal political agendas to color decision-making processes).

Felix Frankfurter said "a judge worth his salt is in the grip of his function." Glendon says today's militant judges have slipped that grip and rationalize their emancipation from restraints this way: "If the house is on fire, it makes no difference who puts out the blaze; the branches of government should be partners, cooperating in the solutions of new social and economic problems." There is, says Glendon, "ill-concealed authoritarianism" in judicial activism, and it exacerbates the nation's irritability, as does the sense that law is suffocating life.

"Americans," Glendon says, "learn more about law and government in the toils of the tax, welfare, or Social Security system than in the jury room, town meeting, or party precinct organization. Such experiences tend to engender feelings of frustration and helplessness, rather than a sense of empowerment. Any parent who has dealt with the educational bureaucracy knows firsthand what it is to be treated like a subject rather than a citizen. We are encountering law more but participating less in its creation and administration." Hence the rising support for such policies as a flat tax and school choice.

Glendon believes "the extended orgy of legal hubris is winding down." Perhaps. If Republicans heed the nation's impatience with the regulatory state, if Republicans deliver "loser pays" and other reforms, and if Senator Orrin Hatch's Senate Judiciary Committee will not confirm judges who will not confine themselves to a judicial function, then in this year's elections lawyers lost.

But Glendon's book suggests that by losing some power, and moving more to the periphery of American life, the legal profession might become not only better but happier.

December 11, 1994

"Extreme Fighting" and the Morals of the Marketplace

Here are some sounds of entertainment in a nation entertaining itself into barbarism:

> I was hitting him to the brain stem, which is a killing blow, and when he covered up I'd swing back with upswings to the eye sockets with two knuckles and a thumb. There was no other place on his body you could hurt him.

> There's the toe stomp! . . . There's an open thigh there—he should do some punching. . . . His tooth went flying out of the ring! . . . He's going to snap his arm—he did, too!

Those are words from a participant and some announcers involved in "ultimate fighting" or "extreme fighting," which involves two combatants in an octagonal pen, governed by minimal rules: no biting or eye gouging. There are no rounds, no judges, no weight classifications. (The man pounding the brain stem and eye sockets was fighting a 650-pound wrestler.) The combatants fight until one is unconscious, disabled, or "taps out"—taps the canvas, signaling surrender. The referee's job is to watch for the tapping, occasionally summon a doctor to see if a participant can continue, and exhort the combatants to pour it on.

Six states have permitted such a spectacle. One permissive state is enough to make this a flourishing amusement on pay-per-view television. Three months ago about 300,000 subscribers paid twenty dollars each to see the seventh Ultimate Fighting Championship.

More are coming, but if you can't wait, your neighborhood Blockbuster, which will not rent sexual pornography, probably offers cassettes of some UFC events like the one in which a man's face was pounded to a pulp while he crawled across the canvas, leaving a broad smear of blood. Especially memorable is slow-motion footage from an overhead camera showing a man pounding the face of a pinned opponent. Aficionados savor full-force kicks to faces and elbows smashed into temples.

Participants in these events are frightening, but less so than the paying customers. They include slack-jawed children whose parents must be cretins, and raving adults whose ferocity away from the arena probably does not rise above muttering epithets at meter maids.

Senator John McCain (R., Ariz.), a former naval aviator who was a boxer at Annapolis and spent more than five years being tortured as a prisoner by the North Vietnamese, knows appropriate manliness and is exhorting governors and local officials to ban "extreme fighting" events because they pose "an unacceptable risk to the lives and health of the contestants." To the objection that the contestants are consenting adults, McCain, arguing within the severe limits imposed by our society's respect for choice, contends that the consent may be somehow illusory. He says perhaps a contestant is "driven by profits or the enticements of publicity associated with it and unknowingly is placing his or her life at risk."

To which libertarians respond: If you ban being driven by profits and enticed by publicity, what remains of modern life? Besides, no one has yet been killed in "extreme fighting," which is more than can be said for boxing.

Although in one letter to a governor, McCain says he is "solely" concerned with damage done to combatants, he also worries about the "glorification of cruelty," which raises the problem of virtue: What do we want government to do in the name of that?

The historian Macaulay, disdaining the Puritans, said they banned bear-baiting not because it gave pain to bears but because it gave pleasure to spectators. The Puritans were, of course, tiresome, but were they wrong? Surely there are ignoble, unwholesome pleasures.

Washington manages to make even a concern about virtue seem ludicrous, but "extreme fighting" forces a commercial society to decide when the morals of the marketplace are insufficient. Do we really ban cockfighting only because the birds cannot consent? Suppose (one hates to give entertainment entrepreneurs any of the few odious ideas they have not yet had) someone offers a $10 million prize for a Russian roulette competition—winner take all, necessarily. Imagine the pay-per-view potential.

Would—should—we so respect "consumer sovereignty" that we would allow that? The question is hypothetical, but perhaps not for long. In entertainment, competition does not elevate. Competition for audiences in an increasingly jaded, coarsened, and desensitized society causes competitors to devise ever-more lurid vulgarities to titillate the sated. If you think "extreme fighting" is as extreme as things can get, just wait.

November 26, 1995

The Crisis of Character Development

With a tendentiousness that seems characteristic, Hillary Clinton has entered the welfare reform debate by denouncing "the unbelievable and absurd idea of putting children into orphanages because their mothers couldn't find jobs." But the serious idea being considered by serious people is that infants whose mothers are, say sixteen, unmarried, uneducated, unemployed, addicted, and abusive might be better off in institutions. Ms. Clinton should be shown James Q. Wilson's recent lecture to the Manhattan Institute. It demonstrates how to bring intellectual honesty and humility to bear on the problem of character development, the problem that is commonly called the "welfare crisis."

Anxiety about America's communal life largely concerns the intergenerational transmission of poverty in an underclass crippled by family disintegration. The process by which that class reproduces itself severely damages children, and there is no reason to expect the damage to be stopped by a spontaneous regeneration of responsibility, civility, and commitment. Furthermore, says UCLA's Wilson, there is disagreement about whether the problem arises from structural, rational, or cultural causes.

The "structural" explanation is that good jobs have moved to urban peripheries, leaving young men without the sort of work that provides money and self-respect. These men abandon both the search for work and the work ethic. The "rational" explanation is that welfare benefits render the formation of stable two-parent families unnecessary. "These benefits," Wilson writes, "have induced young women wanting babies and a home of their own to acquire both at public expense and have convinced young men that sexual conquest need not entail any personal responsibilities." The "cultural" explanation is that traditional family life organized around child rearing is a discipline subverted by "a culture of radical self-indulgence and oppositional defiance fostered by drugs, television, video games, street gangs, and predatory sexuality." The flight of middle- and working-class people drains cities of the social capital of attitudes, activities, and commitments that are necessary to block the sweep of such pathologies.

All three explanations are pertinent, but Wilson warns that "people define problems so as to make them amenable to solutions that they favor for ideological or moral reasons." Liberals emphasize the structural explanation because it licenses social engineering by government—job creation, job training, even relocating the inner-city poor to urban peripheries. Conservatives favor the rational and cultural explanations because they like the programmatic implications. The rational explanation points toward cutting or abolishing welfare or linking it to behavioral changes by recipients, such as acceptance of work. The cultural explanation encourages attempts to alter the inner-city ethos by means of religious and other private redemptive movements. The government is relegated to a supporting role, perhaps providing, for example, group homes where at-risk children and their young mothers can be sheltered from the culture of the streets while receiving care and guidance.

The principal problem with a structural strategy is the thinness of evidence of a causal connection between the worsening of job opportunities and the weakening of families. Besides, cultural differences seem to account for dramatic differences among racial and ethnic groups regarding the readiness to search for jobs. Mexican-Americans in Los Angeles, for example, are famously diligent. And the government's worker training and job placement programs have had only slight effects on welfare rolls.

The rational strategy is supported by evidence that states with high welfare payments tend to have high rates of birth to welfare recipients. And increases in welfare were strongly correlated with increases in illegitimate births from the early 1960s until about 1980. Then the value of the welfare package stopped rising, but illegitimacy did not. There are large differences in illegitimacy rates between racial and ethnic groups. For example, since the Civil War, blacks have had higher illegitimacy rates than whites, even though there were no federal welfare programs until 1935. However, black illegitimacy rates are low in some northern states where welfare payments are relatively high, and black illegitimacy rates are high in the Deep South, where welfare payments are low. Cultural factors clearly are having consequences.

What, then, of a cultural strategy? Cultural regeneration cannot be legislated; least of all can it be skillfully implemented by the federal government. States are more promising sources for regenerative support, for two reasons. "First," says Wilson, "there are fifty of them." (Trust a past president of the American Political Science Association to notice this.) Therefore, the odds are better for electing a few smart and bold governors whose experiments might teach us something than are the odds of electing a smart and bold president. Second, because there are fifty states, they must compete—for residents, employers, and good credit ratings. "They cannot afford to attack crime and illegitimacy and gang warfare merely by grandiose rhetoric and the signing of bills in the Rose Garden." If the salvation of children is the paramount objective, and it should be, then Wilson believes local jurisdictions might usefully revive the kind of boarding schools—they would serve more than orphans—that earlier in this century provided homes and education for more than 100,000 young Americans. Does Ms. Clinton disapprove of Boys Town of Nebraska, and the many institutions around the country providing similar services?

Attuning child care to healthy communal voices is the central challenge posed by the great cultural change of this century. That change, says Wilson, is "the emancipation of the individual from the restraints of tradition, community, and government." This emancipation has been hugely beneficial to most people, but has been ruinous to people made vulnerable by their lack of the internal restraints of good character. What can government or, for that matter, private groups do for character development? "I do not know," says Wilson, using a four-word phrase that would be a becoming addition to Ms. Clinton's rhetorical repertoire. However, the first step toward progress in solving a problem is precision in the statement of the problem. This Wilson provided.

December 12, 1994

Prepare the Wee Harnesses

As the welfare reform debate begins to boil, the place to begin is with an elemental fact: No child in America asked to be here.

Each was summoned into existence by the acts of adults. And no child is going to be spiritually improved by being collateral damage in a bombardment of severities targeted at adults who may or may not deserve more severe treatment from the welfare system.

Senator Phil Gramm says welfare recipients are people "in the wagon" who ought to get out and "help the rest of us pull." Well. Of the 14 million people receiving Aid to Families with Dependent Children, 9 million are children. Even if we get all these free riders into wee harnesses, the wagon will not move much faster.

Furthermore, there is hardly an individual or industry in America that is not in some sense "in the wagon," receiving some federal subvention. If everyone gets out, the wagon may rocket along. But no one is proposing that. Instead, welfare reform may give a whole new meaning to the phrase "women and children first."

Marx said that history's great events appear twice, first as tragedy, then as farce. Pat Moynihan worries that a tragedy visited upon a vulnerable population three decades ago may now recur, not as farce but again as tragedy.

Moynihan was there on October 31, 1963, when President Kennedy, in his last signing ceremony, signed legislation to further the "deinstitutionalization" of the mentally ill. Advances in psychotropic drugs, combined with "community-based programs," supposedly would make possible substantial reductions of the populations of mental institutions.

But the drugs were not as effective as had been hoped, and community-based programs never materialized in sufficient numbers and sophistication. What materialized instead were mentally ill homeless people. Moynihan warns that welfare reform could produce a similar unanticipated increase in children sleeping on, and freezing to death on, grates.

Actually, cities will have to build more grates. Here are the percentages of children on AFDC at some point during 1993 in five cities: Detroit (67), Philadelphia (57), Chicago (46), New York (39), Los Angeles (38). "There are," says Moynihan, "not enough social workers, not enough nuns, not enough Salvation Army workers" to care for children who would be purged from the welfare rolls were Congress to decree (as candidate Bill Clinton proposed) a two-year limit for welfare eligibility.

Don't worry, say the designers of a brave new world, welfare recipients will soon be working. However, 60 percent of welfare families—usually families without fathers—have children under six years old. Who will care for those children in the year 2000 if Congress decrees that 50 percent of welfare recipients must by then be in work programs? And from whence springs this conservative Congress's faith in work programs?

Much of the welfare population has no family memory of regular work, and little of the social capital of habits and disciplines that come with work. Life in, say, Chicago's Robert Taylor housing project produces what sociologist Emil Durkheim called "a dust of individuals," not an employable population. A 1994 Columbia University study concluded that most welfare mothers are negligibly educated and emotionally disturbed and 40 percent are serious drug abusers. Small wonder a Congressional Budget Office study estimated an annual cost of $3,000 just for monitoring each workfare enrollee—in addition to the bill for training to give such people elemental skills.

Moynihan says that a two-year limit for welfare eligibility, and work requirements, might have worked thirty years ago, when the nation's illegitimacy rate was 5 percent, but today it is 33 percent. Don't worry, say reformers, we'll take care of that by tinkering with the incentives: There will be no payments for additional children born while the mother is on welfare.

But Nicholas Eberstadt of Harvard and the American Enterprise Institute says: Suppose today's welfare policy incentives to illegitimacy were transported back in time to Salem, Massachusetts, in 1660. How many additional illegitimate births would have occurred in Puritan Salem? Few, because the people of Salem in 1660 believed in hell and believed that what today are called "disorganized lifestyles" led to hell. Congress cannot legislate useful attitudes.

Moynihan, who spent August writing his annual book at his farm in Delaware County, New York, notes that in 1963 that county's illegitimacy rate was 3.5 percent and today is 32 percent—almost exactly the national average. And no one knows why the county (which is rural and 98.8 percent white) or the nation has so changed.

Hence no one really knows what to do about it. Conservatives say, well, nothing could be worse than the current system. They are underestimating their ingenuity.

September 14, 1995

Eloise Anderson: Off the Plantation

SAN DIEGO—Obviously, the most important African-American man in public office is a conservative—Justice Clarence Thomas. Less obviously, but surely, the most important African-American woman in public office is a conservative. Meet Eloise Anderson, director of California's Department of Social Services, a $16 billion agency in this state where one-eighth of all Americans live, where one-third of all births are illegitimate, and where until now 12 percent of the population accounted for 27 percent of the nation's spending on Aid to Families with Dependent Children.

Anderson says this about the end of that federal entitlement to welfare: "People say, 'The poor won't know what to do!' Tough. They'll learn." She adds, "When I was young, people did not think the poor were stupid." But, then, when she was young her grandfather was appalled not just by the idea of government provision of health care, but even by employer provision. That seemed to him redolent of the paternalism practiced by "good" slave owners.

It took just a stroke of a pen—the president's—to transform Anderson from someone supposedly on the far right fringe of the social policy debate into someone who had been prematurely correct about where the debate was going. President Clinton signed Congress's repeal of a sixty-year-old federal AFDC entitlement because he had been dragged to where she had been standing for years.

She is fifty-four, her short hair is flecked with gray, and her speech is salted with a bracing bluntness, as when she recounts how she got into government twenty-four years ago. Born on the edge of poverty in Toledo, she became a social worker in Wisconsin and became incensed by the disconnection between the rules cranked out by the state welfare bureaucracy in Madison and the lives led by the people she struggled to help in Milwaukee.

So she drove to Madison, parked outside the state welfare office, and began bombarding the people who worked there with questions: What do you do? Ever worked anywhere else? Ever been to Milwaukee? Soon she was working on Governor Tommy Thompson's welfare reforms, which got her interviewed on public television, where California's Governor Pete Wilson spotted her.

She became a national figure because of fifteen minutes on *60 Minutes,* during which Lesley Stahl asked her, "Will you not concede that you have a large number of unemployable people who are on welfare?" Anderson conceded nothing of the sort, saying there were lots of low-paying jobs that immigrants take but welfare recipients refuse.

Stahl: "But we're talking about sweeping floors."

Anderson: "That's employable."

Sentimental she is not. To the Manhattan Institute's *City Journal* she has said: "If you tell me, 'I'm pregnant and I've never worked,' I would say . . . go talk to your family; go talk to his family. But don't come here, because having a baby is not a crisis. That's a condition, and your behavior caused that."

Why the explosive growth of illegitimacy? People live up—or down—to expectations: "It was accepted. Back in the 1960s, middle-class whites took the *shame* out of a lot of stuff." And there also was "the feminist thing—men are dogs," we can live without them.

For many young girls, she says, the first sexual relationship is involuntary. When the daughter born to a teenager mother becomes a teenager, she is apt to meet in her home the male friends of her mother's man—men in their late twenties or early thirties. And so illegitimacy is transmitted. Dismantle the welfare system, Anderson says, and young women will think differently about men and getting pregnant. We shall see.

"Maybe my time has come and gone," she says. Actually it is just arriving. Given the devolution of federal welfare responsibilities to the states, this is exactly the time for her to be where she is, doing two things.

One is putting in place measures to direct welfare recipients to work, thereby underscoring the transitional nature of welfare. The other is exhorting the poor, and particularly the African-American poor to "get off the plantation"—the intellectual plantation of conventional liberalism, and the closed world of dependency she thinks it produces.

On her way to the mainstream—make that, while waiting for the mainstream to come to her—she has felt the full fury of liberal intolerance of deviations by African-Americans. "It is," she muses, "scary getting off the plantation." She has been sustained, she says, by the example of someone who, like her, rose from near poverty and left that plantation: Clarence Thomas.

October 27, 1996

The Chambers Brothers' Career Choices

The remarkable Chambers brothers rose from grinding poverty in the Arkansas delta to running a retail trade earning $1 million a week in Detroit. This was in the mid-1980s, when the automobile industry was shrinking and the city was losing a quarter of a million jobs and a fifth of its population. The four brothers' enterprise had revenues larger than any other privately held business in the city.

This story of ghetto capitalism is told in a virtuoso exercise in reporting, William M. Adler's new book *Land of Opportunity*. Adler details how the brothers, without benefit of education beyond their high school in the nation's sixth-poorest county, identified a market niche, mastered whole-sale buying and mass production and risk analysis, monitored cash flows, devised employee benefit plans, performance bonuses, and customer incentive plans. Adler admires the way the brothers' leader, Billy Joe, "refused to settle for passivity and hopelessness" in Lee County, Arkansas.

Billy Joe is now earning five dollars a month in the kitchen of a federal prison where he will be for at least another twenty years. Yet Adler, a terrific reporter and a terrible ethicist, says Billy Joe and his three brothers, who also are in prison, made "a rational career choice" when they became pioneers of the age of crack cocaine.

Adler is not averse to moral judgments. He vigorously disapproves of "the Reagan-Bush era's domestic spending politics," "the wealth-obsessed culture," "the decade's cult of money," and so on. But Adler's honest reporting vitiates his ideological judgments.

Billy was sixteen in 1978 when he bought a one-way bus ticket to Detroit where his brother Willie was a postal worker. Soon Billy was working his way up in the drug business, and with some help from Willie.

"By 1982," writes Adler, "seven years as a letter carrier and his prudent way with a dollar had left Willie with a tidy nest egg." And an eye for cheap real estate he saw as he delivered mail. Willie bought some inexpensive houses. Soon they were distribution centers for the family drug business. By 1984 one was a crack house "pumping" $35,000 a day.

It is a bit much to blame Republicans for Willie's choice of a criminal career. And brother Larry had made that choice in 1969, long before "the decade of greed." When the youngest brother, Otis, came to Detroit to join the moneymaking, crime was a family tradition.

Crack came to the United States from the Caribbean, where a dying crack addict had said to a Bahamian doctor, "When the world tastes this, you're going to have a lot of trouble." It got to Detroit late in 1983. In that year about 100 people were admitted to Detroit clinics for treatment of cocaine use. In 1987, the year the Chambers' business peaked, about 4,500 were admitted. Between 1983 and 1987 emergency room admissions linked to cocaine rose from 450 to 3,811. In 1987, when Detroit's murder rate peaked, half the murder victims under age forty had cocaine in their systems.

By 1986, Adler writes, Billy Joe and Larry were folk heroes, "the Lee Iacoccas of the crack business." Children played games of "B. J. and Larry." Larry ran a drug-dispensing apartment house where the doorman, who carried an Uzi, was admonished by Larry to project warmth to customers: "When a crackhead comes to you and his woman is on his back, his babies don't have no Pampers, he hasn't eaten in two days, and he's about to spend his last five dollars on crack, you have to make him feel good about spending his money."

Larry was stern with disobedient employees (he had hot grease poured on one) and his "wrecking crews" would "hammer" people who displeased him. Adler tells about Dennis, one of Larry's wreckers: "(Dennis and colleagues) grabbed (the victim's) wrists, held them to the concrete floor, and pummeled his hands with hammers. Then they hammered his feet, his knees. The kid lost consciousness. They hammered his ribs. They left him in the garage. Dennis says he heard later the injuries left the young man paraplegic, never to walk again. Dennis says he felt bad about the beating, but that 'I did it because it was part of my job and I wanted to move up in the organization and I wanted a (Ford Mustang) 5.0.' "

To say, as Adler comes close to doing in his otherwise illuminating book, that the Chambers and their friends were only obeying social imperatives or cultural promptings is today's version of the Nuremberg defense—"I was only obeying orders"—that was offered in 1946 by people who for a while thought they had made rational career choices.

May 18, 1995

Replaceable Product, Fungible People

Bill Mockler is one of the fortunate few for whom there is no clear distinction between work and play. "I love," he says, "the challenge of trying to put people in jail." It is especially challenging because, he says, he is "dealing with some of the craftiest people in the criminal world." It is a measure of Mockler's professionalism that he can acknowledge the skills of his Colombian adversaries while despising the activities the skills serve.

Mockler, who speaks in the Flatbush accent of his native Brooklyn, is fifty-one, six years from mandatory retirement from what is largely a young man's business, the Sisyphean task of disrupting the distribution of illegal narcotics. He has risen through the ranks of the Drug Enforcement Administration to be director of special operations. Those operations usually target what are called "drug kingpins," people like the man known as Zorro, who also was known as "the Mayflower Mover" for the Cali cartel in Colombia, moving a ton of cocaine a week across the United States from Los Angeles. That cartel controls more than 80 percent of the cocaine sold in America.

It took thirty-one concurrent investigations during two years to identify and arrest Zorro because the Cali operatives use technologically sophisticated systems of fax lines, cellular communications (to foil wiretaps they use computer software to "clone"—steal—the telephone numbers of unsuspecting individuals), and segmented organizations. As a result Zorro rarely met anyone in his distribution network. When someone like Zorro is arrested, much of his operation is rolled up—much, but not all of it. One or more of his operatives may be left in place so that law enforcement can follow them and identify the new leadership that replaces those arrested.

But replacements always appear. That is why the high morale of men and women like Mockler—he has been with the DEA and predecessor agencies since 1968—is remarkable. DEA agents routinely devote twelve-hour days to seizing a product that is replaceable and arresting people who are fungible.

The government has spent many years and billions of dollars fighting drugs on the supply side, yet the price on the street is falling, and the purity of cocaine and heroin is rising. There are fewer casual users of cocaine than there were a decade ago, but total consumption is as high as it was then because the number of heavy users has increased. Heroin often is 65 percent pure rather than the 6 percent fifteen years ago. Thus it can be inhaled, which cleanses the drug of the stigma associated with needles. One sign of the increased purity is the increasing rate of fatal overdoses. The strength of marijuana is often fifteen times what it was in 1980.

James Q. Wilson, writing in *The American Enterprise* magazine, explains the depressing mathematics of cocaine interdiction: "Experts at the RAND Corporation estimate that the price of cocaine in transit to the United States is $17,000 per kilo, but on U.S. streets that same kilo is worth $129,000. That enormous spread means that even if authorities manage to seize one out of every ten kilos shipped (which seems to be about as much as can be hoped for) the street price on the supplies that get through need only be raised by 1.5 percent to make up for the lost shipment."

So, how do the DEA men and women like Mockler avoid the despair to which people are prey when assigned to bail an ocean with a sieve? They know that law enforcement is just one leg of a three-legged stool—the other legs are education to prevent drug use, and rehabilitation to cure addiction—but also know that law enforcement performs an educative as well as deterrent function that reduces addiction rates. And perhaps the most sustaining sense they have is of preventing individual, anonymous tragedies.

Mockler remembers a night in 1987 during a cocaine seizure operation in upper Manhattan when he was startled by the traffic congestion in side streets caused by drivers, many from New Jersey, stopping to transact business with young men waving small plastic bags. It was an open-air market at the beginning of the crack epidemic, and its brazenness mocked the resources of law enforcement.

And yet, he thought, if one arrest is going to prevent a young person from taking narcotics back to a party where another young person might be tempted to step onto the slippery slope to addiction, that alone is worth all his efforts. Such efforts by many unsung agents have earned more of the nation's gratitude than they have received.

May 11, 1995

A Colombia Within America's Borders

SAN DIEGO—The phrase recurs in discussions of the drug problem: "source country." As in, Colombia is the source country for much of the cocaine that comes to America. A drug now making the mean streets even meaner is methamphetamine, and the "source country" for America's supply is San Diego County.

The fact that there is, in a sense, a Colombia within America's borders illustrates the complexity and intractability of the drug problem. Make that plural: drug problems. Methamphetamine shows how the problems multiply faster than solutions can even be imagined, let alone implemented.

Drug Enforcement Administration agents waging semimilitary operations against manufacturers and distributors of that drug describe its effects as similar to, but longer lasting—up to twelve hours per hit—than those of cocaine. Users are called "tweakers." The term is borrowed from mechanics, who speak of "tweaking" an engine to make it perform better.

One DEA agent's laconic description of methamphetamine's effect: The user is mowing his lawn at three A.M.

Or the user unintentionally kills his or her baby by shaking it too hard. It gets users so wired they can stay awake for three or four days. Which makes them crazy, and dangerous. Eighty percent of the people arrested here have drugs in their systems, and more than half are on methamphetamine.

The street value of one pound—which can provide 90,000 "hits"—is $8,000 to $12,000 here, $25,000 in the East. It takes at most $500 worth of chemicals to make that pound. Fifty to seventy pounds of the stuff can be manufactured in twenty-four hours in primitive "kitchens" that can be quickly assembled and disassembled in shacks in the hills and ravines of this sprawling county which contains the nation's sixth most-populous city and is larger than Rhode Island. The chemicals can be smuggled in large quantities. The recipe for the product can be found on the Internet.

California's motorcycle gangs used to control the methamphetamine trade, but various fallings-out and other business turbulence opened the way for a hostile takeover by people from—let it not be said there are no entry-level jobs for new arrivals—Mexico. They have lowered the tone of the business using violence beyond the ken of the relatively demure motorcyclists. The DEA office here has a horrifying slide show detailing some of the practices, including the distinctive signature on assassinations: bullet holes in the pattern of a cross on the victim's face.

Fashions change regarding drugs. Workers digging the Erie Canal received a quart of whiskey a day in eight four-ounce portions, beginning at six A.M. Harry Truman drank whiskey before breakfast. And alcohol is not the only recreational drug concerning which mores have changed. In his *Letters from an American Farmer* (1782), Hector St. John de Crevecoeur noted among Nantucket ladies "the Asiatic custom of taking a dose of opium every morning."

Then nineteenth-century developments in organic chemistry began what Pat Moynihan calls yet another hard, continuing lesson about the impact of technology on society. In 1885 the Parke-Davis pharmaceutical company declared cocaine a "wonder drug" that could "make the coward brave, and the silent eloquent." Cocaine and heroin (it was advertised in the *Yale Alumni News*) could be purchased without prescriptions until 1914.

Perhaps society's first, shall we say, chemical crisis concerned distilled alcohol, which Moynihan calls the "combined result of the invention of distillation and an agricultural revolution that produced a relative abundance of grain." Devastation wrought by cheap gin contributed to a stunning phenomenon: London's population grew hardly at all in the first half of the eighteenth century.

In the first half of the next century, London's population tripled. It did for many reasons, but one was that society became better at living with a new product of technology. What happened? Among other things, John Wesley happened. A religious movement seized the culture by the lapels and shook it.

The hope for some similar cultural shaking is small comfort to DEA agents crawling through the underbrush toward drug labs defended by heavily armed people whose volatile behavior suggests they have been sampling their product. These admirable agents, realists all, know they are no match for the storm. They are improvising levees against surging rivers of substances, and as long as millions of Americans seek wilder living through chemistry, real flood control will require cultural revival, not just law enforcement.

What sustains agents is their correct conviction that enforcement signals society's seriousness, a prerequisite for revival. Besides, causing bad things to happen to bad people is a pleasure.

September 19, 1996

At the Border: Arduous Lives
of Honorable Frustration

SAN YSIDRO, CALIFORNIA—Before uttering a syllable about "winning" the "war" on drugs "at the border," politicians should spend a day here, a twenty-minute drive from downtown San Diego. They should join the men and women of the Customs Service on the broiling concrete, in the fog of exhaust fumes, as they struggle with a twenty-four-lane, twenty-four-hours-a-day crime wave in plain view. These people lead arduous lives of honorable frustration, leavened by frequent successes that can be spectacular without being quite calculable.

At this, the world's busiest land border crossing (40 million people a year; think of screening the population of Spain in a traffic jam, every year), about 130 cars per hour, per lane pass into the United States. Recently one of them, a ramshackle red Nissan, attracted a trained American eye. The driver was nervous. Should have been. The forty-three pounds of heroin under the floorboard had a street value of $20 million.

But how to estimate what is not being interdicted? Various indices, from satellite photos of crops in the Third World, to emergency room reports of overdoses in America's inner cities, make possible rough estimates of the quantities of drugs being produced and reaching America's streets. If the war waged on the supply side were being won, drug prices would be rising and drug purity would be falling. The reverse is true. However, there are successes short of victory. For example, calculate the consequences for price and purity if 110 tons of cocaine had not been interdicted around the nation last year.

Seventy percent of the cocaine sold in America comes across the southwest border. Two sights near here—a tunnel and a building—prove the siphoning power of billions of dollars of American demand for compact, concealable packages of cocaine, heroin, and marijuana.

The 1,467-foot tunnel under the border, large enough for a man to walk through in a crouch, was dug to carry drugs north and cash south. Before it was discovered, a rash of murders of engineers and construction workers helped keep it secret. The building is a huge vault—its steel-reinforced walls are sixteen inches thick—in which the stale air has the sour reek of drugs, sometimes $2 billion worth, seized nearby.

High technology is employed against the poor people and lowlifes who smuggle. A $3.5 million X-ray machine for vehicles can spot a brick of cocaine secreted among thousands of regular bricks on a flatbed truck. Every license plate at the San Ysidro crossing is scanned electronically and in 1.5 seconds a computer spits out pertinent information, if there is any, about each.

But the best law enforcement weapon is a dog's nose, which has an olfactory acuity 700 times as great as a human nose. Back and forth through the congealed traffic the dogs scamper, drawn by the slightest drug scents in the cones of air behind cars. The dogs cannot even be consistently defeated by smugglers who hide drugs in truckloads of fish or rotting leather. The rule is that any especially rank load is a reason for searching a truck.

Sixty yards into Mexico, smugglers' accomplices with cell phones communicate with cars creeping with contraband through the congestion, directing drivers away from lanes that look problematic. And on the U.S. side, officers watch the northbound pedestrians, looking for those walking awkwardly. The hollowed-out soles of Nikes can carry enough heroin to buy a Mercedes to drive back to Mexico.

The scene at the border—part Hieronymus Bosch, part P. T. Barnum— is a brew of fear, cunning, and animal spirits, and is not what anyone intended when the nation decided that one recreational drug, alcohol, was providing as much devastation as American society could stand, and so proscribed heroin and cocaine. Today we understand the irreducibly tragic dimension of the decision, as Mark Kleiman of the Kennedy School of Government describes it: The choice between criminalization and legalization of drugs is a choice between a serious but localized crime problem (in certain shattered urban neighborhoods) and a general public health problem.

Having reasonably chosen the former, interdiction—attempts to control supplies—is implicit in drug policy. But any politician who watches the craftsmanship and stamina of the men and women doing the interdicting will understand this: The only way to cut supplies substantially is by dampening the demand that draws the supplies to and, inevitably, through the border.

Indignation is a natural response to what is seen here—America under assault. But our rich nation makes it economically rational for poor nations to grow the crops from which drugs are produced. Blame Americans first.

September 22, 1996

The "Growth Model" and the Growth of Illiteracy

Summertime, and the living is easy. Schools are empty, so the damage has stopped. During this seasonal respite from the education system's subtraction from national literacy, consider why America may be graduating from its high schools its first generation worse educated than the generation that came before. Particularly, why is it common for high school graduates to be functionally illiterate, uncertain when reading, and incapable of writing even a moderately complicated paragraph?

Heather Mac Donald knows one reason: More and more schools refuse, on the basis of various political and ethical and intellectual theories, to teach writing. Her essay, "Why Johnny Can't Write," in the summer 1995 issue of *The Public Interest* quarterly, is a hair-raising peek into what she calls "one overlooked corner of the academic madhouse."

Mac Donald, a contributing editor of the Manhattan Institute's *City Journal*, explains how the teaching of writing has been shaped by "an indigestible stew of 1960s liberationist zeal, 1970s deconstructionist nihilism, and 1980s multicultural proselytizing." Indeed many teachers now consider the traditional idea of teaching to be intellectually suspect and morally offensive because it is tainted by the authoritarian idea that there are defensible standards and by the inegalitarian idea that some people do things better than others.

At a 1966 conference organized by the Modern Language Association and the National Conference of Teachers of English, the "transmission model" of teaching composition was rejected in favor of the "growth model." The idea of transmitting skills and standards was inherently threatening to the values of that decade—spontaneity, authenticity, sincerity, equality, and self-esteem. Education in the new era of enlightenment was to be not a matter of putting things into students—least of all putting in anything that suggested a hierarchy of achievement—but of letting things out. Nothing must interfere with the natural, undirected flowering of the student's personality. One interference would be a teacher cast as an authority figure rather than in the role of supportive, nurturing friend.

The "growth model" was, Mac Donald notes, impeccably liberationist: Who was to judge anyone else's "growth"? And that model "celebrated inarticulateness and error as proof of authenticity." This was convenient for evolving racial policies. In 1966 the City University of New York began the first academic affirmative action program. Open admissions would soon follow, as would the idea that it is cultural imperialism to deny full legitimacy to anything called "Black English." Simultaneously came the idea that demands for literacy oppress the masses and condition them to accept the coercion of capitalism.

"Process" became more important than content in composition. Students would "build community" as they taught each other. A reactionary emphasis on the individual was replaced by a progressive emphasis on the collectivity. But, says Mac Donald, there have been difficulties: "Students who have been told in their writing class to let their deepest selves loose on the page and not worry about syntax, logic, or form have trouble adjusting to other classes." Thus a student at St. Anselm's College complains that in her humanities class, "I have to remember a certain format and I have to back up every general statement with specific examples."

Academic fads have followed hard upon one another, all supplying reasons why it is unnecessary—no, antisocial—to teach grammar and style. The deconstructionists preached that language is of incurably indeterminate meaning. The multiculturalists, who preach the centrality of identity politics in every endeavor, argue that the rules of language are permeated by the values of the dominant class that makes society's rules and also makes victims. Mac Donald says, "The multicultural writing classroom is a workshop on racial and sexual oppression. Rather than studying possessive pronouns, students are learning how language silences women and blacks."

As student writing grows worse, Mac Donald notes, the academic jargon used to rationalize the decline grows more pompous. For example, a professor explains that "postprocess, postcognitive theory . . . represents literacy as an ideological arena and composing as a cultural activity by which writers position and reposition themselves in relation to their own and others' subjectivities, discourses, practices, and institutions."

Nowadays the mere mention of "remedial" courses is coming to be considered insensitive about "diversity," and especially insulting and unfair to students from American "cultures" where "orality" is dominant. So at some colleges remedial courses are now called ESD courses—English as a Second Dialect.

The smugly self-absorbed professoriate that perpetrates all this academic malpractice is often tenured and always comfortable. The students on the receiving end are always cheated and often unemployable. It is summertime, and the nation is rightly uneasy about autumn.

July 2, 1995

Multiculturalism as Compulsory Chapel

The high school test asked students to identify the "Hellenic epic which established egotistical individualism as heroic." The correct answer was *The Iliad,* the message of the question being this: Individualism is egotistical and egoism, rather than anything more noble, defines Western civilization. When a University of Pennsylvania student wrote of "my deep regard for the individual," an administrator underlined the word "individual" and wrote back: "This is a RED FLAG phrase today, which is considered by many to be RACIST. Arguments that champion the individual over the group ultimately privileges (*sic*) the 'individuals' belonging to the largest dominant group."

Asked what her fifth and sixth grade pupils learn about George Washington, a teacher says: "That he was the first president, that he was a slave owner, that he was rich—not much." She does teach about another white male: Eli Whitney. She says her pupils "know that he stole his invention from a woman who didn't patent it." How does the teacher know this? "Another teacher told me."

During the 1992 quincentennial, a public education group produced a study guide, "Rethinking Columbus," with chapter titles such as "Once Upon a Genocide" and "George Washington: Speculator in Native Lands." A Cornell residence hall director removed pictures of herself and her husband when she was accused, because of the pictures, of heterosexism. At a Cornell training session for resident advisers, an X-rated homosexual movie was shown and pictures were taken of the advisers' reactions, to detect homophobic squeamishness.

Some Brookline, Massachusetts, parents were denounced by public school officials as "censors" because they wanted to put back into the curriculum an advanced placement course on European history. The course had been found "incompatible with multiculturalism," presumably because it did not "validate" the self-esteem and contribute to the cultural "legitimization" of non-Europeans. Here is a multiple choice exam question from Brookline: "A characteristic of the thirteen English colonies was (a) complete religious freedom, (b) free high school education, (c) class distinctions, or (d) universal voting." "C" is the correct answer to this sly question that Richard Bernstein rightly says is "designed to demonstrate that something negative was the sole feature all the colonies had in common."

Critics of Bernstein's invaluable new book, *Dictatorship of Virtue: Multiculturalism and the Battle for America's Future,* from which these stories are culled, dismiss his meticulous reporting as "anecdotal," which is today's preferred denigration of inconvenient evidence. But a multitude of anecdotes makes a pattern and the book frames with an explanatory theory the ugly picture of the depredations done in the name of "diversity." Bernstein, a reporter for *The New York Times,* is a liberal who is angry about the multiculturalists' attempts to smother intellectual diversity beneath "a thick glue of piousness."

What explains "the middle-class bureaucrats and education entrepreneurs, the guilty white liberals and aging flower children of the 1960s who most aggressively press the multiculturalist agenda"? Says Bernstein, "Thirty years ago, something shifted in the national mind." The broad contours of America's demography have not changed radically since the mid-1960s, and the foreign-born percentage of the population is much smaller than in 1920. What, then, accounts for today's multiculturalist frenzy?

Bernstein flinches from baldly stating the simple fact that many cultural institutions (including the Smithsonian, busy with vilifications of American history) have fallen into the hands of people who despise America. However, when he dissects the so-called "massive increase in hate crimes" in Minnesota—yes, Minnesota—he concludes, "There is a sizable industry of exaggeration that combines with a fear of appearing complacent about racism to create a misleading impression of American life." In fact, multiculturalism is a campaign to lower America's moral status by defining the American experience in terms of myriad repressions and their victims. By rewriting history, and by using name-calling ("Racist!" "Sexist!" "Homophobe!") to inhibit debate, multiculturalists cultivate grievances, self-pity, and claims to entitlements arising from victimization. Hence the education trend that Bernstein calls "the curriculum as expiation of guilt."

Multiculturalism attacks individualism by defining people as mere manifestations of groups (racial, ethnic, sexual) rather than as self-defining participants in a free society. And one way to make racial, ethnic, or sexual identity primary is to destroy alternative sources of individuality and social cohesion, such as a shared history, a common culture, and unifying values. Hence the multiculturalists' attempts to politicize and purge higher education curriculums. Once universities are reduced to therapeutic institutions, existing to heal victimized groups and reform the victimizing society, our trickle-down culture produces similar distortions in primary and secondary education.

The multiculturalists' mantra is "diversity," but, as Bernstein demonstrates, their assumption is that all authentic groups will share the sour leftism of the multiculturalists. Authoritarian politics and banal careerism have blended as "diversity" has become a growth industry, guaranteeing academic employment for the otherwise unemployable. Multiculturalists demand more jobs, honors, attention, and subsidies, all in the name of the ultimate entitlement—a "right" to adore yourself and to make others express adoration of you.

The multiculturalists are invariably humorless and often ignorant, but these are not disabilities in today's academic settings. However, multiculturalists do have a fatal flaw as a political force: They manage to be simultaneously boring and ludicrous. Multiculturalism is, as Bernstein says, a kind of compulsory chapel. Yet in spite of all its bullying and occasional cruelties, it may by now be doing more good than harm because it is producing a libertarian backlash, of which Bernstein's not-at-all boring book is a splendid example.

November 14, 1994

The Paradox of History Standards

Until now it has seemed both paradoxical and axiomatic that a nation that needs national standards for the teaching of its history should not seek such standards. This is because those who are apt to be called upon to write such standards will be teachers of history, the shortcomings of whose teaching have occasioned the call for standards.

That is, a profession riven by intellectual disputes arising from political differences cannot be counted on to come to an acceptable consensus concerning what and how students should learn. But given a second chance to write standards, after a fiasco of a first attempt vindicated skeptics (the Senate voted its disapproval 99–1), the profession has produced revised standards that perhaps merit a passing grade.

The idea of national standards, even voluntary ones, is a departure from the traditional conservative emphasis on educational localism. However, the idea became national policy when the Bush administration gave a grant to UCLA's National Center for History in the Schools to develop such standards. The result was evidence for the proposition that educational localism is prudent because at least state and local mistakes are confined, rather than continental, mistakes.

The first standards reflected the multiculturalists' mentality: America is an incoherent bazaar of cultures (the document referred to "the American peoples") and a cafeteria of values, all cultures and values being of equal importance and worth. But the standards also radiated the idea of therapeutic and affirmative action history—history taught to give various victim groups special representation in the national narrative in order to make them feel good about themselves.

And the standards reflected the intellectuals' self-congratulatory understanding of themselves as constituting an "adversary culture." Their adversary is the benighted complacency of most Americans, who do not recognize American history as a gloomy manifestation of the disease called Western civilization.

So the first standards described the Cold War in terms of the moral equivalence of the two sides—as "swordplay" between "two superpowers . . . competing for power and influence." McCarthyism was mentioned nineteen times, the Ku Klux Klan seventeen times, the 1848 Seneca Falls Convention (which launched the women's suffrage movement) nine times, Harriet Tubman six times. The foundings of the National Organization for Women and the Sierra Club were mentioned, but not the First Congress.

Westward expansion was explained in terms of the avarice of "restless white Americans." And there was what one distinguished and disgusted historian (John Diggins of the City University of New York) called "the *Dances with Wolves* kind of history where Native Americans are depicted as living in peaceful tribal solidarity, at one with nature, with no sense of possessiveness and competitiveness." Students were encouraged to analyze JFK's "accomplishments" and LBJ's "leadership" and the "legacy" of both, but also Coolidge's "trickle down" policies. You get the picture.

In the revised standards produced by the UCLA center, partisanship has been purged from descriptions of modern presidents, the Cold War is related to dangerous internal and external dynamics of the Soviet Union, McCarthyism is related to Soviet espionage and other U.S. security anxieties. Gone are the suggested classroom activities, such as a mock trial of John D. Rockefeller.

How improved the standards are is a matter of opinion. What is indisputable is that the revision was prompted and shaped by fierce criticism, some of it by distinguished liberals in academia (such as John Diggins and Arthur Schlesinger), much of it by conservatives not on campuses. Which suggests an interesting reversal: Today many defenders of cultural standards are out in the world, and many philistines are in the academies.

It has been said that the trouble with the younger generation is that it has not read the minutes of the last meeting. That is, it has not been taught history in a way that makes them reliable legatees of a shared and valuable culture. But the question remains: Should there be national standards?

Recently the president, meeting with governors, embraced their preference for state standards. The president is a former governor; he is a supple bender to conservative breezes. But there is a two-part conservative case to be made for national standards.

One part is that the revision of the standards proves that the historians' profession is not incorrigible or impervious to arguments congenial to conservatives. The second part is that national standards should annoy multiculturalists. That is, standards assert the reality of what many multiculturalists deny—the existence of a unifying common culture worthy of conserving. The annoyance of multiculturalists is a nearly irresistible reason.

April 7, 1996

Intellectual Cotton Candy

Novelist Walker Percy defined a "deconstructionist" as an academic who claims that the meaning of all communication is radically indeterminate but who leaves a message on his wife's answering machine requesting pepperoni pizza for dinner. Deconstructionists read things like *Social Text*, which will never again be called a "learned journal."

In it Alan Sokal, a New York University physicist, has perpetrated a hilarious hoax that reveals the gaudy silliness of some academics. He submitted to *Social Text* for publication an essay that was a tissue of pseudoscientific solecisms and gaseous philosophical rhetoric, flecked with the political jargon that causes leftists' pulses to race. *Social Text* published his parody as serious scholarship, thereby proving that any nonsense, however prolix and preposterous, can win academic approval if it includes "progressive" murmurings about feminism and the baneful effects of "the Western intellectual outlook."

Sokal's essay was intellectual cotton candy—the mere appearance of nourishment—spun from the patois by which certain charlatans disguise their lack of learning. He laid down a fog about "liberatory" this and "postmodernist" that, "nonlinearity" and "emancipatory mathematics" and "transformative hermeneutics" and the "morphogenetic field," and did not neglect that old reliable, "the crisis of late-capitalist production relations." All this supposedly pertained to physics.

Any competent undergraduate physics or math major would, Sokal says, recognize the essay as a spoof. So what, beyond ignorance, explains why *Social Text*'s editors swallowed it? Arrogance, for starters, the arrogance of what Sokal calls a "self-perpetuating academic subculture." It is defined by its ideology, which holds that ideology permeates everything, so there is no truth, only "sublimated" power relations "encoded" in various "texts."

Social Text's editors never thought to ask scientists to review Sokal's "argument" because to do so would be to "privilege" a point of view and concede the existence of objective truths. After all, the editors were smitten by Sokal's ridicule of the "Western" notion that "there exists an external world" the physical laws of which can be discovered by the "so-called" scientific method. And the editors surely liked the political tone of Sokal's exhortation "to demystify and democratize the production of scientific knowledge."

He is indeed a leftist, having taught mathematics for Nicaragua's Sandanistas. But as he says in *Lingua Franca*, the magazine of academic affairs in which he revealed his spoof, the left has become hospitable to intellectual sloppiness.

Actually, he is too kind. Something more sinister than sloth is involved. The lumpen Marxists and other theory-mongers begin with Nietzsche's assertion that there are no facts, only interpretations. They proceed to belabor certain banalities, such as that developments in science are influenced by political and social forces and that literature is conditioned by writers' contexts. And they arrive at an encompassing relativism, by which they justify seeing everything through the lens of politics.

Everything, they assert, from science to sexuality, is a "social construction," and thus arbitrary. The issue of *Social Text* containing Sokal's parody includes excruciatingly serious essays that read like parodies, such as "Gender and Genitals: Constructs of Sex and Gender," which reports that "transgender theorists and activists" are refuting the "Western assumption that there are only two sexes," and are promoting "increased fluidity" and "a 'rainbow' of gender" purged of "the binary model." No wonder *Social Text*'s editors nodded approvingly even as Sokal strained to be, as he says, "especially egregious" in his conclusion concerning "the dialectical emphasis" of "catastrophe theory" becoming a "concrete tool of progressive political praxis."

Well, if, as academics who read things like *Social Text* like to say, we are all captives of racial, sexual, and class conditioning, and if any "text," properly "interrogated" (sorry, but they talk this way), reveals not the writer's intention but power relations and the hidden agenda of our phallocentric society's dominant cliques, then let's get on with the agenda of academic victimology. That agenda involves using higher education's curricula to dole out reparations to "underrepresented cultures."

Sokal's spoof became still more entertaining when Professor Stanley Fish shoved his oar in. Fish is professor of English and executive director of the Duke University Press, which publishes *Social Text*. Sokal having demonstrated the comic potential of *Social Text*'s poverty of intellectual standards, Fish denounced Sokal as a threat to, of all things, "intellectual standards."

Say what? Science, says Fish, is a "communal effort" but because of Sokal, communal efforts may be more difficult because there may be "a deep and corrosive attitude of suspicion" in the offices of learned journals.

Learned people hope so, and hope especially for suspicion of the likes of Fish.

May 30, 1996

Intellectual Segregation

In 1993, Dr. Yosef A. A. Ben-Jochannan, who was advertised as "a distinguished Egyptologist" although he is not a scholar of Egyptian language or civilization, delivered the Martin Luther King Memorial Lecture at Wellesley College. Unfortunately for him and for other "Afrocentrists," and fortunately for the rest of us, Mary Lefkowitz, a scholar of antiquity, teaches there and attended the lecture.

He offered the Afrocentrist's usual litany about how Greek civilization was stolen from Africa, as when Aristotle acquired his philosophy by plundering the library at Alexandria. When she asked him how Aristotle could have done that, considering that the library was not built until after Aristotle's death, and that there is no evidence that Aristotle ever went to Egypt, he said he resented the tone of the question. Several students accused her of racism and of having been brainwashed by white historians. The occasion, she says, was less like an academic lecture than a political rally.

Which did not make it aberrant on a campus today. And it was not a novel experience for Lefkowitz, who was accused of leading a Jewish "onslaught" on Afrocentrism in defense of Eurocentric hegemony when she questioned whether Socrates, Hannibal, and Cleopatra were Africans. Once when she suggested that Afrocentrists should give evidence for such claims as that Plato visited Egypt and acquired his philosophy there, she was told that her attitude was "McCarthyite in its intolerance." Such experiences moved her to write her new book, *Not Out of Africa: How Afrocentrism Became an Excuse to Teach Myth as History.* Talk about using a howitzer to slay a hamster. Except the hamster, the Afrocentrist fable, is unslayable by mere evidence.

With heroic patience and goodwill she brings her formidable erudition to bear on the Afrocentrists' assertions, which are rarely more than that. If truth mattered in this controversy, her book would end the debate. But what makes the debate important and sinister is that it is not really a debate—not a dispute between scholars in agreement about professional standards. The disputants have no shared sense of what scholarship is or what the ethics of argument should be. On one side are scholars, with a traditional understanding of how truth is acquired and respected. On the other side are political activists wearing academic gowns. They believe that the truth of a proposition about history is less important than the proposition's therapeutic effect on the self-esteem of people whose ethnic pride might be enhanced by it.

Actually, Afrocentrism rests on something even worse than the idea that the truth of a proposition matters less than the utility of the proposition in serving a political agenda. Afrocentrism is another weed fertilized by the idea that there is no such thing as truth, only competing "narratives"; that power decides which narratives prevail; and that people of color are oppressed because the Eurocentric narrative has been "privileged" by the "hegemony" of white racism. Afrocentrists begin with, because Afrocentrism depends on, disdain for historical methodology.

Drawing upon ancient texts, European history, and contemporary archaeology, Lefkowitz meticulously demonstrates why "arguing that Afrocentric writers offer a valid interpretation of ancient history is like being comfortable with the notion that the earth is flat." What do we know of Socrates' physical appearance? (Not much, and nothing that suggests he was African, any more than there is evidence for the Afrocentrist canard that Napoleon shot the nose off the Sphinx because it was recognizably

African.) Was Cleopatra black? (With the possible but improbable exception of one grandmother, her known ancestry was fully Macedonian Greek.) What of the cultural dependency of the Greeks resulting from Egypt's invasion of Greece in the second millennium B.C.? (A cultural transaction that never occurred, the invasion never having occurred.) Lefkowitz deals with evidence but Afrocentrists partake of the Oliver Stone mentality, according to which the utter absence of proof for a proposition *is* proof—proof of a successful conspiracy to destroy all proof.

One prominent Afrocentrist teaches that Beethoven was "Afro-European." Afrocentrism is sometimes based on merely incompetent interpretations of facts, but more often is based on aggressively meretricious misrepresentations of facts for ideological purposes. They are the purposes of identity politics, which preaches that in arguments about history, the important thing is not the historians' evidence but the historians' motives, which are explained by racial or ethnic determinism.

Afrocentrism is not new. The most influential book espousing it was published in 1954. And Marcus Garvey, who died in 1940, said that because of "thousands of Negro professors," ancient Egypt "gave to the world civilization," that Greece and Rome "robbed Egypt of her arts and letters" and whites "resort to every means to keep Negroes in ignorance of their history." But today the teaching of Afrocentrism illuminates the distinction between freedom of speech in society and academic freedom in institutions devoted to the dissemination of knowledge. "Academic freedom," writes Lefkowitz, "is the right to profess a discipline according to its recognized content and procedures, free from constraints and considerations extraneous to that discipline." It does not encompass "the right simply to cease to be an active member of the intellectual community" and does not give anyone "the privilege of teaching what is beyond his or her range of proven competence." People who believe the teaching of Afrocentrism is protected by academic freedom must recognize the "right" to teach creationism.

Afrocentrism is an attempt to "empower" African-Americans with a "transforming" myth. But the myth is self-inflicted intellectual segregation, and the entire project is condescending to African-Americans: tell them inspiring stories, just as parents tell moralizing fairy tales to children. The truth is grander than the myth. "The Negro is an American," said Martin Luther King. "We know nothing of Africa." That is why African-Americans alone are entitled to the robust pride that W.E.B. Du Bois expressed: "There is nothing so indigenous, so completely 'made in America' as we."

February 19, 1996

The Abuse of Excuses

O. J. Simpson has begun to pay the price of double murder: He must surrender his silverware. And this is not the most dismaying recent outcome from the criminal justice system.

On August 18, 1989, the Menendez brothers, Erik and Lyle, drove from Los Angeles to San Diego to buy shotguns and birdshot, using false identifications. That night they slept in their wealthy parents' Los Angeles home, and the next morning exchanged the birdshot shells for more deadly buckshot. Later that day they went boating with their parents. The next day they fired fifteen shells—they had to reload—into their parents while the parents were watching television. The brothers collected $700,000 in life insurance and went on a shopping spree.

When they admitted the killings they argued that they killed because they were frightened victims of sexual and emotional abuse. About half the jurors were convinced by the excuse (convinced that the brothers had an honest but unreasonable fear for their lives) and refused to convict of murder.

This has moved James Q. Wilson, the social scientist especially knowledgeable concerning crime, to publish a timely, disturbing, and valuable book, *Moral Judgment: Does the Abuse Excuse Threaten Our Legal System?* His answer to that question is: Increasingly it threatens not only the legal system but society's moral equilibrium and tranquillity. It undermines the concept of personal responsibility. And the legal system's increasing susceptibility to "abuse excuses" weakens the law's character-building capacity because it diminishes the law's power to strengthen the individual's often attenuated self-control.

It is a juror's duty to judge human behavior. It is a human tendency to want to explain behavior. Jurors are human. Hence a tension between judging and explaining. Into this tension intrudes, increasingly, the "expert witness." He is arguably a scientist and certainly an expert at making murky—on behalf of clients wealthy enough to hire him—the fundamental assumption of our legal system, that people are responsible for their actions.

What Wilson calls the "struggle between science and law" is often first a struggle between competing scientific claims, often with less real science involved than when experts clashed about DNA evidence during the Simpson trial. And what causes a judge to admit testimony such as that of the expert who testified that research on snails explained that the Menendez brothers' brains had been "rewired" by their experiences, as snails' brains can be?

One reason is the fear that, given our obsession with procedural perfection, cases that are not plea-bargained are ripe for appeal. Hence judges struggle to minimize grounds for appeals. Hence the circus of jury selection, which takes minutes in England and in the Simpson trial *began* with prospective jurors filling out seventy-three-page questionnaires. Hence permissiveness toward "expert witnesses."

Another reason for excessive deference to "experts" is the therapeutic ethic—policy must cure, not judge—that arises from a disposition to assume that crime is socially or biologically caused. Plausible science (the proposition that all behavior is in some sense caused) can produce perverse law (the notion that, if behavior is caused, the individual is not responsible for it).

For example, when, as in the past, the law assumed that culpability was intensified when a crime was committed by someone intoxicated or caught up in mob hysteria, the law taught a duty to avoid loss of control. Now both intoxication and mob hysteria (remember Damian Williams and others beating the truck driver Reginald Denny nearly to death with bricks during the Los Angeles riots) are apt to be thought to mitigate guilt.

Indeed, many factors other than abuse of various sorts are said by "experts" to correlate with crime, hence to cause crime, hence to lessen responsibility for crime. These factors include—among many other things—low verbal IQ scores, low levels of serotonin, elevated levels of testosterone, lead, and manganese, the XYY chromosome pattern in men, fetal alcohol and fetal drug syndromes, extreme poverty, living in a single-parent family, and use of anabolic steroids.

Wilson believes the law should hold (as the second Menendez trial held) that individuals are responsible for their actions "unless those actions are caused by a pure reflex or a delusional state utterly beyond rational control." Otherwise we will increasingly have what Wilson calls "a decline in the willingness of citizens to assume and ascribe personal responsibility for their actions."

This begets a tendency "to deny guilt, to expect rewards without efforts, to blame society for individual failings, and to exploit legal technicalities to avoid moral culpability." Thus does doubt about the capacity of individuals to govern themselves erode society's capacity for self-government.

April 6, 1997

Coney Island and the Guiding Arithmetic of Delusion

NEW YORK—In broad swaths of this high-rise city the horizon of hope is defined by a steel hoop hung ten feet above the concrete. Basketball, the game of kinetic grace in a confined space, combines, like urban living itself, high energy and barely controlled contact. Today it exemplifies both the exhilarations and pathologies of urban life, as a new movie and a new book make shatteringly clear.

Hoop Dreams is a documentary tracing the five-year journey of two black Chicago teenagers through the downward trajectory of their extravagant hopes for salvation through basketball. Even better than the movie—score one for print journalism—is Darcy Frey's slender book *The Last Shot: City Streets, Basketball Dreams,* an elegantly told sad story of young black men playing with literally life-and-death desperation in Brooklyn's Coney Island wasteland, where there are two basic career paths—drugs, and a basketball scholarship to college.

See the movie. But first read Frey's book so you will better understand the sorrows you see as two Chicago lives hang by threads as thin and fragile as knee ligaments.

Nasty neighborhoods are nothing new in the human story but Coney Island, a lunarscape of warehoused poor, drug markets, and basketball courts, bears the distinctive stigma of government's infliction of good intentions. In the 1950s, in the name of "urban renewal," planners had the lunatic idea of piling up poor people fourteen-stories deep in apartment blocs built where organic neighborhoods were bulldozed to make room. The result, startling only to the planners, is concentrated misery.

The players Frey befriended attended Lincoln High School. In better days it produced three Nobel laureates in physics, but now it almost never produces among its famously gifted athletes any who can get the 700 SAT score necessary for an athletic scholarship at a Division I school. Your heart will be in your throat as you read about Russell Thomas's attempts to get to 700.

Clutching SAT review books and vocabulary cards the way a shipwrecked sailor clings to a spar, Thomas is caught in the surrealism of a system that promises a young man glittering prizes if he perfects a jump shot, but prevents him from rising on its arc because nothing in his home or school prepared him to know the synonym for "panache." Thomas aims not for the NBA but for "a nice small tight school where they'll look after me and I can get my degree in nursing and I'll never have to come back to Coney Island." How did Thomas do? Buy the book and find out.

A summer meat market called a "camp," run by the Nike shoe company and attended by drooling college coaches, almost all white, displays the talents of 120 players, almost all black, ninety-seven of whom read below the ninth-grade level. As Frey says, all have the athletic skills to play big-time college basketball but most of those who will make their SAT 700 will arrive on campuses "with no idea how to take lecture notes, read a college text, use a library, or write a research paper."

Coaches recruit with a ruthlessness commensurate with the billions of dollars of television fees, ticket sales, shoe contracts, and other revenues sloshing through the entertainment industry called "amateur athletics" that has been grafted onto America's system of higher education. A measure of the coaches' minuscule moral awareness is that they unblushingly made their smarmy pitches to the Lincoln players in front of Frey. Their oily quarter-truths and robust lies give a dark new meaning to the axiom that sport does not just build character, it reveals it.

If the purest immorality is to treat another human being as a mere means to the achievement of one's ends, big-time college athletics—there are honorable exceptions, as at Georgetown University—achieves a ghastly purity as it wrings wealth from young bodies and then discards their possessors at age twenty-two, with minds untrained for the rest of their lives.

The grinding arithmetic of delusion is this: Fewer than 1 percent of the more than 500,000 high school basketball players get Division I athletic scholarships. However, given where young inner-city men start, and how little their homes and schools give them to start with, a long shot can look like the only shot they have at escape. Hence the intensity of their pursuit.

Long ago Bayard Rustin, the civil rights leader, pausing to watch teenagers playing basketball on a Harlem court, said it was heartbreaking how good they were. He understood the desperation that is the goad to such grace in a confining space.

November 24, 1994

The "Decent" Against the "Street"

All at once Sherman was aware of the figure approaching him on the sidewalk, in the wet black shadows of the townhouses and the trees.

The "Decent" Against the "Street"

Even from fifty feet away in the darkness, he could tell. It was that deep worry that lives in the base of the skull of every resident of Park Avenue south of Ninety-sixth Street—a black youth, tall, rangy, wearing white sneakers.—Tom Wolfe, *The Bonfire of the Vanities*

PHILADELPHIA—But in real life the black youth probably would be worried more often than Sherman McCoy. In inner cities, where life is a slow-motion riot, young black men live worried, which is one reason why they often live briefly. Elijah Anderson understands why they worry.

Anderson, a black professor of urban sociology at the University of Pennsylvania, and a superb reporter of real life, says the inner-city black community is divided, socially, between two orientations, "decent" and "street." The street code is a quest for "respect" by people who are apt to have thin skins and short fuses because they feel constantly buffeted by forces beyond their control. Writing on "The Code of the Streets" in *The Atlantic Monthly*, Anderson says respect in the streets is hard won and easily lost, and losing it leaves the individual naked to the aggression of others seeking to acquire or preserve respect.

Amid the congenial academic clutter of an office overlooking the campus, itself an island of calm in urban turmoil, Anderson says lack of confidence in the police and criminal justice system produces a defensive demeanor of aggression. This demeanor expresses a proclivity for violent self-help in a menacing environment. A readiness to resort to violence is communicated by "facial expressions, gait, and verbal expressions—all of which are geared mainly to deterring aggression" and to discouraging strangers "from even thinking about testing their manhood."

Inner-city youths are apt to construct identities based precariously on possessions—sneakers, jackets, jewelry, girlfriends. The taking and defense of them is part of a tense and sometimes lethal ritual. It has, Anderson says, a "zero-sum quality" because raising oneself requires putting someone down. Hence the low threshold of violence among people who feel they have no way of gaining or keeping status other than through physical displays.

The street is the alternative source of self-esteem because work experiences are so often unsatisfactory, partly because of demeanors and behaviors acquired in the streets. A prickly sensitivity about "respect" causes many black youths to resent entry-level jobs as demeaning. And, Anderson says, employers, black as well as white, react with distrust to a young black man "with his sneakers, 'gangster cap,' chain necklace, and portable radio at his side."

For such a person, work becomes a horizontal experience of movement from one entry-level job to another. And the young person's "oppositional culture" is reinforced by the lure of the underground economy of drugs.

Furthermore, says Anderson, some young people develop "an elaborate ideology in order to justify their criminal adaptation" to their situation, an ideology portraying " 'getting by' without work as virtuous."

Anderson's father brought his family north from Arkansas to do war work in the Studebaker plant in South Bend, Indiana (making fighter planes that anticipated the look of postwar Studebaker cars), and by 1948 was making $5,500 a year, equivalent to more than $30,000 today. Such jobs are scarce now in cities, even for youths who have not adopted the demeanor, or succumbed to the temptations, of the street.

Also, says Anderson, many inner-city parents who love their children nevertheless parent harshly to prepare their children for the harsh world beyond the front stoop. A child who comes home from a losing fight may be sent out to refight it, and parents yell at and strike their children for small infractions of rules. As a result, says Anderson, children "learn that to solve any kind of interpersonal problem one must quickly resort to hitting or other violent behavior."

Anderson is not censorious of the black middle class which could have leavened the ghetto with role models and encouragement, but which instead has produced what Anderson calls "a kind of diaspora." However, Anderson, who lives where gunfire occasionally disturbs his family's sleep, has various family experiences with the violent possibilities of urban life.

During the 1992 rioting in South Central Los Angeles, his brother's restaurant was burned down because it was sandwiched between two Korean shops targeted by black rioters. Elijah Anderson and his brother both know that the fictional worries of Sherman McCoy are as nothing next to the real-life worries the decent black majority has about the minority that lives by the code of the streets.

September 15, 1994

Ambiguities of Assimilation

SAN DIEGO—Here, hard by Mexico, and with the surf's concussions rhythmically reminding natives of the ocean across which Asian immigrants now come as Europeans once did across the Atlantic, the debate about immigration rages. It is silting up with misunderstandings, according to Wayne Cornelius, director of the Center for U.S.-Mexican Studies at the University of California, San Diego.

He believes one of today's problems may be too much rather than too little "assimilation." Certainly the nightmare of many immigrant parents is that their children are becoming too much "like us"—like the native populations they are closest to.

The alleged failure of, or resistance to, assimilation is the basis of the cultural, as distinct from the economic, criticism of current immigration. But Cornelius asks, suppose today's immigrants were importing a dangerous culture value—say, advocacy of authoritarian government. Or, more pointedly, Cornelius says: Suppose native-born Americans today had the 1960 rate of illegitimate births and immigrants were importing the soaring illegitimacy rates that native-born Americans now have (68 percent for African-Americans, 30 percent for society as a whole). Then the cultural critique of immigration would be understandable. But one problem concerning today's immigration, says Cornelius, "is with domestic minorities," a conclusion supported by other research on the other side of the continent, among Haitian and other immigrants in Miami.

In their essay, "Should Immigrants Assimilate?" in *The Public Interest,* Alejandro Portes of Johns Hopkins and Min Zhou of Louisiana State University note that children of nonwhite immigrants usually live at close quarters with inner-city minority youths who have an "adversarial stance" toward the white mainstream culture. And "joining those native circles to which they do have access may prove a ticket to permanent subordination and disadvantage." The subculture of marginalized native-born youths often instills "skepticism about the value of education as a vehicle for advancement, a message that directly contradicts that from immigrant parents."

Cornelius concurs. "Pick your indicator," he says. School dropout rates? Involvement in gangs? Indicators are apt to become worse as "assimilation" of young inner-city immigrants becomes "better." Cornelius says America's aversion to immigration rises as the "first generation effect" wanes among immigrants. That effect is the shaping of young people by conservative families with faith in education and the work ethic. Indeed, immigrant parents in cities are terrified of what their children are apt to learn at school—sex, drugs, petty crime.

The idea that millions of immigrant parents are resisting assimilation is, Cornelius says, a myth. "Cultural maintenance" of the immigrants' old identity is more apt to be a goal of Anglo intellectuals than of immigrants. "Lack of English," says Cornelius, "is the single most important factor working against improvement of immigrants' economic condition—and they know it."

Immigrant parents who remain monolingual do so primarily for two reasons. Working dawn to dusk, they are too exhausted to attend "ESL"— English as a second language—classes. And there is an acute shortage of such classes.

Americans' rhetorical aversion to today's immigration masks their ambivalence about immigration, ambivalence rooted in economic rather than cultural calculations. There always will be, Cornelius says, jobs that "Americans do not raise their kids to do." It is, to say no more, rare to see an Anglo working in a car wash. Chances are, a non-Anglo will serve you in a Southern California restaurant. There are similar realities in other industrial nations. Japan's 300,000 illegal immigrants are less than 0.5 percent of the workforce but are indispensable to Japan's economy because Japanese parents, even more than American parents, do not want their children performing some work that society wants performed. In Spain, child care is done largely by Dominicans and Peruvians.

As America's population ages, the shortage of entry-level workers, especially for small- and medium-size businesses, will deepen America's ambivalence about immigration. But Cornelius argues that if by "effective control" of immigration we mean equilibrium between the supply of immigrants and the demand for their labor, we may have that now. There may be places (e.g., Los Angeles) and sectors (e.g., agriculture) where equilibrium does not exist, but nationally there is no large pool of unemployed immigrant labor.

Americans, says Cornelius, would prefer that immigrants do their jobs and then disappear at the end of the day. But they won't, and Americans won't do without the work the immigrants do. So Americans, conflicted and with slightly guilty consciences about immigration, will, he says, continue to be wrong—sometimes willfully—about facts and their inferences from them.

August 11, 1994

Our Towns

In the twelfth century, when Paris, with a population of 100,000, was Europe's largest city, the city of Cahokia was about as populous as Florence (40,000). But Cahokia, sprawling over almost six square miles, was much less densely populated than compact Florence. And much less durable. It seems to have had no walls or other fortifications, its domestic architecture was made of logs and bark, and it vanished before Hernando de Soto arrived in the region in 1539. Cahokia was in what is now southwestern Illinois.

Cahokia, as archaeologists describe it, shows just how early there was a distinctively New World style of urban living. Puzzlement about the differences between American and European cities is as persistent as the differences. "Why aren't our cities like that?" was the question a friend put to Witold Rybczynski when she returned from Paris. Ask a professor (Mr. Rybczynski is professor of urbanism at the University of Pennsylvania) a straightforward question and you are apt to get a long answer. Mr. Rybczynski's answer to his friend's question is a book—not a long one, but one packed with common sense, subtlety, and observations that illuminate our always evolving urban landscape. Readers who allow Mr. Rybczynski to take them on a brisk stroll through *City Life: Urban Expectations in a New World* are apt to understand—and like—their cities more than they do when they begin the stroll.

The trouble is, Americans do not think they are supposed to like cities. They like living in the sort of nation Hamilton wanted—urban, industrial, dynamic—but they want to talk like Jefferson, who said, "The mobs of great cities add just so much to the support of pure government as sores do to the strength of the human body," and "I view great cities as pestilential to the morals, the health, the liberties of man." Jefferson exemplified the American ambivalence about cities. As Mr. Rybczynski dryly notes, Jefferson may have lived on an isolated mountaintop but he lived there in a house he radically designed to resemble a fashionable Parisian residence, the Hôtel de Salm, and he furnished it with a lot of French furniture that was not exactly rustic. Sherwood Anderson chose to live in Chicago while writing *Winesburg, Ohio*. And for several generations, Americans have been fleeing to suburbs situated near highways and railroads that expedite flight back from crabgrass to city concrete five days a week.

Americans, Mr. Rybczynski says, have bestowed the title "city" exuberantly and promiscuously. In 1872 the grandly named Dodge City had a few adobe houses, about a dozen frame houses, and about two dozen tents. Miami had 343 voters when it declared itself a city in 1896. By 1920 it had 30,000 residents; seventy years later it was the core of the eleventh-largest metropolitan area in the United States. Such swift transformations are the key to Mr. Rybczynski's understanding of American urban experience: No large European city was founded after the sixteenth century, and no American city was founded before that. Which is to say, American cities came along in a context of new ideas, like democracy and toleration, new materials, such as structural steel, and new technologies, like elevators, automobiles, and telephones.

Paris, he writes, reflects the aesthetic visions of various planning elites over four centuries. The only American city that makes similar grand gestures, Washington, was designed by a Frenchman. (Never mind that when another Frenchman, Alexis de Tocqueville, visited Washington in 1831 the third largest building, after the Capitol and the White House, was a tavern.) Above all, the American city, Mr. Rybczynski says, has been "a stage for the ideas of ordinary people." And arguably the most American city—the first example of twentieth-century urbanism—is the one famously disparaged as the second city: Chicago.

It was laid out on the grid system that is suited to American cities that have commercial downtowns, not cathedrals or royal precincts, as their focal points. What Mr. Rybczynski calls "the anonymous American grid" became "an ideal accommodating device for a more tolerant society," to the extent that a wide variety of beliefs and ethnicities could flourish, with none privileged by an act of urban planning. In 1880 almost 90 percent of Chicagoans were first- or second-generation immigrants. Chicago then and after exhibited the tension between "horizontal ideals and vertical aspirations." Adjacent prairies invited, and electric trolleys facilitated, growth of the grids toward the horizon. But in 1871 a useful fire provided a tabula rasa for downtown builders. This extraordinary opportunity (which is how jaunty Chicagoans regarded their calamity) occurred just as structural steel, elevators, and telephones were emancipating urban architecture from limits imposed by the weight-bearing capacity of stone walls and the stair-climbing endurance of people.

Manhattan, particularly the Manhattan encouraged by geology (bedrock, the most economical base for skyscrapers, is near the surface at the tip of the island, around Wall Street, and in Midtown south of Central Park), exemplifies one striking contrast between New World and Old World cities. In the New World, the most impressive urban buildings are not public works like Saint Paul's Cathedral or the Eiffel Tower, but private enterprises like the Chrysler Building with its eagle gargoyles evoking the hood ornaments on the company's cars.

However, a humble occurrence in Memphis in 1916—just as Henry Ford's Model T was making personal mobility a universal aspiration and (hence) an inalienable right—did more than skyscrapers to presage the future of urban living. What happened was the founding of Piggly Wiggly, the first self-service grocery store chain and model for future supermarkets.

Mr. Rybczynski, who has a gimlet eye for the mighty consequences of mundane connections, says refrigerators made it possible to store food in quantity, and automobiles made it possible to carry food purchased in weekly rather than daily shopping trips. Soon such trips were being made to supermarkets unsuited to downtowns: "Unlike department stores, supermarkets are spread out on one floor and, especially when parking is taken into account, require large building lots, which are more affordable on the edge of town." Today long-distance trucks, traveling on federally subsidized highways, deliver their goods at the edge of town, not down-town near the old railroad depots. They arrive at large shopping centers. In 1946 there were eight such novelties. But between 1970 and 1990 Americans opened 25,000 new shopping centers—one every seven hours. Today some malls have playgrounds and skating rinks.

Mr. Rybczynski, who hasn't gotten the word that everything modern must be discouraged, says: "I think that what attracts people to malls is that they are perceived as public spaces where rules of personal conduct are enforced. In other words, they are more like public streets used to be before police indifference and overzealous protectors of individual rights effectively ensured that *any* behavior, no matter how antisocial, is tolerated."

There is nothing quite like a dose of unvarnished history for inoculating people against the tendency to indict the present for failing to measure up to a sentimental notion of the past. Although Mr. Rybczynski has robust complaints about our urban living, he is wonderfully dry-eyed about the passing of cities of the sort that existed before there were "the urban technologies we take for granted. . . . The mud in the street was mixed with horse manure, and domestic waste was scattered everywhere, for there was no trash collection. Garbage simply accumulated outside and was trampled into the street, which explains why the oldest Manhattan streets are anywhere from six to fifteen feet higher than their original levels."

Mr. Rybczynski has written a wonderfully informative, entertaining, and nuanced answer to the question why our cities aren't like Paris. In the process he has shown readers how to receive the answer—we have the cities we have because we have the attributes we have—with minimal regrets.

A **New York Times** *book review, September 17, 1995*

The Great Divide

CLEVELAND—About fifteen years ago—this was after the Cuyahoga River caught fire—this city defaulted on some bonds, the city council president and a handful of other members were indicted in connection with a kick-back scheme, the president of the school board was arrested for "mooning" on his way home from a rock concert, and the mayor, in a snit of some sort, withdrew his personal checking account from the Cleveland Trust the day his brother was arrested for robbing a branch of that bank.

Today things are going well, up to a point. The reason they are, and the point at which they are not, are topics about which Mayor Michael White has volcanic opinions.

A five-foot seven-inch cauldron of energy, he seems to pace even when sitting. He became mayor in 1990 at age thirty-eight and was reelected last year with 85 percent of the vote, an achievement that glitters like, and is a reward for, Cleveland's revived downtown. The symbols, and perhaps the catalysts, of the revival are two new venues for professional sports—Jacobs Field, the Indians' new ballpark, and Gateway Arena where the Cavaliers soon will play basketball.

The economic justification for public investment in sports emporiums is easier to believe than to demonstrate. The calculation is complex because it is unclear how much of the money spent in connection with the sporting events would otherwise be spent locally anyway. In any case, new sports facilities are a trickle-down approach to building up cities: The viability of downtown facilities depends on the rental of luxury "skyboxes" or suites to corporate clients from nearby office towers.

That said, this too must be: The sense of pulsing viability that new sports facilities, and recurring crowds, impart to a downtown, has a cash value, albeit one difficult to calculate. And it has other values as well.

Crowded streets are safe streets. With eleven new restaurants having opened near the ballpark, and a new Ritz-Carlton a few blocks away, and the Rock and Roll Hall of Fame, White, an African-American from the inner city, says happily, "The suburbs are beginning to be played out." People are moving back into the city, he says, "for the same reason a fifty-five-year-old buys a Stingray after driving around in an Olds 88 for ten years."

Rhetorically, he does not crawl along in second gear. He is a paradigmatic urban politician, a materialist optimist: "Take care of economic problems, and two-thirds of social problems go away." Hence his recipe for recovery in the rest of the city, the part away from the line drives and jump shots, is: jobs. Jobs, he says, will cure "addiction to the mailbox"—monthly welfare checks.

How, then, does he explain the fact that the explosion of social pathologies since the 1960s—welfare dependency, drug addiction, and, especially, family disintegration and illegitimacy—has coincided with prosperity? He says the prosperity passed by the inner cities where there has been a "depression" for ten years.

But there have been severe, protracted economic hardships before that did not result in anything remotely like the revolution in values represented by the 80 percent rates of illegitimate births in many inner cities. The numbers denote the starkest tragedy in contemporary America. However, regarding the possibility of reversing the collapse of the stigma hitherto associated with illegitimacy, White says with finality: "We are no more going to go back to the stigma against having sex at thirteen than we are going to start wearing chastity belts again."

Well. Here is the great divide in American politics in the tenth decade of the twentieth century. On one side there are those who assert the primacy of material factors, such as the availability of jobs. On the other side are those who believe in the sovereignty of moral values in determining the destinies of communities.

White argues, correctly, that an emphasis on jobs has a moral dimension. Work is indeed central to the culture of freedom because work requires, and hence teaches, responsibility, discipline, and such useful habits as punctuality and grooming. Also, the availability of jobs, which nourishes the hopes that sustain secondary education, is a prerequisite for a successful society.

However, so, too, are well-parented children. Neither the children who have children, nor the children, are a promising workforce for today, or tomorrow. Glistening sports facilities and commercial towers, however numerous, are insufficient to sustain cities in which there is fatalism about thirteen-year-olds having sex and, inevitably, babies.

October 6, 1994

Ignition in Sandtown

BALTIMORE—Winter's cutting cold acquires a serrated edge from the harbor's dampness, and in the Sandtown-Winchester neighborhood winds whipping through gaping empty windows in abandoned row houses suggest spring never comes here. These seventy-two square blocks of blight give the impression that all commercial and social energies have congealed like oil in the crankcase of a jalopy: Ignition will be impossible.

That impression is wrong. There is a quickening of community life because Jim Rouse willed it. He knows a thing or two about urban resuscitations.

Building sparkling urban projects around the nation—for example, Harborplace, the commercial development crucial to the revival of Baltimore's downtown—was a piece of cake compared to the challenge of reversing the downward trajectory of this neighborhood where about 10,300 people live.

Almost 13,000 would live here were it to reacquire its vanished strengths. Time was, this was a working-class neighborhood where Thurgood Marshall went to school and jazz clubs resembled Harlem's.

That is the way it was as recently as the 1950s. Then came the 1960s. Manufacturing jobs departed. (Sandtown got its name from sand trucks passing through from a quarry, en route to Bethlehem Steel's plant that no longer makes nearly as much steel as it did.) Drugs arrived. Social pathologies exploded.

What is wrong today? Everything. Where do you start fixing things? Everywhere. "Everything at once" could be the motto of Community Building in Partnership, the most ambitious model for neighborhood transformations in 150 cities, that was launched by the Enterprise Foundation that Rouse created. Its premise is that poverty is a seamless web and must be combated comprehensively: Low-cost housing will not stabilize a community where there is no commerce; there will be no commerce where crime is rampant; crime will be rampant where schools are bad, drug treatment is inadequate, and recreation facilities are negligible. So, everything at once.

Seventy percent of Sandtown-Winchester families are headed by single women. The neighborhood has four times the nation's rate of low birthweight babies and infant mortality, and many babies are born addicted. Forty-four percent of the adults are unemployed or underemployed (receiving neither a living wage nor benefits). Twenty-two percent of the neighborhood's houses are vacant, and occupants of houses cannot get insurance if they are next door to an unoccupied house, or on a block with three such houses: Insurers know that trouble eventually fills such voids.

Four years ago, Rouse's initiative entered the void of community that Sandtown-Winchester had become. Its strategy has demonstrated the strengths and insufficiencies of different dimensions of Jeffersonian doctrine.

What is needed "to close the circle of our felicities?" asked Jefferson, who never saw a place where felicities are as scarce as they are in Sandtown-Winchester. All that is needed, he said, is "a wise and frugal government" that restrains men from injuring one another but leaves them otherwise free to regulate their own "industry and improvement." Would it were so.

Here children have babies and the elderly would have to walk past open-air drug markets to get to the supermarket if there were a supermarket; here four years ago 91 percent of the three elementary schools' pupils scored below minimal state standards; here 9,000 tons of debris (cars, stoves, sofas—everything, including kitchen sinks) had to be trucked away from seven square blocks before new housing units could be constructed. Here scarcities of material resources and deficits of social skills are so severe that federal, state, and city governments toil to empower people to participate in their own improvement.

However, the high rate of participation—residents comprise a majority of the board of CBP; 100 block captains, some with walkie-talkies, supplement police patrols; neighbors whose encouragements of pregnant women to receive prenatal care at the new clinic have dramatically reduced infant mortality—may be what Jefferson had in mind as democracy. By one definition of freedom, the participating residents of Sandtown-Winchester are among the freest Americans.

If freedom is more than freedom from restraints imposed by others, if freedom is a consequence of self-government, if freedom is active engagement in the affairs of a community controlling its fate, then the energized residents are free in a way that most Americans, who in most ways are more fortunately situated, are not. The residents of Sandtown-Winchester lack many things but have something Jefferson sought when he said: Divide the nation not just into states and counties, which are too large for meaningful self-government, divide it into "wards."

"Residents"? Call them citizens of the Republic of Sandtown-Winchester.

December 31, 1995

Harlem's Pink Hallways

NEW YORK—Driving along the edge of East Harlem, Seymour Fliegel points to a public school building, says, "There's an interesting story," and tells it.

In 1934, when the city had three kinds of high schools—commercial, general, and academic—an Italian-American politician named La Guardia gave an elite academic high school to what was then an Italian-American neighborhood. In those days there were people who wondered aloud what Italian-Americans would do with such an institution. Never mind. For years it excelled, and not just for Italian-Americans, as a graduate named Pat Moynihan can attest.

But time passed, East Harlem changed, and by 1982 the graduation rate was 7 percent and attendance averaged 44 percent. But the school was the state basketball champion, so there was resistance to Fliegel's proposal that the building be given to the school district educators who specialize in creating alternative schools. Resistance was overcome and three schools sprouted in the building—an elementary school, a math-science junior high, and the Manhattan Center for Science and Math, which four years later graduated every member of its first class, all of whom went to college.

What is the secret of such success? Fliegel is a former teacher and superintendent now associated with the Center for Educational Innovation at the nation's most fecund think tank, the Manhattan Institute. He says there is no secret. Just give a school autonomy in exchange for accountability and allow it to have a single vision embraced by pupils, parents, and teachers.

Which brings us to Fliegel's destination this day, an eleven-story building on 106th Street, where the sparkling top three floors are the home of The Young Women's Leadership School. It opened two weeks ago to its first class, fifty seventh-graders, mostly black and Hispanic, immaculate in the uniforms they unanimously choose to wear.

Naturally the New York Civil Liberties Union and the National Organization of Women object to the city allowing a single-sex public school. Why have these organizations worked themselves into a swivet? "That's what they do," is the scientific explanation of a laconic young female science teacher at TYWLS, fresh from Berkeley.

Call that the Oscar Hammerstein explanation, which is correct: Fish gotta swim, birds gotta fly, and the likes of NOW gotta litigate. Their organizational DNA dictates a damn-the-evidence, full-ideological-speed-ahead objection to single-sex institutions. (The theory is that they violate prohibitions on discrimination based on sex, and the Constitution's guarantee of "equal protection of the laws.") Never mind the abundantly demonstrated fact that many young girls are less reticent and more apt to flourish academically in a single-sex setting than in the hormonal hurricane of a coeducational high school.

Get this. About 91,000 of the more than one million pupils in this city's 1,095 public schools do not even have desks. Classes are being held in locker rooms. And what makes the civil liberties fetishists furious? A few parents and their daughters can exercise the freedom to choose TYWLS.

However, various little flowers like that are sprouting through cracks in the concrete—cracks, that is, in the bureaucratic slabs of public education. Fliegel and his fellow innovators have planted fifty-two imaginative schools in twenty buildings in East Harlem. And last week Mayor Giuliani endorsed acceptance of an offer made five years ago by this city's Catholic Archdiocese: Catholic schools will educate 1,000 public school students who are in the bottom 5 percent of their classes.

Because civil liberties groups object that any mechanism for using public funds for this would be unconstitutional "establishment" of religion, private funding may have to be found. If so, it will be, and the outcome will be (redundant) proof that public schools as traditionally configured and tenaciously defended by traditionalists are not producing the best possible results.

The fifty fortunate girls walking the pink hallways of their new school are a little platoon illustrating a large event—the end of an era of public policy. The assumption was that there can be national and material solutions to society's big problems, that the national government can supply what poor people need, which supposedly is a materially improved social environment.

The premise of people like Fliegel is that many big problems begin with a scarcity of inner resources in little people, a scarcity that can be cured only by bite-size programs. Glenn Loury, an African-American economist at Boston University who writes superbly about such things, titled his latest book *One By One from the Inside Out.* That is the slogan of today's real reformers, and could be the motto of TYWLS.

September 15, 1996

"Tipping the Forty":
Growing Up in Jersey City

Before the big December dance at St. Luke High School (not its real name) in Jersey City, New Jersey, Sister Peter, a woman of abundant faith but few illusions, advised newcomers to the staff, "Their dancing might get a little explicit, but there is nothing we can do about it—until it resembles foreplay. Then stop it." The tenth-graders in Mark Gerson's five American history classes knew what would happen if they did things he wanted to stop. They would "get a Frank." They would be given after-school detention, during which they would have to listen to recordings by Gerson's hero from nearby Hoboken, Frank Sinatra.

Gerson, then twenty-two and fresh from Williams College, had grown up twenty miles from Jersey City, in, effectively, another country—affluent Short Hills. He had wanted to spend the 1994–95 academic year teaching in an inner-city public school before going on to Yale Law School. However, he could not get so much as an interview from the sclerotic public system. (Jersey City has the nation's highest percentage of public school teachers who send their children to private or parochial schools.) So Gerson, who is Jewish, applied to Catholic schools.

There are more non-Catholics than clergy teaching in Catholic schools nationwide, and St. Luke hired him for $15,600. Now comes his memoir of that year, *In the Classroom: Dispatches From an Inner-City School That Works*, a high-spirited and moving antidote to the plague of education fads. What works is not Ebonics, or history taught as self-esteem therapy for "victims." What works is discipline, mutual respect, moral seriousness, high standards, and no condescension dressed up as compassion.

Jamal: "I ain't care about no SATs, Mr. Gerson. They are culturally biased."

Gerson: "Yes, Jamal, they are biased, biased against people who don't study."

Jersey City, hard by Ellis Island, is the nation's most ethnically diverse city. St. Luke's 430 students came from forty-two countries. More than half their families were on welfare. Gerson decided that what his students needed most was standard English. "We be going" was unacceptable. So were double negatives and slang phrases such as "Word is bon" and "Word up" (both meaning "That's the truth!"). But he could not connect with his students without coming to terms with their experience of America. What, he asked, do you find interesting in your life? A girl answered, "Who is having sex with who, who shot who, crimes."

When a student asked classmates, "How many of you have tipped the forty?" most raised their hands. Gerson was puzzled. The student explained. "It happens when someone you know real well is killed. You go to the spot they was killed with a forty-ounce beer. You spill some of it on the spot and you drink some. You spill some and you drink some. You ain't ever did that?" Short Hills teens do not "tip the forty." Gerson found that St. Luke students were shaped by "intimate contact with premature, violent death . . . a normal thread in the fabric of inner-city life." However, his students could be mordantly funny about the social chasm between Short Hills and Jersey City, as when a student said, "Glee club sings too loud, and the Short Hills police are all over them. But if I got a problem here, I gonna cap the bastard. Or else he gonna cap me."

Most St. Luke students are not Catholic, and religious orthodoxy at St. Luke is restricted to posters such as GOD RULES: ALWAYS HAS, ALWAYS WILL! END OF DISCUSSION! and required attendance at periodic Masses. But Gerson noted a kind of piety by osmosis: "Every one of the best classes I taught all year came after a Mass." The parents who scraped together tuition to get their children into St. Luke were motivated by the moral consensus of the school's staff. As a result, the parents backed the staff when the children were disciplined.

A durable myth of American education, nurtured by the public education lobby, is that financing is the best predictor of a school's performance: increase monetary inputs and you will increase cognitive outputs. Jersey City spends about $10,000 per public school pupil, with miserable results, as measured by such indices as truancy, graduation rates, and post-secondary education attainment. St. Luke spends about a third as much, with much better results. The year Gerson was there it mobilized the entire school community for a fund-raising party that netted the gratifying, even astonishing sum of $13,420, enough for a down payment and a few subsequent payments on a van. Because there was a community to mobilize.

Gerson's epiphany was that the word "community" denotes something about St. Luke that is entirely different than "when people gave a 'right' to be a member of a 'community' by virtue of residing in a particular location or sending a check to the proper authority." A federal bureaucrat, defending her department's $14 billion budget, says, "By having a Department of Education you're saying the kids are number one, and there's someone in Washington who's their friend, who's pulling for them." Gerson responds that the kids at St. Luke have never heard of that department and hardly need a stranger in Washington declaring herself their "friend" and them "number one." He adds: "A great tragedy of the modern welfare state has been in inculcating the belief that one can discharge his social responsibility by sending a big check to the tax man every April 15. . . . It is much simpler to send money than to spend time. . . . What is needed is not monetary gifts but social intercourse."

The concrete of bureaucratized compassion that the welfare state has poured over society is cracking, and through the cracks are coming, like crocuses after winter, small sprouts of successes, like Gerson's and St. Luke. Ella Fitzgerald, one of the "big four" (with Sinatra, Glenn Miller, and Duke Ellington) Gerson recommended to his rap-addicted students, once sang, "I've seen the charm of Jersey City, but first let me remark, I've seen it from the Empire State solarium." Gerson's report from the ground is both charming and heartening.

January 20, 1997

Atoms to Molecules in Dorchester

BOSTON—Eugene F. Rivers 3rd thinks of himself as part Jesuit and part marine and answers to "Yo, Reverend." He answers at all hours because he and his associates, many of them graduates of fine colleges who think of themselves as "paramedics of civil society," find that business is brisk for healers in a neighborhood where there are fifteen-year-old mothers and twenty-nine-year-old grandmothers, and many unparented adolescent males, and, Rivers says, it is "easier to get into a crackhouse than a church on Friday night." More of the former are open.

Rivers, a compact forty-six-year-old intellectual with wire-rimmed glasses and gray-flecked hair, was not "called," in any traditional sense, to minister to the approximately sixty-two square blocks of this city's Dorchester section. He just came, fresh from Harvard and full of faith that something like a 1930s settlement house could thrive where almost nothing else did.

Hence the house on Washington Street. Five years ago it was a burned-out shell. Today its interior sparkles, proving the power of paint and enthusiastic occupants. Rivers's enthusiasm has had to survive defeats, such as Sal.

Life prepared Rivers to deal with young men like Sal. Rivers had been one. Drawn into Philadelphia gang life at twelve, at fourteen Rivers was given a .38-caliber revolver and told to kill a member of a rival gang. He did not. He managed to achieve what physicists call "escape velocity," which enables particles to break out of the prison of an orbit and attain their own trajectory. Sal never did.

Sal was a precocious young drug dealer—his customer lists were computerized—who expressed his disapproval of Rivers's arrival in Dorchester by shooting into Rivers's home. It was Sal who taunted Rivers, saying, "When Johnny goes to school in the morning, I'm on the corner and you're not. When he comes home, I'm there, you're not." Sal is not there anymore. A drug overdose—perhaps laced by rivals with battery acid—killed him just as he seemed to be reaching escape velocity by means of a downtown job Rivers had arranged.

Rivers and his associates try to be there on the streets when they are not visiting prisons, or buying someone a suit for a court appearance, or soliciting financial support from private sources and political help from government. From government they seek basics—stop signs, community policing, scissors to slice through red tape that prevents capital, land, and buildings from coming together as businesses.

The modesty and practicality of Rivers's political agenda testifies to the subordinate place politics takes when in harness with serious religion—religion unlike the pallid Christianity that gives a slightly stained-glass tint to whatever is the Democratic Party's most recent platform. Rivers named his son after Malcolm X and his daughter after Sojourner Truth, and is a prolific participant in the polemical exchanges along the Charles River about the primacy of race or class in the urban crisis. Although he considers himself a man of the left, he is mistaken, because he says the crisis can best—indeed only—be understood in terms of a third category: secularization, enemy of hope.

His message is not "Arise ye prisoners of starvation!" or "Workers of

Atoms to Molecules in Dorchester

Dorchester, unite—you have nothing to lose but your chains!" Rather, his message is aimed not at categories but at that adolescent girl standing there on the corner at eleven P.M.—the one holding the hands of a small boy and a small girl who are not her siblings but her children. The message is: We think you are important.

In Scott Turow's new novel *The Laws of Our Fathers,* a judge broods about the endless parade of young black defendants before her bench, each an "atom waiting to be part of a molecule":

> I've been struck by how often a simple, childish desire for attention accounts for the presence of many of these young people. Most of these kids grow up feeling utterly disregarded—by fathers who departed, by mothers who are overwhelmed, by teachers with unmanageable classrooms, by a world in which they learn, from the TV set and the rap of the street, they do not count for much. Crime gathers for them, if only momentarily, an impressive audience: the judge who sentences, the lawyer who visits, the cops who hunt them—even the victim who, for an endless terrified moment on the street, could not discount them.

Rivers and his associates comprise an attentive audience, a molecular unit amid one city's atomized population, telling as many of them as they can reach, one by one: You count.

December 12, 1996

CHAPTER FOUR

POLICY

The First Amendment
and the Speech-Rationers

Surveying the constitutional and political damage done by two decades of campaign finance "reforms," friends of the First Amendment feel like the man (in a Peter De Vries novel) who said, "In the beginning the earth was without form and void. Why didn't they leave well enough alone?" Reformers should repent by repealing their handiwork and vowing to sin no more. Instead, they are proposing additional constrictions of freedom that would further impoverish the nation's civic discourse.

The additions would be the Forbes-Perot Codicils, abridging the right of a rich person to use his or her money to seek elective office. This will be called "closing a loophole." To reformers, a "loophole" is any silence of the law that allows a sphere of political expression that is not yet under strict government regulation.

Jack Kemp, Bill Bennett, Dan Quayle, Dick Cheney, and Carroll Campbell are among the Republicans who were deterred from seeking this year's presidential nomination in part by the onerousness of collecting the requisite funding in increments no larger than $1,000. You may or may not regret the thinness of the Republican field this year, but does anyone believe it is right for government regulations to restrict important political choices?

There are restrictions on the amounts individuals can give to candidates and on the amounts that candidates who accept public funding can spend. Limits on individuals' giving force candidates who are less wealthy than

Forbes or Perot to accept public funding. Such restrictions are justified as necessary to prevent corruption and promote political equality. But Professor Bradley A. Smith of Capital University Law School in Columbus, Ohio, demolishes such justifications in an article in the *Yale Law Journal*, beginning with some illuminating history.

In early U.S. politics the electorate was small, most candidates came from upper-class factions, and the candidates themselves paid directly what little campaign spending there was, which went for pamphlets, and for food and whiskey for rallies. This changed with Martin Van Buren's organization of a mass campaign for Andrew Jackson in 1828. Democratization—widespread pamphleteering and newspaper advertisements for the increasingly literate masses—cost money. Most of the money came from government employees, until civil service reform displaced patronage.

Government actions—Civil War contracts, then land and cash grants to railroads, and protectionism—did much to create corporations with an intense interest in the composition of the government. Then government created regulations to tame corporate power, further prompting corporate participation in politics. Smith says that in 1888 about 40 percent of Republican national campaign funds came from Pennsylvania businesses, and by 1904 corporate contributions were 73 percent of Teddy Roosevelt's funds. Democrats relied less on corporate wealth than on the largesse of a small number of sympathetic tycoons: In 1904 two of them provided three-quarters of the party's presidential campaign funds. By 1928 both parties' national committees received about 69 percent of their contributions in amounts of at least $1,000 (about $9,000 in today's dollars).

Only a few campaigns have raised substantial sums from broad bases of small donors. These campaigns have usually been ideological insurgencies, such as Barry Goldwater's in 1964 ($5.8 million from 410,000 contributors), George McGovern's in 1972 ($15 million from contributions averaging about $20) and Oliver North's 1994 race for a U.S. Senate seat from Virginia (small contributors accounted for almost all of the $20 million that enabled North to outspend his principal opponent four to one in a losing effort).

The aggressive regulation of political giving and spending began in 1974, in the aftermath of Watergate. Congress, itching to "do something" about political comportment, put limits on giving to candidates, and on spending by candidates—even of their personal wealth. Furthermore, limits were placed on total campaign spending, and even on political spending by groups unaffiliated with any candidate or campaign. In 1976 the Supreme Court struck down the limits on unaffiliated groups, on candidates' spending of personal wealth, and on *mandatory* campaign spending ceilings. The Court said these amounted to government stipulation of the permissible amount of political expression and therefore violated the First Amendment.

But in a crucial inconsistency, the Court upheld the limits on the size of contributions. Such limits constituted deliberate suppression by government of total campaign spending. And such suppression constitutes government rationing of political communication, which is what most political spending finances. Furthermore, in presidential campaigns, limits on the size of contributions make fund raising more difficult, which coerces candidates (at least those less flush than Forbes or Perot) into accepting public funding. Acceptance commits candidates to limits on how much can be spent in particular states during the nominating process, and on the sums that can be spent in the pre- and postconvention periods.

Now, leave aside for a moment the question of whether the "reformers" responsible for all these restrictions remember the rule that Congress shall make no law abridging the freedom of speech. But why, in an era in which the United States has virtually eliminated restrictions on pornography, is government multiplying restrictions on political expression? (Here is a thought rich in possibilities: Would pornographic political expression be unregulatable?)

When reformers say money is "distorting" the political process, it is unclear, as Smith says, what norm they have in mind. When reformers say "too much" money is spent on politics, Smith replies that the annual sum is half as much as Americans spend on yogurt. The amount spent by all federal and state candidates and parties in the 1991–92 election cycle was approximately three-quarters of the *annual* sum of the private sector's two largest advertising budgets (those of Procter & Gamble and Philip Morris). If the choice of political leaders is more important than the choice of detergents and cigarettes, it is reasonable to conclude that far too little is spent on politics.

The $700 million spent in the two-year election cycle that culminated in the November 1994 elections (the sum includes all spending by general-election candidates, and indirect party-building expenditures by both parties, and all indirect political spending by groups such as the AFL-CIO and the NRA) amounted to approximately $1.75 per year, per eligible voter, or a two-year sum of $3.50—about what it costs to rent a movie. In that two-year cycle, total spending on all elections—local, state, and federal—was less than $10 per eligible voter, divided among many candidates. And because of the limits on the size of contributions, much of the money was not spent on the dissemination of political discourse but on the tedious mechanics of raising money in small amounts. Furthermore, the artificial scarcity of money produced by limits on political giving and spending has strengthened the incentive for the kind of spending that delivers maximum bang for the buck—harsh negative advertising.

Does a money advantage invariably translate into political potency? Try telling that to Forbes, who spent $440 per vote in finishing fourth in the Iowa caucuses. True, the candidate who spends most usually wins. But as Smith notes, correlation does not establish causation. Money often follows rather than produces popularity: Many donors give to probable winners. Do campaign contributions purchase postelection influence? Smith says most students of legislative voting patterns agree that three variables are more important than campaign contributions in determining legislators' behavior—party affiliation, ideology, and constituent views. "Where contributions and voting patterns intersect, they do so largely because donors contribute to those candidates who are believed to favor their positions, not the other way around."

Smith argues that limits on campaign giving and spending serve to entrench the status quo. As regards limits on giving, incumbents are apt to have large lists of past contributors, whereas challengers often could best obtain financial competitiveness quickly by raising large sums from a few dedicated supporters. If today's limits had been in place in 1968, Eugene McCarthy could not have mounted his antiwar insurgency, which depended heavily on a few six-figure contributions. As regards spending limits, the lower they are the better they are for incumbents: Incumbents are already well known and can use their public offices to seize public attention with "free media"—news coverage.

The rage to restrict political giving and spending reflects, in part, the animus of liberals against money and commerce. There are, after all, other sources of political influence besides money, sources that liberals do not want to restrict and regulate in the interests of "equality." Some candidates are especially articulate or energetic or physically attractive. Why legislate just to restrict the advantage of those who can make or raise money? Smith notes that one reason media elites are apt to favor restricting the flow of political money, and hence the flow of political communication by candidates, is that such restrictions increase the relative influence of the unrestricted political communication of the media elites.

To justify reforms that amount to government rationing of political speech, reformers resort to a utilitarian rationale for freedom of speech; freedom of speech is good when it serves good ends. This rationale is defensible; indeed, it has a distinguished pedigree. But it has recently been repudiated in many of the Supreme Court's libertarian construings of the First Amendment. Those decisions, taking an expansive view of the First Amendment in the interest of individual self-expression, have made, for example, almost all restrictions on pornography constitutionally problematic. And such libertarian decisions generally have been defended by liberals—who are most of the advocates of restrictions on campaign giving and spending.

But liberals of another stripe also advocate campaign restrictions. They are "political equality liberals" rather than "self-expression liberals." They favor sacrificing some freedom of speech in order to promote equal political opportunity, as they understand that. Such liberal egalitarians support speech codes on campuses in the name of equality of status or self-esteem for all groups, or to bring up to equality groups designated as victims of America's injustices. Liberal egalitarians support restrictions on pornography because, they say, pornography deprives women of civic equality by degrading them. And liberal egalitarians support restrictions on political expressions in order to achieve equal rations of political communication for all candidates.

Professor Martin Shapiro of the University of California's Law School at Berkeley writes that "almost the entire first amendment literature produced by liberal academics in the past twenty years has been a literature of regulation, not freedom—a literature that balances away speech rights. . . . Its basic strategy is to treat freedom of speech not as an end in itself, but an instrumental value." And Bradley Smith says that "after twenty years of balancing speech rights away, liberal scholarship is in danger of losing the ability to see the First Amendment as anything but a libertarian barrier to equality that may, and indeed ought, to be balanced away or avoided with little thought."

Fortunately, more and more people are having second thoughts—in some cases, first thoughts—about the damage done to the political process, and the First Amendment, by the utilitarian or "instrumentalist" understanding of freedom of speech. Campaign "reforms" have become a blend of cynicism and paternalism—attempts to rig the rules for partisan advantage or the advantage of incumbents or to protect the public from what the political class considers too much political communication. Any additional "reforms," other than repeal of the existing ones, will make matters worse.

April 15, 1996

The Outlaws at KTOZ-AM

Autumn, season of mists and mellow fruitfulness, this year will also be a season of mayhem as congressional Republicans reach the climax of their attempt to get the government on a shorter leash. To get in the mood to enjoy this blood sport, consider the way the people at radio station KTOZ-AM in Springfield, Missouri, spent their summer. They spent it suffering the attentions of the U.S. Department of Labor, which caught KTOZ's people committing the unspeakable faux pas of doing volunteer work.

Last year the little 500-watt daytime station, which covers an eighty-mile radius, was bankrupt, but was cherished by a smattering of people fond of its music format of big bands, jazz, and blues. Nineteen of them who fancied the chance to be amateur disc jockeys scraped together $35,000 to buy the station from a bankruptcy court, invested $60,000 in new equipment, and began volunteering their time to keep it on the air.

This came to the attention of a commissar in the Labor Department's Kansas City outpost. He was gnawed by the fear that this volunteerism was a low and cunning dodge to evade the rigors of the Fair Labor Standards Act of 1938, thereby mocking justice and jeopardizing American prosperity. So he saddled his charger and rode to the rescue of the volunteers, undaunted by the fact that they, in their unregenerate state, did not want to be rescued.

They were having fun, and that was not even the worst of it. They were not being paid the minimum wage of $4.25, and the law is quite strict about the fact that all "employees" of a for-profit business must be paid at least that so America can be a land fit for heroes and so the government can collect its FICA taxes.

Speaking as if to a particularly dim five-year-old—slowly and with precise enunciation—the people at KTOZ explained that they were not employees and the station was not making a profit and would the commissar enjoy hearing some Glenn Miller? But your tax dollars buy bureaucrats made of sterner stuff than the Springfield scofflaws supposed; the bureaucrats cannot be deflected from their duties merely by reasonable explanations.

The commissar told them that the government is large-spirited and latitudinarian, willing, when the spirit moves it, to give specific exemptions to the minimum wage requirement. But KTOZ's volunteers had not tugged their forelocks and said, "Mother may I?" to the government. Therefore the station might have to pay back wages and interest and maybe a fine. The implication was that they should thank their lucky stars that Alcatraz has been closed.

Now, you might think that even a commissar would have sufficient sense of the absurd to note this: It is pathetic but true that the achievement of which President Clinton is proudest is AmeriCorps, the oxymoronic little program that seeks to enkindle the spirit of volunteerism in this country (in which about 90 million people do volunteer work) by hiring about 20,000 "volunteers." So why is his Labor Department trying to stamp out true volunteerism in Springfield?

Because it is all so unfair, as an unrepentant Labor Department official in Washington stoutly insisted in a letter to the congressman from that district, explaining that the investigation of KTOZ has been discontinued but was virtuous: "The department's decision not to pursue this matter should not be viewed as condoning work for no pay. There are very good and strong policy reasons why for-profit companies are not allowed to employ people for no pay. First of all, those practices take wages out of worker's (*sic*) pockets and force everyone's wages down."

Amazing, is it not, how migraine-inducing the government's reasoning can be? Yo, Labor Department: What do you—what can you—mean by the phrase "employ people for no pay"? Let's take this slowly: They. Are. Not. Employees. (Are we going too fast?) Concentrate: V-o-l-u-n-t-e-e-r-s. And what wages are being taken out of whose pockets by people donating labor without which the station would be stone silent?

KTOZ's listeners burn with the spirit that chased the redcoats back to Boston from Concord bridge. One listener suggested organizing a KTOZ fan club: "To get the feds' attention, we could call it the 'KTOZ Militia.' " Many lawyers volunteered—that dread word again—to help defend KTOZ without pay. Can they be disbarred for that offense?

This week a congressional committee will consider changes to the 1938 law to make volunteerism less obnoxious in the squinty eyes of the government. And if in coming weeks you wonder whence springs the passion behind the grinding down of government, remember KTOZ's story, and imagine how many Americans have had comparable experiences.

October 22, 1995

How Bad Law Begets Bad Law

ATLANTA—Northeast of here, hard by the South Carolina border, in Toccoa, Georgia, Waymon Earls, a tow truck driver, and his wife, Sharon, have started something that demonstrates the deep roots and strong sinews, but also some ambiguities, of today's conservatism. However, the Earls don't think they started the fight they are waging here with the help of the Southeastern Legal Foundation, a nonprofit public interest law firm spoiling for fights on behalf of conservative causes.

The Earls think, reasonably, that they are acting in self-defense. The aggressors who started the fight are the people in the school district who, without consulting the Earls, gave the Earls' daughters, ages fourteen and fifteen, a bag of condoms, prescriptions for birth control pills, Pap smears, and tests for AIDS.

Last June the *Athens* (Georgia) *Banner-Herald* quoted the Toccoa district school superintendent: "Schools are now taking over responsibilities that aren't being covered in the home. When parents won't do it, we have to." Won't do what—give their teenagers condoms? The Earls are seeking monetary damages for what they say were violations of school rules, state law, and the state constitution.

Furthermore, they allege violations of their rights under the U.S. Constitution, including their First Amendment right to the free exercise of religion (which they say encompasses child rearing) and recognized Fourteenth Amendment "due process" rights to parental sovereignty. The Earls say they are just trying to get policy to conform to precedents.

They cite a line of cases beginning with two from the 1920s. In one the Supreme Court overturned a Nebraska law (passed as a result of World War I hysteria) prohibiting foreign-language instruction to schoolchildren. The Court said the prohibition impermissibly infringed parental child-rearing rights. In the other case, the Court overturned an Oregon law requiring parents to send children to public schools. The Court said the law unreasonably interfered with the liberty of parents "to direct the upbringing and education of children under their control."

These cases were examples of "substantive due process," which those conservatives who stress judicial restraint have generally considered a contradiction in terms. Such conservatives oppose wringing policy substance, even conservative substance, from a clause they say has merely procedural meaning. And a lawyer for the Southeastern Legal Foundation cheerfully says, "We are out to make bad law in order to provoke legislatures to repeal bad laws."

The foundation believes that for too long liberals have been defining the substance of substantive due process, so conservatives should get into the game. The foundation has been in the game for twenty years. Similar organizations practicing conservative judicial activism—yes, many conservatives do not consider that an oxymoron—have proliferated since the early 1970s, when the first of them was formed with the help of a California lawyer named Ed Meese.

One can sympathize entirely with the Earls and applaud the social policies organizations like the foundation advocate while regretting the zest with which some conservatives are succumbing to the temptation to seek judicial relief from offensive policies. That often means judicial relief from the rigors of politics.

Consider the rapidly spreading movement to pass "parental rights amendments" to state constitutions. The most common formulation is: "The right of parents to direct the upbringing and education of their children shall not be infringed." Those seventeen words are rich in potential for breeding litigation about matters that should be settled by legislation, or by processes of political persuasion.

Both politics and social accommodation are discouraged by casting issues in the brook-no-compromise language of rights. Is the parental right to "direct" the "upbringing and education" of children infringed by school curricula or texts or dress codes that parents disapprove? Do we want to turn every parent's grievance into grounds for suing?

Representative Steve Largent, a freshman Republican from Oklahoma, has 125 cosponsors for his "Parental Rights and Responsibilities Act," which says, among much else, that "No federal, state, or local government . . . shall interfere with or usurp the right of a parent to direct the upbringing of the child of the parent." At first blush, that may seem unexceptional. And it is reasonable to execrate the many governmental provocations, from condom distributions to propagandizing curricula, that have moved Largent and other good people, including the Earls, to seek to codify parental rights.

However, there is a competing consideration: It is injurious to democracy to write into law language certain to breed litigation that will draw courts even deeper into the unjudicial business of reviewing and rearranging the details of social life.

February 11, 1996

"Wacko" Hurley Gets His Way

A unanimous Supreme Court, speaking through Justice Souter, cleared its throat and said, "If there were no reason for a group of people to march from here to there except to reach a destination, they could make the trip without expressing any message beyond the fact of the march itself. . . . Hence we use the word 'parade' to indicate marchers who are making some sort of collective point. . . . Parades are thus a form of expression, not just motion."

Such truisms can be steppingstones to important truths, and were so on Monday when the Court held that the organizers of Boston's St. Patrick's Day parade had a First Amendment speech right to exclude from the parade GLIB, an organization of Irish-American gays, lesbians, and bisexuals eager to express pride in their heritage and sexual orientation, and to express solidarity with similar people who have tried to march in New York's parade.

The annual parade is organized by an association of South Boston veterans groups headed by John J. "Wacko" Hurley, who does not cotton to being lectured by lower courts about the virtues of "diversity." GLIB sued him and the other parade organizers, citing, among other things, the state public accommodations law which prohibits discrimination on the basis of sexual orientation relative to the admission of any person to "any place of public accommodation, resort, or amusement."

Two Massachusetts courts sided with GLIB, praising diversity. They argued that the parade includes so many patriotic, moral, religious, commercial, and public service themes, from denunciations of drugs to denunciations of (naturally) the British, that the parade is "eclectic" and lacks "genuine selectivity." Therefore it lacks an expressive purpose and is not entitled to protection under the First Amendment. It is an open recreational event and subject to the public accommodations law.

Not so, said the Supreme Court, which is rarely unanimous these days. If constitutional protection were accorded only to narrow, succinct, and harmonious messages, such protection would be denied to (for example) Jackson Pollock paintings and newspaper opinion pages. There is no evidence of any intent of the parade organizers to exclude individual homosexuals from the various participating groups. Rather, they objected to the GLIB unit, which wanted to conscript the parade into transmitting an ideological message the organizers did not want to transmit.

Said the Court, a parade is an inherently expressive activity and the First Amendment protects a speaker's "autonomy" in choosing the content of his message, including what not to express as well as what to express. If the parade organizers did not want to celebrate what GLIB wanted to celebrate, their First Amendment right not to be coerced into doing so cannot be abridged by a state's public accommodations law.

This is not a new notion. In 1977 the Court upheld the right of a Jehovah's Witness in New Hampshire to edit, with metal shears or tape or something, his license plate, which bore the state slogan LIVE FREE OR DIE. He said "life is more precious than freedom" and the Court said New Hampshire could not compel him to "foster" any religious or political "concepts" with which he disagreed.

The Court implied that only mottoes "not ideologically neutral" were editable, so presumably Idaho can deal roughly with anyone who obliterates from his plates the ringing words FAMOUS POTATOES. Justice Rehnquist, dissenting in 1977, said the logic of the Court's ruling was that the words "In God We Trust" on the currency violate the First Amendment speech autonomy rights of atheists. But the 1977 majority said *au contraire*, currency is generally in pockets, not "displayed."

But back to Boston. "Our tradition of free speech," said the Court Monday, "commands that a speaker who takes to the street corner to express his views in this way should be free from interference by the state based on the content of what he says." GLIB wanted Massachusetts to, in effect, edit the parade as an expressive event.

GLIB's suit against the parade organizers is illustrative of the "progressive" agenda. It was just one more skirmish in a struggle—conducted in the name of enlarged rights, naturally—to break more and more private organizations to the saddle of the state. As such, the suit illustrates how the language of rights is used in attempts to diminish freedom by making more and more of life government-supervised and mandatory. It vindicates the wit who said that liberals do not care what you do, as long as it is compulsory.

June 21, 1995

VMI R.I.P.

'Twas a famous victory women won last week. The Supreme Court gave them the right to enroll in an educational institution which, the moment they enter it, will essentially cease to exist.

Virginia Military Institute's men-only admission policy was put on a path to extinction fourteen years ago when the Court held that men denied admission to Mississippi University for Women's nursing program were denied what the Constitution promises, "equal protection of the laws." After the Court's ruling against VMI's male-only admissions policy, it is probable that all single-sex public education has been put on the path to extinction by the logic of the Court's VMI ruling. So perhaps have all private single-sex institutions of higher education that receive significant government aid. (Such aid provides an average of almost 20 percent of their budgets—not counting direct government aid to students.)

In the hands of any willful Supreme Court—and the judiciary is not becoming less willful—the logic may forbid single-sex classes or sports teams in public schools, and government support for such single-sex programs as shelters for battered women and boot camps for young male offenders. What else? We will know when our robed masters tell us what single-sex programs have "exceedingly persuasive" justifications. The VMI ruling establishes that vacuity as the judiciary's latest "standard."

VMI, one of Virginia's fifteen publicly supported four-year colleges and universities, enrolls just 1,300 of the 160,000 students in the state's public higher education system. It features an "adversative" education system emphasizing physical rigor, mental stress, military etiquette, absence of privacy, and minute regulation of behavior. Virginia's attempt to shield VMI from the "equal protection" challenge by creating at a women's college an analogous program for women was inherently implausible.

Justice Ginsburg, writing for the Court and joined by Stevens, O'Connor, Kennedy, Souter, and Breyer (Rehnquist concurred separately and Thomas did not participate because his son attends VMI), sought to portray the ruling as narrow by emphasizing VMI's uniqueness—its special prestige and its origins in 1839 in a context of male chauvinist stereotypes about women. Purging society of unacceptable stereotypes is the point of the Court's ruling. The Court engaged less in construing the Constitution than in what is called "consciousness-raising."

Justice Scalia, dissenting, said the majority believes, against considerable evidence, that no substantial educational value is served by all-male military academies. He said inherently ambiguous constitutional texts such as the equal protection guarantee should be construed in ways that reflect respect for "constant and unbroken national traditions" such as educational diversity that includes some single-sex schools, including male-only military schools.

He noted that the majority criticized the "fixed notions" of our forebears regarding women's education, but that the majority favors its own notions so fixedly that it fixes them as constitutional mandates. He notes that the majority faults the "closed-mindedness" of our forebears regarding women, but the majority wields judicial power to abort the system of democratic persuasion by which the public's mind is kept open, and changed: "That system is destroyed if the smug assurances of each age are removed from the democratic process and written into the Constitution. So to counterbalance the Court's criticism of our ancestors, let me say a word in their praise: they left us free to change. The same cannot be said of this most illiberal Court, which has embarked on a course of inscribing one after another of the current preferences of the society (and in some cases only the counter-majoritarian preferences of the society's law-trained elite) into our Basic Law."

This dispute divides Americans into two camps, those who do and those who do not think women are to men as blacks are to whites. VMI's premise, put with maximum compression, is that sexual differences are radically unlike racial differences, particularly in the high-risk and high-stress environment of a military context, because of two things—differences of physical capacities, and eros. Current intellectual fashion is dismissive of this premise. A pity.

Earlier this year *The New Republic*'s Jeffrey Rosen interviewed VMI's superintendent, General Josiah Bunting III, a Rhodes scholar and author of an acclaimed novel about his Vietnam experiences. Bunting lamented, "Our opponents aren't even trying to see this institution as it really is; they're not interested in what Coleridge called 'imaginative sympathy.' "

Rosen wrote that "almost everyone concedes" that women will never benefit from VMI's distinctive virtues because with the admission of women, that VMI "will no longer exist." To Rosen, Bunting described the sadness felt by VMI students and graduates about the impending extinction of a 157-year tradition: "They realize that once it's gone it can never be recovered. *Nescit vox missa reverti*—the voice which sent can never be recalled. . . . This is everything that is good in our culture, and it's going to change irretrievably if they bring in women."

The people most pleased by the Court's killing of the unique institution for which Bunting mourns are people who describe themselves as defenders of "diversity" and "choice."

June 28, 1996

And Now, a Right to Be Obnoxious

Compassionate government has recently rained new rights and entitlements so rapidly that you may have missed this beauty: You have a right to be a colossally obnoxious jerk on the job.

If you are just slightly offensive, your right will not kick in. But if you are seriously insufferable to colleagues at work, you have a right not to be fired, and you are entitled to have your employer make reasonable accommodations for your "disability." That is how the Americans with Disabilities Act of 1990 (ADA) may yet be construed.

This is explained in the Spring 1996 issue of *The Public Interest* quarterly by G. E. Zuriff, professor of psychology at Wheaton College and a clinical psychologist at MIT. His essay, "Medicalizing Character," suggests that the ADA, as elaborated by regulations, threatens "to undermine our culture's already fragile sense of personal responsibility."

The ADA is generally thought of in terms of guaranteeing wheelchair access and other provisions for the physically disabled. But the ADA's definition of disability includes "mental impairment that substantially limits one or more major life activities." During the ADA's first fifteen months, complaints of violations pertaining to mental disabilities were nearly 10 percent of all complaints, second only to complaints pertaining to back problems.

Regulations say "mental impairments" include "any mental or psychological disorder such as mental retardation, organic brain syndrome, emotional, or mental illness." But no regulation defines what constitutes emotional or mental illnesses. For that, as the ADA's legislative history and court cases arising from the ADA demonstrate, the authority is the fourth edition of the *Diagnostic and Statistical Manual of Mental Disorders* *(DSM-IV)* published by the American Psychiatric Association. In the context of the ADA, the *DSM-IV*'s nearly 900 pages have the potential to produce legal chaos and moral confusion.

Consider the *DSM-IV*'s definition of "oppositional defiant disorder" as a pattern of "negativistic, defiant, disobedient, and hostile behavior toward authority figures." Diagnostic criteria include "often loses temper," "often deliberately annoys people," "is often touchy," or "spiteful or vindictive."

The *DSM-IV*'s list of "personality disorders" includes "antisocial personality disorder" ("a pervasive pattern or disregard for . . . the rights of others . . . callous, cynical . . . an inflated and arrogant self-appraisal"); "histrionic personality disorder" ("excessive emotionality and attention-seeking . . . inappropriately sexually provocative or seductive"); "narcissistic personality disorder" ("grandiosity, need for admiration . . . boastful and pretentious . . . interpersonally exploitative . . . may assume that they do not have to wait in line"); "avoidant personality disorder" ("social inhibition, feelings of inadequacy"); "dependent personality disorder" ("submissive and clinging behavior"); "obsessive-compulsive personality disorder" ("preoccupation with orderliness, perfectionism . . . may be excessively conscientious, scrupulous . . . mercilessly self-critical . . . rigidly deferential to authority").

It is, as Zuriff says, momentous for society to decide that what once were considered faults of mind and flaws of character are "personality disorders" akin to physical disabilities that demand legal accommodation. Suggesting some of the real-world consequences of the psychiatric profession's success in medicalizing emotional problems, Zuriff asks: "How will workers react when they see chronically late, socially difficult, temperamental, or unlikable colleagues being given special privileges? What will workers think of sensitivity-training sessions that encourage them to tolerate, and even empathize with, a coworker who is rude or lacks self-control?"

Because lots of people manifest, at one time or another, many of the traits associated with various "disorders," judgments must be made about what is "excessive" manifestation. That will vary with particular cultures and contexts. Furthermore, we are, says Zuriff, far from knowing biological or psychological causes of "personality disorders" understood simply in terms of observed constellations of personality traits.

Zuriff believes that people manifesting these traits "should be held morally responsible for them. They should be encouraged to accommodate to society rather than the reverse." Instead, the ADA, as elaborated with regulations that inadequately clarify and limit the definitions of mental disabilities, encourages the proliferation of claimed disabilities. Thus does life imitate art. Read on.

In a satiric novel published just thirteen years ago, Peter De Vries wrote, "Once terms like identity doubts and midlife crisis become current, the reported cases of them increase by leaps and bounds." And, "Rapid-fire means of communication have brought psychic dilapidation within the reach of the most provincial backwaters, so that large metropolitan centers and educated circles need no longer consider it their exclusive property, nor preen themselves on their special malaises."

So it now is with mental disabilities. Name them and they will multiply, particularly if people who acquire them acquire power in the bargain. How long is thirteen years in modern America? Long enough to turn satire into solemn law.

April 4, 1996

Judges and the Definition of Marriage

Earlier in this century, Judge Learned Hand decried conservative judges who used the Constitution's "due process" guarantee to strike down economic legislation they disliked. This temperate man even suggested repeal of the "due process" provisions of the U.S. and state constitutions, or that a two-thirds majority of the Supreme Court be required to declare a law unconstitutional on due process grounds.

Today the consensus-building processes of democratic persuasion are again threatened by judicial abuses, this time of the "equal protection of the laws" guarantee in the U.S. and state constitutions. In Hawaii, judges seem likely to tickle from their state constitution's "equal protection" clause a right to contract same-sex marriages. Such a judicial preemption of political deliberation would come at a moment when that deliberation is being enriched by some thoughtful homosexual advocacy of same-sex marriage.

Serious arguments for such marriages, although not ultimately persuasive, merit political debate and legislative judgments on their merits. They should not be rendered irrelevant by some court's epiphany concerning a hitherto undetected constitutional right.

An example of the formidable advocacy of same-sex marriage is Jonathan Rauch's essay in the May 6 issue of *The New Republic*, wherein he concludes that the most important arguments for heterosexual marriage also justify homosexual marriage. Rauch, who is homosexual, comes to that conclusion with reasoning more nuanced than the syllogistic argument favored by many homosexual rights advocates: Marriage is for people who love, homosexuals love, therefore marriage is for them.

Rauch concedes that there is a burden of proof on those who, like himself, propose to change a settled practice of many cultures, religions, and centuries. But, he notes, the burden has been successfully dispatched by opponents of such settled practices as slavery, segregation, and antimiscegenation laws.

And, he asks, how settled is marriage? Traditions have relatively recently been unsettled by laws allowing women to own property independently of their husbands and to charge their husbands with rape. Will the institution of marriage, which has been manifestly unsettled by society's sudden embrace of no-fault divorce, be comparably unsettled by making marriage a status for which the homosexual 3 to 5 percent of the population is eligible?

An incapacity to have children cannot, any more than an unwillingness to have children, establish ineligibility, otherwise sterile men, postmenopausal women, and couples uninterested in child rearing would be ineligible. In a secular setting, such as American lawmaking, a sufficient justification of marriage, says Rauch, is its utility in "taming," "domesticating," "civilizing" men, who arguably are not naturally monogamous. Another sufficient justification is to formalize the caretaking necessitated by life's vicissitudes and old age. Both justifications pertain to homosexuals.

Vulnerabilities of Rauch's argument include: Same-sex marriage might aggravate the trivialization of marriage as a mere "lifestyle choice" or a mere means of acquiring benefits from employers and the welfare state. And Rauch does not adequately adumbrate a principle by which polygamy can be proscribed if marriage is justified in terms of the fact of loving commitment and the functions of taming and caretaking.

Furthermore, it is a mere hypothesis, and a dubious one, that same-sex marriage would have the domesticating effect associated with heterosexual marriage. Same-sex marriages would lack a central component of domesticity: offspring.

Rauch writes that "heterosexual society would rightly feel betrayed if, after legalization, homosexuals treated marriage as a minority taste rather than as a core institution of life." The betrayal might be more profound than that. Andrew Sullivan, a homosexual advocating same-sex marriage in his book *Virtually Normal*, casually writes that homosexual relationships may have facets that could "nourish the broader society," such as "greater understanding of the need for extramarital outlets." Sullivan writes that "the lack of children gives gay couples greater freedom." But marriage is more about responsibility than freedom. Why call what Sullivan wants, with its "outlets," marriage?

Whatever conclusion America comes to, it should reach by political debates that are resolved in representative institutions. The alternative is too costly.

Before the Supreme Court in 1973 arrogated to itself the setting of abortion policy, a vigorous national debate was underway, and many states were modifying abortion laws. The abrupt truncation of that democratic process by judges wielding a newly discovered "fundamental" right contributed to the embitterment of politics.

Worse will come if another eruption of judicial authoritarianism similarly shoves representative institutions away from the shaping of policy regarding marriage. Surely judges should heed Learned Hand's warning against "anticipating a doctrine which may be in the womb of time, but whose birth is distant."

May 19, 1996

Animosity and the Constitution

This is what constitutional law has come to. On Monday a six-person majority of the Supreme Court held that America's traditional and majority opposition to homosexuality is bigotry akin to racism. The Court held that this is not just a moral principle to which it subscribes, it is a principle suddenly excavated from the Constitution, a principle to which the nation must conform. So although a state may (under a 1986 ruling, mendaciously unmentioned by the majority) constitutionally criminalize homosexual conduct, it is suddenly unconstitutional for a state to prohibit granting special protections to homosexuals.

The six justices (Kennedy writing, joined by Stevens, O'Connor, Souter, Ginsburg, and Breyer) said all this when they held that the U.S. Constitution's guarantee of "equal protection of the laws" was violated when the people of Colorado enacted by referendum an amendment to their state constitution prohibiting state and local laws banning discrimination based on sexual preference. Justice Scalia, dissenting and joined by Rehnquist and Thomas, noted the majority's "heavy reliance upon principles of righteousness rather than judicial holdings," and accused the majority of concocting a constitutional impediment to a legitimate and traditional social goal, that of preventing "piecemeal deterioration of the sexual morality favored by a majority."

In 1992 a majority of Coloradans became provoked by the aggressive and successful campaigns of homosexuals and bisexuals for state and local laws protecting them against discrimination in jobs, housing, public accommodations, and other transactions. Supporters of the amendment said such laws violate privacy, associational, religious, and economic rights and liberties, and cumulatively constitute endorsement of the idea that homosexuality is a matter of moral indifference.

Colorado's supreme court declared the amendment an unconstitutional infringement of the right of homosexuals to "participate" in the political process. But the amendment did not prevent homosexuals from pressing their agenda. It simply meant that to do so, they must counter the success of their opponents by amending the state constitution. (The Court's reasoning has preposterous implications. For example, by that reasoning the Establishment Clause of the First Amendment is incompatible with the "equal protection" guarantee because a class of people defined by a single trait—people who favor establishment of religion—are denied equal "participation" in politics because in order to achieve their agenda they must amend the Constitution.)

In affirming the Colorado court's decision, the Supreme Court stressed that the amendment was a mere act of "animosity" against homosexuals, unrelated to a legitimate governmental purpose. The Court said it is "impossible" to believe that Coloradans really were worried about their associational rights, and implies that protecting traditional sexual mores is not a legitimate governmental goal.

The Court falsely asserted that the Colorado amendment's disqualification of a class of persons identified by "a single trait" from the right to obtain specific protection in the law is "unprecedented." Under the Arizona, Idaho, Utah, New Mexico, and Oklahoma constitutions, polygamy is "forever prohibited." Since Monday, either those provisions are unconstitutional or polygamists have fewer constitutional rights than homosexuals.

Scalia notes that Colorado, far from being seized by blind intolerance, is one of twenty-five states that have repealed laws criminalizing homosexual behavior, and that 46 percent of the voters opposed the amendment, which only prohibits giving homosexuals favored status because of their conduct. Homosexuals, Scalia argued, have the right of all Americans to seek, as they have done, to use democratic persuasion to change the legal system for "reinforcement of their moral sentiments." But they should be subject to democratic countermeasures, such as Colorado's amendment, which was a "modest attempt . . . to preserve traditional sexual mores against the efforts of a politically powerful minority to revise those mores through use of the laws."

The Court, says Scalia, has departed from anything recognizable as constitutional reasoning. Instead, it has taken sides in a cultural struggle on behalf of the views prevalent in a particular class and against the views represented in Congress, which has repeatedly refused to extend to homosexuals the protections of federal civil rights laws. Because the Constitution is silent on this subject, "it is left to be resolved by normal democratic means," and the Court "has no business imposing upon all Americans the resolution favored by the elite class from which the members of this institution are selected, pronouncing that 'animosity' toward homosexuality is evil."

To what has constitutional law come? "Terminal silliness," says Scalia. Monday's decision indicates that the condition is indeed terminal if constitutional law is supposed to be the application of principles derived from a respectful reading of the Constitution's text, and an interpretation of its structure, in the light of the Framers' intentions.

May 22, 1996

Dead End: From Topeka to Kansas City

Kansas City is just down the road from Topeka, where the crusade against school segregation began with what became the *Brown* v. *Board of Education* Supreme Court decision of 1954. Kansas City may henceforth be known as the end of the road for the crusade that went awry.

Last week the Supreme Court began to pry loose the grip of judicial arrogance from Kansas City, where a judge's unbridled willfulness has produced one of the most spectacular abuses of power, and failures of policy, in American history. After nine years and a cost of approximately $1.5 billion, a program with the one goal of increasing the nonminority enrollment in the city's schools has produced a school system in which such enrollment is lower than ever—below 25 percent. Furthermore, test scores are down, the dropout rate is up, and the principles of separation of powers and self-government have been violated. The only good that has come of this is Justice Clarence Thomas's concurring opinion when the Court emphatically reasserted that "local autonomy of school districts is a vital national tradition."

Missouri schools were segregated by law until 1954. In 1986, after nine years of litigation about removing the "vestiges" of segregation, a district judge, Russell Clark, decided that that goal justified judicial Caesarism. He seized control of not only the schools but also, in a sense, the city itself and a portion of the state's budget. He could not just order the usual futility—forced busing to shuffle children around to achieve a school-by-school racial balance pleasing to the judiciary. That social engineering has provoked black as well as white flight, reduced public support for public schools, and failed to prevent the proliferation of schools in which minorities are the majority. But in Kansas City there were not enough white children to shuffle because so many families had moved to the suburbs or across the state line into Kansas. Clark's solution was to decree "suburban comparability" in order to achieve "desegregative attractiveness." He ordered the creation within the city of "magnet" schools so attractive that white pupils from out of the district would enroll.

He ordered that money be lavished on fifty-six such schools. While wielding this executive power, he also exercised the legislative power to tax. When state constitutional and statutory limits on taxation prevented the school district from paying its judicially decreed share for the capital improvements, Clark enjoined the laws limiting taxes. The U.S. Supreme Court, in its first go-around with this case five years ago, approved this judicial overreaching. With Clark cracking his whip, various schools were endowed with Olympic-size swimming pools, planetariums, vivariums, greenhouses, a model United Nations wired for language translation, radio and television studios with an animation and editing lab, movie editing and screening rooms, a temperature-controlled art gallery, a dust-free diesel mechanics room, and much more. He ordered pay raises for all but three (what did *they* do to offend His Majesty?) of the approximately 5,000 employees of the school system. This delighted the teachers' union, which was spared the rigors of collective bargaining. Clark found in the U.S. Constitution a mandate that parking lot attendants, trash collectors, and food handlers be paid particular amounts.

But last week the Supreme Court, ruling against the wishes of four justices and the Clinton Justice Department, held that Clark improperly pursued "suburban comparability" and could not use the failure of the district's students to achieve national norms on standardized tests as an excuse to continue commandeering the state budget. The Court noted that per pupil expenditures in Kansas City far exceeded those in surrounding suburban districts. This is another blow to the theory, promoted by the public education lobby, that the best predictor of a school's cognitive output is the financial input into the school.

Fireworks came from Justice Thomas, who traced the cause of Clark's policy to the jurisprudence of liberal racism. "It never ceases to amaze me," wrote Thomas, "that the courts are so willing to assume that anything that is predominantly black must be inferior." The mere fact that a school is predominantly black does not, said Thomas, prove that the school is the product of, or is, a constitutional violation. It is not surprising that there will be predominantly black schools in a district where population is predominantly black. Such "racial isolation" long after de jure segregation has ended may reflect voluntary housing choices and other private decisions, not impermissible state actions.

But, Thomas wrote, the assumption of black inferiority, buttressed by dubious social science, has given rise to the notion that black students suffer some unspecified psychological harm when they are not in school with white children. "This position appears to rest upon the idea that any school that is black is inferior, and that blacks cannot succeed without the benefit of the company of whites."

Thomas said Clark misread the *Brown* decision as saying that "racially isolated" schools are inherently inferior. Actually, the harm *Brown* identified was linked entirely to the stigma of inferiority imposed by state action establishing de jure segregation. Said Thomas, "After all, if separation itself is a harm, and if integration therefore is the only way that blacks can achieve a proper education, then there must be something inferior about blacks." Under this theory, even de facto segregation injures blacks—but not whites. So, according to Thomas, the theory must be that "blacks, when left on their own, cannot achieve. To my way of thinking, that conclusion is the result of a jurisprudence based upon a theory of black inferiority."

The road from Topeka to Kansas City is straight and smooth. But the road from *Brown* to this most recent school-related case—a case ostensibly about segregation but really about using racial patterns as pretexts for social engineering—has been winding and bumpy. The decision to restrain Judge Clark is one more sign that the nation is escaping from the intellectual dead end of solving social problems—including the most intractable ones, regarding race—by allowing judges to bend the Constitution to the service of their political agendas.

June 26, 1995

The Dangerous Cult of Cultural Diversity

The ruling of the U.S. Court of Appeals for the 5th Circuit concerning affirmative action in the admissions process at the University of Texas Law School may or may not be momentous. Unless and until it is appealed to and affirmed by the Supreme Court, it applies only to Texas, Louisiana, and Mississippi. But if it is affirmed, its significance will transcend constitutional law.

The dynamite in the circuit court's ruling is the assertion that racial preferences can never be justified as a means of achieving "diversity." This means affirmative action policies, which often are referred to as "race-based remedies," must be just that—remedial, narrowly tailored to correct specific discrimination by the particular institution, not by society generally.

The diversity rationale for affirmative action has served the double purpose of broadening the racial spoils system by severing it from mere remediation, and making it permanent by putting it in the service of an endless project. But the deeper significance of the cult of "cultural" diversity in higher education is that it denotes an aggressive ideology concerning the meaning of culture, the aims of education, and the merits of the United States.

It is serendipitous that the circuit court's ruling coincides with the publication, in *The Public Interest* quarterly, of Clifford Orwin's essay "All Quiet on the (Post) Western Front?" Orwin, an American political scientist at the University of Toronto, unpacks from "diversity" the full agenda of multiculturalism.

Before the ascendancy in academic circles of what Orwin calls the relativistic understanding of culture, the idea of culture was connected to the idea of intellectual cultivation, which is a difficult attainment, not a democratic entitlement. But, says Orwin, cultural relativism asserts that every "people" (nowadays this means every racial, ethnic, or other group organized around a grievance) has a culture, understood as the totality of its social practices, and all cultures are equal in the sense that there are no neutral principles—no principles that are not themselves mere emanations of a culture—for evaluating them.

Multiculturalism is a fact; Americans have various racial and ethnic backgrounds and experiences. But multiculturalism as a policy is not, Orwin argues, primarily a response to that fact. Rather, it is an ideology, the core tenet of which is this: Because all standards for judging culture are themselves culture-bound, it is wrong to "privilege" Western culture, and right to tailor university admissions and curricula to rectify the failure to extend proper "recognition" and "validation" to other cultures.

The Dangerous Cult of Cultural Diversity

Orwin says this "inclination to treat students ascriptively rather than as individuals" translates into the right of ever-more recondite "cultures" (for example, "gays and lesbians of color") to "construct a playground of their own at university expense"—a course of their own, a department, a dormitory. Because supposedly "marginalized" cultures are defined in opposition to the oppressive dominant culture, Orwin says multiculturalism has less to do with the serious study of other cultures than with promoting a particular interpretation of American culture.

As a result, "multiculturalism is not ecumenical but adversarial." And "one will rarely encounter a more efficient engine of intellectual sameness than this ideology which celebrates difference."

Multiculturalism does not mean the replacement of the familiar by the strange. Rather, says Orwin, it means the replacement of the strange by the familiar as popular culture gains in panache as a subject of supposedly serious study. This is because popular culture—for example, movies and other entertainments—is understood either as a conspiracy by which the masses are controlled or the means by which the masses express resistance to control.

In contrast, old books have two defects: they are old and they are books. Being old, they are mere representations of power relations (all works of the mind are merely such representations) in irrelevant social orders. And because there are no permanent standards, it is fallacious to think that old things can be what Orwin calls "permanent beacons for thoughtful human beings." Being books, they require reading and what Orwin calls "the habits of rumination appropriate to them." This explains "the aversion of today's students to reading."

All this may seem distant from the question of the unconstitutionality of different law school admissions standards for different races. But behind the seemingly bland and benign celebration of "diversity" there simmers an ideology of disparagement regarding this nation, and an agenda of what the circuit court calls "racial social engineering." The full resonance of the court's ruling could make the ruling an event as important as the presidential election.

March 28, 1996

Arizona, a Conquered Province

President Clinton, toiling to re-reinvent himself, says he is rethinking racial policies and restraining Washington's overreaching. However, because of appointees he drew from among his party's unchastened and unreconstructed liberals, his administration's tendencies continue, regardless of his rhetoric.

Consider the Justice Department's remarkably meretricious attempt to coerce two Arizona counties into racial gerrymandering. The attempt annoys some of its supposed beneficiaries, local Native Americans who understand something that Justice's social engineers either cannot comprehend or consider irrelevant: The change Washington wants to impose would be injurious to the Native Americans' interests.

Because population growth has produced crowded court dockets, Coconino and Navajo counties each want to add two elected judges. But because of past discrimination, since 1972 Arizona has been one of sixteen states entirely or partially "covered" by a portion of the Voting Rights Act that requires it to seek Justice Department approval for all voting "changes."

Deval Patrick, who became head of Justice's civil rights division when Lani Guinier didn't, insists that merely adding judges constitutes voting "changes." Actually, the only changes relevant to the section of the act that Patrick cites are voting process changes that cause "retrogression" in minority voting strength. By his tendentious reading of the act, Patrick imposes on the counties the burden of justifying their long-standing method of electing judges (in countywide elections) before implementing an increase in the number of judges.

Patrick's next intellectual somersault is to say that elections in the two counties "are characterized by racially polarized voting." The ostensible proof of this is that although Coconino and Navajo counties are 29 percent and 51 percent Native American respectively, no Native Americans have been elected to county offices under at-large voting. To remedy this supposed denial of "equal opportunity to participate in the electoral process and to elect judicial candidates of their choice," Patrick, sitting in his Washington office proposes Balkanizing each county into judicial districts, one of which in each county would have a huge Native-American majority.

Patrick's premise is a non sequitur: The absence of Native-American judges proves that Native-American voters have insufficient voice in judicial selections. Each of the following three facts refutes that.

First, there are probably fewer than half a dozen Native Americans in each county who have been members of the Arizona bar for five years, a legal prerequisite for judges. Second, tribal and federal courts have jurisdiction over almost all cases concerning Native Americans living on reservations (where 90.6 percent of Navajo County and 74.2 percent of Coconino County Native Americans live). Thus even if there were created a judicial district with a Native-American majority that regularly elected a Native-American judge, that judge would have few cases involving Native Americans. Third, in the past decade no judge has been elected in either county without winning more Native-American votes than any other candidate.

This last explains the opposition Patrick's plan provokes among some Native Americans who actually live where Patrick seeks to rearrange things. By ending countywide voting and carving within the county a Native-American majority district, Patrick's scheme might well produce a Native-American judge (on a court to which no Native American has ever sought election). But the scheme would do so at the cost of eliminating the decisive influence that Native-American voters currently have on all the countywide judicial elections.

This absurd outcome would flow from the peculiar premise (necessary to justify blocking the counties' new judgeships) that increasing the number of judgeships decreases the likelihood of a Native American winning a judgeship. But such is the politics of diversity-mongering.

Somebody in Washington decides that there is something wrong with the racial composition of the judiciary in two Arizona counties, and that therefore there must be something illegal about the judicial selection process, and suddenly neither logic nor the plain meaning of words or laws can inhibit the extremism of the diversity enforcers. So now Arizona learns how prescient Justice Hugo Black was when, looking askance at some provisions of the Voting Rights Act, he warned that states required to "entreat federal authorities in faraway places for approval of local laws" seem to be "little more than conquered provinces."

This skirmish in the federal government's ongoing assault on reason and Americans' sensibilities will not measurably decrease the president's chances of carrying Arizona, the only state to vote Republican in every presidential election since 1948. But the skirmish illustrates why when the president talks moderation, people everywhere will do well to remember this adage about judging a politician: Don't watch his mouth, watch his feet.

March 12, 1995

The Case Against
Categorical Representation

When Sir Arthur Stanley Eddington (1882–1944), the astrophysicist, was asked how many people understood his theory of the expanding universe, he paused, then said, "Perhaps seven." That may be more people than fully understand how we got from the Voting Rights Act of 1965 to the notion that racial gerrymandering is not only virtuous but also mandatory under that act.

Such gerrymandering to create "minority-majority" electoral districts is the quintessential "outcome-based" racial policy and a provocative political entitlement. The purpose of drawing lines to create districts in which minorities constitute a majority of the voters is to assist, virtually to the point of ensuring, the election of minorities to offices to which they presumably are entitled by virtue of their race or ethnicity. The result is "political apartheid," to use Justice O'Connor's phrase from the 1993 ruling invalidating North Carolina's districting scheme that produced the 160-mile-long district that straggled down Interstate 85 and for most of its length was no wider than the highway. Other racially concocted districts have shapes like roadkill—like raccoons that have had run-ins with eighteen-wheelers. All such districts rest on the assumption that people of a particular race will and should think and act alike. This assumption undergirds the doctrine of categorical representation, which holds that the interests of people in certain racial, ethnic, or sexual categories can be understood, sympathized with, articulated, and advanced only by other people in those categories.

The 1965 act was written to guarantee to blacks the right to vote, a right long denied by many devices such as discriminatorily administered registration requirements or literacy tests, or naked violence. The act was passed after the civil rights march to Montgomery from Selma, a town where the population was 42 percent black but less than 1 percent of voters were black. The act was a swift success. Between 1964 and 1969 the number of blacks registered to vote in the eleven states of the former Confederacy more than doubled. In 1963 there had been fewer than 100 black elected officials in those states. In 1973 there were 191 in Mississippi.

But in the hands of lawyers who regard legislation as merely the launching pad for litigation, the act was increasingly construed to mandate government measures to ration political power among certain preferred groups. Amended with opaque language in 1982, it was subsequently read to entitle certain groups to political set-asides—offices they were sure to win. It was read to guarantee not just each individual's right to vote but certain groups' entitlements to win quotas of offices. It was read to mean that for blacks and Hispanics, the *reality* of the right to vote could be proven only by certain electoral results. Republicans, particularly President Bush's Justice Department, connived at this misconstruction of the act for partisan advantage: When blacks, who generally are reliable Democratic voters, are swept from many districts into one district, all the districts contiguous to that new "minority-majority" district become easier for Republicans to carry. The liberal transformation of the act since 1965, recently abetted by cynical Republicans, is one reason Newt Gingrich is Speaker of the House on the thirtieth anniversary of the act.

The transformation was somewhat reversed last week when the Supreme Court held, 5–4, that the act cannot compel what the Constitution forbids. At issue was Georgia's Eleventh Congressional District, a splatter on the map from Atlanta all the way to Savannah (to within a few miles of Justice Thomas's birthplace in Pin Point). The Court held that the district violates the fourteenth Amendment's guarantee of equal protection of the laws because race was the "predominant" factor when the state legislature drew the district's meandering lines—lines that can have no other explanation. Under pressure from the Justice Department, which was supporting the ACLU's "Max-Black" plan to produce a third black majority district, Georgia's legislature subordinated to racial considerations such traditional race-neutral districting principles as compactness, contiguity, and respect for political subdivisions and communities defined by actual shared interests.

Justice Kennedy, writing for the majority and joined by Justices Rehnquist, O'Connor, Scalia, and Thomas, detected in Georgia's districting "the offensive and demeaning assumption" that voters of a particular race will, because of their race, have the same political preferences. But to give Georgia its due, the state did not claim to be acting to implement any theory, such as categorical representation, or to remedy past discrimination. It did what it did just to get the Justice Department off its back. Makes you wonder why it is called Justice.

Justice Ginsburg, joined in dissent by Justices Stevens, Souter, and Breyer, correctly notes that legislatures have often been respectful of ethnic bonds in drawing district lines that produce such entities as are routinely referred to as "the predominantly Italian wards of South Philadelphia" or a "Polish district in Chicago." But what the dissenters elide is the distinction between somewhat trimming a district's lines to conform to a compact racial or ethnic community, and drawing race-driven lines to create an illusory political "community" that the organic life of society has not created.

The creation of "minority-majority" districts expresses the ideology of "identity politics": You are whatever your racial or ethnic group is. But that ideology, promulgated by political entrepreneurs with a stake in the racial and ethnic spoils system, is false regarding the facts of human differences, and bad as an aspiration and an exhortation. Furthermore, such districts are bad for the public weal because they reduce the incentive for politicians to form coalitions by reaching across racial lines.

Last week's ruling will make the Justice Department and courts less involved in allocating political offices by predetermining election results. As a result there may be fewer "minority-majority" districts. But that does not necessarily mean there will be fewer minority members of Congress. One of Speaker Gingrich's loyal soldiers in the House is J. C. Watts, a freshman from Oklahoma's fourth district. Watts is black. Only 7 percent of the fourth district is black. Obviously the people of that healthy district have not embraced the principle of categorical representation.

July 10, 1995

Dismaying Good News About Race

Professional auditors of racial rectitude seem dismayed by the good news. They insist, with the ingenuity characteristic of ideologues defending theories from discordant facts and the tenacity of factions defending their functions, that the news is not as good as it appears.

When the Supreme Court ruled that bizarrely shaped congressional districts are unconstitutional if race—the goal of collecting minority voters to produce a majority—was the predominant factor in the drawing of them, Jesse Jackson said this limit on racial gerrymandering would produce an "ethnic cleansing of Congress," an ACLU leader foresaw "the bleaching of Congress," and an NAACP leader, summoning memories of lynchings, said, "the noose is tightening." But this year all five black incumbents whose districts were redrawn—two each in Texas and Georgia, one in Florida—were reelected, with majorities ranging from 54 percent to 77 percent, in districts where nonblacks are from 56 percent to 65 percent of the population.

Those who had argued the necessity of racial gerrymandering say the five were reelected because of the power of incumbency, which was the result of such gerrymandering. But the NAACP official who said incumbency "gives you the ability to raise money and get your message out" was conceding the decisiveness of message rather than race.

Why, in the face of good news, insist on the unabated malignant salience of race in the nation's life? Because modern liberalism has a stake in that fiction. Such liberalism, the rationale for the regulatory state, postulates that America's masses have deficits of competence and goodness that require remedial government.

Such liberalism was born with the century, at the high tide of confidence in science, including political science (a former professor of which was elected president in 1912), and in the reign of experts. Liberalism held that, given the complexities of modern life and the anachronistic—or worse—nature of local institutions and attachments, the average American needed succor and supervision from the central government. Power must be concentrated in Washington, and Washington power concentrated in the presidency rather than Congress, which is a concentration of parochial people.

The 1930s were happy days for liberals—"Happy days are here again!"—because the Depression heightened Americans' feelings of dependency. But six decades later, a leader of liberalism (Hillary Rodham Clinton) still insists "it takes a president" to raise a child and an act of Congress is needed to help Americans get pets to vets. When the postwar boom and the democratization of higher education increased Americans' sense of social competence, the civil rights movement rescued liberalism from irrelevance by giving government a new mission, that of improving the behavior and, by doing so, improving the character of Americans regarding race. It was liberalism's finest hour. Statecraft became soulcraft, successfully. But today liberals discount the success, lest irrelevance loom again.

To guarantee an unendable crisis for liberalism to cope with, liberals encourage "identity politics," the premise being that identities, and rights, derive from group membership, and special rights are owed to grievance groups composed of America's myriad victims. A corollary is "categorical representation," the theory that the interests of particular groups can be articulated only by members of those groups. Such thinking produces racial gerrymandering and other racial preferences, including O. J. Simpson's acquittal.

Liberalism's self-serving obsession with race is not only irrational (if the skin color of everyone in Harlem were changed, would their life prospects markedly improve?), it threatens the rule of law, as Jeffrey Rosen argues in a trenchant essay in *The New Republic*. He argues that the essentially lawless act of the Simpson jury was sediment from our trickle-down culture. The defense's argument—insinuation, really—was that objectivity is impossible and hence willfulness is permissible. This invitation to anarchy that produced the jury's low act flowed from high theory—"critical race theory"—that flourishes in prestigious law schools. It says: The civil rights movement was futile because futility is foreordained in a society where endemic racism defines everyone's experiences and conditions perceptions. Each group explains reality as it experiences it, through "narratives" that are unintelligible, or at least unpersuasive, to other groups. Racism is so institutionalized that all blacks, Simpson included, are victims by definition, not by anything so mundane as identifiable acts of discrimination. Race is "socially constructed," so blacks who deviate from group thinking are (to use Lani Guinier's words) not "authentic" but merely "descriptively black."

Given contemporary liberalism's intellectual and political investment in racial fatalism, it dismisses as delusions developments that less-clouded minds see as simply good news.

November 28, 1996

Gotham Gets "Reality Therapy"

NEW YORK—When students at the city university recently jammed streets around city hall to vent indignation about budget cuts that portend tuition increases, they carried signs denouncing Mayor Giuliani, but misspelling his name, as well as "tiution" and "priorty." Those signs were indications either that more money is needed for higher education, or that less money should be entrusted to the people responsible for that university. Whichever, the turmoil was just one manifestation of resistance to budgets that Giuliani calls "reality therapy."

It is an old axiom that in politics if you have no choice, you have no problem. That is the only sense in which Giuliani has no problem. He has no choice but to cut continuously at the city's government because the alternative is implosion. That occurs when rising taxes and declining quality of life drive more and more of a city's tax base—people and businesses—to flee the city, leaving the remainder of the steadily shrinking base to bear a steadily increasing burden.

Last year the city budget was smaller than the year before, and this year Giuliani has proposed a still smaller budget achieved by spending cuts of a severity not seen here since the depths of the Depression. He says his aim is to make New York "more like a normal city." That is the reverse of what New York has, through much of this century, striven to be politically, but it is a worthy aspiration for a city that has more people on welfare (1.2 million—more than one in seven people) than in public schools and that has three times more admissions to Rikers Island jail each year than to the freshman classes on the city university campuses. Normality would be welcome in a city where in a recent year there were 78,000 calls—one every seven minutes—to the 911 emergency line reporting gunshots, which are so common that many go unreported.

New York in its proud abnormality spends twice as much per capita on its residents as Chicago or Boston, twice as much per capita on welfare as Los Angeles. Chicago has approximately fourteen city employees for every 1,000 residents. New York has fifty. Giuliani proposes privatizing three of the sixteen city-run hospitals. It is a rare city that operates even three hospitals. The city owns a television station and two radio stations. Why? Because for decades the political culture here was not receptive to the question, "Why is government doing this?"

What the city government was trying to do was teach the rest of the nation how to be progressive. The city was proud to be "the capital of the American century" and "the world's destination," and part of this chosen role was to extend the New Deal idea—largely a product of New York political and intellectual circles—of government that is omnipresent and omniprovident. One result is that today New Yorkers must bob and weave to avoid paying twenty-three different taxes.

Giuliani, required to balance the budget, has asked Governor George Pataki to cut spending on welfare and Medicaid even more than Pataki has planned, because the city must match such spending. There is a proposal for earning $10 million by selling advertising in city parks—on basketball backboards and softball field fences. And then there is the matter of taxis.

The fleet of yellow cabs numbers 11,787. It has been that size since 1937. As a result of this government restriction of entry into the business, a taxi medallion—a license to operate a taxi—now sells for about $175,000. The city could raise more than $60 million by selling 400 new ones, but that would depress the value of existing medallions, so the taxi interests will fight to keep the city forever in 1937.

Want to buy a city-owned golf course? A city-owned hotel? One of those radio stations? Do policemen, who can retire on full pensions after twenty years in uniform, really need a paid day off each year to purchase uniforms? If all the public school teachers were actually teaching, the pupil-teacher ratio could be sixteen to one instead of thirty to one. But inch after agonizing inch, Giuliani is making progress. For example, prompted by the prospect of privatization, garbage collectors now work more than six hours a day.

New York in its political vanity used to be called "the city that longs to belong to another country." Today the municipal government that once fancied itself the nation's moral model is reduced to scrambling for small sums, like an indigent groping for change between the cushions of a sofa in the lobby of a seedy hotel.

April 9, 1995

New York, Between Singapore and Dodge City

NEW YORK—Seven million souls live here, doing New York things—littering, jumping over subway turnstiles, saying how boring it must be to live in New Jersey, and being rude to one another. But until recently approximately seventy-five New Yorkers were making the city even more neurotic than it normally is. They were the "squeegee men."

Given the media attention to them, and the anxiety caused by them, people were astonished to learn that there were not 7,500 of them. Their story says a lot about urban living, and policing, and how little things mean a lot.

Squeegee men hung around a few congested intersections and bridge and tunnel toll plazas, "offering" to wash windshields for a fee. They relied on intimations of vandalism to vehicles whose drivers did not accept their offers. Most squeegee men were neither homeless nor poor; most had arrest records. Now they have mostly gone into another line of work, because the police decided that they contributed to the city's demoralizing atmosphere of incipient disorder.

Police rousted the squeegee men on the grounds that they were obstructing traffic. Didn't any civil liberties lawyers have a conniption? No, says Police Commissioner William Bratton, people "are tired of 'anything goes.' "

The mayor, Rudy Giuliani, is a former prosecutor. Bratton is a kindred spirit. This place is still a far cry from Singapore in its commitment to order, but neither is it, as it until recently was, a combination of Dodge City and Calcutta.

Just a few years ago, intellectuals, who are more plentiful here than is healthy (and who rarely ride subways), were praising as folk art the graffiti that gang members and other preintellectual New Yorkers were spraying on subway cars. Most subway riders considered it vandalism producing an atmosphere of menace. Today, says Bratton, the city's 6,000 subway cars are virtually free of graffiti. Some intellectuals probably see this as a sign of the suffocation of the masses' creativity. The masses find it reassuring.

New York, Between Singapore and Dodge City

Like a corporate CEO with his eye on the bottom line, Bratton knows his numbers, such as: 307. On a recent day that was how many fewer New Yorkers had been homicide victims this year compared with the same date last year. This is the biggest numerical one-year drop in the city's history. It is a somewhat alarming triumph, given what it says about the level from which the decline began. (There were 1,946 homicides in 1993.) There is similar mixed comfort to be taken from the fact that there have been 820 fewer shootings and 11,000 fewer robberies so far this year.

The decline is partly the result of preventive policing, particularly in pursuit of guns. But the city should brace itself for a demographic bump in the road to bliss: In 1997–98 there will be a bulge in the size of the unruly fourteen-to-nineteen age group.

However, Bratton is inoculated by experience against the despair that afflicts people bailing oceans with thimbles. As head of the transit police from 1987 to 1990, he oversaw substantial success policing the city's subway system.

The system never was, he insists, as dangerous as its reputation suggested. Only about twenty homicides occurred in the subways each year, a reassuring number here, which tells a lot about the city. Bratton rightly emphasizes that the system handles 3.5 million riders a day and they are protected by 4,000 transit cops who respond to about forty-five crimes a day.

Forty-five, that is, not counting the 80,000 fare-evaders who jump turnstiles daily. Until recently, the 80,000 were not defined as a police problem. Hence there was a problem of police morale—too many cops concerned with a few crimes, while turnstile jumpers produced a climate of chaos.

Bratton knew there couldn't be a cop at every turnstile, but there could be "sweep teams" swooping down on fare-evaders. And guess what was swept up: One in seven was the subject of an arrest warrant. One in twenty was carrying an illegal weapon. Subway crime is a "crime of opportunity" and suddenly, because the police were more active, there were fewer opportunities. Subway crime declined for thirty-eight consecutive months, 48 percent overall.

Until recently Bryant Park behind the Public Library in midtown was a drug market, as were some public places around Wall Street. Until recently it took twenty-seven hours to process the paperwork—twelve forms—for an arrest. With computers it takes less than four hours, so more police are out policing, and more New Yorkers can safely go around behaving the way they usually do, which is not a crime, quite.

December 1, 1994

Shaming

A New Hampshire state legislator says of teenage vandals, "These little turkeys have got total contempt for us, and it's time to do something." His legislation would authorize public, bare-bottom spanking, a combination of corporal punishment and shaming—degradation to lower the offender's social status.

In 1972 Delaware became the last state to abolish corporal punishment of criminals. Most states abandoned such punishments almost 150 years ago, for reasons explained by professor Dan M. Kahan of the University of Chicago Law School in an essay to be published in the spring issue of that school's law review. But he also explains why Americans are, and ought to be, increasingly interested in punishment by shaming. Such punishment uses the infliction of reputational harm to deter crime and to perform an expressive function.

Around America various jurisdictions are punishing with stigmatizing publicity (publishing in newspapers or on billboards or broadcasting the names of drug users, drunk drivers, or men who solicit prostitutes or are delinquent in child support); with actual stigmatization (requiring persons convicted of drunk driving to display license plates or bumper stickers announcing the conviction and requiring a woman to wear a sign reading I AM A CONVICTED CHILD MOLESTER); with self-debasement (sentencing a slumlord to house arrest in one of his rat-infested tenements and permitting victims of burglars to enter the burglars' homes and remove items of their choosing); with contrition ceremonies (requiring juvenile offenders to apologize while on their hands and knees).

In "What Do Alternative Sanctions Mean?" Kahan argues that such penalties can be efficacious enrichments of the criminal law's expressive vocabulary. He believes America relies too heavily on imprisonment, which is extraordinarily expensive and may not be more effective than shaming punishments at deterring criminal actions or preventing recidivism.

There are many ways to make criminals uncomfortable besides deprivation of liberty. And punishment should do more than make offenders suffer; the criminal law's expressive function is to articulate society's moral condemnation. Actions do not always speak louder than words but they always speak—always have meaning. And the act of punishing by shaming is a powerful means of shaping social preferences by instilling in citizens an aversion to certain kinds of prohibited behavior.

For most violent offenses, incarceration may be the only proper punishment. But most of America's inmates were not convicted of violent crimes.

Shaming

Corporal punishment is an inadequate substitute for imprisonment because, Kahan says, of "expressive connotations" deriving from its association with slavery and other hierarchical relationships, as between kings and subjects.

However, corporal punishment became extinct not just because democratization made American sensibilities acutely uncomfortable with those connotations. Shame, even more than the physical pain of the lash and the stocks, was the salient ingredient in corporal punishment. But as communities grew and became more impersonal, the loosening of community bonds lessened the sting of shame.

Not only revulsion toward corporal punishment but faith in the "science," as it was called, of rehabilitation produced America's reliance on imprisonment. And shame—for example, allowing the public to view prisoners at work—occasionally was an additive of incarceration. It is so today with the revival of chain gangs.

Recent alternatives to imprisonment have included fines and sentencing to community service. However, both are inadequately expressive of condemnation. Fines condemn ambivalently because they seem to put a price on behavior rather than proscribe it. The dissonance in community-service sentences derives from the fact that they fail to say something true, that the offenders deserve severe condemnation, and that they say something false, that community service, an admirable activity which many people perform for pleasure and honor, is a suitable way to signify a criminal's disgrace.

Sentences that shame not only do reputational harm and lower self-esteem, their consequences can include serious financial hardship. And Kahan argues: "The breakdown of pervasive community ties at the onset of the Industrial Revolution may have vitiated the stake that many individuals had in social status; but the proliferation of new civic and professional communities—combined with the advent of new technologies for disseminating information—have at least partially restored it for many others."

Today America has 519 people imprisoned for every 100,000 citizens. The figures for Mexico and Japan are ninety-seven and thirty-six respectively. America needs all the prison cells it has and will need more. But policies of indiscriminate incarceration will break states' budgets: The annual cost of incarceration is upward of $20,000 per prisoner and $69,000 for prisoners over age sixty. It would be a shame to neglect cheaper and effective alternatives.

February 1, 1996

Corrections Cocktails and Supermax

JESSUP, MARYLAND—The winter wind seems as lacerating as the razor wire through which it whistles. Upward of 100 miles of such wire, atop the several high fences and in coils between those fences, discourage inmates from trying to leave the maximum security prison here.

But some of the prisoners are more easily confined than controlled in confinement, and a few must be controlled by the threat, or fact, of confinement elsewhere, in what is called supermax. That is an even more strict regime prison that fills a block in downtown Baltimore.

Maryland's Division of Correction, and the men and women who do the dangerous daily work in the cellblocks here, say supermax is "the pressure release valve on a pressure cooker" and is indispensable. President Clinton's Justice Department says it, and others like it around the country (John Gotti is in a federal supermax in Marion, Illinois), may be unconstitutional. But, then, the Justice Department's lawyers may never have been exposed to a "corrections cocktail."

In the last decade, Maryland added more than 1,000 prison beds a year. It now has more than 22,000. None of the 1,800 men here should be on the streets now. (The recidivism rate for persons released from this prison is almost 45 percent: Recidivists are back inside within three years.) About 1,300 of the 1,800 will not be out for a long time—if ever. They are lifers, 98 percent of them murderers. They would be hard to control even if the culture and politics were not making matters worse.

Corrections officers and older inmates are similarly appalled at the increasing viciousness of younger convicts. And a political development has complicated the task of controlling the lifers among them.

Until recently, life-with-parole sentences meant an average time served of twenty-two years, if the inmate were paroled at all, which gave at least some prisoners a faint horizon of hope which, though distant, exerted a benign controlling influence. However, in 1994 the current governor, Parris Glendening, came here to pledge that no lifer would be paroled while he was governor, unless the lifer were elderly, or terminally ill.

Some national corrections professionals—hardly a sentimental lot— tersely describe this pledge, which is apt to become standard for Maryland's gubernatorial candidates, as "troubling." One official says, "It shut off the light at the end of the tunnel." So now institutional behavior has less meaning for the futures of 1,300 demonstrably dangerous lifers.

Now, says one prison administrator, the younger, most frightening prisoners (there currently are two fifteen-year-olds in the system), particularly the lifers, come inside convinced that "all they can do is get a reputation," the coin that purchases prestige and safety (in prison argot, preventing someone from "making me a girl"). The quickest way to get that coin is to hurt someone—usually another prisoner, sometimes a correctional officer.

Then there is the explosive force of boredom. Aside from making license plates, there are too few jobs for the mostly young males whose failures of self-restraint got them here. In the cellblock reserved for the most recalcitrant, the officers offer to walk a visitor down the cell-lined hallway, but warn him about "corrections cocktails"—mixtures of feces and urine sometimes thrown at officers for the sheer sport of it.

For the few untamable prisoners, there is supermax. There prisoners are in their cells twenty-three hours a day, without radios or televisions until those amenities have been earned by good behavior. Prisoners eat in their cells, the food coming through slots in solid metal doors. When they come out for showers or exercise, they back up to their cell doors, are shackled and accompanied by two officers. No prisoner even sees another prisoner. The average stay is sixteen to eighteen months. The only prisoners permanently there have killed while in prison, or are under sentence of death. Before California built a supermax, one in 1,200 prisoners was murdered. Now the rate is one in 12,000.

The Justice Department's apparent theory is that, even absent evidence of physical abuse, Maryland's supermax, and presumably similar institutions in twenty-nine other states, are inherently unconstitutional ("cruel and unusual punishment"). A thirteen-page Justice Department letter to Glendening lists various violations of constitutional rights, including insufficient exercise equipment and food insufficiently hot.

However, the crux of the case against supermaxes is that they do not produce rehabilitation, which supposedly is a prisoner's "right." To which the answer is: The primary function of prisons is safety—that of society outside, but also of prisoners and the prison staff. Besides, a precondition of rehabilitation is conformity to the regime of incarceration, which supermaxes teach to the teachable.

January 12, 1997

1937: Leviathan's Birth

In Nathaniel Hawthorne's day, as today, and as usual in America, the voices of various "experts" and "realists" gravely warned that society's problems were more daunting than ever and demanded that old principles yield to new realities. Hawthorne, however, kept his head. It was time, he said, to consult "those respectable old blockheads who still . . . kept a death grip on one or two ideas which had not come into vogue since yesterday morning."

Two weeks ago the Supreme Court dusted off an idea that has not been in vogue since 1937, an idea that went out of fashion exactly 150 years after the Constitutional Convention of 1787 made it a bedrock principle of the Republic. Now the Court has reaffirmed it, but only by a 5–4 vote. Still, the decision in the Lopez case indicates, more strongly than all the fermenting rhetoric from the political branches of the federal government, that 1995 really might be remembered as a year of restoration.

"We start with first principles," said Chief Justice Rehnquist, who enjoys doing just that. "The Constitution creates a federal government of enumerated powers." The case that occasioned Rehnquist's exercise in intellectual archaeology began in 1990 when Congress, seized by one of its frequent fits of grandstanding about crime, passed the Gun-Free School Zones Act, criminalizing possession of firearms in or near schools. Obviously gun-free schools are a good idea, which is why forty states already have such laws. Congress's largely redundant law was remarkable neither as a further step in its almost absentminded federalization of criminal law, nor as yet another careless assertion by Congress that there is no problem too local to be beyond its purview. But Congress's 1990 law is now remarkable for having aroused the Court from its dogmatic slumbers and moved it to give a jerk on the leash that Congress is astonished to learn that it still wears.

In 1992 Alfonso Lopez, a San Antonio twelfth-grader, was arrested under the Texas law banning guns in schools. Federal prosecutors elbowed aside Texas authorities, and Lopez responded with a question that seemed like a constitutional impertinence: Where does the federal government get the right to exercise what are essentially local police powers? The federal government gave the answer it has routinely, almost reflexively, given to many such questions since 1937: We get it from the Commerce Clause, so pipe down.

In what has come to be known as "the constitutional revolution of 1937" the Supreme Court stepped out of the way of the New Deal's drive to expand the reach of federal power. It essentially stopped enforcing limits to the Constitution's grant of power to Congress to "regulate commerce . . . among the several states." Almost any activity could be said to have "substantial effects" on interstate commerce, and so Congress could regulate almost any activity. But this was an invitation to, indeed an incitement to, constitutional sophistry. It threatened to rationalize the annihilation of the distinction between national and local problems, and between federal responsibilities and state and local responsibilities. Thus it went far toward making a mockery of the idea of limited government.

In a muscular concurrence with Rehnquist's opinion for the majority, Justice Thomas minced no words: "Apart from its recent vintage and its corresponding lack of any grounding in the original understanding of the Constitution, the substantial effects test suffers from the further flaw that it appears to grant Congress a police power over the nation. When asked at oral argument if there were *any* limits to the Commerce Clause, the government was at a loss for words. Likewise, the principal dissent insists that there are limits, but it cannot muster even one example."

The author of that dissent, the newest justice, Breyer, essentially accepted the argument made by the government that schools can be considered to be engaged in commercial activities, and that therefore the possession of a gun by an individual near a school can be regulated by Congress because—take a deep breath—the gun might produce violence which would affect the economy by spreading insurance costs throughout the population, and by reducing the willingness of individuals to travel, and by injuring the learning environment and thus resulting in a less-productive citizenry. But as Rehnquist said, Breyer's rationale could classify child rearing as a commercial activity that Congress can regulate. Given Breyer's willingness to justify constitutional permissiveness because of the extended ripple effects that any activity can have on commerce, how could he argue against a Commerce Clause rationalization for, say, a federal law requiring all students to eat their spinach and do their homework?

Breyer says the Court's opinion "threatens legal uncertainty" about Congress's reliance on the Commerce Clause as a justification for its activism. Indeed it does, but the alternative is to allow Congress to be the arbiter of its own limits. Given Congress's promiscuous use of the Commerce Clause, there would then be virtually no limits. But some conservatives who are pleased by the Court's decision are going to have to trim their sails regarding a related issue. They have made hay politically by criticizing "judicial activism" that supposedly violates the democratic ethos by showing insufficient deference toward the discretion of the legislative branch. But the task of relimiting government requires, in some instances, a Court less limited by deference than it has been for fifty-eight years.

In 1937, under the pressure of public opinion and FDR's threat to "pack" the Court by enlarging it, the Court adjusted its jurisprudence to the impulse of the 1930s here and abroad, the expansion of the state. "Beginning in 1937," writes historian William E. Leuchtenburg, "the Supreme Court upheld every New Deal statute that came before it" and "legitimated the arrival of the Leviathan State." The decision in the Lopez case will not by itself seriously inhibit that state, but it may cause Congress to pause now and then and think about the fact that the Constitution's enumeration of the federal government's powers presupposes some powers that are not enumerated and therefore are reserved to the states or to the people.

May 15, 1995

The Equity of Inequality

A monk asks a superior if it is permissible to smoke while praying. The superior says certainly not. Next day the monk asks the superior if it is permissible to pray while smoking. That, says the superior, is not merely permissible, it is admirable. The moral of the story is that much depends on how a thing is presented.

Consider, for example, this lead paragraph from a *New York Times* news story: "New studies on the growing concentration of American wealth and income challenge a cherished part of the country's self-image: They show that rather than being an egalitarian society, the United States has become the most economically stratified of industrial nations." But the same data could be reported as demonstrating that the United States, more than any other industrial nation, values equality, sensibly understood. And as demonstrating that this nation's distribution of wealth is an incentive to rational behavior in contemporary economic conditions.

The studies purportedly show that the wealthiest 1 percent and wealthiest 20 percent of American households have a larger portion of the nation's wealth than they used to have, and a larger portion than the wealthiest households in other industrial nations have. Furthermore, the least wealthy 20 percent of Americans have a smaller portion of the nation's wealth than the bottom 20 percent have in other industrial nations.

Now, let's assume the data is accurate, although income and wealth statistics involve judgments that can skew comparisons with other eras and nations. However, the data, even if accurate, need not compel the essentially political judgment expressed in the *Times* paragraph above.

In it, note the word "egalitarian." What the country's self-image actually celebrates is broad if imperfect equal opportunity for striving—for the pursuit of happiness. Americans have never been egalitarian in emphasizing equality of outcomes. Concerning that, elsewhere in the *Times* story there occurs this essentially political assessment: "Most economists believe that wealth and income are more concentrated in the United States than in Japan. But while data show that wealth is more equitably distributed in Japan, the government there has not released enough detailed information to make statistical comparisons possible."

Note the use of the phrase "more equitably" as synonymous with "more equally." That peculiar usage flows from an idea that Americans have generally considered peculiar—the idea that equality of condition is a key component of social justice.

A society that values individualism, enterprise, and a market economy is neither surprised nor scandalized when the unequal distribution of marketable skills produces large disparities in the distribution of wealth. This does not mean that social justice must be defined as whatever distribution of wealth the market produces. But it does mean that there is a presumption in favor of respecting the market's version of distributive justice. Certainly there is today no prima facie case against the moral acceptability of increasingly large disparities of wealth.

This century's experience with government attempts to use progressive taxation to influence the distribution of income suggests the weakness of that instrument and the primacy of social and cultural forces in determining the distribution of wealth. Consider three things that might conduce to a smaller gap between the most and least affluent households. Stopping immigration would reduce downward pressure on wages. A stock market crash would devalue the portfolios of the wealthy. And curtailing access to college and postgraduate education would limit the disparities in the marketable skills that increasingly account for income disparities.

But to suggest such "solutions" is to understand that the problem of increasing inequalities of wealth is not a problem we will pay just any price to remedy, and may not be a problem at all. In an increasingly knowledge-based economy, education disparities drive income disparities, which are incentives for the rising generation to take education seriously as a decisive shaper of individuals' destinies.

In today's deregulated global economy, with highly mobile capital and an abundance of cheap labor, the long-term prosperity of an advanced nation is a function of a high rate of savings—the deferral of gratification that makes possible high rates of investment in capital, research and development, and education. All these forms of social capital are good for society as a whole and are encouraged by high rewards for those who accept the discipline.

That is why promoting more equal distribution of wealth might not be essential to, or even compatible with, promoting a more equitable society. And why increasingly unequal social rewards can conduce to a more truly egalitarian society, one that offers upward mobility equally to all who accept its rewarding disciplines.

April 23, 1995

Here We Go Again:
Is Economic Dynamism Desirable?

In 1802 Alexander Hamilton, seething about President Jefferson's rejection of Hamilton's plans for a national highway system and other stimulants of economic dynamism, wrote acidly: "Mr. Jefferson is distressed at the codfish having latterly emigrated to the southern coast, lest the people there be tempted to catch them, and commerce, of which we have already too much, receive an accession."

The policy argument that helped prompt formation of two parties concerned what kind of economy was desirable. The argument was about what kind of people Americans should be, sturdily independent rural yeomen of Jefferson's agrarian vision, or restless, urban entrepreneurs of the nation envisioned by Hamilton's "Report on Manufactures."

In Andrew Jackson's war against the Bank of the United States, or the pre-Civil War debate about "free labor" versus "wage labor," or later debates about laissez-faire versus unionization, and free trade versus protectionism, political leaders did what Republican presidential candidates and others are now doing. Because of the resonance of Pat Buchanan's promises to assuage middle-class anxiety and protect job security, the candidates and others are rekindling a debate as old as the Republic, a debate about how much economic dynamism is desirable, and what are dynamism's costs to the tranquility of individuals, the stability of communities, and the nation's character.

Herewith three propositions pertinent to today's debate: One of the best things that ever happened to African-Americans was the mechanization of agriculture that destroyed so many of their jobs. One of the best things that ever happened to America's automobile industry is Japan's automobile industry. One of America's economic afflictions has been the idea of the compassionate corporation.

Time was, in places like rural Mississippi, African-Americans lived in stable, traditional, organic communities of a sort often praised by intellec-

212

tuals from afar. They led lives of poverty, disease, and oppression, but they had security, albeit the security of peonage.

Then came machines that picked cotton more efficiently than stooped-over people could, so lots of African-Americans stood up, packed up, got on the Illinois Central, got off at Chicago's Twelfth Street station, and went to the vibrant South Side where life was not a day at the beach but was better than before. Destruction of a "way of life" by "impersonal" economic forces can be a fine thing.

Before the "invasion" of America's market by Japanese automobiles, American automobiles were about what you would expect from an unchallenged industry grown fat on a continental market. Today's American cars, made by fewer but more productive workers, are more reliable, cheaper to operate, less lethal, and much less expensive than they would have been but for the "invasion."

What happened to former autoworkers? They became other kinds of workers in an America where, writes Robert Bartley, *The Wall Street Journal*'s editor, the unemployment rate is "about 5 percent, half that in Europe, where governments have tried to protect jobs by, for example, making it nearly impossible to lay off workers."

Congressional Democrats and other kindred spirits of Buchanan are concocting various measures, from presidential hectoring to social engineering by tax incentive, to prevent things like AT&T's shedding of 40,000 workers. What are they thinking? Surely not that AT&T is mistaken about efficiency and actually needs the 40,000. So they must be thinking that political pressure and economic bribery should be used to encourage AT&T and other corporations to be inefficient.

Time was when various "model corporations" advertised their "social conscience." As recently as the early 1980s IBM told employees: "In nearly forty years, no person employed on a regular basis by IBM has lost as much as one hour of working time because of a layoff." No more. IBM's layoffs have been especially severe because the corporate culture of IBM's private-sector welfare state made it so very vulnerable to leaner firms like Intel and Microsoft. Who thinks America would be better without job-creating, wealth-producing corporations like those?

"Populists" promising to protect Main Street from Wall Street are confused. *Wall Street Journal* columnist Holman Jenkins Jr. notes that when Wall Street, meaning capitalist pressure to maximize profits, enforces efficiencies on corporations, the beneficiaries include Main Street, meaning most Americans, who own stocks directly or through their pension funds. Often the Wall Street enforcers are agents of Main Street—managers of the pension funds, investing the money that flows from Main Street.

Jenkins says that after announcing the 40,000 layoffs, AT&T gained

$4 billion in market value. This benefitted, among other stockholders, the college professors' pension fund, but do not expect expressions of gratitude from the faculty clubs.

March 3, 1996

Malthus Reversed

PARIS—A proper Cassandra probably should not be quite as comfortably situated as Sir James Goldsmith is here in his house that once was home to a king's brother and later, and more impressively, to Cole Porter. But Goldsmith, sixty-one, can't help being a billionaire and won't mute his political lamentation, which is nothing if not comprehensive. He has drawn an indictment against most of modernity.

Shortly before the 1987 stock market crash Goldsmith got out of the market, went to earth—opulently, in several homes around the world—and thought. Now his sabbatical is over. Pausing here recently between campaign stops in his Gulfstream jet during his quest for a seat in the European Parliament, he poured forth his worry that unless the new GATT free trade pact is scuttled, it will produce social divisions "deeper than anything Marx anticipated."

Goldsmith is a capitalist worried that the equilibrium achieved between capital and labor during the last century is about to be tilted radically in capital's favor. The great fact of our age is, he says, the sudden—because of political and technological changes—entry of four billion people into the international labor market, people from low-wage areas such as China, India, Bangladesh, the former Soviet Union, and Latin America. In a world of instantaneous international communication and movements of capital, almost anything can be made almost anywhere. The result under global free trade will be, Goldsmith warns, the "proletarianization" of the labor forces of advanced nations.

Marx falsely prophesied that a "reserve army of the unemployed" would produce the immiseration of the masses and a revolutionary crisis of capitalism. With similar certitude, Goldsmith asserts that global free trade will produce chaos for the many but financial bliss for a few.

The world GATT will produce will be, he says, "economic paradise for an elite"—for those with capital to invest where low labor costs maximize its return. This world also will be a politician's dream, making possible lax monetary policy with minimal inflationary effects because of downward pressure on wages from what Goldsmith calls "the reservoir of the under-employed."

Insisting he is not a protectionist but a regionalist, he favors free trade among comparable economies. To those who say the rapid ascents of South Korea, Taiwan, Hong Kong, and Singapore prove that trade between dissimilar economies can produce "leveling up," he rejoins that those successes were produced by the Cold War and involve trivial numbers of people—70 million. But he seems to postulate an improbable permanence—two hermetically sealed blocs of nations, one of high wages, the other low, forever.

Still, he has an attention-arresting vision, particularly of the possible consequences—reverse Malthusianism, a crisis of agricultural abundance—of intensive, high-technology agriculture. Goldsmith will not call such agriculture "efficient," because of the social and economic costs he sees coming from it. Those costs include the deracination of populations and the destabilization of cities.

Currently 3.1 billion people live on the land. Free trade in the foods and fibers that could be produced worldwide by agriculture as efficient as, say, Canadian, Australian, and American agriculture could, Goldsmith says, drive two billion of those people into cities, with staggering infrastructure, welfare, and police costs. Imagine, say, São Paulo with a population of 45 million. Goldsmith's language acquires Old Testament resonance as he envisions rural communities worldwide "washed away as if by a flood" in "the greatest migration ever" that would "make Stalin's collectivization look like child's play."

Goldsmith's prophecy may seem like "Marxism of the right," but it rejects the sovereignty of economic forces and the primacy of merely economic values. We have heard such refrains before, even in cheerful capitalist America where "change" is considered a synonym for "progress"—remember the southern "agrarians" taking their stand against industrialism. And ever since the Industrial Revolution, some European conservatives have blanched at capitalism's revolutionary power to dissolve traditional social arrangements.

Goldsmith, a child of an Anglo-French marriage, is allied politically with some representatives of old Catholic France. Some will say Goldsmith is a political aesthete, recoiling from the ugliness of an urbanized world. But if so, so what?

Asked whether, by standing athwart history crying "Halt," he is rejecting most of the West's experience and values since the Renaissance made man the measure of all things and made science his servant, Goldsmith answers, equally: "More or less." He is mistaken about both possibilities and inevitabilities, but by darkly sketching a world in which all values are sacrificed to a specious "efficiency," he leavens the conversation of nations.

June 12, 1994

First, Sell the Prison to Yourself

In 1916 the national debt could have been paid off by the nation's richest man, John D. Rockefeller. This year the two richest Americans, William Gates and Warren Buffett, working together would go broke trying to pay even two months' interest—approximately $50 billion—on the national debt.

Does that get your attention? It is from John Steele Gordon's lively little book, *Hamilton's Blessing: The Extraordinary Life and Times of Our National Debt*. This 198-page primer appears just in time for the beginning of the great debate of this year, and perhaps of the remainder of the decade.

The debate is about the proposed constitutional amendment to require a balanced budget—or, to be precise, to require supermajorities of 60 percent in both houses of Congress to authorize a deficit. Gordon's subject is debt, a subject for which few people have had anything nice to say since Alexander Hamilton said in 1781 that "a national debt, if it is not excessive, will be to us a national blessing."

So it has frequently been, and a blessing to the world, too, in two world wars. Establishing sound public finance was the first challenge of the new nation, which is why the Treasury Department had forty employees when the State Department had but five. The sale of government bonds to banks was crucial to expanding the money supply, which ignited commerce, which united the regions.

Not, of course, without the Civil War. But it was won by the men and materiel financed by a forty-two-fold increase in the national debt between 1860 and 1866. War, a wise man once said, is the health of the state. It certainly has fattened up the national debt, which went from $1.2 billion in 1916 to $25.4 billion in 1919, and from $48 billion in 1941 to $269 billion in 1946.

There have been, Gordon notes, seven periods in which the debt steadily increased, six when it declined, and three when it was stable. Six of the seven periods of increase involved either a major war or depression.

It is the seventh period, which began in 1960, that is ominously different and has driven the nation to the brink of constitutionalizing the pay-as-you-go principle.

In the last thirty-six years business fluctuations have been, on balance, remarkably mild and the Vietnam War was, relative to the size of the economy, a small burden. Yet the national debt has increased seventeen times more than in all of the nation's first 184 years. In the past fifteen years federal revenues have increased 25 percent (largely because of, not in spite of, the Reagan tax cuts and reforms) and our principal foreign adversary has imploded, yet the debt has soared.

Why? Here is a hint: In 1985, the year the deficit finally became a large political issue and Congress passed the Gramm-Rudman law that was supposed to control it, Congress also enacted fifty-four new benefit programs, bringing the total then to 1,013.

Why are there now debt service costs of more than $1,000 per American per year? Because, Gordon writes, debt has served "the political self-interests of a few thousand people"—federal elected officials in these thirty-six years.

Gordon does not explicitly endorse term limits as part of his recipe of reforms but he does cite "the transformation of politics into a lifelong profession" as part of the problem, along with the proliferation of political action committees and a tax code full of vote-buying deductions and credits—a code that has been amended more than 4,000 times, an average of more than an amendment a day, in the ten years since the Reagan simplification of the code. Gordon proposes campaign finance reforms and a flat tax.

He emphatically does not endorse the "chimera" of a balanced budget amendment, which he considers an invitation to gimmickry of the sort New York State used in 1992 when $200 million was needed to meet the constitutional requirement of a budget balanced out of current income. Were taxes raised or spending cut? Not exactly.

Instead, the state sold Attica Prison to itself. A state agency established to fund urban redevelopment borrowed in the bond market, gave the money to the state, and took title to the prison. The state recorded as income the $200 million its own agency had borrowed, declared the budget balanced, then rented the prison from the agency for a sum sufficient to service the $200 million debt.

Imagine the potential for fiscal prestidigitation at the federal level. Alas, one moral of Gordon's highly entertaining and informative story is this: The very habits of governance that make a balanced budget amendment tempting make such an amendment problematic.

January 26, 1997

The Case for a Supermajority

The properly reverent reason for amending the Constitution is to revive those of the Framers' objectives that have been attenuated by political developments since the Framers left Philadelphia. An attempt at such an amendment will be voted on in the House on Monday, April 15, tax day.

It would require a two-thirds supermajority to raise taxes. The House may pass it, but only because some members who oppose it will vote for it knowing that the idea is popular but that the Senate will defeat any such amendment—partly because the amendment would inconvenience the political class, partly because the amendment is problematic.

Any amendment that contains language the meaning of which is unclear is apt to result in mendacious evasions by the political branches of government and excessive supervision by the judicial branch. Consider the key language of the amendment as originally offered by Representative Joe Barton (R., Texas): "Any bill to levy a new tax or increase the rate or base of any tax may pass only by a two-thirds majority of the whole number of each house of Congress."

Is a tariff a tax? Is a user fee? If one decreases an entitlement by increasing a cost (such as a Medicare premium), is one raising a tax? Such questions may not be insoluble. Ten states with one-third of the nation's population manage to function with some sort of supermajority voting requirement regarding some taxation.

But anxiety about the prudence of loading such questions into the Constitution was one reason why the key language has been replaced with this, also problematic, language: "Any bill, resolution, or other legislative measure changing the internal revenue laws shall require for final adoption in either house the concurrence of two-thirds of the members present, unless that bill, resolution, or measure is determined at the time of adoption, in a reasonable manner prescribed by law, not to increase the internal revenue by more than a de minimis amount."

Polls show that people would be more ready to risk the uncertainties inherent in any radical transformation of the tax code (to a flat tax, or a national sales tax, or a consumption-based income tax) if there were a supermajority provision to reduce the risk that thorough tax reform would be a cover for raising taxes. However, the amendment's original language probably would have enabled a minority in either house to block such reform. It is unlikely that any new system could be put into place without constituting a "new tax" or increasing the "rate or base" of a tax.

Supermajority requirements, which reward both the intensity of a minority and the breadth of a majority, are hardly inconsistent with the

American system. Federalism, a bicameral legislature, and other facets of the constitutional system of separation of powers were designed to temper simple majoritarianism. And the Constitution's Takings Clause and Contracts Clause expressed the Framers' desire to give special protection to that which taxation can threaten—the right to enjoyment of property that results from enterprise.

Unfortunately, the Supreme Court's expansive construction of the Constitution's Commerce Clause has given Congress powers not envisioned by the Framers of American federalism. And property rights have been substantially compromised by the rules and regulations of the administrative state. Thus two supporters of the supermajority amendment, John McGinnis of Yeshiva University's Cardozo Law School and Michael Rappaport of the University of San Diego Law School, say the amendment "should be seen as an attempt to revive the original values of the Constitution rather than as a radical innovation."

And as an attempt to replace what cannot be revived—the fiscal morality that said government should borrow only during recessions and wars. Nowadays the political class spends as much as it can with the politically least risky mix of taxation and debt. McGinnis and Rappaport argue that if the supermajority requirement "forces Congress to finance spending with larger deficits that are even more unpopular than higher taxes, this will induce Congress to spend less than it otherwise would."

Senator Jon Kyl (R., Texas), the Senate's leading proponent of a supermajority requirement, says it would incline the political branches toward wholesome policies. By making tax increases more difficult, a supermajority requirement would force the political class to look to economic growth to raise revenues. And growth reduces the temptation of the class to engage in the divisive politics of envious redistribution.

Some such amendment could represent reverent restoration of the values embodied in what the Framers did at Philadelphia.

April 11, 1996

The Case Against

David Skaggs, a thoughtful Democratic congressman from Colorado, has filed a lawsuit charging that virtually the first thing the House of Representatives did on January 4 after its members swore to defend the Constitution was to violate the Constitution. And not in a peripheral matter, but by overthrowing the constitutional principle of majority rule.

The flaw in his argument is that there is no such explicit constitutional principle, and it is problematic extracting even an implicit principle. But if his constitutional reasoning is unpersuasive, his prudential reasoning deserves more attention than it received on Congress's hectic opening day.

That day Congress performed the usual housekeeping chore of readopting, with some amendments, the rules that would govern legislative proceedings. But several amendments were unusual. For example, the House decided that no legislation containing "an income tax rate increase shall be considered as passed" unless it receives the votes of three-fifths of the members voting. (The House also voted that it cannot even consider a retroactive tax increase.)

Skaggs argues that this unconstitutionally empowers a minority to defeat legislation. He says that because the Constitution contains some supermajority provisions (consent to treaties, impeachment, and so on), this implies that a simple majority is mandatory wherever the Constitution is silent. He also notes the provision that the vice president votes in the Senate when it is "equally divided." He says this means the Framers intended the Senate, and surely not just the Senate, to operate by simple majority rule. Finally, he notes that the Constitution says that "a majority of each (house) shall constitute a quorum to do business."

Defenders of the new supermajority rule argue that the Framers who wrote the quorum clause clearly assumed that in the absence of such a stipulation, Congress could do as it pleased. And there is no stipulation that all legislation shall be passed by simple majorities. Furthermore, the Constitution says, "each house may determine the rules of its proceedings." And the Supreme Court has held that "congressional practice in the transaction of ordinary legislative business is of course none of our concern."

However, the new supermajority rule's supporters, most of whom are Republican, are in a weak position to wax indignant about Skaggs and others taking the rule to court. When in 1993 the Democratic majority in the House voted to permit delegates from the territories and the District of Columbia—all Democrats, of course—to vote in the House when it is functioning as the Committee of the Whole, Republicans challenged this in the D.C. Court of Appeals. There they lost, but not because the court declined to review the House action. And that court said "there are limitations to the House's rulemaking power."

Still, no court has ever held a rule of either house unconstitutional. Even in this age of judicial overreaching it would be an unusually rash judge who would put courts into the business of examining House and Senate procedures (the Senate three-fifths requirement to limit debate, the "holds" senators can place on bills, the restrictive rules under which legislation can come to the House floor, various powers of committees and subcommittees) that can impede a majority eager to act.

There is nothing anticonstitutional about giving protective empowerments to minorities, or about complicating the way majorities work their wills. A supermajority requirement is one way of building into democratic decision making a measurement of intensity of feeling as well as mere numbers. Furthermore, supermajority requirements are devices for assigning special importance to particular matters, and perhaps taxation is properly so regarded.

However, everyone considers something, and not always taxation, especially important. Skaggs worries that supermajority provisions will multiply as various factions use them to give imprimaturs of moral seriousness to this or that. Indeed, already the House has voted to require a three-fifths vote to repeal rules and regulations on the new "correction days" devoted to such repeals. Some of the people who opposed the supermajority provision regarding taxation wanted the supermajority provision for "corrections."

What a House majority has done regarding supermajorities and taxation, a subsequent majority can undo, but perhaps not easily. From now on congressional candidates will be asked how they will vote on the supermajority rule. A majority of each new Congress may come to office committed to keeping the rule.

Conservatives' pleasure about this should be, but does not seem to be, tempered by concern about the damage that may be done to future defense budgets by measures like the House supermajority rule that institutionalize today's particularly acute taxaphobia. The world is still a dangerous place, full of things more unpleasant than taxes.

July 9, 1995

Bilingual Ballots: A Seriously Bad Idea

John Silber, the sandpapery president of Boston University, might have been governor of Massachusetts—he was the Democratic nominee in 1990—were he not given to speaking his formidable mind as bluntly as he did when a voter asked what we should teach our children. "Teach them that they are going to die," he said. And have a nice day.

His point was that children need a sense of reality, beginning with the fact that life is short and that living nobly may depend on an early understanding of that brevity. He never tried, as most politicians do, to be a ray of sunshine.

Recently he was here among the politicians, displaying his penchant for uttering discomforting truths. He is a philosopher by academic training and his testimony in favor of repealing bilingual ballot requirements was a model dissection of ill-conceived compassion.

The 1965 Voting Rights Act, as amended in 1975 and subsequently, requires bilingual ballots in jurisdictions with certain demographic characteristics pertaining to linguistic minorities, English deficiency, illiteracy, and low voter turnout. But as Representative John Porter (R., Ill.), another advocate of repeal, noted in testimony, all this is patently peculiar because since 1906 any immigrant seeking citizenship has been required to demonstrate oral English literacy, and since 1950 has been required to "demonstrate an understanding of English, including an ability to read, write, and speak words in ordinary English." Applicants over fifty-five who have lived here at least fifteen years are exempted.

Porter said that if immigrants are gaining citizenship without knowing how to read English, the law is not being enforced. And if eighteen-year-old citizens born and raised here are illiterate in English, the education system is failing.

Deval Patrick, who as President Clinton's assistant attorney general for civil rights is paid to inflate the rhetoric of civil rights while trivializing the subject, testified against repeal of the bilingual ballot requirement, warning of "the pernicious disenfranchisement resulting from a lack of English proficiency." He regards bilingual ballots as instruments of compassion for people who are "limited-English proficient" and exhorted one and all to "recognize, respect, and celebrate the linguistic and cultural variety of our society." He said repeal would "resurrect barriers to equal access to and participation in the democratic process for American citizens who do not speak English very well."

"Very well"? Good grief. Talk about inadequate use of the language. How can bilingual ballots produce "equal access to and participation in the democratic process"? What is at issue is accommodations for people who cannot read English-language ballots, and the law of the land is supposed to be a barrier between such people and citizenship.

It fell to Silber to say why bilingual ballots are of "constitutional consequence, amending in effect the very concept of United States citizenship." The naturalization statutes clearly presuppose that English is the language indispensable for life in America, where all the founding documents, and all the laws and all the proceedings of legislatures are in English. Citizens not proficient in English are, Silber said, "citizens in name only" because they cannot follow a political campaign, talk with a candidate, or petition a representative, and providing them with a bilingual ballot merely makes a mockery of civic life.

The financial cost of this unfunded mandate is not trivial. (New York City has had to acquire new voting machines to cope with the required Chinese characters. In the 1994 general election, Los Angeles County spent $67,568.87 accommodating 692 voters who speak Tagalog—$97.64 per voter.) However, as Silber testified, the intolerable cost is the degradation of the concept of citizenship when applied to "someone lost in a country whose public discourse is incomprehensible to him."

Silber stressed that in no other nation do so many people, spread over so large an area, speak the same language. This nation, which Lincoln said is dedicated to a proposition, is a creedal nation, founded on shared affirmations, not on ethnicity. Here, Silber said, ethnicity is "a private matter." Various ethnic groups celebrate their saints and other sources of communal pride. Such private and voluntary undertakings are splendid. However, the government properly recognizes only Americans, not ethnic groups. In opposition to that principle, bilingual ballots "represent a dangerous experiment in deconstructing our American identity."

But of course. For some of the diversity-mongers who advocate bilingual ballots, such deconstruction is precisely the point. They think it is oppression for one American identity to be (in the jargon du jour of the multiculturalists) "privileged."

Silber says such deconstruction is how nations die. Have a nice day.

May 2, 1996

Voting by Mail: Another Improvement That Isn't

Oregon, a progressive place, is pioneering a new wrinkle in democratic practice. The primary and general elections that will choose a successor to Senator Packwood will be the nation's first elections of a federal official conducted entirely by mail.

Like most improvements, this is atrocious. It is another step away from what should be the practice for people morally sturdy enough to deserve democracy—oral voting. How did we sink to the shabby business of choosing leaders behind drawn curtains? What are cloistered voters afraid of? What good comes from practices designed to get the fearful to vote?

We will recur to those questions anon. First, however, to Oregon's folly.

Oregonians have conducted many local elections entirely by mail and last June the legislature voted to conduct all elections this way. However, the governor, a Democrat, with encouragement from both parties, vetoed the measure, saying study is needed.

Some Republicans worry that shoving ballots through everyone's mail slot will merely stimulate voting by people too slothful to bestir themselves for public business if doing so requires them to get to a neighborhood polling place. The premise of many Republicans is that sloth is a Democratic attribute. That is one reason Republicans opposed the "motor voter" law which requires states to offer voter registration where people get their driver's licenses or welfare services.

Democrats seem to share the Republicans' bleak view of Democrats, which is why Democrats adored "motor voter" and why they probably would favor a "pizza voter" bill requiring pizza delivery guys to register their customers. But surely Republicans should rethink their assumption that increasing turnout disproportionately increases the turnout of Democrats: In 1994 turnout surged and so did Republicans.

Some Democrats worry that Republicans, who Democrats think are better organized (is there a chromosome that controls this?), will benefit from mail voting because they will organize churches and other groups to pressure members to vote as a bloc. One Oregon political scientist says, "You can easily see the potential for families sitting down together and deciding how to vote, and what scares everybody is the churches sitting down together and saying you can vote however you want—hell is an option." But families will talk together, even about voting, confound them, and congregations will congregate, with or without mail voting.

Mail voting is a bit cheaper than setting up polling places, but mail voting abolishes a communitarian moment that is a valuable part of our civic liturgy—the Election Day coming together for the allocation of power. However, what really worries opponents of mail voting is the specter of "ballot-marking parties" where voting is not secret. Another Oregon political scientist says he not only worries about churches saying, "On Sunday, everybody bring your ballots and we'll mark them together," he even frets that "you may have a domineering spouse more or less enforcing his or her views on someone else. We'll never know if that happens."

Oh, gosh, let's hazard a guess that it happens occasionally even without mail voting. Now let's get to the real question: Are not secret ballots decadent? Paper ballots themselves are, although for many decades in the nineteenth century the parties printed their own ballots, in distinctive colors, with full slates of candidates, so there was little secrecy about how individuals (who sometimes had to sign their ballots) were voting—which party's ballots did they mark?—and there was no ticket-splitting.

But back when democracy was vigorous and the results did not make you wince—back when voters were electing Washington, Adams, Jefferson, Madison, Calhoun, Clay, and Webster—oral voting, often conducted around a whiskey barrel, was common. It persisted in virtuous Kentucky until after the Civil War. Why should a crucial public activity—participation in the allocation of public power—be done furtively, behind a curtain, as though some shameful transaction is occurring?

As Cicero said, lamenting the end of oral voting, "The people should not have been provided with a hiding place, where they could conceal a mischievous vote by means of the ballot." Cicero wanted people to vote knowing that the most virtuous people in polity would know what they had done. Do today's voters want to make their choices in secret because they fear the disapproval of acquaintances? Such voters should stay in bed with the covers pulled over their heads.

Abolish secret voting, have every voter call out his or her choice in an unquavering voice, and have the choice recorded for public inspection. You probably will have a smaller electorate, but also a hardier, better one.

October 26, 1995

Artistic Dependency

"Our job," says Everett Albers, "is to get the people of North Dakota busy writing to Congress." In defense of agriculture subsidies? No, Albers, quoted in *The Chronicle of Higher Education,* is executive director of the North Dakota Humanities Council and wants North Dakotans to rally in defense of the National Endowment for the Humanities.

Extinction may be the fate of the NEH and its Great Society siblings, the National Endowment for the Arts and the Corporation for Public Broadcasting. Extinction will be their fate if Republicans mean a syllable of what they say about rethinking federal functions.

Because government breeds more government, and develops a lobbying infrastructure to defend itself, every state now has a humanities council. By these, and the travels of peripatetic culture bureaucrats, and by the spreading of subsidies across the continent, culture agencies build constituencies of articulate letter-writers.

Jane Alexander, head of the NEA, is proud as punch of having visited all fifty states in her less than two years tenure. Dante Ramos reports in *The New Republic* that Alexander considers this travel "her best accomplishment." Alexander believably reports that wherever she goes disbursing money, she is warmly received. Headlines generated by her campaigning for her agency ("Alexander Brings Message of the Arts' Balm for Society," *Arizona Daily Star;* "Arts Touted as Solution to Violence, Racial Strife," *Fort Worth Star-Telegram*) cause Ramos to conclude that in her utilitarianism—art as social improvement—"there's a point where art gives way to social work."

And it becomes just another jobs program. Directing Ramos's attention to a pot, Alexander says its maker "is already a professional and he intends to make a career as a ceramicist." Absent the NEA, would the pot not have been made? If so, just how very interested is that fellow in becoming a ceramicist? Ramos says Alexander has "improved the mood of the agency and the artists who depend upon it." What sort of "artist" develops such dependency?

The current head of the NEH, Sheldon Hackney, is organizing a "national conversation," the implicit supposition being that Americans converse too little, or too clumsily, or come to incorrect conclusions, and need government guidance. Thanks to NEH funding, guidance galore has come for teachers of history, in the form of new "standards." Writing in the same issue of the *Chronicle*, Arnita Jones, executive secretary of the Organization of American Historians, exults that the teaching standards "offer nothing less than an escape from the rote learning of factual matter." Now there's a problem for government to tackle—American students knowing too many historical facts.

Jones warns that the standards will be "expensive." She says they will be "meaningless" unless lots of money is spent on the appropriate training of teachers and the writing of appropriate texts. This money that must be spent because of the money already spent will promote the predictable— "history" as ethnic boosterism, and as reparations for various victimizations, past and present.

The standards for American and world history miniaturize great men (because they were men, and because it is democratic to celebrate common people) and marginalize Western civilization. Students are asked to study, for example, "the achievements and grandeur" of the fourteenth-century West African monarch Mansa Musa. Note that in this "inclusive history" certain "grandeur" is stipulated, not questioned.

Defenders of public television in this era of abundant cable choices cloak themselves in "concern" for "the children," arguing, with antic illogic, that *Sesame Street* and *Barney* serve huge audiences but could not find alternative broadcast venues. Regarding public radio, in a nation with almost 9,500 commercial radio stations, exactly why is it necessary to give federal subsidies to about 600 public stations? The answer from Leonard Garment, President Nixon's counsel, is: to preserve stations like WVMR in Dunsmore, West Virginia, which "offers local programming that no commercial station would consider: lost dog ads, funeral announcements, school closings, junior high sports broadcasts." Actually, some commercial stations do some of that, and even if none did, that fact would not generate a federal lost-dog-ad responsibility.

The hysteria about proposals to terminate the CPB, NEH, and NEA seems synthetic, as when *The New York Times* says that to "cripple" the CPB would be "barbaric." What adjectives does the *Times* hold in reserve to describe, say, ethnic cleansing? If Republicans merely trim rather than terminate these three agencies, they will affirm that all three perform appropriate federal functions and will prove that the Republican "revolution" is not even serious reform.

January 8, 1995

A Case Study of Contemporary Government: "Rent Seeking" with the "Perimeter Rule"

The national pastime, at least in Washington at the seat of the national government, is a game economists call "rent seeking." It has many permutations, one of which has produced the "perimeter rule" concerning National Airport, which sits on the Virginia bank of the Potomac, a short drive from the Capitol, the Yankee Stadium of rent seeking.

Rent seeking is the attempt by a private faction, in league with compliant public officials, to bend public power to private advantage by conferring either an advantage on that faction or a disadvantage on that faction's competition. Rent seeking is usually an attempt to evade market forces, so it sows inefficiencies in society's allocations of resources.

Consider the rule that planes taking off from National may not have as their initial destination any airport more than 1,250 miles away. Begin by drawing on a map a circle with a radius measuring 1,250 miles. The perimeter of the circle will cut just deep enough into Texas to include the Dallas-Fort Worth Airport. The perimeter rule was set at 1,250 miles in 1986, when the speaker of the House was Jim Wright of Fort Worth.

This story began in the 1960s, when airlines serving National agreed to combat congestion at National by limiting nonstop flights from there to destinations within 650 miles, with exceptions for seven more distant cities that already were receiving nonstop flights from National. The federal government, which then operated National and, much farther out in Virginia, the new Dulles Airport, which had opened in 1962, supported the rule as a subsidy for Dulles: The rule conferred on the less convenient airport a monopoly of long-distance flights.

In the early 1980s the perimeter rule was revised to permit 1,000-mile flights, covering the seven cities that had been granted exceptions to the 650-mile limit. But by 1986 some airlines responding to that inconvenient (as governments often consider it) idea called consumer sovereignty, were evading the perimeter rule by taking off from National, touching down briefly at Dulles about twenty-six miles away, then flying on to Dallas-Fort Worth.

Texas's congressional delegation proposed exempting Dallas-Fort Worth from the 1,000-mile limit. But Houston, which still would have been without nonstop flights from National, was not amused. Neither were cities within the 1,000-mile perimeter that stood to lose flights that would be rerouted to Dallas-Fort Worth.

Texas prevailed with the 1,250-mile perimeter rule that swept in Houston and Dallas-Fort Worth. The effect was to permit some flights to land there and to compel many others to land there. This benefitted two large airports and many commercial interests. But the law in its majesty still forbids nonstop flights from National to, for example, Denver and Salt Lake City.

And to Phoenix, home of Senator John McCain, who has an old idea and a new position from which to advance it. The idea, which pertains to government involvement in the economy, is: When in doubt, get it out. His position, a result of last November's election, is the chairmanship of the aviation subcommittee of the Commerce, Science, and Transportation Committee.

The perimeter rule is, eighteen years after the deregulation that produced today's highly competitive airline industry, an obviously anomalous federal interference with the market's ability to reflect consumer preferences. Erasing the rule would cause a redistribution of flights between National and Dulles, and would have ripple effects, some of them disadvantageous to various interests, in cities that have been hubs for flights forced by law to terminate within 1,250 miles of National. So there is much talk about this "wrecking" air traffic patterns around Washington and around the nation and hurting Dulles as a feeder of transatlantic flights, some of which, say pessimists who are confident of their clairvoyance, would be canceled.

This small controversy about an obscure rule illuminates how regulatory government produces resistance to the reform of itself. By making decisions that markets would not make, government creates or strengthens interests that become dependent on government not letting markets work. These interests defend their government-conferred advantages by playing upon two impulses that are becoming stronger in reaction against conservative attempts to prune government.

One impulse is a flinching from the unpredictability of freedom's consequences. Another is to assert the entitlement mentality—interests that become dependent on government policies are entitled to have those policies continue forever. Thus does the perimeter rule demonstrate how activist government, responsive to rent seekers, creates, in the end, constituencies for inertia.

March 16, 1995

Moralism and Cynicism in Rhode Island

Perhaps in 1956 Rhode Island, which began as an outpost of Protestants too turbulent to get along in other colonies, was still smarting from Cotton Mather calling it "the sewer of New England." When in 1956 the state banned price advertising of alcoholic beverages, perhaps it really was worried, as a nanny should be, about the morals and livers of Rhode Islanders. Only cynics, meaning students of government and human nature, suspect that the ban was imposed at the behest of owners of small liquor stores, to protect them from the competition of larger stores that can afford to spend more on advertising.

In any case, on Monday the Supreme Court unanimously struck the forty-year-old fetters from Rhode Island's liquor dealers, holding that the ban on price advertising violates the First Amendment. This pleases conservatives who believe that granting less protection to commercial speech than to political or artistic speech is part of a dangerous derogation of economic liberty and property rights. But the decision should disturb conservatives who believe judges should strive to be deferential to legislative judgments, even some dotty ones.

This case began when a liquor store ran a newspaper advertisement that

229

did not state the prices of beverages but did place the word "wow" next to pictures of vodka and rum bottles. Reasoning that this implied bargain prices, the state fined the store $400.

Rhode Island argues that banning price advertising inhibits competition, thereby raising the prices of alcoholic beverages, thereby reducing consumption. Thereby promoting virtue. That is, some ignorance is good for us.

Well, not ignorance, exactly. Prices can be displayed in liquor stores if the information is not visible from the street. So the ban on price advertising does not enforce ignorance, it increases what economists call "transaction costs." Customers must expend more time and energy—visiting various stores—for price comparisons they cannot make by reading advertisements.

(Did Rhode Island's legislators consider the possibility that comparison shoppers traipsing from store to store may work up fearful thirsts, so the ban on price advertising may militate against its objective, which is temperance? Rhode Island ranks high among the states in per-capita alcohol consumption, above many of the thirty-nine states that allow price advertising.)

Under the Twenty-first Amendment, which repealed the Eighteenth and Prohibition, any state has the power to ban alcoholic beverages. So why does not Rhode Island have the power to ban information (even truthful, nonmisleading information) about a commodity it could proscribe?

Because, says the Supreme Court, the Twenty-first Amendment does not limit the sweep of the First Amendment. And twenty years ago the Court held that a "consumer's interest in the free flow of commercial information . . . may be as keen as, if not keener by far than, his interest in the day's most urgent political debate."

(Some Americans may be more interested in learning about a beer bargain than about politicians' views on gas prices? Indeed.)

Writing for the Court, Justice Stevens washes away Rhode Island's law with a torrent of adjectives and adverbs. The state, he says, has not successfully managed its "heavy burden" of showing that the ban on price advertising will "directly" and "to a material degree" promote temperance by "significantly" reducing alcohol consumption. Stevens even speculates that alcoholics may respond to higher prices by reducing purchases of other things. Do tell.

In a robust concurrence, Justice Thomas says that when government's asserted interest "is to keep legal users of a product or service ignorant in order to manipulate their choices in the marketplace," that interest no more justifies regulation of "commercial" speech than of any other kind.

Some conservatives have another view. It is that the First Amendment is part of a political document, the point of which is self-government. Hence the amendment, properly construed, gives special protection to political speech. It may well be sensible policy generally to refrain from restricting truthful communication about legal products, but the amendment does not require that policy. And it is paternalistic of the Court to protect the people of Rhode Island from paternalistic laws they can petition their legislators to repeal.

Of course cynics suspect that the paternalism is a pretense, a way of rationalizing protection for an interest group. They note that the Rhode Island Liquor Stores Association, representing small retailers, joined the state's defense of the ban on price advertising, arguing that without the ban, the association's members "would be obliged to participate in the advertising arena." For a description of cynics, recur to the first paragraph.

May 16, 1996

Sheep and Supply-Side Government

It is an old axiom that the meek shall inherit the earth but the strong shall retain the mineral rights. An analogue of that axiom is that even when Washington gets really, no kidding, this-time-we-truly-mean-it serious about getting serious, the organized will get theirs. To see the axiom in action, as it were, turn to page 253 of the farm bill the president recently signed into law. Note the new National Sheep Industry Improvement Center. To appreciate the rich symbolism of this, some history helps.

During the Second World War, American wool producers could not produce as much as the military needed for uniforms. In 1954, with the nation mobilized for the containment of communism, Congress decided wool production should be stimulated with subsidies financed by duties on imported wool and woolen goods. Hence the National Wool Act.

Time passed. Synthetic materials came along. The Cold War was won. And still the wool subsidy survived—until it received the attention of Jonathan Rauch, a gimlet-eyed reporter for the *National Journal*. The wool subsidy then became a symbol of the mindless immortality of government programs, and in 1993 Congress voted to phase it out. But the import duties remained, producing hundreds of millions of dollars for the Treasury each year.

Now, there is demand-side government and supply-side government, and Washington features both kinds. In demand-side government, groups demand programs, and government provides them. In supply-side government, the government supplies programs that call into existence groups that benefit from the programs, groups that then work to preserve and, if possible, enlarge them. The origins of the wool subsidy are shrouded in the mists of history, so it is unclear whether this was supply-side or demand-side government or a bit of both. In 1954 wool producers presumably were paying attention and showing proper gratitude to the legislators who created the subsidy.

In 1955—the date suggests the supply-side dynamic—the American Sheep Industry Association was founded. It has 110,000 members and an annual budget of more than $5 million. It is headquartered in Englewood, Colorado, but it has found, which is to say it has hired, a friend in Washington. He is Fran Boyd, a lobbyist, who (as reported by David Hosansky of *Congressional Quarterly*) says, "There's a feeling on the Hill that the sheep industry got dealt a pretty tough hand." The tough handling was the phasing out, after four decades, of subsidies that sometimes amounted to $200 million annually, and paid sheep ranchers up to $150,000 annually.

Compassion, meaning the prevention or amelioration of pain, is the core value of contemporary liberalism, and hence of the Democratic Party. But Democrats have not cornered the market on compassion. Consider the example of Senator Larry Craig, a Republican from Idaho, where the deer and the antelope play and lots of sheep work at making wool. Idaho is among the most conservative states. After the 1994 elections, the governor, both senators, and both congressmen were all Republicans, for the first time since the magic year of 1954.

Craig, who is in his first term, is about as conservative as they come. In 1994 the American Conservative Union rated him a perfect 100. His rating by the liberal Americans for Democratic Action was zero. The *National Journal* rated him tied with his Idaho colleague, Dirk Kempthorne, as the most conservative senator. But he and Senator Max Baucus joined to put the National Sheep Industry Improvement Center into the farm bill. Baucus is a Democrat from Montana, Idaho's neighbor, and another state well stocked with sheep.

The law says the center shall "promote strategic development activities . . . to maximize the impact of federal assistance," and shall "optimize" this and that, and shall work on "infrastructure development" for the sheep industry, and shall "empower" the industry to "design unique responses" to the industry's "special needs," and shall "adopt flexible and innovative approaches to solving the long-term needs" of the industry. It shall do all this with a revolving fund starting with $20 million in public funds and up to $30 million in coming years, plus private funds.

Craig stresses that the cost is a small fraction of what the wool duties continue to generate. Baucus justifies all this with a principle as capacious as Montana: "It's helpful to support all American industries generally."

Well, Democrats generally are shaky about the distinction between the public and the private. But conservatives like Craig are supposed to think more clearly. Lobbyist Boyd says of the new National Center, "I think it's the kind of thing you look to for an industry that no longer has any support whatsoever as a direct payment." Oh. So, an industry not getting a direct payment is such a novelty, and such a victim of manifest injustice, that it must be compensated by some other payment. And the president who signed the farm bill says "the era of big government is over."

Of course the National Center is not big. As a portion of the public sector, neither is Amtrak or public broadcasting or the arts endowment or ethanol subsidies. Even cumulatively, these and scores of other little undertakings do not amount to much of the government. But the mentality that produced the National Center is the big reason that the public regards the government with disdain and itself with a measure of self-loathing.

It is a mentality of simultaneous industriousness and laziness of earnestness and frivolousness. It involves the unsleeping pursuit of advantages for friends, and slothful refusal to think about what are and are not proper functions of government. This mentality produces severe dissonance. It is dissonance between the rhetoric of limited government—the rhetoric of the public and the political class alike—and the actual expectations of the public and the behavior by the political class that the public rewards with reelection. The result of this dissonance is cynicism all around. That is unchanged after nearly 500 days of the Congress that was supposed to change things.

April 29, 1996

Maryland Sacks Itself

Art Modell made dumb business decisions and needed the money, or at least wanted it more than he wanted the affection of his community where he once was a leader and now is a pariah. But what is Maryland's excuse for one of the most peculiar acts of government in memory?

In 1961 Modell bought 51 percent of the Cleveland Browns for $4 million. The team is now worth an estimated $160 million. During the last decade the Browns have averaged 70,000 fans a game, fourth best in the league. The NFL has equal sharing of TV revenue, generous sharing of gate receipts, and a (porous) payroll cap. No wonder the Packers can thrive in little Green Bay. But Modell says that he managed to lose millions and that Cleveland is so stingy with subsidies that he had to succumb to Maryland's blandishments and move to Baltimore, a city salivating for a team since 1984, when its Colts skedaddled to Indianapolis, which then had a domed stadium in need of a tenant.

Maryland, which probably would have gift-wrapped the Bay Bridge if Modell had thought to demand it, promises to build a $200 million stadium with 108 luxury boxes, usually bought by corporations, and 7,500 club seats where affluent patrons pay premium ticket prices in order to be pampered with various services, lest they be stuck with only football for amusement. But that is just the beginning of Maryland's largesse. Modell will get, to use for paying some team expenses, up to $75 million generated by the sale of "personal seat licenses." (Purchasers acquire the right to purchase season tickets.) Modell will pay a minimal sort of rent and will get all revenues from ticket sales, concessions, parking, and stadium advertising. When the stadium is used for college football games, rock concerts, and other events, Modell will collect a 10 percent management fee and half the profits. No wonder Maryland has added an estimated $60 million to the value of the Browns, who even under Modell's guidance probably will be unable to avoid making an annual profit of $30 million.

Modell's move is part of the new trend of NFL teams moving to smaller cities. This year the Los Angeles Raiders and Rams moved to Oakland and St. Louis respectively. The Raiders were returning to where they started. St. Louis got the Rams to replace the Cardinals, whom St. Louis got from Chicago and then lost to Phoenix, which may soon lose them to another city on the make. Baltimore might have got them for less than the Browns are costing. Long ago, the Rams belonged to Cleveland. And the beat goes on. The Houston Oilers will light out for Nashville when that city's $292 million stadium (eighty-two luxury suites, 9,600 club seats) is ready in 1998. The Tampa Bay Buccaneers are flirting with Orlando.

This "socialism of sport" is explained—rationalized—as what is known as "industrial policy," a strategy for urban economic development supervised by interventionist government. It began in 1953 when Milwaukee built a stadium to lure the Boston Braves, the first major-league baseball team to move in fifty years. After twelve years the Braves defected to Atlanta, so Milwaukee plucked the Pilots from Seattle, renamed them the Brewers, and now in order to keep them is going to build a better (definition: more luxury suites for "fans" more interested in canapés than double plays) ballpark. To mollify litigious Seattle, baseball invented the Mariners, who recently were on the verge of migrating until last year's success on the field revived interest in building them a new park.

There is a high ratio of bald assertion to serious demonstration in most arguments purporting to prove that sports franchises give cities large economic benefits. One reason Maryland is committing football folly is because Baltimore clearly benefitted when the Orioles (on whose board of directors I serve without compensation) moved into a gem of a ballpark Maryland built for them near Harborplace, the development that sparked the city's downtown revival. But the Orioles play eighty-one home games a year and average attendance at the new park has been more than 40,000, so the park is putting 3.5 million people a year into a commercial setting, generating what economists call "multiplier effects" of spending on restaurants and hotels. The Baltimore Ravens will use the stadium just ten times a year (two preseason and eight regular season games). Besides, much of the money spent on sports would otherwise be spent on other things in the local economy.

The argument that a particular project will be "self-financing" is usually the first refuge of politicians defending the indefensible. So Maryland says the Browns will mean $123 million a year to the local economy, a figure ginned up with dubious assumptions, such as that 20 percent of the people attending games will spend a night in a hotel. (Where will those people be coming from in a region with NFL teams in Pittsburgh, Philadelphia, and Washington?) Maryland says the Browns will create the equivalent of 1,400 full-time jobs. But if the cost of the stadium and other inducements is $250 million, that comes to $178,000 per job—rather pricey, even if the 1,400 figure is not inflated and even if many of the jobs are not low-wage (ushers, food services) and seasonal.

Downtowns as different as those of Baltimore, Cleveland, and Phoenix are benefitting from new sports facilities. And major-league sports can give a rising city a cachet that has a cash value in attracting other businesses. And it only takes a few cities in search of such cachet to create a sellers' market for team owners eager to move, or to feign eagerness in order to extort more subsidies from their home cities. Still, hats off to Houston's mayor, Bob Lanier, who, asked to sink $150 million in a new stadium to keep the Oilers out of Nashville's clutches, said, "Can you ask the average guy to build luxury suites for rich people, so they can support rich owners, so they can pay rich players?"

If litigation in Cleveland and indignation in Maryland do not derail the deal, it will make Modell the latest proof that there often is no penalty for failure in America. Maryland's role in this farce is the latest proof that government often is the servant of those strong enough to wheedle it cleverly.

January 22, 1996

AIDS: The Evolution of an Epidemic

The AIDS epidemic is "one of those cataclysms of nature that have no meaning, no precedent, and, in spite of many claims to the contrary, no useful metaphor." So wrote Sherwin Nuland, who teaches medicine at Yale, in his book *How We Die: Reflections on Life's Final Chapter.* No metaphor, perhaps, but the epidemic's evolution underscores a grim truth: life is regressive. That is, people with problems have a high probability of acquiring more problems.

This truth can be tickled from numbers provided by Philip Rosenberg in *Science* magazine. The numbers show that even good news about the epidemic is infected with alarming connotations. His good news has two parts, one of which is that previous estimates of the prevalence of HIV— the virus that is the precursor of AIDS—among Americans were too high. Rather than 800,000 to 1.2 million infected persons, there probably were 630,000 to 900,000 as of January 1, 1993. The second part of the good news is that the incidence of AIDS has slowed and the epidemic seems to be approaching a plateau.

But the bad news also has two parts. One is that the plateau is terribly high, particularly for a disease transmitted almost entirely by behavior that, for more than a decade, has been abundantly publicized as putting people at risk. (The median incubation from HIV infection to the onset of AIDS seems to be about nine years.) This year approximately 50,000 people will die of AIDS-related diseases. Between 40,000 and 80,000 will be infected with HIV. Less than 5 percent of them will live long enough to be examples of "long-term nonprogression" in the destruction of their immune systems. The epidemic is too young for us to know its trajectory, but people in even that "long-term nonprogression" category probably will succumb.

The other part of the bad news is that the epidemic's dynamism is now devastating a different cohort of the population. From the first appearance of AIDS in America in the late 1970s, through the middle of the 1980s, the epidemic was driven by white homosexual men in major metropolitan areas, particularly New York, Los Angeles, and San Francisco. Now it is increasingly concentrated among racial minorities, involving more and more women, not only in cities but in rural areas, especially in the South, and is increasingly linked with drugs. That is, it is spreading among people inadequately constrained by social norms, including the criminal law pertaining to drugs, and impervious to even the aggressive dissemination of public health information.

The arrival of AIDS was shocking. It struck, Nuland says, just as biomedical science was beginning to believe that the conquest of infectious bacterial and viral diseases was in sight. It is doubly shocking that today the disease has become endemic even though it is difficult to acquire and is almost entirely preventable. "AIDS is a disease of low contagion," writes Nuland. "HIV is a very fragile virus—it is not easy to become infected with it." It has been transmitted only by blood, semen, vaginal fluid, and breast milk.

Yet in early public commentary about AIDS, there were absurd comparisons to the Black Death of the fourteenth century. People contracted that plague by eating food, drinking water, breathing the air. In the United States, AIDS is contracted primarily by anal receptive sex among men having sex with men, by dirty needles used by IV drug abusers, and by people who have heterosexual sex with infected bisexuals or IV drug abusers. Worldwide, heterosexual sex is the dominant mode of transmission and before long may be in America.

In the last two years the proportion of newly reported AIDS cases among men having sex with men fell below 50 percent and 27 percent of newly reported AIDS cases were ascribed to drug injections. The spread of AIDS is further linked to drugs by women who turn to prostitution to support crack habits. HIV-related illness is the leading cause of death among young adults between twenty-five and forty-four years old. In 1994, a third of all deaths among black men in that age group were the result of such illnesses. Rosenberg estimates that by 1993, 3 percent of black men and 1.5 percent of Hispanic men between the ages of thirty and forty-four and 1 percent of black women in their late twenties and early thirties were infected with HIV. In something of an understatement, Rosenberg calls it "sobering" that one of every fifty black men eighteen to fifty-nine may be infected.

The Economist notes that black Americans, even more than most Americans, are having sex at younger ages. "By the age of fourteen, more than a third of black males have had sex, five times the rate among white and Hispanic boys." The earlier one starts, the more partners one is likely to have. That fact, and the fact that most Americans have sex with people of the same race and socio-economic condition, and the fact that many HIV cases are diagnosed only after the onset of AIDS, mean that there could be an explosive spread of AIDS among inner-city blacks. But not only there. For example, in Georgia the prevalence of HIV among childbearing women in some rural areas exceeds that in Atlanta.

The main reason for hope regarding AIDS is what it has always been: an epidemic driven by behavior can be contained by changing behavior. But one reason for not hoping extravagantly is the experience we have had with another, simpler behavior-driven epidemic, that of smoking-related diseases such as lung cancer. Smoking involves the powerful pull of nicotine. But AIDS often involves a tangle of sexual impulses and heroin or cocaine addiction. Thirty-two years have passed since the first surgeon general's report asserting a causal connection between smoking and cancer, and one lesson is clear: knowledge is not enough. A full-court-press campaign of public education has achieved considerable success in curtailing smoking, but in the process it has demonstrated something depressing. Aggressive public education and stigmatization have made smoking less common but also have made it increasingly concentrated among poorer and poorly educated Americans who are more susceptible to tobacco marketing than to medical warnings. Life really is regressive.

February 5, 1996

The Real Opiate of the Masses

In the escalating war against smoking—a habit that has taken many more lives than all of America's wars combined—some states are seeking compensation from tobacco companies for medical expenses for smoking-related injuries, and prosecutors are contemplating perjury and conspiracy charges against tobacco executives who testified to disbelief in the obvious—the addictive nature of nicotine. In this war, ironies and paradoxes abound.

Smokers shiver outside their workplaces, pariahs in a country the father of which was a tobacco farmer. Probably the most powerful disincentive for smoking—peer pressure—is also the most powerful incentive for people to start smoking. Most smokers start before age eighteen and start because of peer pressure in the search for status and glamour. However, smoking now seems dumb and déclassé.

Cigarettes are the world's most heavily taxed consumer product. U.S. state taxes range up to Washington's 81.5 cents a pack, and in twenty industrialized nations cigarette taxes are even higher, sometimes five times higher. The ideal revenue yield from such taxes would be zero.

By some calculations, the social costs of smoking (in health care, lost productivity from illness and shortened lives, and fire damage) about equal the sum produced by cigarette taxes plus the savings that smoking produces in the form of reduced spending for Social Security, pensions, and nursing home care for smokers. If every smoker quit today, that would be a crisis for Social Security and all pension plans that incorporate actuarial assumptions about millions of smokers dying before they can receive benefits they otherwise would collect.

Cigarettes generate interesting product liability litigation because cigarettes are harmful when used as intended. The fact that cigarettes are harmful has been broadly understood for several generations and today is almost universally acknowledged. (The one-fourth of smokers who die prematurely because of smoking lose on average twenty years of life expectancy, or twenty-nine minutes per cigarette.) The consensus about this, combined with the warning labels on cigarette packs and advertising, has helped immunize tobacco companies against liability for damage their products do. Juries have spurned plaintiffs who have said they deserve recompense from tobacco companies because "everyone knows" smoking is harmful.

Government subsidizes tobacco farming and the treatment of illnesses tobacco causes. Government pays for these things from a Treasury diminished by revenues lost because of productivity lost as a result of 1,164 smoking-related deaths a day. Think of three jumbo jet crashes, 365 days a year. Or think of three smoking-related deaths in the time it takes to read this column. Yet the cigarette war is a substantial government success.

In the mid-1950s half the nation's adults smoked. Today one-quarter do. Democracy presupposes the efficacy of information. Regarding tobacco, more people are behaving reasonably, largely because of government's most cost-effective activity, the dissemination of public health information. Is there in all of government in the last three decades a life-enhancing success comparable to the stigmatizing of smoking since the 1964 surgeon general's report affirmed a causal connection between smoking and cancer?

In *Ashes to Ashes*, Richard Kluger's Pulitzer Prize-winning history of America's tobacco industry, he writes that there has long been an intuitive, commonsense consensus that filling one's lungs with smoke is unhealthy. So why do a quarter of Americans over eighteen smoke, and smoke heavily—twenty-five cigarettes a day on average, which means about 70,000 nicotine "hits" per year?

Smoking, says Kluger, is a highly sensual experience costing about a penny a minute. No wonder it is the century's preferred pacifier, "the truest, cheapest, most accessible opiate of the masses" as they cope with "the careening velocity of life." Yes, smoking kills, but, says Kluger, the smoker's catechism is: Smoking hastens the death of only one in four smokers, so the odds are on the particular smoker's side; you must die of something, so the something might as well be a pleasure; smoking takes years off the end of life, which is not quality time; life is risky, so seize pleasure whenever possible.

Recently the Liggett Group Inc., which has less than 3 percent of America's cigarette market, agreed, under the pressure of a class action suit from smokers, to accept various government regulations and fund some programs to help smokers kick the habit. A small advance in the war.

It is a war with a long past that suggests a long future. A Russian czar used torture, Siberian exile, and executions to discourage smoking, a Mogul emperor of Hindustan had smokers' lips split, and a Turkish sultan, convinced that careless smoking caused a conflagration in Constantinople, made an example of some smokers by having pipes driven through their noses, sometimes just before, sometimes just after beheading them. "And yet," writes Kluger, "the custom thrived."

March 21, 1996

Gambling: "The Pathology of Hope"

Diana Cooper, a live wire in British society between the wars, always edited the Lord's Prayer when reciting it, refusing to say "Lead us not into temptation" because "it's no business of His." As today's Americans yield, even more than Americans always have, to the temptation to gamble, libertarians say this vice, if such it is, is none of the government's business to disapprove, particularly because governments almost everywhere are inciting it.

Still, Congress may commission a study of the causes and consequences of the changed public attitude that underlies this fact: Today only two states—Utah and Hawaii—do not have legalized gambling, the status of which has changed in just a generation from that of social disease to social policy. Perhaps the study should begin with the thoughts of J. H. Plumb, the British historian, on the pandemic wagering in eighteenth-century Britain.

Life, including the law, was often cruel and many people lived in unspeakable poverty in slums where epidemics slaughtered children and many men survived two or three wives. The British "took these things in stride as part of life's vast gamble," wrote Plumb, adding: "Living so close to death, they grew to love risk. Betting provided an outlet. Raindrops running down a windowpane, the fertility of a Dean's wife, horse races, cricket matches, dogfights, dice, and cards—all were fit subjects for a bet."

Perhaps the gambling fever in late twentieth-century America arises in part from contrasting conditions: So many of life's risks have been removed or palliated, living is not stimulating enough without gambling. But there is much more than that behind the change since 1935, when Grand Rapids, Michigan, police jailed the woman who organized bingo games for Catholic charities. Or since 1950, when the first great television spectacle from Washington, the Kefauver Committee investigation of organized crime, focused on the menace of gambling.

Massachusetts Puritans passed America's first law against gambling in 1631. At about the time General Washington was distressed by rampant gambling among soldiers at Valley Forge, Harvard and other universities were doing what all the colonies had done—using lotteries to raise funds. (President Washington supported a lottery to finance construction in the District of Columbia.)

In 1964, notoriously taxaphobic New Hampshire launched the first state lottery. Seventeen of that year's eighteen winners were from out of state. One reason state lotteries have multiplied is self-defense—to keep the money at home. Today state governments spend upward of $400 million a year advertising the lotteries that raise upward of $40 billion in "voluntary taxation."

Big government now depends on big gambling. Government needs gambling to help siphon government's total take—35.6 percent of GDP—from the economy. So governments exploit what Robert Goodman, a student of gambling, calls "the pathology of hope," which is particularly strong and poignant among the poor who have lost confidence in work as a means of upward mobility. Kim Phillips, a Chicago journalist, reports that one South Side liquor store sells 2,700 lottery tickets a day when the state jackpot reaches $20 million.

Of course gambling also satisfies something inherently human—a desire for play. More than 70 percent of Americans gamble in a given year, many of them putting money at risk for the same reason people ride roller coasters and see horror films—for an adrenalin rush not attained elsewhere in lives lacking intense experiences.

There can be different dimensions to the pleasures of gambling in different social milieus. At the turn of the century, when adoration of science gave rise to depressing philosophies of determinism, gambling was a way of asserting the reality of randomness, another name for luck.

At the end of this century, with the weed of pessimism growing in profusion in the national garden, gambling may be for many people a fatalistic assertion of the belief that most of life is luck. If in the new economy the rewards of life go increasingly to the intellectually gifted, and if that gift is to a significant extent conferred by genetic inheritance, then life is to a significant extent a lottery won or lost at conception, so one might as well roll the dice as life rolls along.

The pursuit of wealth without work is not new to this vale of tears. However, to the extent that "players" (as the gambling industry, which calls itself the "gaming industry," prefers to call gamblers) regard gambling not as play but as a utilitarian activity, and one tinged with despair or desperation, the proliferation of gambling is deeply depressing.

January 4, 1996

CHAPTER FIVE

(Epi)Phenomenal Politics

1994: 1938 Redux

Thirty years ago this Thursday, on the evening of October 27, 1964, supporters of Barry Goldwater's presidential candidacy bought half an hour on NBC for a prerecorded speech by a private citizen, who said: "This is the issue of this election: whether we believe in our capacity for self-government or whether we . . . confess that a little intellectual elite in a far distant capital can plan our lives for us better than we can plan them ourselves." A few hours after the broadcast the speaker was awakened at his Los Angeles home by a call from Washington informing him that the Goldwater campaign's switchboard was still clogged at three A.M. Eastern time by callers contributing $8 million ($38 million in 1994 dollars). Sixteen years after that, the speaker was elected president.

In 1964 President Johnson won a landslide victory by using one of the first and most effective negative television campaigns, and by telling Americans that "greater government activity in the affairs of the people" would produce a Great Society. But soon there came a conservative tide that has not yet crested. In 1966 Republicans rebounded, gaining forty-seven House seats. In 1968 the combined Nixon-Wallace vote was 56.9 percent. In 1972 Nixon carried forty-nine states. In 1976 Democrats, facing a Republican Party still reeling from Watergate, won, but barely, and only by nominating the most conservative candidate who sought the nomination. Republicans won the next three elections. Then Bill Clinton won a 43 percent victory by advertising himself as a semidemiconservative ("New Democrat").

The 1994 elections could resemble those of 1938. Those produced a powerful reaction against a president who had overreached his mandate—FDR had tried to enlarge the Supreme Court so he could pack it. Republicans gained eighty-one House seats, almost doubling their total, and joined with conservative Democrats in a coalition that generally prevented a liberal legislating majority until 1964 produced a two-year liberal episode.

Historian Alan Brinkley believes that Republicans crossed a Rubicon in the late 1970s. They took their cue from Californians who in June 1978 took government into their own hands, using Proposition 13 to slash their property taxes. Until the late 1970s conservatives had argued, as Goldwater did, that many government programs, although popular, must be opposed because they take an intolerable toll on freedom. But the "Reagan Revolution" rested on the premise that Goldwaterite opposition to government programs was politically futile. So conservatives would attack taxes rather than the programs they support.

This was Republican accommodation to the fact that voters were ideologically conservative but operationally liberal. Voters were conflicted, which is a polite way of calling them hypocrites: They talked a much more conservative line than they were prepared to have their politicians hew to. So, how about now?

The election results two weeks from now will be sifted for signs that the country's still-waxing conservatism is at last producing an electoral sorting-out. Beginning in 1968 Republicans won five of six presidential elections but could not translate their presidential majorities into realignments farther down the ballot. For example, ten years ago Reagan carried 375 of 435 congressional districts, but only 182 of the 375 elected Republican representatives. And in 1992, 103 congressional districts voted for Bush and a Democratic representative or for Clinton and a Republican representative. However, there is evidence that more and more voters are becoming operationally as well as ideologically conservative. The evidence is anecdotal, but enough anecdotes make a pattern, and here is one from Speaker Tom Foley's campaign for a sixteenth term.

His campaign theme is that he brings home the bacon from the far distant capital. For example, he recently announced that his hometown of Spokane (population 178,000) is getting a larger law enforcement grant than San Francisco (population 724,000). However, a Spokane voter tells a reporter, "The man has done a lot of great things, you have to give him credit. But you have to wonder how corrupt Washington is if a man can bring that much money from Washington."

One reason for the public's steadily deepening disdain for government is the increasing reliance by politicians on negative advertisements of an increasingly scabrous sort. These usually are thirty-second snarls that preclude subtlety. Such campaigning, which is now the norm because it is effective, serves conservatism, for two reasons. First, campaigning in such short televised bursts is survival of the briefest, and conservatism's message, distilled to its essence, often is: No, less, stop that, cut it out. What that message lacks in poetry it makes up in concision. Second, conservatism considers distrust of government, and of people who crave political power, a virtue. Today's acidic campaigning breeds such distrust. Consider California's Senate race.

That state is so large (its population of 32 million is larger than the nation's population was when it elected Lincoln) that the only campaigning that matters is done via paid television. That is expensive and the biggest bang for the buck comes from accusation, denunciation, excoriation. Six months ago Dianne Feinstein, former mayor of San Francisco and now Democratic senator, was California's most-admired public official, regarded favorably by two-thirds of the voters. Her challenger, Michael Huffington, was an unknown freshman congressman. But by now each has driven up the other's "negatives" so high that whoever wins will be the most disliked official in the state.

This is part of what Jean Bethke Elshtain calls the "spiral of delegitimation." Vile campaigning deters many decent people from entering electoral politics. Thus the talent pool from which elected officials are drawn is small and brackish. Many of those who plunge into that pool are coarse to begin with and become more so by doing what it takes to win. With campaigns sounding like fingernails scraping across blackboards, voters come to despise all the authors of the awful noise, winners and losers alike.

Perhaps there are lessons to be drawn from this fact: During this thirty-year decline in the public's trust of government, polls have measured a marked increase in trust only during the presidency of the man who thirty years ago denounced the overbearing nature of the far distant capital.

October 31, 1994

Thermidor

Thermidor, the name of the month in the French Revolutionary calendar in which Robespierre fell and the Reign of Terror ended, has become the name by which historians denote an era of waning revolutionary ardor. Conservative critics of the 104th Congress complain that it went directly from the *ancien régime* to Thermidor, without any intervening revolution.

The deflation of their aspirations is symbolized by Newt Gingrich bran-
dishing buckets in which ice had been delivered to congressional offices
since before the invention of refrigeration. The Commerce and Education
departments may not be finished, but ice deliveries are, so there.

Some depressed conservatives—one of them calls the 104th "the Bush
administration in drag"—may think that the end of the 104th was in its
beginning, in its opening day hoopla, which included, among much else, a
children's party featuring the Mighty Morphin Power Rangers and Newt
Gingrich. Back then it was hard to have any Washington gathering of two
or more without having the speaker speak, and at the children's party he
stuffed into the wee minds this explanation of the event's Larger Meaning:
"We wanted the Power Rangers here because they're multiethnic role
models in which women and men play equally strong roles."

There has been too much blather, much of it from Gingrich, who has
paid dearly for his refusal to heed the advice given to him—early and
often—that he ration the portions of himself that he serves to the public.
Still, measuring the 104th against history rather than its own rhetoric, it
was remarkably consequential.

Intelligent people differ concerning the prudence of the 104th's most
important act—the repeal of a sixty-year-old entitlement to welfare. But
the repeal ranks with the 1981 tax cuts, Medicare, the 1964 and 1965 Civil
Rights Acts, and the Taft-Hartley Act as one of the most momentous legislative acts of the last six decades.

The 104th has demonstrated the constitutional fact of congressional
supremacy. Bill Clinton began his presidency talking only about "rein-
venting" government so that it could be more efficient while doing more.
He now accepts, at least rhetorically, that government should do less. This
underscores the fact that Democrats are more "out of power" today than
when George Bush was president but George Mitchell and Tom Foley ran
Congress.

Regarding spending, the actions of the 104th have been more conservative than even the aspirations of the Reagan administration. Last year, for
the first time since 1969, discretionary domestic spending was reduced.
From telecommunications to agricultural policy, regulations and subsidies
have yielded ground to competition and market forces. Sixty-five percent
of the Contract with America's seventy-four legislative provisions are now
laws or congressional rules. Of the major provisions, the House passed all
but the term-limits constitutional amendment.

The 104th's impressive record has been obscured by the fog of war
rhetoric from its leader, for whom politics is war carried on by other
means. *Roll Call*, the newspaper of Capitol Hill, has obtained tapes of
some of Gingrich's frequent conversations with army officers. They are

filled with military jargon ("after-action reviews," "small unit cohesion") and allusions, such as, "I think our budget fight is a lot like [the Duke of Wellington's] Peninsula Campaign."

Gingrich must know what Wellington said of some troops sent to him for that campaign: "I don't know what effect these men will have upon the enemy, but, by God, they terrify me." It might be harmless hyperbole for him to say, "I am in combat everyday," but he scares people when he says things like: "The left at its core understands in a way Grant understood after Shiloh that this is a civil war, that only one side will prevail. . . ." That makes people yearn for a rhetorical Thermidor.

He is wise to brandish the ice buckets, for reasons Senator Pat Moynihan learned when campaigning in 1994. Moynihan found little public interest in the failure of the Clintons' gargantuan health care proposal, but got warm recognition when he mentioned he had "decriminalized baby-sitting."

You remember: Clinton's first two choices to be attorney general came a cropper because they, like millions of others, had violated the law requiring payment of Social Security taxes on domestic workers' wages of more than $50 per quarter (a sum unchanged since 1950). Sally nextdoor baby-sits for $5 every Saturday and you forget her payroll taxes, you are an outlaw.

Moynihan helped get the $50 changed to $1,000 annually. "Here was something (people) could relate to, that mattered to them *personally*." Ice buckets and baby-sitting reflect the miniaturization of politics, itself a conservative achievement.

October 3, 1996

Bob Dole: The Ledger of His Daily Work

When Democrats were thinking of offering their 1948 presidential nomination to Dwight Eisenhower, taciturn Speaker Sam Rayburn said of him, "Good man, but wrong business." Does Rayburn's estimate of Eisenhower suit Bob Dole? Rayburn, who later revised his assessment of Eisenhower sharply upward, worried that the soldier, shaped by the military's command environment, might not be sufficiently rhetorical and wily for the political environment of persuasion and negotiation. Today even many people who wish Dole's candidacy well worry that his lifetime as a legislator—he was elected to Congress when Eisenhower was president, in 1960—has revealed, or developed, proclivities that would be disabilities in a president.

Dole is one of the large figures of America's legislative history. However, the gravamen of the argument against him is this: One thing that has made him effective—the ideological fuzziness that helps him build legislating coalitions by rubbing the sharp edges off issues—would prevent him from reaching presidential greatness, one ingredient of which is a zest for polarizing conflicts over principles. Of course, greatness in the presidency is not necessary, which is fortunate considering its scarcity. And a subliminal theme of any campaign against Bill Clinton is bound to be "let's bring back the grown-ups." That is one reason Dole's age—he will be seventy-three in 1996, older than anyone ever elected to a first presidential term—will not matter.

Another reason is his almost alarming energy. He is (as John Updike describes a character in one of his novels) "an athlete of the clock." It is said talent is a species of vigor. Dole is immensely talented at many political crafts. It also is the case that, like a lot of politicians, he can't sit still. It almost seems that a kind of attention deficit disorder is an occupational hazard of—or an advantage in—high-level politics.

In his public speaking (at least until now; he seems to be trying to reform) he has had the disconcerting habit of improvising, which requires a fluency not natural to him. His aversion to written texts reflects, among other things, the fact that he, like many legislators, is comfortable only with the conversational, unstructured, almost cryptic discourse by which colleagues in a small, face-to-face, legislative setting communicate with each other. His capacity for rhetoric that is even coherent, let alone inspiriting, either has atrophied from disuse or never existed. Whichever, this could be a problem in the presidency and will be perhaps his principal defect as a candidate.

After four years of the oppressively talkative current president, Americans may want an anesthetizing reticence rather than the ointment of presidential eloquence. But before Dole can be president, he must be a candidate who has the steely will to stay "on message." That is doubly difficult for Dole, because he does not have the restraining bridle of a clear agenda dictated by a crisp ideology, and because he is a proud and intelligent man who bridles at attempts to subdue his spirit, of which his untameable wit is an admirable manifestation. There may be admirable aspects to the obduracy of a candidate who refuses to be broken to the saddle of campaign discipline, but there also may be arrogance—and the laziness of someone who is indefatigable when doing what he enjoys, but only when doing that.

Dole, this unrhetorical, almost anti-rhetorical man, is seeking an office whose constitutional powers are weak but whose rhetorical potential is great. Of necessity he will try to stress what has been called "the charisma of competence." But the presidential election will occur two years after the most ideological off-year elections in American history. And the Republican Party is more ideological than at any time in its history. The 1996 political season will not be hospitable to the dotty notion that served Michael Dukakis so poorly—that we should have an election "about competence, not ideology." Dole's message must be that all God's Republican children now have essentially the same ideology—that of limited government—but that he is especially competent to implement it. That may ring true.

Dole's preeminence at the moment may reflect a yearning for surcease from the manifold incompetence of the incumbent president and from the unceasing eruptions of the human Vesuvius who is speaker. Can the country learn to yearn for someone sometimes described as acidic? Dole does have a "dark side," but the idea that it defines him illustrates the axiom that fame is the accumulation of misunderstandings around a well-known name.

He does have some grievances against life's close calls. If he had been a few yards away from where he was on that Italian hill on April 14, 1945, or if the war in Europe had ended twenty-five days sooner, he would not have endured the horror of the wounding, the long agonies of rehabilitation, or the daily pain ever since. A wafer-thin margin of votes cost him the vice presidency in 1976. And if he had stayed on his conservative message in the week before the 1988 New Hampshire primary, he would have beaten Bush there and today might be midway through his second presidential term.

Yet far from being bleak about life, he may be, if anything, too sanguine to suit the nation's mood of the moment, and especially the mood of the Republican nominating electorate. Although he is unlike Reagan in many ways, they both are midwestern boys, fated to a fundamental cheerfulness about America's possibilities. He seems to have only a faint notion of the anger and anxiety many people feel about the coarsening of American life. He has no feel for the intellectual currents in today's controversies about the deleterious consequences government is having on the culture and on the character of the individual. He does not dislike the city where he has worked for thirty-four years. Others may talk of turning the ship of state hard to starboard. Dole thinks a better touch on the tiller should suffice.

Say what you will about this fixture in our national life, he is not one of those puffed-up politicians who always act as though they are unveiling statues of themselves. It has been well said (by Beryl Markham) that "if a man has any greatness in him it comes to light, not in one flamboyant hour, but in the ledger of his daily work." Dole has no flamboyant hours, but his ledger of work is long and honorable and its bottom line is not yet written.

March 6, 1995

Taking Conservatism Slumming

Just fifteen months after the 1994 elections, the high-water mark of modern conservatism, the conservative party is under assault from a man who clearly despises it and disdains the conservatism of its most successful modern president. Ronald Reagan spoke constantly of freedom. Pat Buchanan speaks of restrictions and proscriptions, closing ports to imports, closing borders to immigrants. Reagan imparted confidence to Americans. Buchanan, a whiner liberals can love for his litany of victimizations, presents America as the crybaby of the Western world. Buchanan wants to erase the Reaganite smile from the face of conservatism and replace it with his snarl of resentment about people "sitting on the corner playing bongo drums" in downtown Washington, about the economic onslaught from mighty Mexico, about the voicelessness of "Euro-Americans," about the teaching of "Godless evolution," and other affronts to this "Christian country."

Buchanan's is the only important candidacy this year, because only it can have big consequences, including a ruinous redefinition of conservatism. Most presidents' second terms are even less successful than their first terms, so if Bill Clinton is reelected, and (as is likely) Republicans control Congress, he will be even less consequential than he has been while being the least consequential president since Coolidge. Neither Bob Dole nor Lamar Alexander would significantly alter, retard, or accelerate the conservative agenda that is well defined and advancing. Clinton's latest budget is much more conservative than the one twelve months ago. For the first time since the 1960s spending on government programs (everything but debt services) is less than the government is receiving in revenues. Conservatism has carried the day against liberalism. Now comes Buchananism, wrecker of what Reaganism has wrought.

Buchanan, whose candidacy gives a patina of validity to media caricatures of conservatism, says, "We are taking our party back." From whom? From virtually everyone with conservative credentials. From the spirit of Reagan, champion of free trade. From William F. Buckley, who has judged some Buchanan statements anti-Semitic. From William Bennett who, long before endorsing Alexander, said Buchanan "flirts" with fascism. From Phil Gramm, who doesn't need his Ph.D. in economics to know that protectionism "is a dagger aimed at the heart of everything we stand for. . . . [There] has always been a recessive gene in the American character that has found protectionism appealing." From Newt Gingrich, a student of history who surely recognizes in Buchanan's brew of nativism and protectionism a recipe concocted by the European right—statism in the service of xenophobic nationalism. Says Gingrich, Buchanan is an "isolationist" and a "reactionary": "He is not a conservative. He does not represent Ronald Reagan or Barry Goldwater or anything that we understand as conservatism."

Buchanan has some interesting supporters. Asked recently, with reference to a neo-Nazi newspaper's raptures, "What have you done to generate such enthusiasm among the Nazis?" Buchanan replied: "I have done nothing." Oh?

He repeatedly has expressed impatience with prosecutions of accused Nazi war criminals. When the United States apologized to France for having sheltered Klaus Barbie, the "butcher of Lyons," Buchanan was contemptuous of "all this wallowing in the atrocities of a dead regime." In 1989 he denounced as "moral bullying" the ostracism of Austria's President Kurt Waldheim, whose offense was, Buchanan implied, trivial: "Like others in Hitler's army, Lieutenant Waldheim looked the other way." Hitler's army did much worse than look away; it was deeply complicit in genocide. And in 1988 an Austrian commission concluded unanimously that Waldheim was close to persons committing atrocities, "repeatedly went along" with his unit's atrocities, and that his passivity when knowing of criminal plans facilitated atrocities.

In 1990 Buchanan, blithely misrepresenting "1,600 medical papers," ridiculed the "so-called 'Holocaust Survivor Syndrome,' " which he said involves "fantasies" of martyrdom and heroics. He said that "reportedly" half the survivor testimonies on file at Yad Vashem memorial in Jerusalem are considered "unreliable." He did not say who reported that.

Regarding the use of diesel engine exhaust to asphyxiate Jews at the Treblinka concentration camp where 850,000 died, in 1990 Buchanan wrote: "Diesel engines do not emit enough carbon monoxide to kill anybody." How did he know? "In 1988, ninety-seven kids trapped 400 feet underground in a Washington, D.C., tunnel while two locomotives spewed diesel exhaust into the car, emerged unharmed after forty-five minutes." The source of that anecdote? "Somebody sent it to me." It had already appeared in a publication specializing in Holocaust denial.

Buchanan's eagerness to use such stuff that comes in, as it were, over his transom is telling. And as Jacob Weisberg wrote in *The New Republic*: "Carbon monoxide emitted by diesel engines is sufficient to asphyxiate people when they are crammed by the hundreds into thirteen-foot chambers. According to the *Encyclopedia of the Holocaust*, suffocation at Treblinka took as much as half an hour; Buchanan's comparison only proves that the children he described had sufficient oxygen to survive whatever length of time they were trapped in the tunnel." Even though the tunnel was open at both ends, some children were made sick.

Diesel exhaust was used for killing at several other Nazi death camps and by the *Einsatzgruppen,* roving death squads. By saying it cannot kill, and by saying survivors' testimonies are unreliable, Buchanan abets the principal neo-Nazi obsession—Holocaust denial. The deniers, says Weisberg, focus on Treblinka: "Because the camp was destroyed and most witnesses murdered before the Allies arrived, a smaller quantity of conclusive evidence survives than from Auschwitz. The revisionist case is therefore harder to discredit." The Holocaust deniers' lot is not easy. They reciprocate assistance, such as Buchanan's.

Just fifteen months after conservatism captured the constitutional high ground, Capitol Hill, a reckless presidential campaign is taking the name of conservatism slumming. It could get terribly soiled.

March 4, 1996

Buchanan won the first primary, in New Hampshire. He lost the rest.

A Weird Sincerity

Senator Bob Kerrey, the Nebraska Democrat, spoke with measured malice. Asked if he trusts President Clinton's promise that he will not betray Democrats by coming to a budget agreement with Republicans without the support of Democrats, Kerrey said, "I trust him because [Senate Minority Leader] Tom Daschle trusts him." In 1993, after much agonizing, Kerrey cast the decisive vote for the Clinton budget that Clinton recently said raised taxes too much. But Kerrey is not unusual in his unconcealed disdain. Among congressional Democrats there is scant affection and less respect for Clinton.

The Senate welfare bill, which Clinton has warmly endorsed, is, says Senator Pat Moynihan, "an obscene act of social regression." Charging that the administration has suppressed a study showing that more than a million children would fall into poverty as a result of the bill (which is marginally less severe than the House bill), Moynihan says with icy fury, "Just how many millions of infants we will put to the sword, is not yet clear. There is dickering to do. . . . Those involved will take this disgrace to their graves. The children alone are innocent." Columnist Murray Kempton once wrote that the absence of honest passion is the distinguishing feature of professional wrestling and American politics. Not anymore.

As Washington braces for the climactic battle over the budget, passions range from exhilaration, tinged with anxiety, on the Republican side, to rage among Democrats. Their reserves of rage are almost depleted because they are directed at both Republican measures and Clinton's character. Today's bipartisan consensus is that Clinton is neither bad nor dangerous, just silly. Plainly put, almost no one thinks he believes a word he says. Or, more precisely, he believes everything he says at the moment he emphatically says it, and continues to believe it at full throttle right up to the moment he repudiates it. He has the weird sincerity of the intellectual sociopath, convinced that when he speaks, truth is an option but convenience is an imperative.

As of Saturday, Clinton aides said he was "rethinking" his support for the Senate welfare bill. Of course. By now few know, or much care, what he means when he says Republicans must change their budget priorities before he can deal with them. They propose to balance the budget in seven years, as opposed to the five years he proposed in 1992 or the ten years, and then nine years, and then seven years he has called feasible. Republicans want to cut taxes and he says he does, too, but differently. They favor a $500-per-child tax credit; he used to favor an $800 credit. They favor cutting the capital gains tax; so, suddenly, does he, but differently, details to follow, someday. They favor limiting the growth of Medicare; so does he, but not as much. This man with a political menu featuring *principles du jour* says his promised veto of the Republican budget will be a matter of principle.

Does this garrulous man have any idea how much he has debased the currency of presidential rhetoric? He has done so partly in the way a currency usually is debased: simply by producing too much of it. De Gaulle said Bismarck was a great man because he knew when to stop. One reason Clinton cannot be even adequate is that he cannot keep quiet.

Carol Gelderman, professor at the University of New Orleans, writing in *The Wilson Quarterly,* says most recent presidents "have been loquacious to a fault." Clinton has broken the record for wretched excess. Gelderman writes that Gerald Ford, whom no one ever called Periclean, delivered a speech on average every six hours during the election year of 1976 (including such things as press conference announcements as well as formal speeches). Jimmy Carter stepped up the pace, addressing his countrymen often enough to add 9,873 single-spaced pages to the *Public Papers of the Presidents of the United States.* Ronald Reagan, who understood that rationing something increases its value, spoke less frequently than Carter but still increased the bulk of presidential papers by an additional 13,000 pages over two terms. Clinton, in his first year as president, spoke publicly three times as often as Reagan did in his first year.

Even before Clinton's recent run of half-baked strategies and quarter-baked thoughts, he had become an object of ridicule even among semi-friends. Six months ago *The New Republic* ran this parody of his penchant for musing aloud:

> The Republicans call for legal reform. I totally oppose this. Well, maybe "totally" is strong and I guess I went overboard on "oppose," but may I make a tiny suggestion? I don't just want legal reform, I want *middle-class* legal reform. In particular, I want to restrict how many lawsuits can be brought against one guy who gets up every day to do the hard work of change and then can't finish his third plate of waffles before some gold-digging bimbo brings charges of sexual harassment against him even though it was obvious to any trooper in the room that she wanted it as much as he did.

Senator Paul Wellstone, an exuberantly liberal Minnesota Democrat, says the coming budget battle will be "a really existential moment" for Clinton. Actually, every moment is an existential moment for Clinton, who is passionate about whatever he is passionate about at the moment. The Book of Genesis saw him coming: "Unstable as water, thou shalt not excel." For Clinton, excelling is out of the question, but survival is not. His hope, and that of congressional Democrats, is that Republicans will come a cropper next year because this year they are not heeding polls that show rising anxiety about budget cuts. Whether or not that comes to pass, and regardless of what one thinks about what the Republicans are doing, it is bracing to have the dominant force in Washington faulted for insufficient reverence for the most recent poll results.

Republicans at the end of their year of living dangerously are not hearing many cheers, but they can take comfort from the axiom that applause usually is the echo of a platitude. Clinton can take comfort from the axiom that success is relative: It is making something of the mess one has made of things. But before he can regain a modicum of respect he must stop seeming to be a miser of accuracy—someone who so treasures the truth that he expends it sparingly.

November 13, 1995

Clinton the Inconsequential

CHICAGO—When Nature was dishing out the ability to blush, Bill Clinton did not hold out his plate, so he will come to his party's convention here unencumbered by embarrassment about the disparity between the presidency he promised and the one he has produced. If he is reelected, that will be largely because the country believes, accurately and contentedly, that he has been notably inconsequential and that a second term will be even less consequential than the first.

Four years ago his campaign featured the promise of a finishing filigree on the Great Society—universal health care. A Congress nearing completion of almost four decades under Democratic control would surely enact a Democratic president's request for the largest new entitlement in six decades, since Social Security. The Democratic Party's happy days would be here again because it would have returned to the Rooseveltian and Johnsonian recipe of programs benefitting the broad middle class, not just the needy.

However, Clinton's extravagant health care proposal catalyzed the 1994 elections that cost Democrats control of Congress. And today Clinton is campaigning unblushingly as, he insists, the proud partner of the Republican-controlled Congress in repeal of a New Deal entitlement, Aid to Families with Dependent Children.

Acknowledging the power of fanaticism during the French Revolution, Mirabeau said of Robespierre, "He will go far, for he believes all he says." Proving the power of cynicism in our time, Clinton has gone far toward reelection because he seems to believe nothing he says. And look what is being said about him.

The media have lately made much of Republican strife concerning abortion policy—policy that has not been altered by either a Republican-controlled Congress or a Supreme Court that includes seven justices appointed by Republican presidents. However, concerning the immediately practical question of welfare, Clinton accepts legislation that has provoked one of his party's most distinguished members, Pat Moynihan, to an acidity unmatched in Republican arguments.

"The current batch [of liberals] in the White House," says Moynihan, "now busily assuring us they were against this [the end of the federal entitlement to welfare] all along, are simply lying, albeit they probably don't know when they *are* lying. They have only the flimsiest grasp of social reality; thinking all things doable and equally undoable." Moynihan praises the opposition to the welfare bill by the Catholic bishops, "who admittedly have an easier task with matter of this sort. When principles are at issue, they simply look them up. Too many liberals, alas, simply make them up."

Moynihan may not be right about the recklessness of the welfare legislation that broadly devolves responsibilities to states and constitutes the most important such devolution of federal power since the end of Reconstruction. But Moynihan is certainly saying what many more timid Democrats are thinking.

They are thinking: Did we go through the barren years (when Democrats lost five of six presidential elections, and but for a few thousand votes in 1976 would have lost six in a row) for this? Of course their only victory in that period was won by a southern governor whose campaign promise of "a government as good as the American people" was an oblique endorsement of the view that government was not good.

Just two years ago Clinton was saying there was a health care "crisis" that justified the largest peacetime expansion of government in American history. Today he talks more about school uniforms than about that "crisis," thereby calling to mind an old axiom: Some people are in politics because they want to *do* something, others because they want to *be* something. Ronald Reagan, who had an adult life before being drawn to politics by the power of his convictions, was one of the former. Clinton, who went almost directly from student life to political life, is one of the latter.

(Then there is Ross Perot, who had an adult life before he went into politics in order to show off.)

In 1987, on the eve of Margaret Thatcher's third trouncing of the Labor Party, one of her confidants told an American journalist: We know Labor will one day win another general election. It is our job to hang on till Labor becomes sane. Today Labor is led by Tony Blair, who is called Clintonesque partly because of the smoothness with which he has jettisoned some of the statism that made Labor distinctive and self-destructive. He seems on the verge of victory in the next election. If Clinton, on the evening of November 5, delivers a victory speech, it will be for many in his party a concession speech, too, implicitly conceding the end of the aspirations that define them as Democrats.

August 25, 1996

It's Over?

At Henry IV's coronation, the archbishop anointed the king with oil said to have been given to Thomas à Becket by the Virgin Mary (and the archbishop found the king's hair aswarm with lice). Republics, favoring simplicity, have less-exotic civic liturgies—no stately ranks of bishops or oceans of ermine and silk. Republics rely on rhetoric to quicken the public pulse. America's pulse probably stayed steady during President Clinton's bland, formulaic Inaugural Address, but he could not expect to excite while declaring the end of political excitements.

It's Over?

The day before the inauguration, a *Washington Post* report of an interview with Clinton carried this headline: "Clinton Sees End of Fight Over Government's Role." Gosh. An argument as old as Plato's *Republic*, over? A great constant of American life, the argument about how much and what kind of government we want, and what we are willing to pay for it in circumscribed freedom and conscripted treasure, over?

Clinton's wish was the father of that thought as it appeared, somewhat hedged, in his Inaugural Address: "We have resolved for our time a great debate over the role of government." "Our time" ends this week.

He used the word "responsibility," or a permutation of it, five times. Americans are in an unusually intense period of debate about the proper spheres of individual and government responsibilities, with a subsidiary debate raging about which levels of government are responsible for what.

Granted, as long ago as the 1944 presidential campaign the Republican candidate, Thomas Dewey, said, "We Republicans are agreed that full employment shall be a first objective of national policy," achieved, if necessary, by government job creation. Dewey's premise was that peacetime politics would be mostly about economics and mostly a matter of consensus. In 1962 President Kennedy declared that arguments about the nation's domestic arrangements now "relate not to basic clashes of philosophy or ideology but to ways and means of reaching common goals," principally through "the practical management of a modern economy."

This is a hardy perennial, this recurring yearning for politics to be supplanted by administration, so we can all take a holiday from history. Clinton's yearning is understandable, given the central symbolism of inaugural ceremonies: Presidents-elect must travel to Capitol Hill, seat of the first branch of government—the subject of Article One of the Constitution. And Congress as currently constituted does not think the debate about government's role has been resolved "for our time."

Clinton chose to echo George Bush's Inaugural Address, in which Bush declared that the people "did not send us here to bicker." Bush then paused and extended his hand to two Democrats, Senate Majority Leader George Mitchell and Speaker Tom Foley. The four-year gnawing they gave that hand did much to prevent a second Bush Inaugural Address.

Clinton on Monday decried "petty bickering," but the adjective hardly modifies the noun: To stigmatize arguing as bickering is to declare it the low activity of small people. But when Clinton, referring to the American people, spoke of the "extreme partisanship they plainly deplore," he denied what is obviously the case: In a nation with two durable parties, when the electorate frequently entrusts the political branches to different parties, it seems to be insisting on partisan clashes, and certainly is guaranteeing them.

Clinton is said to be preoccupied by history's estimate of his greatness. When asked by *Washington Post* reporters whether a president can achieve that without "winning a big fight," he said he has had some big ones, mentioning fights over the budget and trade and even the crime bill. (You remember—midnight basketball and all that.)

He likens himself to two other presidents who served at the dawns of centuries, Jefferson and Teddy Roosevelt. Jefferson projected the nation's sphere to the Pacific. TR, who spoiled for fights as ardently as Clinton longs for love, projected the government into the nation's economic life and the nation into the world in dramatically new ways. The contrast between building the Panama Canal and passing the crime bill is a telling index of two men's contrasting ideas of what is big.

Nowadays, people who have nothing much in mind for next week speak instead about the next century or millennium, as Clinton does. "It's no easy thing," reports the *Washington Post's* front page, empathizing with him, "ushering in a millennium."

Actually, nothing could be easier. Just stand there. One minute it is one millennium, the next minute it is another. Millennia arrive whether or not anyone ushers them in—another blow to presidential pride and a setback for the quest for greatness.

January 22, 1997

Entitlement and Disappointment

In 1930 in America average life expectancy at birth was fifty-eight years for men, sixty-one for women. By 1990 it was seventy-one and seventy-nine respectively. Until the 1930s the average manufacturing worker toiled nearly fifty hours a week with few rights or benefits. In 1996 about 80 percent of all workers have employer-paid health insurance. In 1940 most Americans were renters, most households had neither a refrigerator nor central heating, 30 percent lacked inside running water, coal fueled most furnaces and stoves, wood was the second most-used fuel. More than a fifth of Americans lived on farms, less than a third of which had electric lights and only a tenth had flush toilets. In 1940 one in twenty Americans had a college degree; fifty years later, one in five did. In 1945 most households did not have a telephone. In 1994 (when the typical new home was 40 percent larger than its 1970 counterpart), 81 percent of households had

VCRs, 37 percent had personal computers. As late as 1948 retirement was no certainty: about half the men over sixty-five worked. In 1995, after decades of supposed "deindustrialization," industrial production was 40 percent higher than in 1980, 90 percent higher than in 1970, 350 percent higher than in 1950. In 1964 there were fewer than 100 black elected officials nationwide; now there are 8,000. Between 1929 and 1933 output declined almost 25 percent. In the worst postwar recessions (1973–75 and 1981–82) output declined just 4.9 and 3 percent respectively. In 1976 the average supermarket offered 9,000 products; fifteen years later it offered 30,000. We are richer, freer, healthier, and work at less exhausting jobs than ever before.

So why during this epoch of unprecedented achievement has America become preoccupied with perceived failure? That question is subtly answered in Robert Samuelson's new book *The Good Life and Its Discontents: The American Dream in the Age of Entitlement, 1945–1995.* Samuelson, the *Newsweek* and *Washington Post* columnist, should have Secret Service protection because if anything happens to him, we are sunk.

He says postwar progress bred an entitlement mentality which in turn bred disappointment that the nation was not living up to unattainable promises. The belief was that we were entitled to whatever is possible; that a rapid, uninterrupted, and painless increase in prosperity is possible, and that such prosperity would banish most social ills. Samuelson says this "almost dreamlike concept of progress" was accompanied by a decline in the sense of responsibility.

Samuelson believes that the mobilization of society for the Second World War blurred the distinction between governmental and private responsibilities. The postwar agenda of unideological "problem-solving" politics erased the distinction between problems that can be solved and conditions that must be endured. For example, in 1970 the man who had been Lyndon Johnson's chief economic adviser said recessions are "fundamentally preventable, like airplane crashes and unlike hurricanes."

Thus did economics, once the "dismal science" that explained costs and limits, become the "cheery science," encouraging the delusion that proper politics is (like another postwar chimera, the "science of management") merely a matter of experts' techniques. Such "pragmatism" became embittering: All problems were considered solvable, so enduring problems must be explained in terms of someone's incompetence or wickedness.

As Samuelson says, "Good was no longer good enough." As Lyndon Johnson said, it had to be a Great Society. And why not, John Kennedy having said, "Man holds in his hands the power to abolish all forms of human poverty." The illusion that government is the source of economic growth and is responsible for the "fair" allocation of wealth encouraged a sensibility demanding the ultimate entitlements—to security and peace of mind. The premise was that social conflict and personal discontent arise from material scarcities.

But economics, far from being a "hard" science, like physics, has more accurately been called a "science of single instances"—hardly a science. The hubris of economists professing competence to control America's complex modern economy, combined with democracy's disposition to spend avidly and tax reluctantly, produced inflations that only recessions could quell.

"Compassionate" postwar capitalism featured giant corporations happily serving as welfare states, promising job security and other benefits, and not attending to competitiveness until jobs had to be shed by the tens of thousands. "Compassionate" government, encouraging the expression of personal desires as group grievances, generated public distrust by becoming a fountain of synthetic, and meaningless, "rights," such as the right to "educational equality." Education and health care were, Samuelson notes, more "equal" when there was a lot less of each.

If the electorate can be inoculated with Samuelson's thesis—that "we need to curb our casual use of government" and "either we reconstitute our expectations, or we condemn ourselves to perpetual disappointment"—his book can elevate this year's political argument.

January 18, 1996

Fast Ride, No Driver

A recurring question is, "Where will the winner of the presidential election take the nation?" There is a ton of silliness packed into the verb "take." What is this nation, a brown paper parcel that presidents can pluck up by the twine wrapped around it and take where they wish?

Talk about presidents "taking" the country hither and yon is part of the foam on a presidential election. Such talk is particularly pernicious when it concerns the economy, as in the common polling question about which candidate would be better at "handling" the economy. America's economy involves uncountable billions of daily decisions by hundreds of millions of Americans. America's economy is influenced by hundreds of billions of daily decisions by producers and consumers of goods and services around the world. America's economy is not in any meaningful sense "handled" by anyone.

Such talk encourages what needs to be constantly discouraged—the hubris of government and its delusions of mastery. And such talk subverts something the nation needs, a sense of the velocity and unpredictability of the autonomous forces that are shaping the future.

Consider, for example, the mind-opening thoughts of Louise Yamada, research vice president at Smith Barney, in an interview with *Barron's*. She notes that in Manhattan there is a Levi's store where customers are scanned electronically for perfect-fitting jeans. At another store, customers' feet—both of them—are scanned for custom-made shoes. Perhaps in the future there will be much smaller retail inventories—samples may suffice, or even computerized images in "E-commerce" (marketing, billing, and paying on the Internet). If so, there will be less need for commercial retail space, for trucking to haul inventories, for power to light and heat the retail space, for fuel for the trucks, for all the paper that goes into triplicate order forms—for today's megamalls, for that matter.

So, hard times are ahead? For some, but boom times for others, such as the new companies driving such changes, companies built around digital and Web technologies— 4,200 such new companies in New York City alone.

Time was, coal, iron, and steel were the stuff of economic vigor. Now, says Yamada, the list may be sand, air, and light. "Sand for silicon, lasers, crystals, and fiber optics; gases, separated from air, for semiconductor washes, chemicals for plastics and catalytic processes; and light for fiber optics." Many such raw materials are low cost and will help insulate the economy from inflation.

Industrialization of developing nations may be speeded by the bypassing of traditional heavy infrastructures—going directly to cellular phones rather than laying miles of wire, and using solar power minimizes the need for fuel pipelines. Today's record U.S. agricultural exports reflect the surging demand of post-Third World countries for higher quality food. At a moment when new communication and manufacturing technologies are allowing a dispersal of American living patterns that amounts to a degree of deurbanization, the global demand for food may produce what Yamada calls "the full-circle return of the malls of America to farmland." American farmland is 25 percent of the world's productive capacity and America leads in biotech advancement of agriculture.

The lumbering policy-making processes of government are increasingly mocked by the speed of private-sector responses to economic information. Consider the train of events that began on a June morning two years ago, after an overnight frost in Brazil, when a government official there announced a substantial reduction in projected coffee production.

The news instantly flashed to the Coffee, Sugar, and Cocoa Exchange, where the price of coffee futures immediately began rising. Traders of soybeans and other products did not understand why this was happening but began bidding up their prices, causing the index of commodity prices to rise. This was registered on the computer screens of commodities traders in almost two hundred Wall Street firms, who reported this shiver of inflation to their bond-trading colleagues, who started a sell-off of bonds, which caused bond prices to fall, which caused bond yields to rise, which put upward pressure on interest rates, which caused stock prices to fall.

Elapsed time between the announcement in Brazil and the tremor on Wall Street: less than ten minutes.

Bear in mind Yamada's informed speculations, and the frost-in-Brazil story of high-velocity connectedness, when next you hear chatter about a president "taking" the country where he pleases, and "handling" the economy. America is—always has been—on a high-speed ride. But there is no driver. Never has been. That's the nature of a free society.

October 10, 1996

Sweeney Sends a *Frisson*

"Arise, ye prisoners of starvation!" exhorted the "Internationale," the anthem of the proletariat long ago, when the class struggle was supposed to be the engine of history and the proletariat was supposed to be the vessel of progress. John Joseph Sweeney has risen about as high as an American labor union man can, and as high as Washington's restrictions on high-rise buildings will permit. As the new head of the AFL-CIO, which has seventy-eight affiliated unions, Sweeney occupies an eighth-floor office in the house of labor on 16th Street, looking down on the White House. (Doesn't everybody seem to nowadays?)

Speaking softly, which he can do, and which he does with faint traces of his native Bronx, Sweeney, sixty-one, seems more like someone's Uncle Lenny than like Lenin. However, he was elected to lead labor because he is thought, with reason, to have "fire in the belly." He has sufficient girth to accommodate a conflagration. His suspenders are blindingly red, like the flags that were to flutter over the barricades at the dawn of justice. "Arise . . ."

Sweeney's exhortation to organized labor and to laborers not yet organized is "Arise, ye prisoners of wage stagnation!" It does not have quite the snap of the "Internationale," but it will do in a pinch. And organized labor is in a pinch, not only in Newt Gingrich's Washington but in today's global economy. The U.S. economy is enduring the disciplining rigors of international competition as never before. It is thriving, but only because many companies have become leaner by shedding workers, and workers' benefits. (Last week AT&T announced plans for doing without 77,800 managers—half its supervisors.) And many Americans believe life has become meaner.

It certainly has for organized labor. Union membership as a percentage of the workforce is at the lowest level since the Wagner Act was passed in 1935. (In the six years after that, union membership tripled.) Union membership was 33.2 percent of the workforce in 1955. Today it is 15.5 percent. In the private sector it is 10.9 percent. Since 1979 the United Auto Workers membership has shrunk from 1.5 million to 800,000, the United Steelworkers from 380,000 to 140,000. Much of organized labor's recent growth has been in the public sector, where 38.7 percent of the workforce is unionized. However, it is a mixed blessing for organized labor to be so heavily identified with government. True, government cannot be moved like a textile plant to South Korea, and in spite of the minisemidemicrisis misnamed the government "shutdown," government never goes out of business. But government may yet go through the sort of wringer the rest of the economy has been going through for more than a decade.

Only 3 million of the 70 million jobs added to the economy since 1950 have been manufacturing jobs, so unions have had to seek members in the public sector and in the private sector's service industries. One union that has grown like Topsy—by 500,000 members during the last fifteen years, doubling its size—is the Service Employees International Union. It is now the third largest union, behind the Teamsters and the American Federation of State, County, and Municipal Employees. SEIU represents janitors, doormen, and other support workers in commercial buildings, and service workers such as those delivering home health care. During those fifteen years of explosive growth the SEIU's president was John Sweeney.

His elevation to the AFL-CIO presidency has sent a *frisson* through the remnant of the American left because when his rhetoric is revved up, old leftists (there aren't many young ones) hear echoes of the United Mine Workers' John L. Lewis and other thunderers from the thirties. Sweeney, the son of Irish immigrants, has a flair for blarney, as when he says that "every workplace in America is being turned into a sweatshop" by "greedy employers" (Microsoft? Bill Gates?). Sweeney says workers are "being treated like so much roadkill on the highway of American life."

Such rhetoric strongly implies that the principal threat to the welfare of American workers is the nasty character of American employers. Would that it were. Demonizing bosses may be cathartic, but labor's problems arise from the increasingly open and deregulated world, featuring the unimpeded mobility of capital and the sudden entry into the world labor market of more than a billion Chinese and others. Sweeney and his allies speak of sit-down strikes and other civil disobedience to protest layoffs of resistance to unionization. Such theatrical tactics might help energize attempts to organize the unorganized (for example, poultry workers in the South), but they are no answer to the economic gales sweeping through the global economy.

When asked what he would seek from Congress if he could wave a magic wand and make Gingrich go away, Sweeney first mentions an increase in the minimum wage. As an act of militancy, that would hardly amount to storming the Winter Palace. Labor would like a law banning the hiring of replacements for striking workers, but labor could not get such a law when Democrats controlled Congress. When Samuel Gompers was AFL president for thirty-seven years, he was asked what he wanted for workers. He said "the earth and the fullness thereof" and gave abundant particulars. What many workers want now is security. Congress is power-less to give them that even were it so inclined, which it isn't. The first Democratic president in twelve years relied on Gingrich's Republicans to pass NAFTA, which labor (and a majority of congressional Democrats) opposed. Labor wants protectionism but the only presidential candidate singing from labor's hymnal is Pat Buchanan, whose increasingly weird "conservatism" expands reverence for property rights into the notion that workers have something like property rights to their jobs. James Madison wrote that "a man has a property in his opinions, and the free communica-tion of them. . . . He has a property very dear to him in the safety and lib-erty of his person. He has an equal property in the free use of his faculties." Not a word about jobs.

Bill Clinton, forever trying to square circles, stands foursquare for "change" but against anxiety and insecurity. Organized labor under Sweeney may be more forthright, seeking protection from the wider world and saying that change is not worth the cost in anxiety and insecurity. If so, labor will have the satisfaction of consistency, but only that satisfaction.

November 27, 1995

Incivility and Senator Byrd

Senator Robert Byrd, whose visage is as stony as the mountains of his West Virginia, resembles William Gladstone, of whom it was said he did not lack a sense of humor but rarely was in a mood to be amused. Nowadays Byrd is notably dour because of what he and others consider a steep decline in decorum in Congress.

An example of the "insolence" and "harsh and severe" rhetoric that Byrd finds grating came recently from Pennsylvania's Republican Senator Rick Santorum, a whippersnapper born the year Byrd was elected to the Senate (1958). Santorum said the president was telling "bald-faced untruths" about the budget and Democratic senators know it is "a lie" when they say the Republican tax cuts favor the rich. Senator Connie Mack, the Florida Republican, displeased Byrd by saying that Clinton's "commitment to principle is nonexistent" and that Clinton "broke his word" regarding the budget.

If Santorum and Mack spoke improperly, that may prove that truthfulness is not a sufficient justification for all utterances. Considerations of place and manner also matter. But Congress has seen worse incivilities, as when in 1850 a senator drew a pistol on another senator, or when in 1856 a congressman splintered his cane over the skull of a senator, or when in 1858 a senator called a colleague a "calumniator, liar, and coward," or when in 1863 a senator drew a pistol and threatened to shoot the sergeant at arms, or when in 1902 two South Carolina senators, both Democrats, traded punches on the Senate floor.

All but one of those incidents occurred when slavery and civil war had raised the stakes and temperature of politics. (*Roll Call* newspaper reports that once in the 1850s, a pistol accidentally discharged in a House member's desk and thirty or forty other members drew their weapons on the floor.) Which suggests one reason for Congress's comportment problems today. The issues today are hardly of a gravity commensurate with those of the 1850s and 1860s, but serious change is afoot, muscular interests are being challenged, and first principles of governance are being invoked. Congress now has an unusual number of "conviction politicians" motivated by hot passions, and rhetorical excesses are inescapable consequences of this generally wholesome development.

But there are uglier reasons for shrillness on Capitol Hill. One is that the assault on Robert Bork succeeded. Fueled by lies and by the conceit of 1980s liberalism that it had cornered the market on morality, this success vindicated the tactic of turning political differences into excuses for moral assaults. In the 1980s it was not enough to say that conservatives were wrong; the accusation was that they were wicked—makers of the "decade of greed," as it was known to liberals before enough was known about the Rose law firm and Mrs. Clinton's cattle futures.

This year Democrats have frequently compared Republicans to Nazis. This, shall we say, historical inexactitude indicates that some people have been unhinged by a horror they never thought possible—life in the minority. But today moral vanity is a bipartisan failing. Many Republicans, intoxicated by political triumphalism, and often by religious zeal, tend to regard their electoral successes as (literally) providential, and as vindications of their intellectual insights about social policy. Bullying arrogance is a consequence of the non sequitur that the fact of liberals' foolishness proves conservatives' wisdom. Republicans have at times run the House with a heavy hand, moving legislation under rules that unnecessarily restrict debates and amendments. It does not excuse the Republicans to note that they are doing unto others as they were done unto. Remember that after losing ten House seats in the 1992 elections, the Democratic majority rushed to give the right to vote in the committee of the whole to the five delegates from Guam, American Samoa, Puerto Rico, the U.S. Virgin Islands, and the District of Columbia.

Careerism, the cure for which is term limits, contributes to carnivorous politics. For people who enter politics young, planning to stay forever, electoral defeat means not just the inconvenience of a career change but the terror of annihilation, so campaigning becomes constant and desperate. And because of the toxic presence of TV cameras, the House and Senate floors have become stages for year-round campaigning. Televising Congress has had precisely the effect predicted by those who opposed it: Floor speeches are used to generate an unending stream of pungent sound bites for the evening news. This has a deleterious effect on the deliberative nature of Congress's proceedings.

Because negative campaigning provides the biggest bang for the political buck, it has become so incessant that good politicians are coarsened and coarse people are drawn to politics. How coarse? In 1992 a Democratic congressman, referring to President Bush, brayed, "I say it is time for Congress to tell the president to shove his veto pen up his deficit." The person presiding in the House responded, "The Chair wishes to advise members to be a little more guarded in making analogies to anatomical factors."

Incivility is a consequence of what Congress is and does. Congress, a representative institution, represents the nation's increasing vulgarity and declining self-restraint. Congress does too much. Members are constantly exhausted by long hours and the frustrations of fumbling around with myriad matters that would be beyond government's competence even if the government were not broke. There might be more comity in a Congress legislating for a smaller, more modest government.

Which brings us back to Byrd, who in his speech deploring the rudeness of his colleagues referred to some of them as "pygmies." Byrd is exercised about rhetorical excesses, but exemplifies behavioral excess. He has an unseemly notion of the role of a national legislator. If he wants to understand all the causes of the vulgarization of public life, he should examine his career, which he has conducted as a looting expedition, pillaging the federal budget for the benefit of his voters. The most serious offenses against standards of civilized politics are not words but deeds, and Byrd should not wax so indignant about politicians whose undignified talk does less damage than his deeds do to the dignity of politics.

January 8, 1996

Astronomy Cures Zealotry

Well, better late than never. As the century closes we have come upon a cure for the century's defining disorder, political zealotry. The cure is astronomy. Astronomy's withering rejoinder to zealotry is, What's the use?

Recently two University of Michigan astronomers reported that if the laws of physics as currently understood continue to operate, then in 10,000 trillion trillion trillion trillion trillion trillion trillion trillion years the universe, which is pretty much everything, will run down. Carbon-based life, including us, will long since have disappeared and the entire cosmos will be a thin soup of diffuse particles.

This assumes that the universe will go on expanding. Into what? That is hard to envision because, it has been said, the universe may be not just stranger than we imagine, but stranger than we can imagine. However, back to the end of things, which may come a lot sooner and more abruptly than the two Michiganders suppose.

Lots of old debris and new stuff makes the universe uncomfortably eventful. Earlier this month a "solar belch" (the *Washington Post*'s description) from the sun, a magnetic cloud 30 million miles thick, washed over the Earth at a million miles an hour. It may be what ruined a $200 million AT&T satellite.

However, such clouds are child's play compared with the comets and asteroids that might bump into Earth without bothering to file an environmental impact statement. The impact would be memorable, if any creature with memory survived, which is by no means assured, according to Timothy Ferris, writing in *The New Yorker*.

We have, Ferris writes, located fewer than 1 percent of the millions of asteroids—small planets made of stones and metals—in our little solar system, where impacts are ubiquitous, as the pockmarked surfaces of the moon and Mars attest. More than 150 terrestrial impact craters—there is one 50,000 years old and a kilometer wide near Winslow, Arizona—have been located on the Earth's surface. The surface would be as scarred as the moon's were it not for the erosion by wind and rain, and geological upheavals.

Every hour the Earth, orbiting the sun at 66,500 mph, gains a ton of weight from micrometeorite dust. Fist-size meteors hit about once every two hours. Once or twice a week there are "near hits" like that of the tumbling house-size object that was discovered just a day before it brushed past the Earth in 1994, just 65,000 miles out.

Every once in a million years, Ferris says, Earth collides with an object a kilometer in diameter—large enough to destroy India. If the object that produced the 1908 blast that flattened trees for fifteen kilometers around Siberia had arrived a few hours later it might have destroyed Oslo or St. Petersburg.

Last November only about ten hours may have spared Manila or Bangkok from the impact of the meteor that instead dug a crater 165 feet wide and ignited acres of coffee plants in Honduras. Extrapolating from cratering rates on the moon and other indices, astronomers estimate that about 2,000 asteroids larger than a kilometer in diameter—capable of generating devastating ocean waves and threatening a "nuclear winter" pollution of the environment—are in orbits that come near, meaning closer than the moon, to Earth's orbit. Only a tenth of them have been located.

It is, Ferris writes, widely accepted that 65 million years ago a comet or asteroid perhaps ten kilometers wide hit near Yucatán, creating enough environmental havoc to kill the dinosaurs and nine-tenths of all other species on Earth. If one hit the Atlantic near Bermuda, it would generate a wave that would be 600 feet high when it hit Manhattan at 500 mph and would submerge low-lying regions from Dublin to Hong Kong. Soot from fires started around the world by the exploding comet might blot out the sun for a year, and acid rain would destroy much of the remaining plant and animal life.

"A day will surely come," says a NASA astronomer to Ferris, "when the sheltering sky is torn apart with a power that beggars the imagination. It has happened before. Ask any dinosaur, if you can find one. This is a dangerous place."

Which confirms the wisdom of Arthur Balfour, the intellectual aristocrat who had been Britain's prime minister in 1905 and was still leader of the Conservative Party in 1911 when he suddenly and without explanation quit. He thought the all-consuming nature of modern politics was disproportionate to any good politics could do. As a friend explained, "He knows that there was once an ice age and that there will be an ice age again."

January 30, 1997

CHAPTER SIX

A WORLD STILL MUCH WITH US

America's Lost Sense of the Tragic

Brooding about the cataclysm of 1914 that shattered the long peace produced by the 1815 Congress of Vienna, Henry Kissinger wondered whether the protracted stability "might have contributed to disaster. For in the long interval of peace the sense of the tragic was lost."

America's sense of the tragic, never strong, may have been bleached away by the sunny blink of peace (peace enlivened by the Gulf War) since the end of the Cold War. Or so it would seem from the widespread incomprehension of the conservative Congress's determination to spend more on defense than President Clinton desires.

Liberal critics say this determination reflects the reflexive militarism of the right, or traditional pork barrel politics with the defense budget. Although undoubtedly some supporters of augmented defense spending are doing the right thing for the wrong reasons, it is the right thing.

But it is not actually an increase in defense spending. Rather, the administration's defense cutting—speaking of reflexive policies—is being slowed. The Pentagon may receive about $7 billion more than the president wants, but that will merely hold the fiscal 1996 defense decline to 1.7 percent. And fiscal 1996 will be the eleventh consecutive year of real (inflation-adjusted) decline in defense spending.

Furthermore, although conservatives are generally disposed to prune government, it is hardly a behavioral anomaly for them to favor slowing the erosion of funding for the federal government's foremost responsibility. The contrast between liberal and conservative mentalities is especially sharp regarding defense, which touches core convictions about men and nations.

Liberalism preaches, or at least holds out the hope, that people are infinitely malleable, and hence the present is endlessly manipulable and the future is predictable. From this flows the recurring belief—it recurs after each time events refute it—that peace is the natural relation between nations, and that war is an aberration explainable by the bad character of rulers and by benighted traditions and institutions.

For two centuries liberals have been explaining the obsolescence of war—their explanations have often been hard to hear because of the roar of the cannon—in terms of the spread of democracy. Or the disappearance of religious and ethnic and nationalistic fervor. Or the pacifying power of commerce. Or the increase of travel. Or the communications revolution. Or whatever.

However, as Donald Kagan dryly notes, "Over the past two centuries the only thing more common than predictions about the end of war has been war itself." In his magisterial book *On the Origins of War,* Kagan, a Yale historian, says that "statistically, war has been more common than peace, and extended periods of peace have been rare in a world divided into multiple states." In 1968 Will and Ariel Durant calculated that only 268 of the previous 3,421 years had been free of war. And no year has been since 1968.

Given what Kagan calls war's "ubiquity and perpetuity," the first duty of political leadership is to act on the axiom that "peace does not keep itself," and to understand that war or the threat of it has often been a surprise, from Pearl Harbor to Iraq's 1990 invasion of Kuwait. The years between those two surprises contained such surprises as the Berlin blockade, North Korea's invasion of South Korea, China's intervention in Korea, the 1956 Soviet invasion of Hungary and the Suez crisis, the 1962 Cuban missile crisis, the 1967 Arab-Israeli war, the Tet offensive and the Soviet invasion of Czechoslovakia in 1968, the 1973 Yom Kippur War, the 1980 Iran-Iraq war, among others.

This has been a century of bitter surprises for optimists, such as the editors of the renowned eleventh edition of the *Encyclopedia Britannica,* published in 1910–11. In it the entry on "torture" said that "the whole subject is one of only historical interest as far as Europe is concerned."

Pessimists—realists who are not fatalists—should be guided by Sir Michael Howard, the British military historian. He writes that military power has three functions, deterrence and coercion and reassurance, and the last may be the most important for the preservation of stability because "it determines the entire environment within which international relations are conducted": "Reassurance provides a general sense of security that is not specific to any particular threat or scenario. The best analogy I can provide is the role played by the British Royal Navy in the ninteenth century."

An American version of Pax Britannica will cost money, but will cost less than the ubiquity of war, which our sense of the tragic should tell us could be the alternative.

July 16, 1997

"What Have We Gone Through the Twentieth Century For?"

When Hitler sent Ribbentrop to Moscow in August 1939 to sign the nonaggression pact with the Soviet Union, he sent along his personal photographer with instructions to obtain close-ups of Stalin's earlobes. Hitler wondered whether Stalin had Jewish blood and wanted to see if his earlobes were "ingrown and Jewish, or separate and Aryan." This historical nugget (from Allan Bullock's *Hitler and Stalin: Parallel Lives*) is offered at this juncture in America's debate about Bosnia, as a reminder of a quality European politics has sometimes had in this century. Some American policymakers need to be reminded.

When Serbians took hostages from U.N. personnel in Bosnia and chained them to military targets as human shields, Warren Christopher was puzzled: "It's really not part of any reasonable struggle that might be going on there." While the secretary of state, a sweet man sadly miscast, searches for reasonableness amid the Balkan rubble, there are "peacekeepers" where there is no peace to be kept and "safe zones" where slaughter is random. UNProFor (the U.N. Protection Force) is akin to the Holy Roman Empire, which was neither holy nor Roman nor an empire. The U.N. force isn't forceful, so it needs more protection than it offers.

This war has been misdescribed as Europe's first civil war since that in Greece in the 1940s and the most portentous civil war since republicans fought fascists in Spain in the 1930s. Actually, this war now churning into its fourth summer is a war of Serbian aggression. It has been a war of aggression since 1992, when the European Community recognized Bosnia as a sovereign state, and since Bosnia became a member of the United Nations. Perhaps Bosnia's inconvenient existence is unfortunate, and perhaps Bosnia will yet be sundered by partition. But it is a state and that is why Pat Moynihan, carrying Woodrow Wilson's torch for international law and collective security, says of Bosnia, "Everything is at stake here, if principle is everything." Says Moynihan, if neither NATO nor the United Nations can summon the will to cope with Serbia, "What have we gone through the twentieth century for?" We went through it because we had no choice, but you know what he means: A century that began, in effect, at the Somme and went downhill from there to Auschwitz is ending with a wired world watching rape camps used in the service of "ethnic cleansing." All this eighty minutes by air from Rome.

Europe's first war between nations since 1945 illustrates an astounding fact: In this century of European fighting faiths—communism, fascism, socialism, pan-Germanism, pan-Slavism, and more—the one hardest to extinguish turns out to be the variant of fascism fueling the drive for Greater Serbia. Like pure fascism it asserts the primacy of the primordial and the goal of perfect national unity achieved by the expulsion or murder of "unassimilables." This explains the violent Serbian loathing of Sarajevo, where Christians and Muslims have peacefully coexisted. Hitler and Mussolini thought they were defending old Europe against the modern menace of Bolshevism. The Serbs think this is the year 732 and they are with Charles Martel saving Christian Europe by stopping the Muslim advance at Tours. Or it is 1529 and they are stopping Suleiman at the gates of Vienna. The Ottoman Empire is long gone, but the gunners in the hills surrounding Sarajevo refer to their targets—civilians dashing from doorway to doorway—as Turks.

Serbia is a raw reassertion of premodernity, the idea that uniform ethnicity and shared myths are essential to a political community. This war, which mocks the notion that Europe has become a supranational society, began in 1992, the year the Maastricht Treaty was signed, supposedly to make "Europe" a truly political as well as geographical expression. The United Nations, embodiment of the modern aspiration of a morality of nations, has been no match for Serbia. And the U.N.'s arms embargo against both sides—high-minded, scrupulous neutrality between Serbian slaughterers and their victims—has been a policy of gross immorality.

The embargo was imposed in 1991 against the whole of disintegrating Yugoslavia. When Yugoslavia disappeared the embargo was continued. That favored Serbia, which had ample weapons from the former Yugoslav army and had a large armaments industry. Now the embargo violates the U.N. Charter, which acknowledges every nation's "inherent" right of self-defense. President Bush defended the embargo with a flippancy about the problem in the Balkans not being an insufficiency of weapons. Today defenders of the embargo say it economizes violence because lifting it would prolong the fighting. This argument is especially unpleasant when used by the British, who today might be obeying German traffic laws if Lend-Lease had not prolonged the fighting.

So far the NATO nations have insufficient political will to impose a solution or use force to help restore the integrity of Bosnia. The Serbs are what the NATO nations are not: serious. The NATO nations want to end the game, the Serbs want to win it. Other people with ancient animosities and modern weapons are watching. It probably is not just coincidental that Russian revanchism became bold regarding Chechnya as the NATO nations became, through the embargo, collaborators with Serbian irredentism. If the irredentism goes unopposed when the UNProFor charade ends, the irredentism will become, even more than it already is, genocidal.

Secretary of State James Baker famously said of the Balkan conflict, "We don't have a dog in that fight." But those in the fight are not dogs and by the embargo we have helped make the fight grotesquely unfair. What would be the consequences on our national self-respect—our nation's soul—of a preventable Serbian victory followed by "cleansing" massacres? Bosnian Serbs have seized 70 percent of Bosnia but they are not a mighty military force and will become even less so if the Serbian government in Belgrade can be pressured into leaving Bosnia's separatist Serbs isolated in combat with a Bosnian army equipped at last with tanks and artillery. The Serbs fighting in Bosnia are bullies led by war criminals collaborating with a dictator. If we don't have an interest in this fight, what are we?

June 12, 1995

A Tale of Two Cities: Madrid and Belgrade

The U.S. aircraft carrier in the Adriatic is the USS *Theodore Roosevelt.* The French carrier is the *Foch.* The names recall an American spirit now in abeyance, and a European memory that is not.

At age twenty-four, Roosevelt wrote a book on the naval war of 1812. He served President McKinley as assistant secretary of the navy (as TR's cousin Franklin would serve President Wilson). As president, TR modernized the navy so that America could sail into history. His navy, an instrument for the projection of power, expressed the national confidence that is a prerequisite for world leadership.

When General Foch learned that his only son had been killed in the third week of the war—August 22, 1914—he asked his staff to leave him alone. Half an hour later he summoned them, saying, "Now let's get on with our work." On September 9, during a German attack, he proclaimed to the French forces, "One more effort and you are sure to win." It would be more than four years before Marshal Foch, by then head of allied forces, would announce, "Hostilities will cease on the entire front November eleventh at eleven A.M. French time." By that eleventh hour of the eleventh day of the eleventh month of 1918 Europe had been bled white, a ruinous victory won by generals who had fought machine guns with young men's chests.

Roosevelt and Foch represent polarities of the American and European experiences in this century—triumphalism, and tragedy. Today Foch's war is one reason Europeans are wary of doing more than watch the Balkan war, Europe's bloodiest conflict since 1945. Yet as Europeans and others watch the starvation and destruction of Sarajevo, a city virtually unscathed from 1939 to 1945, they should remember 1936–39 and another besieged city, Madrid.

British, French, and U.S. "nonintervention" decisions effectively embargoed arms to both sides in Spain—the forces loyal to the republican government, and Franco's military insurgents. This may have made formalistic sense because the conflict in Spain was a civil war, which today's war of Serbian aggression against Bosnia is not. And soon the loyalist side was so stained by Stalinism as to make a choice between the two sides unpalatable.

Still, the Spanish cockpit was the scene of two rehearsals—of the arms and military tactics of the dictators, and of the democracies' impotent reliance on diplomacy to defang the dictators. What happened there did not matter only there, and what happens in the Balkans will matter elsewhere—for example, at Brussels, at NATO headquarters, which might soon be boarded up if NATO has no relevance to genocidal aggression in Europe.

When the U.S. president does not lead, NATO does not act. *The New Republic* editorializes that it is hard to think of a major crisis since 1945 in which a president "has wielded less moral and political authority." President Clinton recently said he would ask Russian President Boris Yeltsin "to call the Serbs and tell them to quit [taking hostages and killing civilians], and tell them to behave themselves." *The New Republic* disdainfully says: "To behave themselves. And if that fails, to go to their room. Does Clinton grasp that there is evil in the world? And does he understand that he is not the governor of the United States? It is a requirement of his job that he care about matters beyond our borders, matters such as war and genocide and the general collapse of America's role in the world, matters that will not gain him a point in the polls."

On November 28, 1992, Senator Daniel Patrick Moynihan sent a long memorandum from Zagreb, Croatia, to the president-elect, commiserating about the Balkan disaster bequeathed to him:

Had we seen to it that the sanctions voted by the Security Council on May 30th (1992) were instantly enforced—Serbia imports at least three-quarters of its oil—the Serbs might have got the message to stop. . . . Had we brought the Security Council around to voting "demonstrations" under Article 42 of Chapter VII—taking out every bridge in Belgrade in one bombing raid—we might have sent a message to the Serbs that "ethnic cleansing" wasn't going to be worth it to them. But now we have some 1,600 U.N. troops spread out all over Bosnia. To start bombing Belgrade is to commence the massacre of our peacekeeping forces.

Three years later it is not too late to remove those forces, to remove the embargo on Bosnia's means of exercising its right of self-defense, and to convince Serbia that continued complicity in the genocide being committed by Bosnian Serbs will be bad for its bridges, and more.

June 8, 1995

Sabbatical from Seriousness

Two years ago, when there were reports that a Bosnian Muslim in a Serb concentration camp had been forced to bite off his father's testicles, it was comforting to recall the European tradition of fabricated atrocity stories— German soldiers amputating the hands of Belgian nurses in 1914, and so on. Today, with abundant evidence of rape used as a weapon of war, of Muslims' eyes gouged out and ears and noses sliced off by Serbian "soldiers" (it is disgusting to give that honorable title to snipers killing Sarajevo children), with convincing testimony about heads on stakes and a woman forced to drink blood from her son's slit throat, it is reasonable to suspend disbelief concerning all reports about the cowardly mob called the Bosnian Serb "army," which is a proxy for war criminals in Belgrade.

The Serbs' flaunting of their terror tactics reveals their largest advantage in this war to extinguish the Bosnian nation, this war in which, as Senator Daniel Patrick Moynihan says, "a new kind of war correspondent emerged, reporting massacres rather than battles." The largest advantage is not the mountainous terrain and the fogs that often shroud it, making Bosnia so forbidding to military leaders contemplating intervention. Rather, the Serbs' largest advantage is their realistic contempt for the West.

The West—what exactly does that noun now denote, given the nonre-

sponse to genocidal aggression?—almost preens about having become too
exquisitely sensitive to use force against barbarism. Shall we blame that
peculiar notion of moral progress for the fact that there still are bridges
standing, across which come supplies from Serbia to the Bosnian Serbs?
Why are Serbian computers still serving the Bosnian Serbs' antiaircraft
missiles of the sort that shot down Captain O'Grady? Shoot down an
American plane and the president's response will be to publicize the fact
that he smoked a celebratory cigar when the pilot was rescued. Clinton is
a Teddy Roosevelt for our time: Talk incessantly and smoke a big cigar.

The disarray of the NATO allies and especially the Clinton administration arises in part from military leaders equally nimble in devising arguments for procuring weapons and against using them. The U.S. military,
which purports to be competent to cope with two regional conflicts simultaneously, has an annual budget more than twenty times larger than Serbia's GNP. Before U.S. military leaders tell civilian officials what so many
of those officials want to hear—that U.S. force cannot be effectively used
to change Serbia's behavior—they should ponder some recent words of
Newt Gingrich: "You do not need today's defense budget to defend the
United States. You need today's defense budget to lead the world. . . . If
you are prepared to give up leading the world, we can have a much
smaller defense system."

The White House warns that NATO military action might "reignite the
war"—how does one reignite a conflagration?—and jeopardize the cruelly
misnamed "safe areas." This fatuity calls to mind the 1944 letter in which
the U.S. assistant secretary of war, John J. McCloy, said that one reason for
not bombing Auschwitz and railroad lines leading to it was that doing so
"might provoke even more vindictive action by the Germans." Wouldn't
have wanted to anger the operators of the crematoriums.

Especially scathing criticism of the president is coming from *The New
Republic*, which would like to like him. In the August 7, 1995 issue Zbigniew Brzezinski, the last national security adviser to a Democratic president, offers a presidential speech that could be given "if the post of Leader
of the Free World were not currently vacant." And *The New Republic*'s
editors write:

> The United States seems to be taking a sabbatical from historical serious-
> ness, blinding itself to a genocide and its consequences, fleeing the moral
> and practical imperatives of its own power. . . . You Americanize the war or
> you Americanize the genocide. Since the United States is the only power
> in the world that can stop the ethnic cleansing, the United States is
> responsible if the ethnic cleansing continues. Well, not exactly the United
> States. The American president is an accomplice to genocide. Not so the

American people. The president of the United States does not have the right to make the people of the United States seem as indecent as he is. He has the power, but he does not have the right.

Strong words, but strong feelings are appropriate. Speaking of the Serbs who sacked the Srebrenica "safe area," a survivor said, "They hunted us like rabbits." Reread the first paragraph of this piece. No one treats rabbits that way.

August 3, 1995

A Distinctively Human Activity

Business is brisk at the Holocaust Memorial Museum in Washington. Visitors line up more than two hours before the doors open at ten A.M., and about two million pass through those doors each year, four times more than were anticipated when the museum opened three years ago. Explaining the museum's success, a member of the staff says dryly, "Human nature has been an enormous help."

She means that from Bosnia, where scores of mass graves are being explored, to Rwanda, from Angola to Kurdish regions of Iraq, from Liberia to Sri Lanka, headlines proclaim the continuing prevalence of what visitors hope the museum will help them comprehend: beastliness. But that is the wrong word. Beasts do not do such things. Wanton, gratuitous, even giddily exuberant cruelty (such as one German's game of catching on a bayonet babies hurled from a hospital's windows) in the exercise of exterminating violence against categories of beings—this is a distinctively human activity.

The museum is an institution of memory for the victims of Germany rampant, 1933–45. But it also is a teaching institution, and last week was the scene of a heated symposium about a new book examining the perpetrators of the Holocaust.

Reduced to an epigram, Daniel Jonah Goldhagen's thesis in *Hitler's Willing Executioners: Ordinary Germans and the Holocaust* is that "the road to Auschwitz was not crooked." Elaborating through 619 pages of often shattering anecdotes mined from survivors' and perpetrators' testimonies, Goldhagen's argument is that genocide fulfilled the logic of 150 years of German history.

Hitler's seizure of power, says Goldhagen, was a necessary but not a sufficient condition for the Holocaust. Acculturation came first. When ordinary Germans, products of long conditioning by a culture steeped in anti-Semitism, came under the sway of a totalitarian regime's propaganda that legitimized extermination, they fell to the task with attitudes ranging from dutifulness to relish. Only such thinking, says Goldhagen, can explain the participation of between 100,000 and 500,000 persons who served in the genocide infantry—those who got gore on their sleeves from shooting children at close range.

When Goldhagen, professor of government and social studies at Harvard, says they were "ordinary Germans" who sent photographs of their butchery to loved ones, and even invited their wives to watch them smash skulls with rifle butts, the question becomes: In what sense ordinary? His answer is: Ordinary meaning the routine, predictable products of cognitive determinism. They killed Jews, often with pleasure, because an ideology told them doing so was not merely permissible but virtuous.

This monocausal explanation is made problematic by both the good and the bad that Germans did. If virulent anti-Semitism had such a vicelike grip, what explains the behavior of the significant number of Germans who abstained from, or even resisted barbarism? And if German anti-Semitism was the cause of the barbarism, why did the barbarities engulf so many non-Jews, and why were there so many non-Germans among the barbarians?

The victims of barbarism included the mentally and physically handicapped, Gypsies, three million Soviet prisoners of war, the inhabitants of the Greek village of Komeno, Italian POWs who a few days earlier had been Germany's allies, and others. And although Goldhagen insists that the "quantity and quality of personalized brutality and cruelty" inflicted by Germans on Jews flowed from a German cultural idea, many Croatians, Ukrainians, and others collaborated with Germans in administering the Holocaust.

At the symposium, Christopher Browning of Pacific Lutheran University agreed with Goldhagen concerning the high degree of volunteerism on the part of the numerous ordinary German participants in genocide. But Browning, author of *Ordinary Men*, a stunning study of middle-aged conscripts who became mass murderers in a German police battalion in Poland, argued that the unspeakable cruelties committed by the Khmer Rouge against fellow Cambodians, and by Chinese against other Chinese during the Cultural Revolution, cannot be explained by Goldhagen's model—by centuries of conditioning by a singular idea.

Browning charged that Goldhagen's "unremitting portrayal of German uniformity" makes history one-dimensional and dehumanizes Germans. By making Germans so alien, Goldhagen's thesis is too comforting. Browning believes that mass murder and the ubiquity of cruelty accompanying it suggests the need to seek explanations in "those universal aspects of human nature that transcend the cognition and culture of ordinary Germans."

This Tuesday, April 16, is the Day of Remembrance for Holocaust victims and survivors. Since 1945 the theme of remembrance ceremonies has been "Never again." But again Europe is sifting skulls from the earth over mass graves, this time of Muslims, victims of . . . what? Ordinary Serbs?

April 14, 1996

Fascism's Second Spring

When Leon Degrelle died recently at eighty-seven in exile in Spain, he had lived long enough to enjoy a last laugh at the expense of those who doubted the durability of the dark impulses that define fascism. Founder of a fascist party in Belgium in the 1930s, Degrelle organized a Belgian military unit that fought for Germany in Russia and was integrated into the Waffen SS. Condemned to death by Belgium, he escaped to Spain, where for decades he hosted members of Europe's fascist remnants. He claimed that Hitler had said to him, "If I had a son, I would have liked him to be like you."

Today it seems that Hitler had progeny after all. Who could have guessed in 1945 that half a century later, communism would be a spent force in Europe but that echoes of fascism would be reverberating there. Among the grim astonishments of a century replete with them is the fact that the world has fresh reasons for worrying about the tribalism, irrationality, mythmongering, and cult of purging violence that define fascism.

Never mind that Alessandra Mussolini, granddaughter of the socialist journalist who first brought fascism to power, is a member of the neofascist party's delegation in Italy's Parliament. By now that growing party may merely be xenophobic, and Italy is a stable democracy. The English Football Association was foolish to cancel a soccer match set for Berlin last Wednesday, Hitler's birthday, because of fears of neo-Nazi violence. The firebombing of a Lübeck synagogue last month does not indicate the disposition of Germany, which is a stable democracy.

But in Russia, Vladimir Zhirinovsky's recognizably fascist party recently received 25 percent of the vote. His rantings about restoring Russia's lost status and land, including Alaska, might seem as funny as Charlie Chaplin's portrayal of Hitler as a buffoon seemed until, suddenly, Hitler was no laughing matter. And there is a family resemblance to fascism in the impulses currently fueling Serbian barbarism.

Against Marxism's myth of creative class conflict, with the proletariat the engine of progress, fascism offered the myth of perfect national unification. A nation could be a people purged of internal conflicts and of "unassimilables," such as Jews. History would be powered by the outward projection of strong nations' hostilities against weak nations. Marxism preached that preindustrial factors—race, ethnicity, religion—had lost their history-making power. Fascism asserted the primacy of the primordial. Marxism is a discredited prophecy. Fascism has a future.

As they use "ethnic cleansing" to create "Greater Serbia," Serbs claim, as Hitler and Mussolini did, to be defending both their nation's ancient particularity and "European" civilization. Serbian demolition of mosques is revenge against the Ottoman Turks. Fascism was, and is, projected hostilities and does not just condone violence, it is inextricable from violence—it *is* violence. "The democrats of *I Mondo* want to know our program?" said Alessandra's grandfather. "It is to break the bones of the democrats of *Il Mondo.*" His spirit simmers in those Serbian gunners firing randomly into cities jammed with refugees.

The soil of modern society, including American society, has been fertilized for fascist seedlings. Fascism is a revenge that history takes on an age of mindless moral relativism. You say we should "deconstruct" all truth claims (a founder of "deconstructionism," Paul de Man, whose writings are still influential in American universities, was a Belgian fascist) because there are no facts, only opinions? Well then, if truth is a chimera, let the stronger opinion prevail. Serbian opinions are very strong. You say you favor "ethnic self-determination"? How do you like the Bosnian Serbs' determination?

In the name of "diversity" and "multiculturalism" many American young people are taught to ground their sense of self in their racial or ethnic identity. This repudiates a source of America's success, its creedal identity, grounded in free assent to truths—"propositions," in Lincoln's language—to which the nation is dedicated. History—make that "history"—is increasingly taught not to ascertain truth but to enhance the "self-esteem" of various factions. The result is the manufacture of myths that make this or that group feel good. Or bad. Today more and more groups are taught to cultivate grievances as victims. Fascism flourishes as a doctrine of vengeance.

Fascism favors the visceral over the cerebral—thinking with one's blood. There is a lot of that going on where there should be the least of it—in universities. Khalid Muhammad is a black anti-Semite currently receiving ovations on some historically black campuses, and others. After touring the Holocaust Museum in Washington last week, he referred dismissively to what the Nazis did to "so-called" Jews. (He calls Jews "hook-nose, bagel-eating . . . just crawled out from the caves and hills of Europe.") Then he headed for Howard University to lecture, again.

He says 150 million blacks died en route to the Americas in slave ships. Many historians believe that between 7 million and 15 million Africans came to this hemisphere as slaves, and perhaps 15 percent died during this transatlantic passage. Howard students should hear David Biron Davis, Sterling Professor of History at Yale and an authority on slavery. But

Howard officials persuaded Davis to "postpone" a scheduled lecture there because they thought the anti-Semites—Davis is Jewish—would disrupt the event. Said a dean, "I did not want this man to be embarrassed." Howard cannot protect a scholar from the equivalent of Brownshirts, and the *scholar* might be embarrassed?

This squalid little episode is of course as nothing next to the bloodlust in Bosnia, but it arises from a similar mentality, and is another reason why, fifty years later, the faint smile on the face of Leon Degrelle looks so sinister.

May 2, 1994

History Revs Its Engine

Like a distant forest seen faintly through a fog, the national security concerns that will darken our children's futures have become visible in recent weeks. The concerns are as small as bacteria and as large as the country that contains nearly a quarter of the human race. The concerns are as quiet as a nuclear reactor and as loud as a mortar shell exploding in a Balkan marketplace. All around the world the sound you hear is history again revving up its engine. Our children will not be bored after all.

Recent revelations about Iraq's inventory of chemical and biological weapons, combined with what was already known about the nature of the Iraqi regime, stirred in prudent people thoughts retrospective and anticipatory. One thought was of the gratitude owed to the Israeli government that decided, and the pilots who enforced the decision, to destroy the Baghdad reactor that served Iraq's nuclear weapons program. That occurred in 1981. The world would have a different look and feel today if the Iraq that invaded Kuwait (and menaced Saudi Arabia) in 1990 had possessed nuclear weapons and ballistic missiles to deliver them.

President Clinton has said, "North Korea cannot be allowed to develop a nuclear bomb." Secretary of State Christopher says of North Korea's nuclear weapons program, "Last fall, this administration ended it." There really is no reason to believe that. However, those words represent the administration's intention, which is to elevate the game "let's pretend" to a policy.

The proliferation of weapons of mass destruction, and of the means of delivering them, is driving the suddenly quickened debate about developing ballistic missile defenses for America. Many Americans do not know that the nation has no such defenses and is effectively precluded from deploying even such defenses as could defeat an attack by a few missiles from a rogue state. That is because of a twenty-three-year-old treaty with a nation that no longer exists, the Soviet Union. When focus groups of voters are asked what a president should do if notified that a missile is incoming, the voters say: Shoot it down, of course. When they are told that the nation does not have the capacity to do that, and why it does not, they often are incredulous and indignant. This issue, which Republicans in Congress will highlight with increased funds and strong language in defense appropriation and authorization bills, is ripe for inclusion in the presidential campaign.

Today the nation's attention, or that minuscule portion of it that is allotted to foreign policy, is on events triggered by one Bosnian Serb mortar shell. That shell killed thirty-seven people in a Sarajevo marketplace and could have killed the most successful military alliance in history. If NATO had again dithered and allowed U.N. bureaucrats to keep it bridled and snaffled, an American majority might have begun to ask insistently some awkward questions, such as: Why is the nation bearing the burden of European engagement when such engagement is only depressing and embarrassing? And why, for that matter, does the nation bother to have a twelve-digit defense budget if it still cannot dissuade a tin pot army like the Bosnian Serbs from random terror and systematic war crimes? When, years late, NATO at last used force against the Serbs, it demonstrated how the personnel and materiel purchased by defense budgets can rescue diplomacy from impotence. And if, as seems likely, the final settlement accepts much of what Serbian aggression accomplished on the ground, that will merely demonstrate that diplomacy rarely can entirely reverse what force has established.

The mortar shell forced many Americans to explore the limits of their tolerance of horrors that affect them primarily by disturbing them. The shell caused many Americans to contemplate what might be the consequences—barbarism and anarchy, for starters—of a thorough abandonment of the quest for (in Sir Michael Howard's words) "a world impregnated by American ideals and controlled by American power." Of course, no one really believes the "world" can be "controlled" by American power. However, forty-one months of carnage in the Balkans have demonstrated that without American power, and American leadership that is unembarrassed by that power, the phrase "the West" is no longer a political expression denoting anything coherent or consequential. Caleb Carr, editor of *MHQ: The Quarterly Journal of Military History,* rightly says, "We are, today, farther from a viable international order than we were fifty or even ten years ago, if only because there are fewer sound, powerful nations to support one." With a confident United States leading, there are a few such nations. Without such a United States, there are none.

To see the need for visible American power, look to the Far East, where America went to war three times in twenty-five years. There China, a regime in crisis, is trying to use naked intimidation to control, if not eliminate, Taiwan's freedom of movement on the international stage. The disruption of air and sea traffic by missile tests conducted provocatively near Taiwan was a notably crude attempt to deter Taiwan from trying to raise its international profile, as it did with its president's visit to Cornell University in May. The CIA says China is involved in territorial or maritime disputes with Russia, India, North Korea, Tajikistan, Taiwan, Japan, Vietnam, Malaysia, Brunei, and the Philippines. The influence of China's military, which includes the world's largest army and a rapidly growing blue-water navy, may wax during the coming post-Deng succession crisis. Merrick Carey of the Alexis de Tocqueville Institution and Loren Thompson of Georgetown University report in *Sea Power* magazine that "Chinese military publications routinely assert that nearly two million square miles of land in adjacent countries rightfully belongs to China." And China regards the South China Sea, through which much international military and commercial shipping passes, as Chinese water.

In our children's lifetimes, and perhaps in ours, China (or some large fragment thereof; China, too, could succumb to the centrifugal forces at work in the world) is apt to possess a superpower's arsenal of ICBMs equipped with nuclear weapons. Yes, our children will live in interesting times.

September 18, 1995

America: Rome or Venice?

From the Caribbean to Korea, the gales of crises are gusting, forcing this nation again to choose: Will it be Rome, or Venice, or a bit of both?

Any new republic, wrote Machiavelli, must decide whether to expand her dominion by power, like Rome, or to be like Venice, located "in some strong place" that protects it as it goes about its business, which for Venice was business. During America's first century, broad oceans and placid neighbors enabled it to be Venetian, in a strong place, practicing commerce.

However, even then there was an itch to be Roman, too—but with a difference. America would seek, in Jefferson's words, "an empire of liberty," but without becoming imperial. We would expand our sway by the sparkling example of our institutions, and by what political scientist Gary Schmitt calls Jefferson's "strategy of peaceful coercion." We would use our commercial power to punish disrespect for natural rights.

War, said Jefferson, was "not the best engine for us to resort to" because we had a better one "in our commerce." Thus would America refute Frederick the Great's dictum that diplomacy without armaments is like music without instruments. Using economic power we would pursue Roman potency with Venetian means.

Britain, warring with France, would not respect the rights of neutral shipping? Jefferson would use an embargo to make it in Britain's "interest . . . to do what is just." It was not a success. The embargo stirred commercial New England to talk of secession—a threat duly noted in Dixie—and did not prevent war.

The world has turned over often since then, and still we seek new ways of tutoring the wayward world. Regarding Haiti, the Clinton administration has declared the restoration of President Aristide a "vital" U.S. interest, for no better reason than that Haiti is nearby and badly abused by its government. This policy, so far, is Jeffersonian: It is couched solely in terms of rights and wrongs, and relies on commercial severities.

However, the policy may become mildly Roman. There may be a military invasion, if being Venetian with commercial sanctions does not suffice.

North Korea is a tougher nut to crack. The Venetian approach assumes that our adversaries aspire to be like us, prospering through commerce. However, if that were their aspiration, they would already be like us, because they share our bourgeois values. The utter futility of U.S. diplomacy backed only by commercial threats suggests that the North Korean regime remains unaware of any affinity with us.

There is a vital national interest at stake here. If North Korea demonstrates the impotence of restraints on nuclear proliferation, in fifteen years there could be fifteen more nations with nuclear weapons backing their hatreds. Such is the progress of military technology over the centuries, from an innovation along a river in Central Asia, to a reactor on the Korean peninsula.

In his new *A History of Warfare,* John Keegan says military historians recognize that "the banks of the Oxus are to warfare what Westminster is to parliamentary democracy or the Bastille to revolutions." It was on or near the Oxus River separating Central Asia from Persia and the Middle East that man first learned to turn horses into instruments of war. This development shaped military power and notions of martial ethics and valor—until a second great development, gunpowder. That began the equalization process: In the age of gunpowder, the nature of military materiel mattered more than the nature of military personnel.

Nuclear weapons have pushed this transformation to the point at which North Korea can be a crisis for the United States in its most Roman stance. Roman, that is, in this sense: The United States is attempting to change the behavior of a nation halfway around the world, in order to shape the future all over the world. Call the objective Pax Americana.

Well, perhaps not exactly pax. The aim is a world of merely gunpowder wars—wars without the worst weapons. In which regard, it is well to remember, as Keegan does, that since August 9, 1945, nuclear weapons have killed no one: "The 50,000,000 who have died in war since that date have, for the most part, been killed by cheap, mass-produced weapons and small-calibre ammunition, costing little more than the transistor radios and dry-cell batteries which have flooded the world in the same period."

The calculations confronting the Clinton administration are excruciating precisely because North Korea, which says economic sanctions are acts of war, not alternatives to it, has so much gunpowder and so little inclination to act like us in response to us.

June 16, 1994

Safety and Sanguine Predictions

A tendentious prediction is the Clinton administration's latest justification for its dilatory approach to defending the nation against the sort of ballistic missile attack that could be launched by a rogue nation. The administration says that such a threat is at least fifteen years distant. The historical record of such predictions is not reassuring. Neither is the method by which this one was produced.

In 1906, three years after the flight at Kitty Hawk, Simon Newcomb, an eminent scientist, declared it was demonstrable—"as complete as is possible for the demonstration of any physical fact to be"—that "no possible combination of known substances, known forms of machine, and known forms of force can be united in a practicable machine by which men shall fly long distances through the air." In 1922, a former assistant secretary of the navy, Franklin Roosevelt, said, "It is highly unlikely that an airplane, or fleet of them, could ever successfully sink a fleet of navy vessels under battle conditions." In 1939, an admiral said, "As far as sinking a ship with a bomb is concerned, you just can't do it."

Albert Wohlstetter, a noted strategic thinker, writes that when in 1937 a congressional committee published an ambitious attempt to forecast technological developments of the next ten to twenty-five years, it missed, among other things, nuclear energy, antibiotics, radar, and jet propulsion. In 1945, MIT's Dr. Vannevar Bush, director of the Office of Scientific Research and Development, reported to the Senate concerning the possibility of developing an intercontinental (3,000-mile range) missile capable of delivering an atomic bomb precisely enough to hit a particular city: "I feel confident that it will not be done for a very long period of time. . . . I think we can leave that out of our thinking."

Many experts were wrong about how swiftly the Soviet Union would acquire atomic and then hydrogen bombs. U.S. intelligence underestimated the progress of Iraq's nuclear program.

Now the Clinton administration suggests wagering the nation's safety on a sanguine prediction that seems to have been produced by a premise designed to induce complacency. The premise is that at least fifteen years will elapse before a ballistic missile threat to the forty-eight contiguous states can be developed indigenously by a rogue state such as Iraq or North Korea.

Now, leave aside the oddity of leaving out, as second-class entities, Alaska and Hawaii. And leave aside the imprudence of ignoring the potential of threats from China and Russia, where the regimes could be changed on short notice.

However, note the intelligence estimate's emphasis on indigenous development of ballistic missiles by lesser powers. That scants the possibility that a nation capable of producing a device for mass destruction might be able to purchase on the international market a means of delivering that device to the continental United States.

Fifteen years ago Roberta Wohlstetter, author of a brilliant study of why we were surprised at Pearl Harbor, wrote an essay titled "Slow Pearl Harbors and the Pleasures of Self-Deception." Her subject was the role a victim's cherished beliefs and comforting assumptions often play in deceiving him.

Beginning in 1919 the British, flinching from the thought of another war and eager to minimize military spending, adopted what came to be called "The Ten Year Rule." They predicted there would be no major war in the next ten years. And then they began making the same "prediction"— actually, a thought generated by a wish—annually. Not surprisingly, beginning in 1933 British estimates of the numbers of first-line German aircraft consistently erred on the low side.

Roberta Wohlstetter also cites "the even slower and more reluctant recognition by American intelligence that the Russians were not interested merely in having a minimum deterrent force of 200 ICBMs, nor even satisfied with the same numbers as our own," but instead wanted much more. Far from being reluctant participants in the arms race, they continued to "run along quite smartly long after we had stopped." Not surprisingly, long-term U.S. projections of Soviet ICBM silos were too low from 1962 to the end of the 1960s, and then became even more erroneous. The 1962 prediction was 85 percent of the number that materialized, and in 1969 we predicted less than 20 percent of the number the Soviet Union actually built.

Soothing assumptions about the good faith and shared interests of antagonists are natural to democracies, as is the desire to spend money on things other than defense. Getting a democracy to do what does not come naturally requires leadership. To get that for the defense of this democracy, a different commander in chief is required.

June 27, 1996

A Marvel of Naval Architecture

ABOARD THE USS *COWPENS*, UNDER WAY OFF SAN DIEGO—In the perpetual dusk of the combat information center, which is illuminated by the glow of display screens all around, the soft clicking of computer keys is suddenly punctured by a shrill whistle that signals a disagreeable development: an antiship missile, incoming. Disagreeable, but all in a day's work for the crew of this guided missile cruiser. The *Cowpens* illustrates how the navy fulfills multiplying missions with fewer ships.

Today's drill is simulated war-fighting involving multiple threats, including enemy ships, submarines, aircraft, and missiles. Such training is much of what the armed forces do in peacetime. In his history of the navy, Captain Edward L. Beach estimates that prior to Pearl Harbor the navy had had only fifty-six hours of combat. Most of its time went to training, the fruits of which were reaped after Pearl Harbor.

But ships such as the *Cowpens,* a marvel of naval architecture, do not just defend themselves and nearby ships. Within its 567-foot length, the *Cowpens* bristles with offensive powers such as torpedo launchers, vertical guided missile launchers, and Tomahawk cruise missiles of the sort it fired ten of into Iraq in a post-Gulf War flare-up in January 1993. And such ships are acquiring an ability to defend forces ashore with theater antiballistic missiles. (About twenty-two nations now have Scud or similar missiles.)

America has been a source of fine naval architecture for three centuries, since England, its forests vanishing, began coveting North America's tall, straight pines and firs for ships' masts. And when the British navy was "the wooden walls of England," no wood was harder than that from live oaks from America's South. Today the 11,000-ton *Cowpens,* named for the South Carolina site (then pastureland, now a town) of a 1781 Revolutionary War victory, prances on the ocean's surface like a pony in a pasture. Its gas turbine engines and reverse pitch propellers enable it to go from zero to thirty knots in less than a minute and from thirty knots to a standstill in two ship lengths.

Classic naval doctrine taught the concentration of a fleet in order to bring an enemy fleet to battle, as at Trafalgar (1805) and Jutland (1916). But naval warfare in this century changed from being one-dimensional (surface) to being three-dimensional with submarines and aircraft carriers. The *Cowpens,* crammed with exotic technologies and computers to control them, expresses the navy's adaptation to its many post-Cold War missions. This involves a shift away from operations on the sea, to the projection of power from the sea in order to shape events in littoral regions—on or near the shore.

As an instrument of "expeditionary warfare," the navy, by controlling oceans adjacent to littoral battlefields, can project, with the help of embarked marines, bombs, missiles, shells, bullets, and bayonets. And by being the forward-deployed, on-station forces in an era of fewer foreign bases, the navy, which boasts of being "first to the fight," can help prevent some fights.

Last October, when Iraqi forces moved toward Kuwait, the navy quickly added four Tomahawk-firing ships to the four already in the neighborhood, the eight having more Tomahawks than were fired during the Gulf War. The navy also quickly doubled the aviation power in the region. Iraq pulled back.

Last week, with Jordan perhaps in peril and certainly nervous because it is providing sanctuary to some high-level defectors from Iraq, the navy had twenty-two ships in the Mediterranean, eighteen in the Persian Gulf, and 2,000 marines on four ships in the Red Sea for joint amphibious exercises that were scheduled with Jordanian forces before the defections from Iraq.

This was a timely demonstration of the fact that there is an unencumbered self-sufficiency about U.S. ships. They can remain on station without any host country's permission, they bring a complete package to a crisis and are more easily reversible than an onshore buildup. That is why the navy is such a versatile instrument for preventative diplomacy, for controlling crises and for conventional deterrence by swiftly demonstrating intentions and capabilities.

But that assumes the nation, or perhaps more precisely the national leadership, wants to play a proactive role in shaping a benign security environment around the world rather than merely reacting to regional disturbances after they have erupted. If so, ships like the *Cowpens* come in mighty handy performing tasks from surveillance to missile defense.

Such ships are among the navy's ingenious responses to the shortsightedness of both political branches in reducing the number of ships while the navy's missions are multiplying in an increasingly disorderly world. Such ships and their accomplished crews do not come cheap. Except compared to wars.

August 24, 1995

The Counterculture at Quantico

QUANTICO MARINE CORPS BASE, VIRGINIA—President Truman was a former army captain and given to pungent expression of his prejudices, one of which was against the Marine Corps, which he derided as "the navy's police force" with "a propaganda machine almost equal to Stalin's." He said that in August 1950. Note that date.

During the postwar dismantling of the military, other services grasped for the Marine Corps' missions and budget. Chairman of the Joint Chiefs of Staff Omar Bradley, a Missourian and Truman confidant, said, "large-scale amphibious operations . . . will never occur again." He said that in October 1949.

In the summer of 1950, the Korean War vindicated the Marine Corps' vow to be the most ready when the nation is least ready. While Truman was criticizing the corps, marines were rushing to Pusan to help stop the North Korean sweep, then going to Inchon in September for the great amphibious landing that reversed the tide of the war. The "propaganda of deeds" was the marines' decisive argument regarding their future.

Today, in another military contraction, there again are voices questioning the corps' relevance. Critics should come here, to these 60,000 acres devoted largely to a stern socialization of a few young men and women. The making of a marine officer amounts to a studied secession from the ethos of contemporary America. The corps is content to be called an island of selflessness in a sea of selfishness, and to be defined by the moral distance between it and a society that is increasingly a stranger to the rigors of self-denial.

The commanding general here, Paul K. Van Riper, says Quantico begins by teaching officer candidates four things—discipline, drill, knowledge of the service rifle, and the corps' history and traditions. The last is not least in a small institution that subscribes to Napoleon's dictum that "in war the moral is to the material as three to one."

Marines tell young men and women thinking of joining one of the military services that there are three choices and one challenge—that the corps is a calling, not just a career. On this day, a cluster of young officers— from Harvard, the University of North Carolina, as well as the Naval Academy and other fine colleges and universities—eating a lunch of field rations in a grove of trees agrees. Says one, other people tell you what they do, marines tell you what they are.

A barracks poster portraying the Trojan horse proclaims that "superior thinking has always overwhelmed superior force," and officers are impatient with the stereotype of (as one puts it) "marines with their knuckles dragging on the ground." "Why would the Marine Corps need a library?" asked an incredulous congressman when the corps asked for the one it subsequently got. The answer is that this nation, with its vast human and material resources, has often waged wars of attrition, but the Marine Corps, the smallest military service, must be, like Stonewall Jackson in the Shenandoah Valley, imaginative.

Being so is a tradition. During the 1930s the marines refined the amphibious tactics that soon were used from North Africa to the South Pacific, and after 1945 were particularly innovative regarding the use of helicopters.

True, there has not been an amphibious assault since Inchon, and Iraqi sea mines—inexpensive leverage for second-rate nations—prevented one during Desert Storm. However, the Marines Corps, which fifty years ago was in danger of being consigned to largely ceremonial roles and embassy protection, is the service least affected by the end of the Cold War.

Lieutenant Colonel Thomas Linn dryly estimates that about once every eleven years since 1829 someone in the White House or the other services has declared the Marine Corps dispensable. However, it is the nation's forward deployed expeditionary force and will not want for work in a world increasingly ulcerated by small, low-intensity conflicts fueled by religious, ethnic, and other cultural passions.

Speaking of cultural conflicts, what makes the corps not only useful but fascinating is, again, its conscious cultivation of an ethos conducive to producing hard people in a soft age. Toward the end of their ten-week program, officer candidates arrive in the predawn gloom at the Leadership Reaction Course—a series of physical and mental problems they must try to solve under the stress of short deadlines. The candidates arrive after a two-mile run they make after they make an eight-mile march, which they make after being awakened after just two hours sleep. What is their reward for choosing this steep and rocky path in life? Life and death responsibilities at age twenty-three.

Looking for today's "counterculture"? Look here.

September 28, 1995

Russia's Memory

The palatable result of Russia's presidential voting is that Boris Yeltsin ran slightly ahead of his principal rival, Gennady Zyuganov, a Communist, in the first round of a contest that will be settled in a runoff within thirty days. The depressing news is that Yeltsin, assisted by foreign governments, his government, and Russia's media, ran only slightly 3 percentage points ahead of the candidate promising "communism as the historic future of mankind."

Actually, some people worry that there could be a Pinochet in Russia's future. Or a Franco. More about that anon. But first, remember what caused communism's collapse. Many things did, but most of all ignorance.

Ignorance is socialism's systemic problem. Zyuganov, promising "a great empire and socialism," is ignorant of the fact that socialism must be ignorant of almost everything, such as: How much bread should cost. Socialism cannot know, because it cannot know what flour and other ingredients should cost, or what packaging, transportation, or advertising should cost.

Markets are mechanisms for generating billions of bits of information daily. Markets produce reasonable allocations of wealth and opportunity. Make the market illegal in an industrialized society, and what you get is what the Soviet Union was: "Upper Volta with ICBMs." That is, a Third World economy with pockets of modernity.

Communism's prodigious achievement was to keep a potentially rich nation poor. The Soviet economy remained substantially a hunter-gatherer economy based on extraction industries—furs, oil, minerals. But eventually party officials, the vanguard of the proletariat, noticed that their nation was in the wake not only of Western industrial societies, which had had a head start, but also of Taiwan, Singapore, and other Asian economies of the information age.

However, before mocking Russia's electorate because a significant portion of it would embrace systematic ignorance, consider the insecurities involved in dismantling the socialism that could give the individual the security of a fly in amber. Then consider how much of America's recent political discourse has been devoted to vehement complaints about, and politicians promising relief from, the relatively mild insecurities that come with capitalism's dynamic wealth-creation.

Russia is still experiencing declining life expectancy. For males it is now fifty-nine. *Barron's* reports that entire cities were built around factories that produced military goods for which there is now no market. Inflation is now "under control" at an annual rate of 30 percent. Agricultural and industrial GDP have been halved in five years. The economy has shrunk at least 25 percent. What is remarkable in Russia is not the Communist Party's limited electoral revival but the fact of elections.

In the runoff the man who finished third, Alexander Lebed, can be king-maker and wait for the king to depart. It is said that Lebed, a stone-faced, forty-six-year-old former general, is Colin Powell without the geniality. He has joined forces with Yeltsin. Yeltsin, who is not a martyr to the rules of healthy living, may not last.

General Pinochet interested Soviet leaders because they assumed history's mechanism was a leftward-working ratchet: Socialism's sphere would never contract. Pinochet broke the ratchet when he broke Allende's grip on Chile. Today Chile's Pinochet episode interests some Russians because it combined "social order" with a market-driven economic growth. That resembles Lebed's program, except that Lebed unlike Pinochet participates in elections.

It is said that the example of another general may be apposite. Franco, who was forty-four in 1936 when he led a rising against Spain's disorderly republic, considered himself the defender of Spain's specialness against the West's homogenizing forces. Lebed appeals to many who fear that

Russia's identity will be washed away by the strong solvents of imported capital and popular culture from the West. However, before anticipating "Bonapartism in mufti" from Lebed, note that he has led not a military rising but a political quest for votes, praising private property and dismissing communism as imbecilic. He knows that yet another general, De Gaulle, showed that "authoritarian democrat" is not an oxymoron.

And there is more good news. Writing in *The American Enterprise* journal about "The Coming Russian Boom," Richard Layard and John Parker, two British students of Russia, note that Russia has an educated population and the world's largest reserves of natural resources, it has privatized faster than its East European neighbors, and its agriculture, which was crippled even more than industry was by communism, should experience explosive productivity growth.

And Russia's recipe for democracy and economic growth includes one other priceless ingredient—a fresh memory of socialism.

June 20, 1996

NATO and Russia's National DNA

Displaying the spirit that was to produce victory at Trafalgar, Horatio Nelson once held a firepoker and said, "It matters not at all in what way I lay this poker on the floor. But if Bonaparte should say it must be placed in this direction, we must instantly insist on it being laid in some other one." Similar reasoning, with Russia playing Bonaparte's role, is one argument for proceeding quickly with NATO enlargement.

Regardless of the outcome of Russia's presidential election this Sunday, the United States should lessen its tendency to trim foreign policy to accommodate Russian preferences and phobias. Continuing the stall concerning the inclusion in NATO of the new democracies of Eastern Europe sends a dangerous signal to Russia and a demoralizing signal to those democracies.

To Russia's increasingly truculent rulers it signals that NATO's member nations, and especially the United States, can be coerced. To the Russian people, when NATO hesitates to enlarge because enlargement might seem "provocative," that suggests that the lies the Soviet regime told them for forty-five years—that NATO is an offensive, not a defensive, alliance— were true.

If Russia's rulers have no revanchist aspirations, they have no reason to resent NATO's inclusion of the new democracies. However, those democracies have reasons to fear Russian revanchism waged by diplomacy of intimidation backed by overwhelming military superiority. That could produce Finlandization, meaning pliant neutrality, from, so to speak, Stettin on the Baltic to Trieste on the Adriatic.

Expansionism is in Russia's national DNA. Richard Pipes, the Harvard historian, calculates that for approximately 150 years, the middle of the sixteenth century to the end of the seventeenth, the Muscovite state's territorial acquisitions year by year averaged an area equal in size to modern-day Holland. "Others have built empires," says Pipes, "but no country has expanded so relentlessly and held on so tenaciously to its conquests as has Russia."

Henry Kissinger notes that a nation spanning, as even post-Soviet Russia does, eleven time zones (St. Petersburg is closer to New York than to Vladivostok, which is closer to Seattle than to Moscow) should not feel claustrophobic, yet Russia still manifests "creeping expansionism," exemplified by the two Russian army divisions in Georgia. The Brezhnev Doctrine held that wherever socialism had been planted by Soviet power, there the Soviet Union had a right to preserve it. The doctrine of today's Russian rulers may be that wherever Russians are, there Russian power can go.

Partly to propitiate nationalists, Yeltsin cashiered his "liberal" foreign minister Andrei Kozyrev, but even Kozyrev asserted a Russian right of military intervention in all of the countries containing Russian minorities. Kissinger says that includes at least fourteen states of the former Soviet Union, including the Baltic States.

Given Russia's history and current dynamics, the tardiness of NATO enlargement makes it understandable that the Czech President Vaclav Havel says, "The danger of another Munich is looming over Europe." In Prague, "Munich" is not a mere metaphor. For Prague, the appeasement policy made at Munich in 1938 was the decisive event of this century. Prague is the last place that the specter of Munich would be frivolously invoked, and Havel measures his words.

The word "Munich," says Peter Rodman of the Nixon Center for Peace and Freedom, is shorthand for "Western abandonment." Rodman recalls that when Franco died in 1975, one argument for bringing Spain into NATO was to strengthen Spain's fledgling democracy. Six years later Spain's admission was proclaimed. Seven years have passed since the de-Sovietization of Poland, Hungary, and the Czech Republic.

Spain's traditional isolation from main currents of European history—"Africa begins at the Pyrenees" was a familiar jest—was deepened by almost forty years of Franco's rule, but admission to NATO accelerated Spain's entry into modernity. For forty years Prague, Budapest, and Warsaw were isolated from Europe's democratic civilization. Prague is west of Vienna and closer to Dublin than to Moscow. But NATO, attempting to appease an irritable Russia, has not yet even decided when to decide about admitting the Czech Republic and the other new democracies. This, Rodman reasons, is one explanation for the demoralization of pro-Western forces and the resuscitation of neo-Communists in central Europe.

NATO has been one of modern history's huge successes. The only invasion of the territory of a member nation by armed forces of another nation occurred in the South Atlantic—the Falklands. NATO's first actual combat operation occurred in February 1994—against Serb planes over Bosnia. What would be enlarged with NATO would be central Europe's prospects for two fragile things, deterrence and democracy.

June 13, 1996

China and Curzon's Law

A flick of the dragon's tail last week sufficed to focus attention on the fact that the world is still a dangerous place. A presidential election is the target of the missiles China has sent splashing into international waters close to Taiwan's two largest ports, menacing air and shipping lanes. On March 23 Lee Teng-hui, who already is Taiwan's first native-born president, is expected to become the first directly elected president of the vibrant island nation of 21 million and the first democratic head of state in 4,000 years of Chinese civilization. Lee says he is not seeking international recognition of Taiwan's independence, or permanent separation, and is committed to unification with the mainland. However, Taiwan has been skillfully pursuing an independent stature in international affairs, and an estimated third of Taiwan's electorate favors independence.

When in May 1994 Lee, en route to Central America, landed at Honolulu for refueling, the Clinton administration, out of deference to Beijing's sensibilities, ordered him restricted to the airport. But in November 1994 the U.S. elections elevated Republican supporters of Taiwan to positions of power in Congress. By then American and Taiwanese money had been gathered to endow a professorship in Lee's honor at Cornell, where in 1968 he earned a Ph.D. In 1995 Cornell asked Lee to address an alumni reunion. Secretary of State Warren Christopher, with a wary eye on Congress, reportedly gave Beijing the vague assurance that a Lee visit "would be inconsistent with our policy." Beijing was subsequently infuriated when the Clinton administration allowed what Congress would have demanded: a visa for Lee.

Inconstancy causes misunderstandings, which can cause wars. Granted, there are occasions when carefully calibrated ambiguity can be creative diplomacy, paralyzing an adversary with uncertainty. But on most occasions, and this is one, it is better to heed the advice of Lord Curzon, the British diplomat: Know your own mind and make sure the other fellow knows it, too. The mind of the U.S. government has been somewhat foggy—deliberately so, in part—since President Nixon in his 1972 opening to China embraced the principle of "one China." The policy has been to pretend that Chinese on both sides of the Taiwan Strait want to live under one sovereignty, and that the passage of time will somehow make things come out right. The problem is, as Taiwan passes quickly to democracy and prosperity and confidence, the passage of time is, temporarily at least, working against convergence.

The law of the land is clear. The Taiwan Relations Act of 1979 commits the United States to "resist any resort to force or other forms of coercion that would jeopardize the security, or the social or economic system, of the people of Taiwan." But is the administration clear in, and is it being clear about, its own mind? Careless or misinterpreted words by American diplomats may have encouraged North Korea's invasion of South Korea in 1950 and Iraq's invasion of Kuwait in 1990. One wonders if the administration has privately said to Beijing what the *Washington Post* has said editorially: "If it came to that, the United States would have no choice but to help Taiwan—a flourishing free-market democracy—defend itself against attack by Communist China."

The task is to keep it from coming to that. Surely Beijing would not attempt anything as militarily ambitious, and foolhardy, as an amphibious invasion across more than 125 miles of water under Taiwan's F-16s and other weapons the United States has supplied. But with communist ideology dead as a doornail, the Leninists still running China need nationalism to hold the nation together. That partly explains their attempts to treat the South China Sea as a Chinese lake, something else the United States, with its longstanding commitment to freedom of the seas, cannot tolerate. Other U.S. grievances include Beijing's ghastly human rights abuses, such as the starvation of orphans, Beijing's refusal to honor its obligations regarding intellectual property rights (pirating U.S. software and CDs), and Beijing's sales, in violation of treaty commitments, of nuclear-weapons-related material to Pakistan.

China, our sixth largest trading partner (Taiwan is seventh) and the largest potential market for almost everything, is the key to stability in the crescent stretching from Korea to India. The CIA estimates that in twenty-five years the crescent will contain five of the world's six largest economies (China, the United States, Japan, India, Indonesia, South Korea—with Thailand pressing Germany for the seventh rank). The hope is that China's sizzling economy—growth has averaged 10 percent annually since 1990—will break the political regime to the saddle of civility.

Prosperity and entrepreneurial ferment do not necessarily produce open societies or democratic politics. But sustained economic growth requires the rule of law regarding contracts and other instruments of commerce, the free flow of information, and competition in international markets for an increasingly scarce essential—capital. China may need to invest $1 trillion just in infrastructure in the next ten years and must export furiously to pay for rivers of imported grains. How much is China willing to risk in the form of legal sanctions and other economic losses in order to combat Taiwan's assertiveness?

That question is pertinent to the U.S. presidential campaign. Bob Dole recently said he would support a Taiwan seat in the U.N. and said that would be consistent with a "one China" policy. (In 1945 the Soviet Union was given seats for itself and Ukraine and Belorussia.) He also said, "It would be all right with me" for any president of Taiwan to visit the United States during a Dole administration. President Clinton will be asked about those matters, and about how he uses, or does not use, the Seventh Fleet to support Taiwan.

But the main aim should be to buy time. The most important sound out of China is not the roar of rockets but the death rattle of the regime. Radical economic transformation is never just economic. There may yet be a convergence between the societies separated by the Strait, a convergence less on the terms of Mao's heirs than on the terms of the heirs of Generalissimo Chaing Kai-shek.

March 18, 1996

The Brothers Netanyahu

When Barry Goldwater told the 1964 Republican convention that extremism in defense of liberty is no vice, a scandalized journalist reportedly exclaimed, "He's going to run as Goldwater!" Today comparable exclamations resound concerning Israel's new prime minister, Benjamin Netanyahu.

Some news reports of his government's guidelines make much of the fact that they closely resemble his campaign promises. Well, did you ever.

President Clinton, speaking from his bunker on barricaded Pennsylvania Avenue, says he hopes Israel will continue to take "risks for peace." In the forty-eight years since Israel was founded on one-sixth of one percent of the 7.5 million square miles of land that is too casually called "the Arab world," Israel has not known an hour of true peace. It has suffered four wars (1948, 1956, 1967, 1973). Five if you count the 1969–70 "war of attrition." Six if you count the continuing conflict with various terrorist organizations supported by hostile nations. In three weeks of war in October 1973, Israel's casualties, as a percentage of its population, were three times larger than U.S. casualties in eight years of war in Vietnam. For Israelis, boarding a bus is risky. How grating they must find the exhortations to risk-taking that issue from a powerful nation surrounded by two weak neighbors and two broad oceans.

Jews were 10 percent of the population of the Roman empire, and if today they were the proportion of the world's population that they were then, they would number 200 million. They number 13 million. The world was an especially dangerous place for Jews before they had a national home. And that home was especially vulnerable in its pre-1967 borders, when it was twelve miles wide at the waist.

Netanyahu's guidelines say the Golan Heights, from which tanks poured in 1973, will not be returned to the aggressor Syria. And there will be no Palestinian state or other foreign sovereignty west of the Jordan River. And Israel can act against terrorism "everywhere," and "will act to remove the threat to the northern border." Much as the U.S. government acted against threats out of Mexico in 1916.

The guidelines say Jerusalem shall forever be Israel's undivided capital under Israel's sovereignty. Ask average Americans to name the capitals of Delaware, Vermont, and Israel. More will know Jerusalem than Dover or Montpelier. Yet their government for decades said that locating the U.S. embassy in Jerusalem would "prejudge" the city's status. Indeed. That is a good reason for locating the embassy not just in Jerusalem, as Congress has committed a reluctant Clinton to do by May 1997, but in East Jerusalem, the portion Jordan lost by its 1967 aggression, and which Arafat plans to make the capital of a Palestinian state.

Netanyahu's guidelines say Israeli settlements in the West Bank and elsewhere are important for defense and "Zionist fulfillment." In 1990 Strobe Talbott, who now holds the State Department's second-highest position, compared Israel's West Bank settlement policy to Saddam Hussein's claim to Kuwait because Kuwait and Iraq had been part of the same province under the Ottoman empire. Actually, the settlements are legal because the West Bank, which Jordan seized militarily in 1948–49, is an unallocated portion of the Palestine Mandate of 1922.

It has been nearly half a century since Israel became the first salient of democratic values in an inhospitable region, and the world still waits for an Arab nation to become the first democracy in the history of Arab civilization. While waiting for such developments, the Netanyahu government's unspoken guidelines will be Golda Meir's admonition: Jews are used to collective eulogies but Israel will not die so that the world will speak well of it.

On the eve of the 1967 war, a young Israeli soldier wrote in his diary of an Englishman, an American, and an Israeli caught by cannibals, put in a pot, and offered a last wish: "The Englishman asked for a whiskey and a pipe, and got them. The American asked for a steak and got it. The Israeli asked the chief of the tribe to give him a good kick in the backside. At first the chief refused, but after much argument he did it. At once the Israeli pulled out a gun and shot all the cannibals. The American and the Englishman asked him: 'If you had a gun all the time, why didn't you kill them sooner?' 'Are you crazy,' answered the Israeli, 'and have the U.N. call me an aggressor?' "

So wrote the man who on a memorable date—July 4, 1976—led, and was the only Israeli soldier killed in, the raid that rescued the hostages at Entebbe. Jonathan Netanyahu. Benjamin's brother.

June 23, 1996

The Spectacle of Suffering

Balkan savagery is forcing Americans to think through a moral dilemma that brings to mind one of the great comic figures of English fiction—Mrs. Jellyby in Charles Dickens's *Bleak House*. She makes a brief but telling appearance in a brilliant essay soon to be published in *The National Interest* quarterly. The essay is "Compassion and the Globalization of the Spectacle of Suffering," by Clifford Orwin of the University of Toronto.

Mrs. Jellyby was the ditzy do-gooder who practiced "telescopic philanthropy." Her children were neglected and London's poor went unnoticed outside her window because her gaze was fixed on the suffering natives of Borrioboola-Gha. She had, Dickens wrote, handsome eyes but "they could see nothing nearer than Africa."

Today, writes Orwin, because of television, everyone's gaze can be fixed on—can hardly avoid being fixed on—the plight of distant people. This television "window on the distress of fellow human beings" is often thrown open as the suffering is actually occurring, and humanitarians hope that the instantaneous global dissemination of heart-rending pictures of agony will soften hearts and prompt humanitarian interventions. Orwin has doubts.

Compassion, he says, depends on imagination, which is why children manifest little of it. It is axiomatic: One death is a tragedy, a million deaths are a statistic. We can imagine the former. Television pictures of real victims are "pegs on which to hang our imagination." However, before "looking to television to effect universal moral regeneration," Orwin warns, note that "images of televised suffering trade at a substantial discount."

They can be turned off, or tuned out by people for whom television, always on and rarely noticed, is akin to audible wallpaper. Note the rhythm of the typical newscast, which begins with gravity and, long before thirty minutes have elapsed, is lighter than air, offering bulletins about the effect of beets on balding, and Julia Roberts's views on judicial review. Television audiences, emphatically including audiences of news broadcasts, want to be entertained, "and the right amount of suffering is entertaining—but only the right amount of it."

Television has a large menu of sufferers to choose from, and viewers can choose which to feel compassion for, until compassion exhaustion sets in. There is, as Orwin says, an "interchangeableness of the sufferers" that prevents powerful affective links between the viewers and the viewed and prevents television from developing permanent constituencies for any suffering group.

Mere humanitarianism toward distant victims, as distinct from communal identification by viewers with similar people similarly situated, is, writes Orwin, "fickle and highly unstable. To find, as the Good Samaritan did, a single victim by the roadside is one thing. To confront a succession of them on television, all very far from us and widely scattered around the globe, is something else entirely."

Which brings him to the heart of the matter: "Our humanitarian impulses may fire, but they will also tend to sputter. On the one hand, we wish that we could help; on the other, we are only too likely to feel ourselves absolved by the fact of this very wish."

Humanitarian intervention is noble precisely because it is not urgent—not closely connected to vital national interests. So there is a mixture of high moral content and low practical content to humanitarian commitments that nations make. And Orwin says we resolve this ambiguity by saying that humanitarian interventions justify the expenditure of treasure but not lives. The result is a compound of interventionism and isolationism, expressed in multilateralism, which is analogous to nonpartisanship in domestic matters deemed not serious.

A German commentator says Western initiatives in the Balkans have been intended primarily to ease the sufferings of onlookers. A European diplomat, explaining his country's policy of neither intervening forcefully nor altogether refraining from intervening, cites the "CNN factor." As Orwin explains that, the Balkans are a television tragedy to be coped with on television by using images of symbolic concern to neutralize images of actual suffering.

Recalling Rousseau's dictum that "it is by dint of seeing death and suffering that priests and doctors become pitiless," Orwin warns that "the new abundance of televised suffering" may desensitize rather than sensitize viewers, who become "voyeurs of the global village." Compassion's horizons become broader, but compassion becomes thin gruel.

We have seen something like this before. At the dawn of television, people worried that it would unhinge constitutional balance by making presidents irresistibly powerful. Instead, it has miniaturized most of them by making them promiscuous claimants for the attention of the country, which is indifferent when not disdainful. People hoping that televised suffering will cure hardness of heart may be in for a similar surprise.

November 19, 1995

CHAPTER SEVEN

WEAVERS OF THEIR TIMES

Thomas Jefferson: Clay, but Uncommon Clay

"Man," says Job, "is born unto trouble, as the sparks fly upward." "Use every man after his desert," Hamlet warns, "and who should 'scape whipping?" Verily, we are all made of clay, right down to our feet.

Modern man likes such leveling, deflating maxims because, by stipulating a comforting equality of common sinfulness, they spare him the pain he likes least, the pain in the neck that comes from looking up at those who are rightly on pedestals. One of those made of uncommon clay was, surely, Thomas Jefferson. It is, therefore, a measure of contemporary fevers and confusions that Jefferson's greatness is continually under assault.

A sulfurous new biography of Jefferson asserts: "It is difficult to resist the conclusion that the twentieth-century statesman whom the Thomas Jefferson of January 1793 would have admired most is Pol Pot. . . . We cannot even say categorically that Jefferson would have condemned the bombing of the federal building in Oklahoma City."

The author, the eminent Irish scholar and statesman, Conor Cruise O'Brien, rests his howitzer of vituperation on the slender reed of a single private letter Jefferson wrote in 1793, concerning the French Revolution: ". . . rather than that it should have failed, I would have seen half the earth desolated. Were there but an Adam and an Eve left in every country, and left free, it would be better than as it now is."

It is meretricious to treat an epistolary extravagance as an index of implacable conviction, but, then, O'Brien, alighting upon the obvious—Jefferson was simultaneously a slaveholder and a paladin of political freedom—with a sense of original discovery, has perpetrated a biography of the sort that novelist Joyce Carol Oates calls "pathography," a shrill reduction of a rounded life to a catalog of dysfunctions.

It is bad enough—it is simple-minded elitism—to say, as has been said, that a biographer should be his subject's "conscientious enemy." But O'Brien is conscienceless. For example, he quotes Jefferson's early judgments of blacks' inferiority, but ignores Jefferson's conclusion, twenty years later, that blacks "are on a par with ourselves. My doubts were the result of personal observation on the limited sphere of my own State, where the opportunities for the development of their genius were not favorable." Jefferson anticipated "their reestablishment on an equal footing with the other colors of the human family."

In February 1997, on public television, Ken Burns, whose accomplishments include acclaimed series on the Civil War and baseball, presented a timely corrective, a visually sumptuous and intellectually judicious appraisal of Jefferson.

Burns, using various analysts (this columnist plays a small role), manages to be admiring without being enthralled. He recognizes that heroism is not saintliness, and proves that a cool appraising eye need not be a jaundiced one.

Burns examines, agnostically, the theory that Jefferson, who proclaimed equality when one-fifth of all Americans were owned by other Americans, had a long sexual relationship, and children, with a slave, Sally Hemmings. The film unsparingly notes that Washington freed his slaves, as did Jefferson's cousin John Randolph and Jefferson's neighbor Edward Coles, but Jefferson never did, even as Virginia's population of free blacks was rising in a thirty-year period from 2,000 to 30,000.

The film punctures Jefferson's pose of ambitionlessness. True, he canceled his newspaper subscriptions when he left Washington in 1793. But by 1801, as politically guileful as he was socially graceful, he was president. ("Ambitious as Oliver Cromwell" and "tough as a lignum nut" said John Adams, who was scurrilously attacked by a drunken editor paid by Jefferson.)

Jefferson, symbol of American optimism, died nearly destitute and was preceded in death by his wife, five of his six children, and his best friend— and, in a sense, by the constitutional, political, and social order he cherished. But he produced what one of Burns's interlocutors calls the nation's "making moment"—the Louisiana Purchase—and provided an enduring model of how a free man with a fine mind and great soul lives amid the world's ethical tangles.

"None of us, no, not one," said Jefferson, "is perfect; and were we to love none who had imperfections, this world would be a desert for our love." Many historians and others, in their intellectual crudity, immaturity, and mean-mindedness, respond to complexity with contempt and to excellence with envy. They pander to the democratic spirit gone rancid in resentment of excellence, and they leave our national memory parched. Ken Burns, an irrigator, causes our capacity for political admiration—for love of greatness in public people—to bloom anew.

February 16, 1997

The Passionate Life of William Gladstone

After the young William Gladstone was beaten up by some sports in his rooms at Christ Church, Oxford, he confided to his diary: "Here I have great reason to be thankful to that God whose mercies fail not . . . 1) Because this incident must tend to the mortification of my pride, by God's grace. . . . It is no disgrace to be beaten for Christ was buffeted and smitten. . . . 2) Because here I have to some small extent an opportunity for exercising the duty of forgiveness." His letter proposing marriage to his future wife contained a 140-word sentence about the Almighty. "Oh, William dear," she would later say, "if you weren't such a great man you would be a terrible bore."

But he was a great man and there is nothing boring about Roy Jenkins's wise and entertaining biography of the man who bestrode Britain for an astonishingly long time when Britain bestrode the world. Jenkins, a seasoned politician (he was home secretary and chancellor of the exchequer in Labor governments), calls Gladstone the dominant parliamentarian of the century when British democracy blossomed, and "the most remarkable specimen of humanity" of all the fifty prime ministers since Walpole. "He was in many ways the greatest figure of the nineteenth century, and taken in the round, the greatest British politician of that or any other parliamentary century."

Jenkins's biography is just right for American readers right now. There is a deflating smallness to present-day American politics. Gladstone's story is powerful proof that there is no necessary connection between democracy and vulgarity, and that popular government can accommodate a political career both elegant and passionate.

This biography has the amplitude of a Victorian novel, but not more bulk than is necessary to cover the nearly eighty-nine years of the man who, more even than the Sovereign whose name denotes the era, is emblematic of the era's two dominant traits, earnestness and energy. He could, Jenkins says, do more in four hours than others could do in sixteen, and he worked sixteen hours a day. He played strenuously, too. On a Norwegian vacation at age seventy-five he walked eighteen miles in one day over rough terrain, and on another he started to learn Norwegian. Two years earlier he completed a twenty-mile hike in the Scottish mountains in less than eight hours.

Born in 1809 to a prosperous merchant, he was educated at Eton ("we knew very little indeed, but we knew it accurately") and Oxford (where he earned a double first, and heard Newman's sermons at the University Church, St. Mary's on High Street). He sat in Parliament for sixty-two-and-a-half years with only a twenty-month break in 1846–47. He was a cabinet minister at thirty-three, the third youngest (after Pitt and Harold Wilson) in 250 years of British cabinets. Four times prime minister, the last time at age eighty-three, he twice was prime minister and chancellor of the exchequer simultaneously.

Leaders of democracies generally are enlarged and pulled to greatness only by the demands of office during war. However, Gladstone achieved greatness during the years of almost continuous peace (other than the constant skirmishes of a colonial power) between Waterloo and the Boer War. But the nineteenth century's political and intellectual ferment caused Britain's domestic tranquility to be roiled by controversies large enough to be, as summoners of greatness, the moral equivalents of war. The issues included how church and state should relate, how broadly access to the franchise should be extended, how a civilized nation should respond to genocide that does not implicate the nation's vital material interests, and, regarding the great dilemma of Gladstone's long twilight years, how to respond to the fact that (in Jenkins's words) "the maintenance of the liberal state was incompatible with holding within its centralized grip a large disaffected community of settled mind."

Gladstone began his public career an unbending Tory, convinced that a confessional state was both practicable and desirable. He even believed that anyone who was not a communicating member of the Church of England should be ineligible for public-service jobs. Jenkins notes dryly, "The plenitude of Gladstone's extremity was underlined by his one 'moderate' concession: the doctrine might be difficult to apply in India." Gladstone was, Jenkins believes, "by some criteria the only dedicated Anglican ever to occupy 10 Downing Street." He read the Bible daily, often in Greek (he was able to communicate in all the principal languages of Europe), and usually attended two, and sometimes three, sermons on Sundays.

Religion was for him a constant reproach: "And this day I am forty years old. Forty years long hath God been grieved with me—hath with much long suffering endured me." On his fifty-eighth birthday: "Another year of mercies unworthily received is added to the sum of my days: of wanderings and backslidings." On his seventieth: "Alas the poor little garden of my own soul remains uncultivated, unweeded, defaced."

He felt deeply about, and plunged deeply into, liturgical disputes. And the nation felt deeply when, in 1850, Rome reestablished the Catholic hierarchy in England for the first time since 1584. He was grieved by Newman's embrace of the Roman church, an institution that at one point he denounced as "an Asian monarchy: nothing but one giddy height of despotism and one dead level of religious subservience." He sold 150,000 copies of a pamphlet denouncing ultramontane Catholicism. But in his mature years he lost faith, Jenkins says, "not in God, but in the ability of any government or state to act as the agent of God."

At the beginning of his career his conservatism caused him to write that the fall of the Roman Empire was a result of the corruption inherent in secret voting. By the end of his career he had helped preside over a dramatic broadening of democracy, which took some curious turns, such as repealing duties on paper. This (Jenkins calls it the "removal of a tax on popular knowledge") was detested by the House of Lords because it produced cheap books and newspapers.

Still, Gladstone was never a liberal in the modern manner. Some reviewers of Jenkins's book, looking for what America currently lacks, a heroic liberal, have tried to present Gladstone as a precursor of today's liberalism. They have a lot to ignore, such as: "I am a firm believer in the aristocratic principle—the rule of the best. I am an out-and-out *inequalitarian.*" He certainly did not subscribe to the central tenet of modern liberalism, that state power is properly used to reduce inequality.

As he grew older he did claim to speak "for the masses against the classes" and he vigorously denounced London's "West End." (Today that phrase denotes the theater district; then it was an epithet akin to "inside the Beltway.") But he did not pander to "the people." As Jenkins says, "The flattery lay in assuming their seriousness and judgmental capacity." This "elevated but nonetheless popular politician" was the first great platform campaigner of modern democracy, capable of riveting the attention of a crowd of 25,000—this before electronic amplification. There was, of course, his manner—"his flashing eye and the eagle's swoop of his cadences"—but there was more: "There was also some feeling that he was on their side, not in the sense of an economic class struggle, for he was never strong on the social condition of the people, but in the sense that he was for seriousness against cynicism, for moral purpose against frivolity, for the achievements of industrial and industrious Britain at a time when it was supreme in these respects, and also in some sense for the solid striving of the northern provincial centers as against the glitter of London and the soft landscape and more traditional society of the South of England."

Disraeli's wit, and the cynical flattery ("we authors, Ma'am") with which he won the affection that the queen withheld from Gladstone, are unattractive—indeed, repellent—in the context of the debate about what response Britain should make to Turkish atrocities in Bulgaria. Disraeli sardonically dismissed Gladstone's pamphlet on the subject (it sold 200,000 copies) as "of all the Bulgarian horrors perhaps the greatest" and was skeptical as to whether "torture had been practiced on a great scale amongst an oriental people who . . . generally terminate their connection with culprits in a more expeditious manner."

Compare what Jenkins calls Disraeli's "mordant and provocative flippancies" to Gladstone's "pulsating moral indignation": "There is not a cannibal in the South Sea Islands whose indignation would not rise and overboil at the recital of that which has been done . . . another murderous harvest from the soil soaked and reeking with blood."

Ireland's dark and bloody ground produced Gladstone's grandest moment and greatest failure. Like Peel, who broke with his party for principle (free trade), Gladstone shattered his party over his proposal for Home Rule in Ireland. Unlike Peel, he failed to carry his principle. He believed that Ireland's volatile compound of agrarian and ethnic stresses meant that the only alternatives to Home Rule were military reconquest or the violent break-up of the United Kingdom. Perhaps there never was a realistic hope of derailing the train of events that led to Yeats's "terrible beauty" of Easter 1916. As Jenkins says, Gladstone's Herculean task was to get his largely Nonconformist Liberal Party to hand over Ireland to a Catholic regime that probably would construct a confessional state. What seems clear is that in Gladstone's day Ireland was corrupting the polity much as Algeria corrupted France in the 1950s.

Because of the passions aroused by the Irish question, Gladstone required a bodyguard—the first prime minister to do so since the social unrest following the Napoleonic wars. Once he was knocked down by a cow; the cow was subsequently shot, and its head was displayed in a pub near Gladstone's home. A wreath arrived with a card that read, "To the memory of the patriotic cow which sacrificed its life in an attempt to save Ireland from Home Rule." The wreck of Gladstone's hopes, partly because of Parnell's adultery with Mrs. O'Shea, is the stuff of tragedy.

Tragedy is foreshadowed in Gladstone's last act of obduracy, his resistance to increased naval expenditures: "If I stood alone in the world on this question, I could not be moved: so strongly am I convinced that this large increase to the navy will lead to disaster in Europe." Something sure did. Gladstone's life was replete with episodes that resonate strangely, as in his diary entry about "a beautiful river walk" with "a Führer . . . who was a charming specimen of those bold hardy active South Bavarians." The destination of the walk? Berchtesgaden.

That diary—Jenkins calls it Gladstone's "account book with God for his

expenditure of 'the most precious gift of time' "—makes possible an astonishingly detailed knowledge of Gladstone's life, such as his voracious consumption of twenty thousand books, including the nineteenth century's
torrent of high-quality fiction—*Middlemarch, Vivian Grey, Romola,* and
on and on and on. His life brushed up against the lives of Trollope, Darwin, Hardy. He meticulously noted all his "rescues." Those were his
strange nocturnal wanderings—he kept at them for decades, into his sev-
enties—to find prostitutes he could ply with hot chocolate and reason.
There is no record of his success in getting them off the streets and onto
the path of righteousness. The cauldron of his sexuality—he tormented his
conscience by browsing for pornography in Munich bookstores—seems to
interest today's historians more than his statecraft ever could.

In 1858 he published three volumes on Homer. While chancellor of the
exchequer he wrote a 15,000-word essay on Tennyson. He wrote a long
riposte to T. H. Huxley on the relationship of the Book of Genesis to modern scientific knowledge. Late in his life felling trees with an ax became a
favorite outlet for his overflowing energy. "The forest laments, in order
that Mr. Gladstone may perspire," sniffed Randolph Churchill, and the
forest went on lamenting until Gladstone gave up the ax one week shy of
eighty-two. When his eyesight began to fail (one eye was seriously injured
when struck by a piece of gingerbread hurled by a woman who was angry
about something unrecorded) and nighttime reading became difficult, he
took up backgammon to keep busy.

When his fourth premiership ended in his eighty-fourth year, he published an edition of the works of a favorite bishop, wrote his own 150,000-
word volume of theology, and published his translation of the *Odes* of
Horace. Such astonishments crop up constantly in Jenkins's pages. And
when dry-as-dust pages about, say, the disestablishment of the Irish
church seem about to make you sneeze, Jenkins's wit banishes tedium.

Here is his description of Gladstone's style of courtship: "Gladstone
persuaded himself that her religious position was satisfactory, but may well
have overestimated the aphrodisiacal effect of telling her this." Here is Jenkins on the effect in England of the surge of American exports produced by
the economic recovery from the Civil War, completion of the transcontinental
railroad, and the development of refrigerated ships: "In England this produced falling rent-rolls and the first touches of austerity for those rural mag-
nates who were not able to make up by the importation of rich American
wives for the adverse effects of wheat and beef from the same source."

Jenkins is amusing about Gladstone's often convoluted rhetoric, in
which "the subordinate clauses hung like candelabra." About one speech,
Jenkins writes that "no one was much the wiser at the end, but his opacity
at least had the advantage that the danger of bitterness was drowned in

incomprehension." However, Jenkins gives Gladstone his considerable due as a giant of democracy because of the grandeur his rhetoric gave to public occasions. Here, for example, is Gladstone speaking in the House of Commons about his transition to the Liberal Party:

> I came among you an outcast from those with whom I associated, driven from them, I admit, by no arbitrary act, but by the slow and resistless forces of conviction. I came among you, to make use of the legal phraseology, *in pauperis forma.* I had nothing to offer you but faithful and honorable service. You received me, as Dido received the shipwrecked Aeneas—
> *"Ejectum littore egentum / Excepi"*
> [an exile on my shore I sheltered].
> And I trust that you may not hereafter at any time say
> *"Et regni demens in parte locavi"*
> [and, fool that I was, I shared with you my realm].

To open Jenkins's book is to begin a protracted, but not too much so, stay in the company of a fabulous personality and noble spirit. When you close it you may be melancholy, so stark is the contrast between the best of democratic politics then and now. But perhaps you will be inspirited by the thought that things have not always been, and need not always be, as they are.

A **National Review** *book review, April 7, 1997*

TR: "Steam Engine in Trousers"

He was "a steam engine in trousers," this Harvard-educated patrician cowboy from Manhattan who galloped into the Dakota Badlands wearing spurs and a pearl-handled revolver from Tiffany, and charged up San Juan Hill in a uniform from Brooks Brothers. He was the first president born in a big city, and the first known to the nation as an intimate—by his initials. The toothy grin that crinkled his entire face masked an unassuageable grief that he kept at bay only by action, by living life as "one long campaign." Author of thirty-six books and 100,000 letters, the first intellectual president since John Quincy Adams, he sometimes read two books a day— some in Italian, Portuguese, Latin, Greek, or other languages he knew— and could recite the "Song of Roland." And just as he transformed himself from a frail asthmatic child too starved for breath to blow out his bedside candle, he transformed the presidency.

In the fall of 1996, public television broadcast a four-hour profile of Theodore Roosevelt that is—to use the words he favored—splendid, delightful, bully. It left viewers both inspirited and melancholy—inspirited by the possibilities of human grandeur illuminated by this blast-furnace personality; melancholy about the fact that the modern presidency he pioneered—he set out to improve everything from freight rates to college football—presupposes big people but usually is occupied, certainly not filled, by little ones.

He worshipped his father, a noble reformer in whose arms the infant Theodore was cradled during long nocturnal carriage rides that eased Theodore's asthmatic suffocation, akin to drowning on dry land. His father died suddenly of stomach cancer at forty-six.

Rushing from the state legislature at Albany to his home where his wife Alice, twenty-two, had given birth to a daughter, Theodore was greeted at the door by a sister who said, "Mother is dying and your wife is, too." His mother died of typhoid fever at forty-eight, and his wife died of kidney failure, hours apart.

He wrote, "Black care rarely sits behind a rider whose pace is fast enough." A theme of the television biography, elegantly written by David Grubin and Geoffrey Ward, is that grief was the spur to TR's hyperkinetic life that gave the nation a decidedly mixed blessing—a hankering for heroic presidencies.

This century began for America with the bang of the assassin's bullet that put the boisterous TR, just forty-two, in the chair that had been occupied by a notably sedentary president, McKinley, who had campaigned seated on his front porch in Canton, Ohio. The century has been what John Milton Cooper, University of Wisconsin historian, calls "an era of great presidential expectations." And therefore also of chronic disappointment.

Such expectations have resisted banishment. Harding's promise of "normalcy," and the rhetorical minimalism of his successor, Coolidge, ran counter to the drift toward the omnipresent presidency, which was intensified first by newsreel cameras, then radio, then television. After Coolidge came Hoover, an engineer cultivating the aura of dynamic modernity. Next came TR's distant cousin, master of national media at a moment when the Depression nationalized a sense of dependence on the national government's actions.

Cooper, writing in *The Virginia Quarterly Review*, notes that the emergence of FDR's full-blown heroic leadership under wartime conditions was presaged by the prewar revival of interest in the Civil War, exemplified by the book and movie *Gone with the Wind*, and interest in Lincoln, as exemplified by Carl Sandburg's immensely popular biography-cum-fairy tale, and the Broadway play *Abe Lincoln in Illinois* by Robert E. Sherwood, who in 1940 became an FDR speechwriter.

What began under TR as a serious attempt to make the presidency as large as the problems posed by industrialism and urbanism, reached both an apotheosis and a distinct silliness in the national swooning about President Kennedy's manufactured glamour and patina of high culture. Richard Reeves, a Kennedy biographer, says "watching the Kennedys was self-improvement" for Americans, teaching them "how to act and spend all the new money coming their way, giving the newly prosperous some polish."

Cooper correctly believes that overreliance on the presidency, and longings for heroism, denote "political immaturity among Americans." Furthermore, by inflating the public's sense of political possibilities, and encouraging childish faith that complex problems will yield to charismatic executive "leadership," the heroic presidency encourages passivity in the citizenry at local levels, and has the anticonstitutional effect of subverting limited government.

Today's president, unrestrained by any sense of the ridiculous, and promising to feel our pain and raise our children, may make one lasting contribution to the nation's health by rendering the idea of the heroic presidency laughable.

October 6, 1996

FDR's Heroic Ebullience

Controversies concerning the memorial to Franklin Roosevelt are today's evidence that this is an age in which one cannot find common sense without a search warrant.

Because of trepidation about possible protests by the animal rights lobby, the statue of Eleanor Roosevelt will not depict her wearing her familiar fur wrap. And FDR's cigarette holder, seen in so many photographs, will not be in evidence. That holder, often clenched in a toothy smile illuminating FDR's large upturned head, was emblematic of the infectious jauntiness which was his greatest gift to a shaken country and a precis of his political philosophy. But the cigarette holder must be banished, lest sin flourish.

More seriously wrong is the decision that none of the three statues of FDR in the seven-and-a-half-acre memorial will depict him in a wheelchair. We wallow waist deep in a confessional culture, in which any lunatic can get on television to confess unnatural acts with llamas, yet we will not truthfully depict this century's most important president in a way that is, to say no more, pertinent to understanding him.

The decision has been made to continue in stone a reticence about FDR's disability, a reticence that in his lifetime was required by public sensibilities that now have been happily surmounted. The decision reveals confusion about the proper point of the memorial.

Defenders of that decision say it would be wrong to "revise the record"—that it would be unhistorical to display what FDR successfully concealed from the American people, most of whom did not understand the reality of his affliction. (Thanks to a cooperative press corps, only two of the more than 125,000 photographs in the FDR library at Hyde Park show him in a wheelchair.) But fidelity to FDR's wishes is not guiding the design of the memorial: FDR told Felix Frankfurter he wanted only a starkly simple memorial no larger than his desk, the sort of memorial to him that already exists at the National Archives.

A statement by the FDR Memorial Commission almost implies that the project is a celebration of the New Deal. If that is so, the heck with it. The statement says the memorial "is designed to serve not as a monument to the man, but as a place of remembrance, contemplation, and tribute to his work."

But that is a distinction without a difference. The work of the last thirteen years of FDR's life cannot properly be contemplated without reference to the affliction that left him a paraplegic for the last twenty-four years of his life. He probably would not have become president, and certainly would not have become the long-headed and tough president he was, without passing through the furnace of polio.

One can believe that many of his works were mistakes and still believe he should be celebrated for the gallantry that the disease demanded from him but need not have elicited. No serious person doubts that FDR played a large role in the making of modern America, and it is passing strange to suppose that the disease did not catalyze the transformation of the debonair young swell, skating along on charm and connections, into the brilliant and broadly empathetic politician.

"Too often," FDR once said, "is the biographer tempted to confine himself to that comparatively brief period after the trumpet of fame has directed the eyes of the world upon him whose life story he writes." From that statement Geoffrey Ward derived the title of the first volume of his unsurpassed biography of FDR, *Before the Trumpet.*

Ward's second volume, which recounts FDR's rise from a bed of pain to the seat of power, is titled *A First-Class Temperament.* That comes from Oliver Wendell Holmes's famous assessment of FDR: "A second-class intellect. But a first-class temperament!" No reader of Ward can doubt that the temperament FDR exhibited in the 1930s and 1940s was forged in the

1920s. The iron entered into his soul when he performed, with heroic ebullience, the excruciating exercises necessary to make his legs ready for steel braces.

So, let's see FDR portrayed at the memorial in a wheelchair. Perhaps we should resist the temptation to have him holding something that would accurately depict one of his most noble talents and his unquenchable capacity for pleasure—a martini shaker. But let's see that cigarette holder which, he once breezily explained to an inquiring boy, he used "because my doctor told me to stay as far away from cigarettes as possible."

May 9, 1996

The Greatest American of the Century?

LEXINGTON, VIRGINIA—He was arguably the greatest American of this century, although he never sought elective office and did not receive the position he most wanted, command of Operation Overlord on D-Day. It was his for the asking, but he would not ask for what President Roosevelt was reluctant to grant—permission for George Catlett Marshall to leave his side.

Even this week, with Marshall's name being invoked more than at anytime since his death in 1959, or since he received the Nobel Peace Prize in 1953, he is not really being given his due. But, then, it is difficult to take the full measure of Marshall, the man who became a cadet here at Virginia Military Institute 100 years ago.

The Marshall museum that faces the VMI parade ground is a suitably understated memorial to a man whose starchy reserve ("I have no feelings except those I reserve for Mrs. Marshall") masked a drive and steely impatience that repeatedly served the nation. Before Secretary of State Marshall joined the other honorary degree recipients at Harvard fifty years ago this week (the group on June 5, 1947, included T. S. Eliot, Omar Bradley, and J. Robert Oppenheimer) to deliver the address that would attach his name to an act of statecraft, he had already achieved greatness.

In France in 1917 a furious Major Marshall exploded at General Pershing for what Marshall considered unmerited criticism of another general. Pershing responded by making Marshall an organizer of the American offensive. After the war, in which 116,000 Americans died, the army shrank to 130,000. Marshall, put in charge of the officer training school at Fort Benning, Georgia, refined infantry tactics, stressing mobility and the initiative of junior officers. The "Benning revolution" produced 200 future generals, including Bradley, Stilwell, and Ridgway.

Eighteen nations had armies larger than America's—it had only forty tanks—when Marshall became army chief of staff on September 1, 1939, the day Germany attacked Poland. Less than four months before Pearl Harbor, Congress came within one vote of virtually disbanding the army: The House voted 203–202 to extend conscription. Marshall abolished the seniority system, forcing upward of 500 colonels into retirement to make way for younger men like Eisenhower and Patton.

Rescuing the nation from improvident disarmaments was Marshall's vocation: As secretary of defense he doubled the size of the army in the six months after the outbreak of the Korean War. Yet this man of arms, organizer of victory in mankind's most destructive war, is remembered primarily for an act exemplifying America's modern penchant for "global meliorism."

That phrase is from Walter A. McDougall, professor of history and international relations at the University of Pennsylvania. The meliorist impulse has two premises. First, America has a mission to make the world better, because the American model of a pluralistic commercial republic is universally valid. And exporting the model is in the national interest because spreading bourgeois civilization, with its preoccupation with prosperity, is the way to tranquilize a murderous world.

Fifty years after the genesis of the Marshall Plan, the American model is more broadly embraced than ever before, but Americans are less interested in, or confident about, their ability or even their right to influence the courses of other countries. And some scholars question whether the plan's $13 billion was crucial to Europe's recovery.

Western Europe's agriculture and industry soon exceeded prewar output, but 80 percent of the capital invested in those years was European. And regarding foreign aid generally, an exhaustive study by the London School of Economics concerning ninety-two developing nations concludes that "no relationship exists between the levels of aid and rates of growth in recipient countries." Rather, foreign aid has discouraged the lowering of tax rates and other barriers to growth while "increasing the size of recipient governments and lining the pockets of elites."

Those who subsequently proposed Marshall Plans for the Mekong Delta and America's inner cities and other places have exemplified a governmental hubris that was not characteristic of Marshall or the other giants of their heroic era of American statecraft. Those realists did not think of the Marshall Plan as relevant beyond the shattered societies of Western Europe, with their bourgeois traditions on which to rebuild.

The plan was at least a catalyst of confidence, psychotherapy for a continent in shock, and a presentation of the American model to a world in need of it. If you seek a monument to Marshall, and to America's meliorist impulse in the immediate postwar period, look around and see what you do *not* see—German and Japanese militarism. That is no small monument.

June 1, 1997

Lenin: Man of the Century

Lenin's patience, never plentiful, was exhausted. "Why," he demanded, "should we bother to reply to Kautsky? He would reply to us, and we would have to reply to his reply. There's no end to that. It will be quite enough for us to announce that Kautsky is a traitor to the working class, and everyone will understand everything." So in the name of a favored category of people, the working class, let's have an end to argument, and to Kautsky (a German socialist guilty of deviationism), and, while we are at it, to whole categories of tiresome people.

Today in Bosnia forensic experts are sifting the unquiet earth of mass graves filled with victims of last summer's slaughter of Muslims from what was called the "safe area" of Srebrenica. Saddam Hussein has assaulted a "protected" area established for a category of inconvenient people, the Kurds. So this blood-stained century is sagging to its end true to the tone set for it by its most pioneering political person. And at this propitious moment the Yale University Press is publishing a slender volume of documents that let Lenin's words trace to him the pedigree of two of the twentieth century's defining ideas, totalitarianism founded on terror, and genocide as state policy.

The Unknown Lenin: From the Secret Archive contains documents that the Soviet government never saw fit to publish in the various editions of Lenin's collected works. The regime's reticence was understandable, given the investment it had in the idea that Lenin was a wise and idealistic fellow. It is hard to square the myth of Lenin's wisdom with his long report of September 20, 1920, in which he insists that Western Europe, including Britain, was ripe for a revolution that would sweep away bourgeois institutions. As for Lenin's idealism, his directive of August 11, 1918, will further complicate for his apologists the already daunting task of absolving him of culpability for Soviet crimes by arguing that viciousness began with Stalin. Lenin wrote: "Hang (hang without fail, so the people see) no fewer than one hundred known kulaks, rich men, bloodsuckers. . . . Do it in such a way that for hun-

316

dreds of [kilometers] around, the people will see, tremble, know, shout: they are strangling and will strangle to death the bloodsucker kulaks."

Lenin's rich repertoire of epithets frequently had an entomological motif—"spiders," "insects," "scoundrel fleas," "bedbugs," "leeches." Harvard's Richard Pipes, in his history of the Russian Revolution, suggests that Lenin might have influenced Hitler, who in *Mein Kampf* referred to Germany's leading Social Democrats, whom Hitler considered mostly Jews, as *Ungeziefer,* meaning vermin, fit only for extermination. And when Lenin calls kulaks bloodsuckers, he was following in the footsteps of a founder of Europe's revolutionary tradition, Robespierre, who said, "If the rich farmers persist in sucking the people's blood. . . ." But who were the kulaks?

Pipes, the editor of the Yale volume of Lenin documents, notes that whereas Hitler at least had genealogical criteria for determining who was a Jew, Lenin "had no standards to define a kulak." The term had been in use since the 1860s, denoting less an economic category than the personality type that Americans call a "go-getter." Be that as it may, in 1918 Lenin exhorted workers to "merciless war" against the kulak "vampires." "Death to them." One historian says "this was probably the first occasion when the leader of a modern state incited the populace to the social equivalent of genocide."

Pipes, writing of the Bolsheviks' murder of Nicholas II and his family in an Ekaterinburg basement the night of July 16–17, 1918, says this marked mankind's entry into "an entirely new moral realm." Since then, state-sponsored atrocities have been so huge and commonplace, and so desensitizing, that readers may have to pause to grasp Pipes's point: "The massacre, by secret order of the government, of a family that for all its Imperial background was remarkably commonplace, guilty of nothing, desiring only to be allowed to live in peace, carried mankind for the first time across the threshold of deliberate genocide."

One of Lenin's colleagues recalled arguing with Lenin about a particularly indiscriminate police measure authorizing executions without trials of categories of people defined no more precisely than "hooligans" or "speculators" or "counterrevolutionary agitators." The colleague wrote: "So I called out in exasperation, 'Then why do we bother with a Commissariat for Justice? Let's call it frankly the *Commissariat for Social Extermination* and be done with it!' Lenin's face suddenly brightened and he replied, 'Well put . . . that's exactly what it should be . . . but we can't say that.' "

In the tenth decade of the century, as in the second, there are many things that cannot be said but can be done. The American people, taking a lesson from their current president, have not been paying much attention to the world. And some American leaders, including the president, seem to have skipped school the day twentieth-century history was taught. They seem constantly surprised by the quantity and quality of the savagery still practiced, and by the fact that the savages are not brought to heel by appeals to civility. The State Department has been reminding Saddam Hussein of U.N. Resolution 688, wherein the United Nations "demands" this and "insists" that and instructs Hussein not to be nasty to the Kurds. This is supposed to inhibit the man who in 1988 used poison gas for the genocidal destruction of 3,800 villages and scores of thousands of Kurds.

From Baghdad to the remnants of Yugoslavia (where, in the fall of 1996, democracy was declared, via almost farcical elections, in a Bosnia beset by war criminals and barely sublimated war), there are a lot of little Lenins out there, practicing in public what he preached in secret. If the title is a measure not of morality but of consequentiality, if it belongs to the century's emblematic man, the man of new departures and large echoes, then to Lenin goes the title "Man of the Century."

September 16, 1996

Richard Nixon's Life of Resentment and Tenacity

No matter what its combination of triumphs and tragedies, any life defined primarily by tenacity must seem, at the end, a story of some bravery but even more melancholy. In Richard Nixon's long slog through various valleys of humiliation, to political triumph and disgrace and partial rehabilitation, there were many episodes of glory, but a constant griminess.

His political life turned on five close calls.

In 1948 he had the right hunch about Alger Hiss. Watching the Washington establishment rally around Hiss, Nixon honed his cynicism and stoked his resentments.

In 1952 his place on the ticket with Eisenhower jeopardized by financial dealings of a sort not uncommon at the time, Nixon, steadily more cynical, saved himself with the "Checkers" speech before the largest television audience in history to that time.

In 1960 he lost the presidency by a thin margin and perhaps by fraud.

In 1968, eighteen years after he had last won an election on his own, he won a 43 percent victory.

And if in 1973 his lawyers had not sent the Watergate committee a memo containing an exact quote from a conversation with John Dean, the committee staff might never have thought to inquire about a taping system, and he would have completed two terms. But anyone thinking that Nixon deserved a better fate from Watergate should remember his silence as his brave daughter Julie crisscrossed the country defending him against charges he knew to be true.

He was an intelligent man despised by intellectuals. A man with a gnawing sense of his inferior education, he nevertheless brought into his administration two Harvard professors as foreign policy and domestic policy advisors—Henry Kissinger and Pat Moynihan—and he also enlisted the services of other extraordinarily talented intellectuals, including George Shultz, James Schlesinger, and Arthur Burns.

If we take as a simple but serviceable measure of modern liberalism's program the expansion of the central government's role as society's supervisor, Nixon's administration was more liberal than any, other than Lyndon Johnson's, since the Second World War. In the Nixon years the federal government created the Environmental Protection Agency and the Occupational Safety and Health Administration; it began racial quotas and set-asides; Nixon favored an enormous "industrial policy" project, the federal funding of the supersonic passenger aircraft; he proposed a guaranteed annual income; he instituted wage and price controls, the most sweeping intrusion of the state into society since the New Deal; he was smitten by John Connolly, a Tory Democrat with a zest for government domination of markets.

Nixon's largest achievement was the opening to China. But as the architect of detente he probably prolonged the life of the Soviet Union. And although he fancied himself at daggers drawn with the nation's intellectual elites, he joined the foreign policy elite in making a fetish of arms control with the Soviet Union. That project was impossible until it was unimportant—impossible because of the Soviet Union's hegemonic aims, then unimportant because the Soviet Union was imploding.

Nixon was spectacularly ill-suited by temperament to become president in the late 1960s, a moment of extreme cultural fragmentation. Traditional political preoccupations with economic redistributions were being supplanted by anxiety about the disintegration of the cultural unity of the postwar period. Lacking an articulable defense of the cultural values under siege, he became a vessel of smoldering animosities.

In the House of Representatives, where his ascent to national prominence began with his confrontation of Hiss, his career was closed by the Judiciary Committee's impeachment hearings. His remaining twenty years were spent using his reputation for statecraft to regain some of the public's respect, and even the affection that often accrues to the tenacious.

Until his forced retirement from active politics, the acids of resentments had ulcerated his personality until self-pity was its strongest faculty. Politics is mostly talk, a lot of it small talk with strangers, at which Nixon was never comfortable. Rarely, and never contentedly, employed other than at politics, he measured out his life in forksful of chicken á la king with contributors and county chairmen. That is not good for the soul.

In his nationally televised farewell to his staff in the East Room on August 9, 1974, he read Theodore Roosevelt's words about the death of his wife: "And when my heart's dearest died, the light went from my life forever." That equation of the loss of political office to the death of a loved one was terrifying testimony to the toll ambition can take on character.

April 24, 1994

Frederick Taylor: Busy, Busy, Busy

In November 1910 some railroads were trying to prove, as it had recently become their burden to do, that they merited Federal permission for rate increases. Representing opponents was Louis Brandeis, the future Justice, who questioned railroad officials about their costs. Were new efficiencies in operations an alternative to rate increases? No, said the railroaders. How did they know? Brandeis asked. Trust us, they said.

But Brandeis was in no mood to trust people who trusted their hunches, intuitions, and experiences rather than the rising clerisy of experts. He caused a sensation by asserting that the railroads could save $1 million a day—serious money then—by "scientific management." How did he know? He knew about Frederick Winslow Taylor, who was about to become famous, and frequently unhappy, for the remaining five years of his life.

Taylor is still renowned among historians of American business. Peter Drucker, the well-known student of management, says that Taylor, not Marx, deserves to be ranked with Darwin and Freud in the trinity of makers of the modern world and that Taylorism is perhaps "the most powerful as well as the most lasting contribution America has made to Western thought since the *Federalist Papers.*" Robert Kanigel's judgment is more measured: "The coming of Taylorism made our age what it was going to become anyway—only more so, more quickly, more irrevocably." However, Mr. Kanigel's richly detailed biography, *The One Best Way: Frederick Winslow Taylor and the Enigma of Efficiency,* shows how much drama there was in the mundane when Taylor was making it the stuff of a new "science" of efficiency.

Frederick Taylor: Busy, Busy, Busy

Taylor, whose life (1856–1915) coincided with America's period of pell-mell industrialization, was born into an affluent, landed family in suburban Philadelphia. At the age of thirteen, during extended travel with his parents in Europe, he watched his impatient father use the power of his purse to get reluctant local laborers to repair a bridge so the family's touring could proceed. This was, for young Fred, an intensely practical epiphany: money can make working men move faster.

He was to become one of those men, briefly, and would use his years on the factory floor to achieve moral ascendancy through downward mobility. For the rest of his life he would invoke his laboring experience to claim the moral high ground in the fierce debates about whether he understood, respected, and served working people. At Phillips Exeter Academy (where, the saying was, there were "no rules, only absolute freedom, tempered by expulsion") he passed Harvard's admission exam with distinction. However, he chose to work in a factory making iron castings. There he learned that life is real, life is earnest.

He entered what Mr. Kanigel calls a "world of wood, iron, rope, leather, cloth," a world of steam power transmitted through belts and pulleys that amplified human muscle, which was abundant. Abundant and hence, Taylor saw, squandered. As he rose quickly into the ranks of management, he could act on his one seminal idea: The key to productivity is knowledge, not muscle power—although sometimes the most important knowledge is how to organize the use of muscles.

The instruments of organization included stopwatches, with dials marking tenths and hundredths of a minute for easy calculations. Taylor's interest was less in what could be done in ten hours than in ten seconds. How much time did it take to perform a properly analyzed task—fill a wheelbarrow, drive a nail, shovel coal? Assembly lines, like Ford's, or even disassembly lines, like those of Chicago's meat packers, required the disassembly of work. "Amid the blur of activity of human work," Mr. Kanigel writes, "where did one element end and another begin?" Well, time-and-motion studies would tell. "Now, gentlemen, shoveling is a great science compared with pig-iron handling," Taylor said to a Congressional committee in 1912.

The committee was hostile and Taylor was bewildered. Theatrical in temperament, brimful of certitudes and vehement in expressing them, he was not just offended, he was uncomprehending when politicians and other people reacted furiously to his statements like: "In our scheme, we do not ask for the initiative of our men. We do not want any initiative. All we want of them is to obey the orders we give them, do what we say, and do it quick." Although he could address workers with appalling brutality ("I have you for your strength and mechanical ability, and we have other men paid for thinking"), he considered himself a progressive, as did Brandeis, Ida Tarbell, and other reformers.

This was, after all, a time of self-conscious modernity, defined in part by faith in science. In 1912 the nation would elect a political scientist president. There was a strong paternalistic streak in the progressivism of Herbert Croly, the founder of *The New Republic* and leader of progressivism; Walter Lippmann; and others who believed that modern life was too complicated for the untutored masses to cope with. A tutoring class, in government and business, would lead the people up from backward practices. However, it now seems that such workplace paternalism often is, well, inefficient. The unending search for enhanced productivity now often leads to something like workplace democracy, empowering the workers to help organize their toils.

In Mr. Kanigel's telling, there is much pathos in Taylor's sense of being ill-used by critics. He was sure his system would dissolve tensions between labor and capital by demonstrating that high wages are not a problem but a solution. His mantra was "Men will not do an extraordinary day's work for an ordinary day's pay." So pay better for workers who will pay the price in new techniques for enhanced productivity. However, that price included more than the heightened stress of a more revved up workplace. It also involved the moral insult of diminished prestige inherent in the transfer of all thinking from labor to the new management class. The result was a world of work that felt and even sounded different. As Mr. Kanigel says, "Everything clacked and whirred faster."

Taylor passionately believed Taylorism would raise what has come to be called the "standard of living." However, the controversy that engulfed him demonstrated that that concept is too complex to be reduced to a few indexes of material betterment. The man who helped ratchet up the level of stress in modern life may have had his life shortened—he died the day after his fifty-ninth birthday—by the strain of living with the controversy he caused. This in spite of the fact that in his last years he stopped to smell the roses: One of his final searches was for the one best way to cultivate them.

In 1916, the year after Taylor's death, Lenin passed some of his time in Zurich annotating a German translation of a Taylor book. The year after that, America's entry into World War I secured the nation's embrace of efficiency as a sovereign value and of Taylor as a prophet. In the 1920s a Parisian cleric declared, "The love of God is the Taylor System of our spiritual life." In 1927, at the end of an Italian conference on scientific management, Mussolini gave Taylor's widow a photograph of himself in exchange for one of Taylor. In 1928 the United States elected as president an engineer who had written a report on waste in industry. It has been reported that when Charlie Chaplin's *Modern Times,* with its depiction of a man meshed with a machine and reduced to a machinelike jerkiness of movements, was shown to audiences in industrial Pittsburgh, they did not find it funny.

Mr. Kanigel is an award-winning science writer but his prose could use an infusion of efficiency. (He uses "kid-glove" as a verb.) And he is not as attentive to intellectual history as he should be. His scanting of that allows his narrative to suggest that Taylorism triggered a spanking new anxiety about a Faustian bargain that degrades workers while making them materially better off. Actually, that anxiety is as old as industrialism. Mr. Kanigel does cite Adam Smith's famous hymn to the division of labor in that pin factory where "one man draws out the wire, another straightens it, a third cuts it, a fourth points it, a fifth grinds it at the top for receiving the head," a process "divided into about eighteen distinct operations." Smith was sanguine about this because specialization increases a worker's "dexterity," and hence "the quantity of the work he can perform." However, Marx thought the division of labor produces alienation but that all would be well under Communism, "where nobody has one exclusive sphere of activity." He was vague about the details.

Mr. Kanigel could have lengthened the pedigree of the controversy that engulfed Taylor had he considered the fact that in the second quarter of the nineteenth century, when American industrialism was in its infancy, Alexis de Tocqueville anticipated the ambivalence that Taylor catalyzed early in this century: "When a workman is unceasingly and exclusively engaged in the fabrication of one thing, he ultimately does his work with singular dexterity; but, at the same time, he loses the general faculty of applying his mind to the direction of the work. He every day becomes more adroit and less industrious; so that it may be said of him, that, in proportion as the workman improves, the man is degraded."

Taylor's critics worried about both "deskilling" and the creation of an "aristocracy of the capable," and about work becoming scarce because of what is now called "downsizing"—a productive few displacing the less fit. Mr. Kanigel believes, reasonably, that Taylor's legacy—a new kind of seriousness about enhancing workers' productivity—has been, on balance, benign. It certainly came in handy when Hitler was rampant. Mr. Kanigel quotes Mr. Drucker: During the war, "by applying Taylor's Scientific Management, U.S. industry trained totally unskilled workers, many of them former sharecroppers raised in a preindustrial environment, and converted them in sixty to ninety days into first-rate welders and shipbuilders." One ship, launched in South Portland, Maine, in 1942, was the 7,176-ton SS *Frederick W. Taylor.*

A New York Times book review, June 15, 1997

Alger Hiss's Grotesque Fidelity

Alger Hiss spent forty-four months in prison and then his remaining forty-two years in the dungeon of his grotesque fidelity to the fiction of his innocence. The cost of his unconditional surrender to the totalitarian temptation was steep for his supporters. Clinging to their belief in his martyrdom in order to preserve their belief in their "progressive" virtue, they were drawn into an intellectual corruption that hastened the moral bankruptcy of the American left.

Hiss died last week at ninety-two. The insufferable agnosticism expressed in many obituaries concerning his guilt is proof of the continuing queasiness of "anti-anti-communist" thinkers confronting the facts of communism and its servants.

When Hiss was accused of espionage for the Soviet Union, his background—Johns Hopkins and Harvard Law School; protegé of Felix Frankfurter; aide to Justice Oliver Wendell Holmes; a diplomatic career that carried him to the upper reaches of the State Department, and to Yalta and the U.N.'s birth in San Francisco; at the time of the accusation, president of the Carnegie Endowment for International Peace—made him a perfect symbol of cosmopolitan sophistication under siege from America's paranoid majority of yahoos. And then there was his accuser, Whittaker Chambers.

Porcine, rumpled, and tormented, with bad teeth and a worse tailor, he was as déclassé as Hiss was elegantly emblematic of the governing class. The trouble was that Chambers knew things. He knew Hiss.

When Chambers said that while he had been a communist operative he had dealt with Hiss, Hiss testified that he had never known "a man by the name of Whittaker Chambers." A very lawyerly answer, that. During his protracted self-destruction he was driven to admit to having known Chambers by another name, but not well. However, Chambers knew so many intimacies—from Hiss's household effects to the thrill Hiss, an amateur ornithologist, felt when he spotted a prothonotary warbler—that Hiss was forced to weave an ever more tangled web.

He lied about transferring his car through Chambers to communists, and about not remembering how he had disposed of the Woodstock typewriter on which some incriminating documents had been typed. He lied by omitting from a list of former maids the one to whose family he gave the typewriter. He was convicted of perjury (the statute of limitations saved him from espionage charges).

In 1978 historian Allen Weinstein, who began his research believing Hiss innocent, published his definitive *Perjury: The Hiss-Chambers Case*, based on 40,000 pages of previously classified material and interviews with forty people involved in the case but never before interviewed, including Soviet agents who confirmed Chambers's testimony. Weinstein's conclusion: "There has yet to emerge, from any source, a coherent body of evidence that seriously undermines the credibility of the evidence against Mr. Hiss."

What emerged after the end of the Cold War would have made peace hell for Hiss, had he been susceptible to guilt or even embarrassment. A Soviet general, falsely described as familiar with all pertinent archives, was pressured by a Hiss emissary to say there was no evidence of Hiss espionage. The general later recanted. From Russia came documents confirming Chambers's account of the communist underground in the United States in the 1930s. From Hungarian archives came documentary evidence (from another Harvard-educated American spy) that Hiss spied.

In a 1990 memoir, a former KGB officer asserted that Hiss's Soviet code name was "Ales." Earlier this year, the U.S. government released files from the "Venona Project," which intercepted 2,200 wartime Soviet cables. A March 30, 1945, cable refers to an agent Ales in terms congruent with testimony about Hiss by Chambers and others.

There is no hatred as corrupting as intellectual hatred, so Hiss's supporters always responded to evidence by redoubling their concoction of rococo reasons for believing him framed by a conspiracy so vast and proficient it left no trace of itself. They still require his innocence so they can convict America of pathological injustice. Never has so much ingenuity been invested in so low a cause, or such futility.

Hiss loyalists finally were reduced to proclaiming that their loyalty was self-vindicating. As one of them said, "Alger would not have put his friends and others through what they went through for him if he was guilty." That is, he was either innocent or a moral monster, which is unthinkable. No, indubitable. He, enveloped in his enigmatic fanaticism, and they, impervious to evidence, were all monstrosities, huddled together for warmth in what G. K. Chesterton called "the clean well-lit prison of one idea."

November 21, 1996

Justice for "Engine Charlie"

Justice delayed is not always justice denied, sometimes it is justice to the dead and to the historical record, two constituencies that have their claims on the conscience of a good society. Consider the case of Charles E. Wilson, who was an early casualty of the politics of reputation as practiced in Washington, where justice often is scarce and random.

If you are under fifty you may never have heard of him. If you are over fifty what you know about him, if anything, is that he was "Engine Charlie," famous for saying, "What is good for General Motors is good for the country." He didn't say that, but the fiction that he did say it served a particular political agenda. And journalism, because of carelessness or complicity with the agenda, treated the fiction as a defining fact of the fifties. Wilson died in 1961 but the falsehood goes marching on. Or it did until John Steele Gordon lassoed it in *American Heritage* magazine.

When Eisenhower became president in 1953, the Defense Department was in the public sector what General Motors was in the private sector—much the biggest entity. So there was logic to Eisenhower's decision to pick Wilson, president of GM, for secretary of defense. GM then had 50 percent of the automobile market. Defense got almost 60 percent of the federal budget. "Engine Charlie"—the nickname distinguished him from "Electric Charlie," the Charles E. Wilson who was president of General Electric—seemed like just the man to deliver on the goal of "a bigger bang for the buck."

But the nation's intelligentsia was in a bad mood. Its large liberal heart had been broken by the defeat of Adlai Stevenson, beaten by a military hero whose grin, said the intelligentsia, was his philosophy. How tiresome. And the intelligentsia's and liberals' sense of entitlement to the presidency had been violated. So liberal intellectuals adopted toward the Eisenhower administration an attitude of contempt and condescension. That attitude was characteristic of their stance toward the country's commercial class and would come to color the Democratic Party's attitude about mainstream middle-class values. Eisenhower and his cabinet were "the bland leading the bland," with Wilson identified as the archetypal boring businessman. This liberal bigotry was singularly ignorant about Wilson.

He was born in Ohio in 1890. His father, a toolmaker, was a union organizer and socialist. Son Charles also was a socialist when, as an undergraduate at Carnegie Institute of Technology (now Carnegie-Mellon University), he supported the presidential candidacy of Eugene V. Debs. After graduation, Wilson found his job prospects clouded by his politics. He became a patternmaker and the business agent for that craft's union local in Pittsburgh. Years later, his framed union card adorned his offices at GM and the Pentagon.

Directing GM's labor relations in the 1930s, he facilitated the United Automobile Workers' organization of the workforce. When the war came he was GM's president. He toiled for two years without a day off, then suffered a stroke. He used his recuperation period—just three months—to acquaint himself with the management theories of people like Peter Drucker, to whom Wilson said: "To design the structure and develop the constitutional principles for the big business enterprise was the great achievement of the founding fathers of GM, the last generation. To develop citizenship and community is the task of the next generation. We are, so to speak, going to be Jeffersonians to Mr. [Alfred P.] Sloan's Federalists."

Gordon reports that when Wilson developed plans for a pension system to supplement Social Security for GM workers, Drucker warned him that if the pension funds were invested in the stock market, in a few decades workers would be the owners of American industry. "Exactly what they should be," said Wilson. Writes Gordon, "If life were fair, liberals would hail Charles E. Wilson as a hero." Or if liberals had been fair.

Wilson gave up his $600,000 a year salary for the $22,000 paid cabinet members, paid a staggering capital-gains tax on the GM stock he sold to avoid conflicts of interest, then went to his confirmation hearing, where he was nevertheless asked if he would be able to make decisions that were in the national interest but were adverse to GM's interests. He answered: "I could. I cannot conceive of one because for years I thought what was good for our country was good for General Motors, and vice versa. The difference did not exist. Our company is too big. It goes with the welfare of the country."

Wilson, writes Gordon, could hardly have imagined what would become of his words, which were uttered behind closed doors, when they were distorted by "liberals horrified to find themselves out of power after twenty years and largely replaced with businessmen. . . . They simply twisted what Wilson had said into, 'What is good for General Motors is good for the country,' leaked it to the press, and repeated the lie endlessly, making Wilson sound like some latter-day corporate version of Marie Antoinette."

Gordon tells a cautionary tale about Washington, which is happiest when in indignation overdrive. There was nothing new in 1953 about attempts to build political careers or movements on the rubble of other people's reputations. But Wilson's experience was a new wrinkle. Call it the politics of sensitivity. The purported significance of his supposed statement was that it proved him to be coarse, boorish, generally deficient in the finer feelings, and lacking an elementary sense of right and wrong. Never mind that Wilson, who was more reflective than the average Washingtonian, can hardly be said to have lowered the tone of the capital.

The caricaturing of him was an early brush stroke in the painting of the 1950s as a decade of crass materialism and moral obtuseness. This political painting prepared the way for the 1960s, and for the politics of feelings which is still too much with us. Today, in addition to, or sometimes instead of, debating the wisdom of particular policies, we argue about the moral worthiness—summed up as "sensitivity" to this or that—of the person advocating the policies. Which is why politics seems so dreadfully personal. It is.

February 20, 1995

Zora Arkus-Duntov: Zooooooooooom

It is a truism that journalism often involves reporting the death of a person to a public that has never heard of that person. So: Zora Arkus-Duntov died the other day in Detroit at eighty-six. And if, 700 words from now, you do not mourn his passing, you are not a good American.

The headline on *The New York Times* obituary said Arkus-Duntov "made the Corvette classic." The text of the obituary said he turned that car "into a symbol of power and ostentation in the late 1950s."

Is there a trace of disapproval in those words? Wouldn't be surprised. The *Times* is the keeper of liberalism's conscience, and liberalism, as is well-known, is not fond of fun, or at least of many forms of fun that many people like (such as cheeseburgers, talk radio, guns, fur coats, Las Vegas). Least of all does liberalism look kindly on the fifties, when the wrong kind of fun was busting out all over.

McDonald's franchises were springing up like dandelions, the yahoos (a.k.a. the electorate) preferred Dwight Eisenhower's smile to Adlai Stevenson's syntax, and irresponsible consumers liked cars that were larger than roller skates, did not sip gas the way Aunt Minnie sips tea, and expressed the exuberance of a nation not yet susceptible to liberalism's favorite emotion—guilt.

The Corvette was born, wouldn't you know it, June 30, 1953, year one of the Eisenhower era. Its body was made of fiberglass, a cousin of plastic, which caused the intelligentsia to curl its collective lip. (Remember the scene early in the 1967 movie *The Graduate*, when Benjamin, played by Dustin Hoffman, was fresh from college and in need of a career? Someone doubly repulsive—an adult and, even worse, a businessman—told Benjamin to remember one word, "plastics." Audiences of advanced thinkers adored that summation of American vulgarity.)

But the Corvette was born with a piddling little 150-horsepower engine. Enter Arkus-Duntov, who was born in Belgium but was born to be an American.

Zora Arkus-Duntov: Zoooooooooooom

He became one after retiring as a gold smuggler at age sixteen and then earning an engineering degree in Berlin and fighting with the French air force early in the Second World War. (This information was in Keith Bradsher's *Times* obituary, which actually was splendid.) As soon as he saw the Corvette, he sought and got a job with General Motors, where before he retired in 1975 he designed four-wheel disk brakes for mass production cars and the fuel injection system now standard in many cars.

However, his signal contribution to American civilization was to rev up the Corvette to 195-horsepower in 1955, 240 in 1956, and 283 in 1957. America's first muscle car. You got a problem with that? Go to court.

But not to the Supreme Court. Justice Clarence Thomas drives a Corvette. A 1990 ZR1 that he modified to pump up to 400 horsepower. Its license plates read Res Ipsa. From a Latin phrase meaning, "It speaks for itself."

Arkus-Duntov had colorful company at GM in the fifties. There was Harley Earl, "the Cellini of Chrome" who designed cars that looked, said a disapproving critic, like jukeboxes on wheels.

David Halberstam, in his history of the fifties, writes that whereas Henry Ford (who said people could have cars of any color they wanted, as long as they wanted black) represented America's Calvinist past, Earl was perhaps the most influential shaper of American style and taste in the fifties' years of abundance and indulgence. He loved airplanes (other GM executives drove Cadillacs, he drove a Buick LeSabre, based on the F-86 Sabre jet) and sharks (hence tailfins). Earl sometimes dressed like a negative of a photograph of a GM executive, in a cream-colored linen suit and dark blue shirt, and it was said that if Earl could have put chrome on his clothes, he would have.

And Earl was a great patriot. When his son said he was going to get a Ferrari, Earl said otherwise. Instead, the son drove a Corvette.

The first Corvette rolled off the assembly line ten months after the first Holiday Inn was opened, on the highway between Memphis and Nashville, and twenty-two months before Ray Kroc's first McDonald's was opened in April 1955 in Des Plaines, Illinois. America was on the move and in no mood to linger over lunch. A lunch of cheeseburgers. Today's food fascists must really hate the fifties.

If you seek Arkus-Duntov's monument, look around, at that 'Vette coming on in the passing lane. Or look in Bowling Green, Kentucky, where, at Arkus-Duntov's request, his ashes will be entombed in a display at the National Corvette Museum.

April 28, 1996

Vance Packard's Self-Refutation

Forty years ago Vance Packard, who died last week at eighty-two, touched a national nerve with a book that was, in a sense, self-refuting. He sounded a theme that, elaborated, became part of postwar liberalism and one reason for that doctrine's decline.

The Hidden Persuaders, one of the best-sellers of 1957, warned Americans about what Packard considered their deepening submission to a subtle tyranny of selling. It was the first of a fusillade of Packard books—next came *The Status Seekers* (1959), then *The Waste Makers* (1960)—about the enervation of society by a culture of "consumerism." Americans, he said, were becoming passive clay shaped by the hands of cunning advertisers.

In 1945, after fifteen years of Depression and war, Americans' pent-up demands for almost everything exploded, powering one of the most prodigious economic expansions in world history. This in turn produced a cottage industry of social criticism catering to the anxiety that Americans were becoming a bovine herd characterized by "conformity" and "materialism," mindlessly consuming to slake manufactured appetites, including the thirst for "status" conferred by conspicuous consumption of material possessions. Mind you, the authors of the books, and their readers, exempted themselves from their indictment of everyone else on charges of docility, gullibility, and almost imbecility.

A 1957 novel, *On the Road,* was partly a protest against the supposed death of individualism, spontaneity, and authenticity. Other book titles were telling: *The Organization Man, The Lonely Crowd, The Man in the Grey Flannel Suit.* Oh, for the days when blandness—a surfeit of grey flannel—was considered an American social problem.

As society has become more hierarchical, complex, and opaque, and social processes have come to seem more impersonal and autonomous, more and more people have become susceptible to doubts about individual autonomy. "Do we move ourselves, or are we moved by an unseen hand?" wrote Tennyson. Packard, playing Cassandra at America's postwar banquet, said we are moved by Madison Avenue, which he depicted as an Orwellian force armed with the sinister science of market research, manipulating mass behavior by implanting cravings.

It has been said (by Daniel Boorstin) that whereas Europeans shop to get what they want, Americans shop to discover what they want. Packard's thesis was that advertising constantly prepares Americans for shopping, turning wants into synthetic needs.

In 1957 the Edsel appeared, backed by Ford's full merchandising might. The ensuing proof that the public is not plastic to the touch of "persuaders" did nothing to dampen the warm reception the intelligentsia gave, in 1958, to John Kenneth Galbraith's *The Affluent Society*. Never one to allow mere facts to inconvenience the flow of theories, Galbraith simply asserted that capitalism had become dangerously dominant by emancipating itself from subordination to supply and demand. It had done this by acquiring mastery over demands, which could be tailored by advertising to conform to the capacities and conveniences of producers of goods and services.

Actually, most advertising aims less to increase aggregate demand for a category of goods or services than to increase a brand's market share. Pepsi's primary advertising goal is not to make people thirsty, or to get them to buy Pepsis rather than Pontiacs, but rather to get them to buy Pepsis instead of Cokes. Furthermore, the average American reportedly can recall, without prompting, only about two of the approximately 600 television commercials he sees each week. Even before Americans became armed with remote control wands with mute buttons, they became sophisticated at detecting and dissecting (with the help of books like Packard's) or, more often, ignoring the "persuaders," which are about as "hidden" as the riot of neon in Times Square.

Today's social environment constantly plucks at one's sleeve, even grabs one's lapels. In a normal week the average American probably is exposed to more messages, printed or spoken, from nonacquaintances than a fourteenth-century peasant was exposed to in a lifetime. In response to this blitzkrieg of stimuli, people develop, perhaps in their neurological wiring, filters and blocking mechanisms. Otherwise they would be driven mad by the din.

But one faction clings to the notion of Americans as incompetents, needing the regulatory regime of a nanny state to save them from victimization. Forty years after Packard found a mass market for his thesis that the masses are unconscious victims of guileful advertisers, what sits atop liberalism's agenda? Amending the First Amendment, if necessary, in order to enable the government to protect the vulnerable public from what liberals consider excessive amounts of political advertising. That is, campaign finance reform. The pedigree of an idea can indeed be embarrassing.

December 19, 1996

Al Capone and Huey Newton: Two Styles of Upward—For a While—Mobility

By 1927, at age twenty-eight, Al Capone was among the most famous Americans, master of a complex service industry in a major metropolitan area where he was a power broker with considerable clout. As exercised by Capone, clout could be memorable. But by 1938 Capone was "the Wop with the Mop," swabbing the concrete corridors of Alcatraz, a syphilitic shell of his former self. In 1947, thoroughly demented, he died.

In 1970, at age twenty-eight, Huey Newton was the toast of "progressives" on both coasts, celebrated as the distillation of radicals' yearnings—an intellectual outlaw in politics. But sometime before dawn on August 22, 1989, Newton, by then just another past-his-prime thug, disregarded reports that some drug dealers with a business grievance were gunning for him. He went looking for some crack. His body was found on a sidewalk. At 6:10 A.M. he was pronounced dead at an Oakland hospital.

The lives of Capone and Newton are studies in the dynamics, and costs, of celebrity. Both careers had remarkably compressed trajectories, with steep plunges from apogees that in retrospect seem as much ridiculous as scandalous. Now the simultaneous publication of biographies of Capone and Newton is an occasion for this nation to learn, at long last, a cautionary lesson about the power of the modern engines of publicity to give grotesque twists to the public's perceptions.

Capone, as portrayed by Laurence Bergreen, was a cunning creature more or less sincerely convinced that his enterprises, principally bootlegging but also gambling and prostitution, produced jobs for deserving men and women and satisfied appetites that he did not create and which someone else would satisfy if he did not. The shootings and beatings and other unpleasantnesses were, he thought, just robust solutions to business disputes that, given the irrationality of the time, could not be submitted to more decorous arbitrations, as in courts. Capone seems to have convinced himself that his activities were legitimized by the illegitimacy of the Volstead Act and other laws that gave rise to the markets he served. Mr. Bergreen, who cannot be accused of being too censorious about his subject, suggests that but for Prohibition and other laws interfering with the satisfaction of consensual vices, Capone's entrepreneurial energies would have flowed productively in other directions.

Newton, on whom Hugh Pearson casts a cold eye, was a dismal and difficult-to-decipher tangle of delusion and cynicism. The Black Panthers organization was largely Newton's creation and instrument, and finally one of his many casualties. It began in 1966 as an organization for black self-defense against perceived—and real—police brutality. For years the Black Panthers preserved a patina of social responsibility by running breakfast programs for children. However, at some point, and not long into the life of the organization, Newton almost certainly stopped believing, or trying to believe, or even pretending to believe that he was a "civil-rights activist." Yet for years portions of the American left persisted in regarding him as an idealist whose roughness—murders, rapes, and savage beatings—testified to his "authenticity" as a man of "the streets."

No matter how hard any sympathizers try to locate "root causes" of the careers of Capone and Newton, neither career was necessary. But both careers were symptomatic of national fevers of their eras.

Around the turn of the century, about the time the Capone family booked passage from Naples to New York, it was widely assumed that Italian immigrants, especially those from Naples and farther south, were permanent residents on what today is called the far left slope of the Bell Curve. Mr. Bergreen labors to wring extenuation from the "climate of anti-Italian prejudice" during Capone's formative years.

Mr. Pearson, a young African-American journalist, knows the economic distress and racial tensions of the Oakland where Newton grew up and the Black Panthers were born. After World War II Oakland sent police recruiters across the South seeking officers experienced in keeping blacks subservient. But Pearson's book, which is an act of considerable moral courage, is unblinking in its refusal to give criminality and other pathologies the dignity of politics.

Capone was born in Brooklyn in 1899 and was raised near the stench and disease of the Gowanus Canal. He attended schools where fistfights between male students and female teachers were not uncommon. One such fight between the fourteen-year-old Al and his teacher ended his schooling. He became a minor racketeer, and moved to Chicago in 1921. By then his adolescent encounters with prostitutes had given him syphilis. After years of latency (it was not discovered until a prison examination in the 1930s) it attacked his brain, distorting his personality, which was not nice to begin with. Eventually it produced dementia. No one can say how much Capone's mood swings, from ebullience to the sort of rage that resulted in his bludgeoning to death with baseball bats three business associates at a dinner party, resulted from neurosyphilis. Or how much his personality was shaped by the cocaine that produced his perforated septum, which also was discovered in a prison examination. Bergreen speculates that because tertiary syphilis is associated with megalomania, it was indispensable to Capone's criminal-commercial success: "The Capone we remember was the creation of a disease that had magnified his personality. Syphilis made Al Capone larger than life."

Not really. He became a celebrity by making the most of an irrational social policy, Prohibition, and of the spectacular corruption of the city that H. G. Wells called a "dark smear under the sky." Oh, Chicago, where a popular booklet, *If Christ Came to Chicago!*, was, Bergreen says, a "guide disguised as a diatribe": it included a map locating the better brothels.

In the 1920s, when a president said that the business of America is business, Americans celebrated commercial and industrial bigness—concentration, centralization, organization. Capone, a lifelong Republican, used modern technologies—cars, trucks, machine guns—to help him achieve economies of scale in slaking the thirst of Chicago. There, criminal factions held well-reported conferences in fine hotels. A journalist wrote of the gangsters "thrust up by Volstead" to "the eminence of big businessmen. Here they sat, partitioning Chicago and Cook County into trade areas, covenanting against society and the law, and going about it with the assurance of a group of directors of United States Steel."

This was during the decade in which radio, tabloid newspapers, and the new business of "public relations" produced what has been called "the age of ballyhoo." Suddenly the public had a powerful thirst for "personalities" and "stars" and "heroes" of all sorts.

Bergreen reports that when Capone dined out at Miami restaurants, he "arrived with a retinue of thugs, one of whom lugged a large bass fiddle case, which contained the gold-rimmed plates Al favored and a cache of machine guns, should a show of force become necessary during the meal." In 1930, at Northwestern's Medill School of Journalism, a student poll picked the following list of the world's ten most "outstanding personages": Mussolini, Charles Lindbergh, Admiral Byrd, George Bernard Shaw, Bobby Jones, President Hoover, Gandhi, Einstein, Henry Ford, and Capone.

One year later Capone was brought down. In 1927 the U.S. Supreme Court had ruled against a South Carolina bootlegger who claimed that the Fifth Amendment protection against self-incrimination meant he did not have to pay taxes on earnings from illegal activities. Nice try, said the Court. Capone was eventually convicted of income-tax evasion.

On October 3, 1931, three days before his trial began, Capone, who often had preened and been applauded at boxing matches and other sporting events, was booed at a Northwestern football game. The social climate had changed. In the grimness of the Depression the nation found Capone's flamboyance repellent. And the nation's taste in outlaws was changing. Capone, the urban organization man, was becoming an anachronism. The rising stars were small-town loners striking against institutions blamed for the nation's distress—banks. The new decade belonged to such bank robbers as John Dillinger, "Ma" Barker, "Pretty Boy" Floyd, and Bonnie Parker and Clyde Barrow. It was just ten years since Capone had arrived in Chicago with no money and few prospects. He had become internationally infamous as a symbol of that city, and now was bound for oblivion in the bowels of the federal penitentiary system.

Huey Newton, too, was a brief but emblematic figure. He was produced by the politics of the late 1960s and early 1970s, and by the national media, which were not bashful about manufacturing "leaders" for black Americans. Newton was an inherently perishable product because American leftists are fickle about their political fashions. And Newton was destroyed by three toxic gifts—unearned income, unmerited adulation, and cocaine. The first two he got from white liberals.

Pearson's narrative is as mesmerizing as carnage at the side of a highway—Newton, high on cocaine, watching *The Godfather* over and over; Newton sodomizing Bobby Seale with a bullwhip; Newton receiving a Ph.D. in "The History of Consciousness" from the University of California at Santa Cruz. This story, in which Mario Savio, Tom Hayden, *Ramparts* magazine, and similar relics make cameo appearances, seems to come from a past more distant and less believable than Capone's 1920s.

Remember the famous photograph of Newton sitting in a wicker chair suggestive of an African throne, with warriors' shields on either side, and an animal pelt on the floor? Newton was holding a spear in one hand and a rifle in the other. He was a premature multiculturalist. He also was the Panthers' minister of defense, then supreme commander, then supreme servant of the people, in the sandbox politics of the American left. Still, the Black Panther "party" was a good way to get girls, whose reluctance to sleep with dignitaries was stigmatized as petit bourgeois deviationism.

Newton's move into a posh penthouse was a bad career move if he wanted to continue to be regarded as a tribune of the downtrodden. But he didn't, so what the hell. Pearson describes the disgust he felt in telling the story of Newton and the Panthers. Pearson is angry "at our society and myself, for paying so much attention to an organization that, arguably, in so many ways amounted to little more than a temporary media phenomenon." But by making that clear, Mr. Pearson has performed a signal service. Perhaps the nation will be a little less susceptible to the recurring temptation to inflate criminals into something grander than they are.

In 1965 Al Capone's son, then forty-five, was arrested for shoplifting $3.50 worth of aspirin and batteries from a Miami convenience store. Said he, "Everybody has a little larceny in them." Perhaps, but some people have a lot more than others. When explaining criminals, that is a good place to start, and sometimes to stop.

A National Review *book review, December 31, 1994*

Allen Ginsberg, Symptom

Allen Ginsberg, symptomatic symbol of the "Beat Generation" and other intellectual fads, died last Saturday at age seventy. He once wrote, "I'm so lucky to be nutty." Actually, his pose of paranoia was not luck, it was a sound career move.

It became big box office with his famous declamation of his poem "Howl" in San Francisco in 1955. That was the year "Rock Around the Clock," in the sound track to the movie *The Blackboard Jungle*, helped launch what was to become the third element in the trinity of sixties ecstasies—sex, drugs, and rock 'n' roll. Ginsberg made the first two his projects. He composed "Howl" with the help of a cocktail of peyote, amphetamines, and Dexedrine.

Thirty years later his reward for a career of execrating American values and works was a six-figure contract for a volume of his collected poetry. It is a distinctive American genius, this ability to transmute attempted subversion into a marketable commodity.

The adjective "beat" was appropriated by Jack Kerouac from a drug-addicted Times Square thief and male prostitute, who meant by it the condition of being exhausted by existence. (That man's existence must have been wearying.) Kerouac attached the adjective to the noun "generation," emulating Gertrude Stein's identification of the "Lost Generation" of the 1920s. Soon *Life* magazine, happy to find some titillating unhappiness in a decade defined by Eisenhower's smile, was writing about the beats as "The Only Revolution Around." That's entertainment.

Back then, poetry commanded crowds. In his book *When the Going Was Good!: American Life in the 1950s*, Jeffrey Hart, now a professor of English at Dartmouth, wrote: "Robert Frost strode onto the stage at Carnegie Hall to a standing ovation from an overflow house. . . . One night in 1957, T. S. Eliot was reading his poems to an overflow audience in Columbia's McMillin Theater. Even faculty members had difficulty getting tickets, and people were crowded into the windows and doors, and listening outside to Eliot over loudspeakers. . . . Dylan Thomas stood at the podium . . . his third American tour in two years."

When Ginsberg came to Columbia "there was a vast throng that had been unable to get in. They pounded on the doors and milled around. Ticket-holders entered between lines of police."

Today no poet could cause such excitement on any campus, or any other American venue, so complete has been the supplanting of words, written and spoken, by music and movies as preferred modes of communication. One of Ginsberg's young acolytes, Robert Zimmerman of Hibbing, Minnesota, put the dissenting impulse to music as Bob Dylan.

Some beats wrote the way some jazz musicians made music, in the heat of chemically assisted improvisation. Truman Capote's famous dismissal of Kerouac's work—"That isn't writing at all, it's typing"—had a point. Granted, Kerouac revised *On the Road* for six years before it was published in 1957. However, fueled by Benzedrine, he wrote the first draft of that novel in 1951 in less than three weeks, as one long single-spaced paragraph—120 feet long on twelve-foot strips of tracing paper taped together. Here is its beginning: "I first met Dean not long after my wife and I split up. I had just gotten over a serious illness that I won't bother to talk about, except that it had something to do with the miserably weary split-up and my feeling that everything was dead."

Does that tone of voice seem familiar? Here is the beginning of a novel published in 1951, the year of Kerouac's typing frenzy: "If you really want to hear about it, the first thing you'll probably want to know is where I was born, and what my lousy childhood was like, and how my parents were occupied and all before they had me, and all that David Copperfield kind of crap, but I don't feel like going into it, if you want to know the truth."

Yes, *The Catcher in the Rye.* Holden Caulfield, adolescent scold, strong in disapproving "phonies," was a precursor of the beats with their passion for "authenticity," which to Ginsberg meant howling echoes of whatever constituted coffeehouse radicalism of the moment. ("Slaves of Plastic! . . . Striped tie addicts! . . . Whiskey freaks bombed out on 530 billion cigarettes a year. . . . Steak swallowers zonked on Television!") With a talent that rarely rose to mediocrity, but with a flair for vulgar exhibitionism, Ginsberg shrewdly advertised his persona as a symptom of a dysfunctional society. He died full of honors, including a front-page (and a full page inside) obituary in *The New York Times,* a symptom to the end.

April 9, 1997

Philadelphia's Deliverance

PHILADELPHIA—There used to be a ballpark here, at the corner of Lehigh Avenue and 21st Street. It was an agreeable little bandbox called Shibe Park and then called Connie Mack Stadium, and in it the Athletics and Phillies set records for futility.

In time the Athletics left town and the Phillies left the neighborhood for a new stadium. A few years ago the Reverend Ben Smith, who is now eighty-two, tore down the old one. Relying on prayer and an alarming amount of borrowing, he built the Deliverance Evangelistic Church complex. The church itself seats five thousand, which is more than the Phillies and Athletics often attracted to the old ballpark. And there is no more futility at the corner of Lehigh and 21st, where Smith's achievements are remarkable, if unremarked.

When God gave Smith a barrel chest and a big voice, He must have had a minister in mind. On a recent Tuesday morning Smith's place was rocking with the joyous noise of worshipers and the bustle of staff attending to the thirty-two classrooms and an even larger number of different departments—adult literacy, youth literacy, prison fellowship, one-on-one attention to drug addicts, and much more—of this good works conglomerate. Churches from Georgia to Michigan, with combined memberships of 84,000 and rising, have been spun off from Deliverance, which is one of the three largest churches on the East Coast. The Nation of Islam—"nation" indeed—probably has fewer than forty thousand adherents but registers as huge news on the national media's radar screens.

In a menacing neighborhood Deliverance is an oasis of . . . well, a large sign in the basketball gym says, ABSOLUTELY NO SLAM DUNKING. Deliverance aims to deliver order based on absolutes in an age of chaos arising from relativism. Is that Quixotic? Smith's Sancho Panza does not think so.

He is John DiIulio, thirty-eight, a Philadelphian born and bred, whose attachment to the city can be gauged by the fact that he still lives here while teaching at Princeton, a long commute away. DiIulio, a political scientist, says that accumulating evidence confirms the efficacy of faith-based approaches to social problems.

The data are hardly counterintuitive. Just as the density of liquor outlets in a neighborhood correlates with negative phenomena, the density of churches correlates with positive ones. Indeed, individuals who may not themselves go to church but who live on a block where people go to church are less likely to commit crimes or wind up on welfare. This is why DiIulio is working on a program to coordinate the ameliorative efforts of the leaders of at least fifty African-American churches in the twenty largest cities.

One such leader is the Reverend Eugene Rivers of Boston who at age twelve was "drafted" into "the life"—Philadelphia's gang culture—and at age sixteen was drawn out of that life and into the Reverend Smith's orbit. Rivers, now forty-six, made it from Philadelphia's mean streets to Harvard's shaded walks. He did so, he says, largely because a "thirst for literacy" was for him, as it is for some other young people in culturally barren settings, one result of a conversion experience. He is a sophisticate who really believes that "Sunday school is the most revolutionary institution."

Rivers is nothing if not succinct in his diagnosis of the central affliction of inner-city youths: They have no idea of purpose or destiny arising from a sense of the sacred. He considers himself a man of the left but his cultural conservatism complements his conviction that the condition of inner-city blacks confirms the primary urgency of spiritual, not political, change. He notes that after years of political gains, America now has eight thousand black elected officials presiding over the decomposition of the black community.

A familiar, facile question is, "Can the nation save the inner-city African-American community?" That question may be backward. There are 65,000 black churches with 23 million adherents, most of them in inner cities. The nation thirsts for good news and grounds for hope about the struggles of inner-city African-Americans. Yet Louis Farrakhan becomes a celebrity on the basis of anti-Semitic and other lunatic ravings while Smith and thousands of unsung others like him remain invisible as they perform daily miracles of social regeneration.

The Reverend Rivers says that one of America's best kept secrets is that "Ben Smith exists." Another is that African-American churches may be saving more than their communities' souls. By preaching—and demonstrating—that the solutions of most social problems begin with spiritual rather than material betterment, they may be saving the nation's soul as well.

September 5, 1996

Strom Thurmond, Bringing Pleasure to the Beacon

SPARTANBURG, SOUTH CAROLINA—Let's put it this way: South Carolinians have a habit of going their own way, sometimes with cannon and cavalry, so the Heart Association should save its breath, because Carolinians are going to keep going to the Beacon restaurant, which subscribes to the famous doctrine that if it isn't fried, it isn't food. Stand downwind of the place and your cholesterol count rises forty points. Order any delicacy, such as the chili cheeseburger, and say "aplenty," and the delicacy will come buried beneath an Everest of french fries and fried onion rings.

So what is America's most spectacular advertisement for healthy living doing here, for the second time today? Well, the first time was for breakfast, before the parade, when he tucked so heartily into the eggs and grits—an unusual indulgence—that he is now skipping lunch but pressing the flesh of lunchers. That's what Strom Thurmond is doing.

That is what Thurmond, who turned ninety-three this week, has been doing almost nonstop since he first won elective office the year Herbert Hoover first won elective office. Hoover won the presidency in 1928; Thurmond became a county superintendent. Thurmond, who has served with about one-fifth of the 1,826 people who have been members of the Senate since 1789, today is serving with one, Republican Rick Santorum of Pennsylvania, who was not born when Thurmond came to the Senate.

This month Thurmond, whose age is 45 percent of that of the Constitution, completes his forty-first year in the Senate. In February he will become the oldest person ever to serve in Congress. If next year he wins an eighth term, and serves all of it, he will be 100 years old.

An aide to Thurmond says his boss still sets a pace the aide can hardly keep. The aide is seventy-two. One of Thurmond's foremost supporters in this city says Thurmond is fit as a fiddle. (If you are not careful, Thurmond will tell you what he eats—fruits and vegetables and other healthy stuff—and what he drinks—nothing any fun—and about his calisthenics and swimming and exercise bike and the weights he lifts.) The supporter says Thurmond is hard to keep up with. The supporter is eighty-two and has known Thurmond since 1938.

Only three other states (Mississippi with James Eastland and John Stennis, Louisiana with Allen Ellender and Russell Long, and Georgia with Walter George and Richard Russell) have had what South Carolina has—two senators with a combined service of seventy years. Fritz Hollings, who will be seventy-four on New Year's Day, has been a senator twenty-nine years and is still South Carolina's junior senator.

A sizable majority of South Carolinians say Thurmond should not be running, but that does not mean a majority will vote against him. The last time he had a close race—close by his standards: he got 56 percent—was 1978. It was close enough that during the campaign he promised he would not run again. He was just joshing. Since then he has been reelected with majorities of 66 and 64 percent.

Thurmond, probably America's only remaining politician who has received votes from Civil War veterans (all Confederates, we may assume), in 1971 became the first southern senator to hire a black staffer, and in 1982 voted to make Martin Luther King's birthday a federal holiday. Thurmond earned his reputation for intransigence—he holds the Senate filibuster record, twenty-four hours and eighteen minutes, set in opposition to the mild civil rights bill of 1957—yet has changed as much as his state. And no state has changed more than South Carolina in the last half-century.

In and around this city, for example, unemployment is about 2.6 percent, thanks to the new BMW assembly plant and associated industries. Tax rates and unionization rates are low and business is booming.

Not everywhere, of course. This city has not one but two Wal-Marts on its outskirts, so the downtown looks a bit down at the heels, especially on a day so cold and rainy that the annual Christmas parade cannot draw a crowd. But it drew Thurmond, who dearly loves parades. So as fire engines with sirens blaring lead some soggy marchers and floats through nearly deserted streets, Thurmond waves from a car on which the hand-lettered sign identifying him dangles at an odd angle.

Afterward, back at the Beacon, he is asked why he does such things in his tenth decade. He answers ingenuously that "I like bringing pleasure to people and people like parades." Then he begins working the room, table by table, before heading down the road to tomorrow and the "Chitlin' Strut" in the town of Salley.

December 7, 1995

Paul Wellstone's Political Unitarianism

Walk, with eyes averted, past the eruption of metal that passes for art and dominates the huge atrium of the Hart Office Building. Enter the first-floor office with the portrait of Hubert Humphrey, the office of Minnesota's Democratic Senator Paul Wellstone. There you will find the flame of liberalism. It is not a hard and gemlike flame.

If you are looking for that old-time political religion, you will be disappointed. Wellstone's liberalism is political unitarianism, as mild and inoffensive as Unitarianism itself, which has been defined as the belief that there is at most one God. Or (to change metaphors) if it is political red meat you are after, more disappointment awaits. You have entered a political salad bar.

A Democratic colleague jocularly greets Wellstone in the Senate chamber as "the last liberal in America." Surely Senator Kennedy demurs. However, Wellstone looks the part of the professor in politics, which he is. He taught political science at Carleton College. He is the most rumpled senator, and in a dark blue shirt and flowered necktie he looks like the sixties settled into tenure. In 1996 he won a second term and was the only senator running for reelection who had the kidney to vote the way a number of others felt—against the welfare-reform bill.

That vote was not as risky or otherworldly as it might have seemed, Minnesota being what it is. But what is Minnesota? Liberalism's last redoubt? It does have a long liberal tradition represented by Humphrey, Eugene McCarthy, Walter Mondale, Orville Freeman, and even Republican Harold Stassen. Yet today it has one of the most conservative senators (freshman Rod Grams, Americans for Democratic Action rating: 0) as well as Wellstone (ADA rating: 100). Still, in the era when Republicans were winning five of six presidential elections (1968–1988), Minnesota was the most Democratic state, voting Democratic five of six times. And in 1990 it elected Wellstone, who two years earlier had been state chairman of Jesse Jackson's presidential campaign.

Asked if, ten years ago, he could have imagined a Democratic president like Clinton—one signing repeal of the sixty-year-old federal entitlement to support for the poor; fixated on balancing the budget; proposing to do so by cutting discretionary domestic spending by one-third—Wellstone answers softly and monosyllabically: "No." He says he subscribed to Arthur Schlesinger's cyclical theory of American politics and expected the 1990s to see resurgent government activism. But when he is asked what thunderous change would result if Wellstonism swept the nation, his answer sounds . . . Clintonian.

He recalls, as a kind of epiphany, a town meeting he held in a small Minnesota community where about 150 people braved a frigid winter night to say essentially this: "Give us some capital to work with and get out of the way." He says, "Too many of their experiences with government have been unpleasant" because government is "overcentralized and bureaucratized."

Good grief. You come hungering for high-octane liberalism and get served warmed-over Reaganism. How about revving up the government as an egalitarian engine of economic redistribution, causing fear and trembling among economic royalists? He does say that the distribution of wealth is becoming increasingly "lopsided." However, that may not be true. John C. Weicher of the Hudson Institute, writing in *The Public Interest* quarterly, argues that wealth—the stock of assets that people own—as distinct from income has been growing rapidly but the concentration of it has changed little: "Overall, as a society, we have been getting richer, rich and poor alike, more or less evenly."

Anyway, Wellstone only tentatively proposes an ameliorative program: "I would not preclude restoring some progressivity to the income tax." "Not preclude"? "Some"? By way of extenuation for such tepidness, he says, "There is an old Yiddish proverb: 'You can't dance at two weddings at the same time.'" He means that if balancing the budget is the goal, a bigger agenda must wait.

But his agenda has almost nothing to do with the left's traditional big agenda of using the power of the state to increase equality of condition, of outcomes. Rather, his agenda falls squarely within the traditional American and conservative emphasis on equality of opportunity. The pursuit of that can involve energetic government, but he does not really call for much energy.

His interests are in schools, and especially in early childhood development. However he knows the severely limited relevance of the federal government, which provides only about 7 percent of all the money spent on education at all levels. Besides, he also knows the limited salience of money. The best predictor of schools' performances is the quality of the families from which the children come to school—the number of parents in the home, quantity and quality of reading matter in the home, amount of homework done in the home, amount of television watched in the home. There is precious little that government at any level can do to vary those variables.

He envisions "giant bookmobiles with mentors" and "read-athons in union halls" and "math-athons in veterans' halls" and a program to get discarded computers to the poor, and his is surely the only Senate office where the name John Dewey is heard. Six years from now, Dewey will have no reverberation in the Senate because Wellstone is pledged to serve only two terms. Which means that in 2000 he will be two years from retirement and perhaps receptive to the idea that some of his fans entertain—a Wellstone presidential campaign to give true liberals a nourishing, stick-to-the-ribs alternative to Clintonist, New Democrat, centrist mush. Wellstone's current disavowal—"That's not the plan right now"—is less than Shermanesque.

But what would be emblazoned on the unfurled banner of True Liberalism? "A bookmobile on every block"? As a summons to the barricades, that needs work.

March 17, 1997

Erwin A. Glikes
1937–1994

Erwin Glikes was my friend and the editor of most of my books.

For many years the slogan of the Buick division of General Motors was, "When better cars are built, Buick will build them." It was a wonderfully

American slogan, full of the assumption of progress—the only question was *when*, not *if* better cars would be built—and the promise to deliver it, personally. I have often thought of that slogan and its American zing in connection with the Glikes family Buick. It carried that family from Belgium, south, away from Hitler's motorized warfare, toward France, then to a port and a voyage to freedom.

Blitzkrieg was, as the name proclaimed, fast. But the Glikes family Buick was faster, for which fact all of us are glad. It brought to safety and to our lives a friend, a patriot, and a superb professional. The service rendered by that Buick was a sufficient reason for, but hardly the only reason for, Erwin's wonderfully immoderate love of America.

It has been said that friendship is a talent. Some people are simply better at it than others. Erwin had an abundance of that talent. But even more ample was his many-faceted talent for the deeper, stronger feeling of love.

He was a man of many loves. He loved Carol and he loved his children. He loved ideas, and books as vessels for ideas. He loved conversation and argument. He loved the publishing profession. But all of his loves were framed by another love. I have never known anyone else with such a pure, such a sweet, such a boundless love of this country. The conversation of this country, and not least the conversation of its capital, was leavened and elevated by Erwin.

Early in his adulthood Erwin chose to run the risk of being prematurely correct about something politically discomforting. He came early to the conclusion that this country was descending into cultural wars that would be bitter, protracted, and potentially ruinous to the society. He believed that books could be consequential—sometimes decisive—weapons in such wars. He was right on both counts—about the culture wars, and about books.

The more journalism I commit, and the more journalism I read and hear and view, the more convinced I am that, beyond newspapers and magazines and broadcasting, a fourth medium retains its supremacy. Books are still the primary carriers of ideas. And it is still true that ideas not only have consequences, only ideas have large and lasting consequences.

So it is altogether right that we who loved Erwin, and who learned so much from him, should return to this university to commemorate, and celebrate, what he meant to his friends, his profession, and his country. It was here in the late 1950s that he caught fire, intellectually.

And here in the late 1960s he had some searing political experiences that turned his well-trained intellect to the contemplation of the importance—and fragility—of the institutions that nourish a free society.

Columbia in the late 1950s gave off a constant shower of sparks from some of the finest scholars of the day. Columbia in the late 1960s gave off a different kind of heat, that of the political passions of a culture in crisis. Here, where the young Erwin Glikes had seen the serene face of applied reason, he saw in 1968 the contorted face of a mob. And he saw cowardice, and its costs.

He never forgot any of this, and he put his memories to use. A theme of his subsequent life was civility—its prerequisites and its enemies. And a characteristic of his life was steady bravery as he beat against the cultural currents that he considered dangerous to his country.

He went to work. He became a publisher and, doing so, enlarged that profession. It has been said that some people are so large, they take up space even when they are missing. Erwin, we now see, was simply irreplaceable. He had a genius.

Genius is the ability to see what is latent in a situation but is unseen by most people. Napoleon could, at a glance, see a bucolic landscape's potential as a battlefield. Michelangelo could see the statue in the stone. Erwin could see a book in a confusing welter of the world's events; he could see a book in a writer's seemingly themeless thoughts and insights and judgments.

An editor is a craftsman and a teacher, instructing his writers in the craft of making something as shapely and harmonious as a fine book from the raw material—often the *very* raw material—of the writer's mind and pen. Writers who have not had the experience of being taken in hand by Erwin cannot fathom how much fun it was.

Fun. What a marvelous capacity for fun Erwin had. He was one of the few, the fortunate few, for whom there simply was no discernable line between work and play, between creation and recreation. Every day he spent as a publisher he spent doing precisely what he would have paid to do. And, really, what could be more fun than keeping company with ideas and arguments and the people who make them dance and sing?

Fun. Too many serious people forget that no matter what you are doing, if you are not having fun, you probably are not doing it—working, living, whatever—right. A major-league baseball manager once said, "Baseball has got to be fun, because if it's not fun, it's a long time to be in agony." And when Barry Goldwater first decided to take a fling at politics, he wrote to his brother, "It ain't for life, and it may be fun." For Erwin, life was fun, all the way, and his sense of fun was infectious.

Erwin enriched the lives of his family and his friends and his profession. He also helped shape, profoundly for the better, the conversation of his country. His was a creative and constructive life—not nearly long enough, but like an Erwin Glikes book, the life of Erwin Glikes was shapely, harmonious, fine, and is certain to have lasting resonance.

A eulogy delivered at Columbia University Chapel, May 20, 1994

CHAPTER EIGHT

SWATCHES FROM
THE CENTURY'S END

Hurrying to the Next Traffic Jam

In 1955 Adlai Stevenson, who was the intelligentsia's political pinup and was considered by advanced thinkers to be an advanced thinker, delivered the commencement address to those he called the "gallant girls" of Smith College. He said they had "a unique opportunity to influence us, man and boy." He urged them "to restore valid, meaningful purpose to life in your home" and to address the "crisis in the humble role of housewife." He said they could do all this "in the living room with a baby in your lap, or in the kitchen with a can opener in your hands" and "maybe you can even practice your saving arts on that unsuspecting·man while he's watching television!"

Any speaker talking like that in, say, 1975 would have been hanged from a branch of one of the campus's stately elms by an enraged regiment of women. Which is to say, twenty years is a long time in modern America.

Values change rapidly, a fact demonstrated last week when the Senate, disregarding the White House's characteristic defense of the way things are, set about undoing some regulations imposed twenty-one years ago. It was an instructive study in conflicting priorities and changing political fashions.

In 1974, after the Yom Kippur War of October 1973, and the oil embargo and all that, Congress enacted a national speed limit of 55 mph. Safety was one concern, but not nearly as large a concern as the "energy crisis," which supposedly would be eased if everyone drove slower, thereby using less gasoline. This was the same impulse that led the government to mandate certain fuel efficiency standards for cars. Those standards encouraged the production of smaller and lighter cars, which are generally less safe than larger cars and certainly have cost lives. The "moral equivalent of war" (President Carter's description of the energy crisis) had more than just the moral equivalent of casualties.

The energy crisis went away, partly because the supposedly imminent exhaustion of petroleum reserves was a fiction, partly because producing companies could not maintain their cartel, partly because the U.S. government did some deregulating of the energy industry. The end of the energy crisis made some Americans, mostly liberals, very sad because it had been a grand excuse to boss people around—telling them what and how fast to drive, where to set their thermostats, how to construct buildings, and so on. However, the national speed limit lived on, justified as a safety measure.

Which it was. It also was one of the most widely disregarded laws: Anyone traveling 55 mph on an interstate risked the derision of the 95 percent of drivers rocketing past him, and risked having an eighteen-wheeler in his backseat.

In 1987 the federal limit was raised to 65 mph outside of metropolitan areas. This was not good enough for most Americans, who are always in a hurry to get to the next traffic jam, and it especially irritated the easily irritated people living in the vastness of the West, where it can be a thirty-mile round trip to get a loaf of bread and people do not want to spend more than twenty minutes doing that. Out there where men are men, rugged individualists all, they don't like the feds doing much of anything other than subsidizing their electric power and grazing and water, and building the Interstate Highway System on which they soon—as soon as the House of Representatives gets with the program—can zoom as fast as their state legislatures will let them.

The speed limit issue, having been an energy issue and then a safety issue, now is a federalism-Tenth Amendment-states' rights issue, with antipaternalism in the bargain. So are attempts to repeal federal laws that pressure states into requiring motorcyclists to wear helmets and passengers in private vehicles to wear safety belts.

(Remember the brief period when cars were built not to start unless seat belts were fastened? Some truculent Americans gave their cars hysterectomies to get rid of that wiring.) The vote to repeal the requirement that highway distance signs include metric measurements is a heartening sign of national intolerance of the fetishes of busybody elites.

One lesson of all this is that life is precious but not priceless. If it were, we would set the speed limit at 35 mph, ban left turns (they are dangerous)—and motorcycles, for that matter. And cheeseburgers. And. . . .

Another lesson is that the way we see and talk about all sorts of things is conditioned by the ideology of the day, as the grandmothers who were the gallant girls of Smith College's class of 1955 can attest.

June 25, 1995

Learning to Worry at a Higher Level

Nighttime illumination at the Lincoln Memorial attracted millions of midges, and spiders that fed on the midges, and sparrows that fed on spiders. Scrubbing away the bird droppings and spider webs made the marble vulnerable to exhaust particles. A modern technology, the jet airliner, has democratized tourism, enabling millions to travel to see Michelangelo's restored frescoes in the Sistine Chapel, where the heat of the visitors' bodies and the vapor in their breath combine with dust in the air to produce indoor acid rain. Warm, humidified, insulated, and carpeted modern homes are comfortable not only for humans but also for fleas, which probably outweigh people on this planet.

Laws protecting marine mammals have produced a sixfold increase in the sea lion population, with devastating consequences for their favorite delicacy, steelheads. The proficiency of smoke jumpers at extinguishing small forest fires has produced a "fire deficit" by building up flammable materials that feed intense fires dangerous to the many people who, encouraged by firefighting proficiency, build homes at the edges of forests. Federal water projects made America's arid Southwest able to sustain millions of new residents and air-conditioning made the region attractive to millions, including many seeking relief from allergies. But then the water was used to irrigate lawns, golf courses, and wind-pollinated trees and plants that the new residents wanted in order to feel at home. And the allergy-sufferers began to suffer again.

On Alaska's Mount McKinley, where there are wind gusts of 200 mph near the summit, improved outdoor gear and improved safety technologies such as helicopter rescue have increased the number of climbers—and casualties. Modern improvements—in nutrition, medicine, training—have produced bigger, stronger tennis players who, wielding "improved" (a complex concept in sport) tennis racquets made of modern materials (no wood racquet has been used at Wimbledon since 1982), can hit 125 mph serves, which can produce boring matches that are mere serving contests. (In one Pete Sampras match at Wimbledon the longest rally was eight strokes.)

Safety measures can make sports more dangerous. Early boxers fought bare-knuckle and floored fighters had thirty seconds to get up. Gloves and the ten-second knockout made hands heavier, decreased the risk of a broken hand from a heavy blow to the opponent's head, and increased the incentive to land such blows because a felled fighter was less likely to get up in ten seconds. Furthermore, the friction of leather on a face rotates the head in a way that increases brain damage. Perhaps World War I, the first large modern war in which combatants wore metal helmets, prompted the development of football helmets. In any case, modern football protections, particularly the hard plastic helmet, have enabled larger and larger players (many enlarged by the illegal modern chemistry of steroids) to produce a ballistic game involving kinetic energy greater than human spines and joints and tendons and ligaments are built to bear, producing an epidemic of chronic ailments. In addition, new antiinflammatory drugs and painkillers, and improved rehabilitation techniques and technologies, enable players to achieve relief from pain at the risk of chronic disability.

Armed carjacking has increased in part as the response of frustrated criminals to automobile alarm systems that complicate the theft of parked cars. Power door locks make drivers feel safer but have produced a huge increase in the number of persons locked out of their cars and exposed to the criminals the locks are supposed to protect them against. Home security systems generate so many false alarms, most from owners' errors, that police resources are squandered, making crime easier.

Depressed? Don't be. But do read the book from which these ideas are drawn. Edward Tenner's *Why Things Bite Back: Technology and the Revenge of Unintended Consequences*. It explores what he calls "the strange consequences of nearly everything." Tenner, a visiting scholar at Princeton, is not one of those neo-Luddites who believe, as a wit said, that progress was all right once, but it went on too long. He acknowledges a kinship with Mary Shelley, whose *Frankenstein* "first connected Promethean technology with unintended havoc." But he is, on balance, cheerful, in his mordant manner, about "the tendency of the world around us to get even, to twist our cleverness against us."

One reason he is cheerful is that he believes in the creativity of disaster. To Murphy's Law ("If something can go wrong, it will") he offers a positive corollary: "Sometimes things can go right only by first going very wrong." As when the tragedy of the *Titanic* produced the International Ice Patrol. But Tenner's sober theme is pertinent to our political discontents that arise from impatience with the world's imperfections, and misplaced confidence in our ability to manipulate society.

He notes that we are suffering what Lewis Thomas called "an epidemic of apprehension." "We seem," Tenner says, "to worry more than our ancestors, surrounded though they were by exploding steamboat boilers, raging epidemics, crashing trains, panicked crowds, and flaming theaters." Disasters foster improvements and improvements foster discontent because they establish standards that are hard for fallible humans to sustain. The U.S. Weather Service has been sued for failing to forecast an ocean storm that killed some fishermen. There was scant medical malpractice litigation until medicine became proficient.

But proficiency often arouses anxiety because it requires intense vigilance. For example, the pharmacological revolution has multiplied medical options and encouraged people to seek more treatment, so even a small rate of error can produce a large number of casualties. A single hospital can dispense upwards of 3 million medications a year. An error rate of less than 0.2 percent would mean 5,000 mistakes and perhaps 500 adverse events. Welcome to the world of what Tenner calls "a new level of worrying." It is a world of progress and progress's "revenge effects," a world exhilarating in its complexity but chastening to our hubris.

July 22, 1996

The Ladies in the Tub in the Rotunda

So now we know. The answer to Freud's famous question—"What does a woman want?"—is: An unattractive statue in the Capitol Rotunda.

Of course not all American women have been heard from. There probably are some in, say, Boise, and maybe others in Muncie, who are unaware that the dignity of their sex is implicated in the controversy about what to do with a cumbersome sculpture of three suffragettes. But Washington always echoes with the voices of individuals purporting to speak for people they have not actually consulted.

The sculpture at issue is often called "The Ladies in the Bathtub." This is agreeable but perhaps illegal irreverence: Such talk could contribute to a "hostile environment," hence it could constitute sexual harassment. Anyway, the ladies emerging, as it were, from a thirteen-ton block of marble are Susan B. Anthony, Elizabeth Cady Stanton, and Lucretia Mott.

Let's stipulate that each was a great American. Unfortunately, the supply of greatness is, it seems, infinite, and the supply of choice Washington

351

spots for homage to greatness is not. The supply of alleged greatness long ago exceeded the supply of space for statues in the Rotunda. For thirty-two years the marble ladies have languished in the Capitol basement, seen only by scurrying congressional staffers and tourists exceptionally diligent in their touring. But society, say those claiming to speak for it, has had its consciousness raised and has decided that the statue kept in the basement is, like the madwoman kept in the attic in *Jane Eyre*, symbolic of Put-Upon Woman.

So plans were made to move it to the Rotunda in time for the 1995 commemoration of the seventy-fifth anniversary of the Nineteenth Amendment, which enfranchised women. However, Congress was so busy not balancing the budget that relocation of the statue was not authorized until the 104th Congress. That's right, during the Gingrich Terror. In the spirit of that Congress, private money—$75,000 of it—was raised to pay for moving the rock, which is about the size of Rhode Island.

That state was founded by Roger Williams (1603–1683), a turbulent divine banished from Massachusetts in 1635 because his theological and political views were a stench in Puritans' nostrils. (He said civil authorities had no right to enforce religious principles and, even more provocatively, he said Native Americans had rights, including the right to be paid for land taken from them.) In 1872 the statue of Williams was placed in the Capitol's Statuary Hall. It was moved to the Rotunda in 1979.

Guess what statue is supposed to be removed from the Rotunda to make room for the ladies? Rhode Island's Senator John Chafee, a model of the "moderate" Republicanism so beloved by journalists who don't like Republicans, is immoderately unamused.

The Rotunda contains a reproduction of the Magna Carta, busts of Washington, Lafayette, and Martin Luther King, and statues of Williams, Washington, Garfield, Lincoln, Grant, Hamilton, Jefferson, and Jackson. So, which should go so that we can improve the representation of X chromosomes in the Rotunda?

Garfield is the least distinguished person represented there, but he was assassinated, so picking on him would be adding insult to the ultimate injury. Jackson was an unpleasant fellow, as nasty to Native Americans as Williams was nice, but he is one of the Democratic Party's saints. Chafee suggests moving the Magna Carta, which isn't even American, but that might displease a woman (Queen Elizabeth II, whose Bicentennial gift it was in 1976).

Anyway, any such solution will leave the Rotunda, one of the nation's great public spaces, diminished by the addition of an unattractive sculpture. And it will be a monument less to past heroines than to present fixations. One fixation is identity politics: You *are* your group—your race or gender or sexual orientation or whatever. Another is the entitlement mentality: Every group is entitled to recognition—a kind of government seal of approval—and it is women's turn beneath the Capitol dome.

The problem is not confined to the Capitol. The clean geometric beauty of the Mall is threatened by monumentitis. Advocates of various causes, from large events (the Second World War) to small factions (veterans of various ethnicities) seek recognition in stone. The background music of contemporary politics is the whine of axes being ground by groups claiming to be victims by virtue of having been ignored.

As government becomes ever more minutely attentive, everything in Washington, from causes to motives, seems to be becoming smaller. Everything, that is, except the grievances of groups that feel neglected.

February 23, 1997

Chief Illiniwek: In a Hostile Environment

CHAMPAIGN-URBANA, ILLINOIS—Come for a walk on the wild side, in the hostile environment of the law pertaining to hostile environments. Actually, "law" may be a misnomer, as we shall see in the controversy concerning Chief Illiniwek, yet another example of how compulsory compassion threatens freedom.

At halftime of a University of Illinois football game in 1926 a student of Indian culture performed a dance dressed as a chief. Since then Chief Illiniwek has become the symbol of the university that serves the state where once lived the Illini tribe that was virtually annihilated by an enemy tribe in the 1760s.

In 1930 the undergraduate then portraying Chief Illiniwek traveled to South Dakota to receive authentic raiment from the Oglala Sioux. In 1967 and again in 1982, representatives of the Sioux came here to present outfits for Chief Illiniwek to wear in his performances at halftimes of football and basketball games. Until the mid-1980s the chief was an uncontroversial and revered tradition keeping alive the memory of the vanished Illini tribe.

Then came the rise, particularly on campuses, of identity politics, with grievance groups claiming special rights as reparations for historic wrongs. This produced in government a compassion industry backed by sensitivity police and thought vigilantes. Since then Chief Illiniwek has been under attack.

Compassion, contemporary liberalism's core value, involves the pre-

vention or amelioration of pain, including the pain of offended sensibilities. Groups compete to be the most offended, and compassion referees
must decide which offenses to which groups matter. A few people, mostly
but not exclusively Native Americans, say Chief Illiniwek is offensive, a
racist Little Red Sambo who must be banned in the name of tolerance and
respect for multicultural diversity. Permanent exclusion of the chief is "the
only ethical solution," according to a university body called the Inclusivity
Committee.

In a complaint to Illinois's Human Rights Commission, a Native-American nonstudent activist cited the state law making it a civil rights violation
to "deny or refuse to another the full and equal enjoyment" of any public
accommodation. He said the symbolism of the chief as "mascot" was so
offensive to him that he could not enjoy himself at the stadium or elsewhere on campus.

The commission replied that the relevant definition of "enjoy" as used in
the law is not "to get pleasure from" but "to have the use or benefit of." The
commission noted that if the complainant prevailed, African-American
groups could get the state to prevent showings of the film *Birth of a Nation,*
Jewish groups could wield the law against performances of *The Merchant of
Venice,* and Native-American groups could prevent screenings of many
cowboy movies.

The chief's tormentors have tried to thwart him with The American
Indian Religious Freedom Act, but unfortunately for them that law does
not make it illegal to impersonate an Indian. They tried the Migratory Bird
Act, which makes some possession of eagle parts illegal, but it turns out the
chief's headdress is made of turkey feathers. So now the chief's enemies
are turning to Title VI of the 1964 Civil Rights Act, which prohibits racial
discrimination in federally assisted educational institutions.

In democratic theory, the legitimacy of a law depends on the authorship
of it by elected representatives. But in contemporary America, after representative institutions have done their work, regulation writers, unelected
and anonymous, take over, filling page after page of the Federal Register
with additional "law," as in the edition of March 10, 1994.

There the U.S. Department of Education said Title VI prohibits not only
discrimination but harassment; that harassment includes the existence of a
"hostile environment"; that the environment is hostile if it would seem so
not just to a reasonable person but to "a reasonable person, of the same age
and race as the victim, under similar circumstances." That comes close to
making any claim of felt hostility in the environment a self-validating
charge of racial discrimination.

Chief Illiniwek probably will survive because the arguments against
him are so strained, and because many Native Americans recognize in his

role a compliment from the university to their heritage. But attempts to wield the government against him demonstrate how freedom is under siege as spurious "rights" are asserted. (Says one Native American, "Native people should have the right to determine how their image is used.")

The controversy illustrates how the forces of political correctness pressure government to grow in size and arbitrariness in order to pursue a peculiar compassion mission. That mission is to assuage the hurt feelings of groups for which taking offense is a political agenda, and to reform the psyches of any individuals slow to conform to the new sensitivity. No wonder liberalism's work is never done.

March 9, 1995

Pennsylvania Excitements

Two hundred years ago this Independence Day, Western Pennsylvania was acting altogether too independent. It was up in arms and jeopardizing what had been accomplished in Eastern Pennsylvania at the Constitutional Convention seven years earlier. This Independence Day let us remember the Whiskey Rebellion, with its interesting echoes.

In exchange for Hamilton's agreement to a national capital where Washington now is, Jefferson and Madison agreed to federal assumption of state debts. An excise tax on whiskey was considered the least objectionable means of financing assumption. The initial grievances of people near the coast were palliated by reductions of the tax, but the West, across the Allegheny Mountains, was unassuaged.

Out there, folks didn't cotton to tax collectors. And as to the theory that the cost of the tax could be bumped along to consumers, well, the tax was collected at the still and owners of stills often were consumers, there being few other amusements at hand. Furthermore, currency was scarce so whiskey sometimes served as currency. And because canals were few and roads were problematic, it was difficult getting grain to market in bulk, so grain was turned into something more transportable: whiskey.

Taxing this staple proved that taxation with representation was not much more tolerable than taxation without. It was unfair, for several reasons, said these early populists.

Some large distillers, who could pay the tax more easily than their small rivals, rather liked it. (Just as today some large corporations accept government burdens that will cripple their smaller competitors.) And the westerners felt they were being taxed to fatten the purses of eastern speculators who had bought at a discount the state debts the federal government was paying off with the whiskey tax.

And what were the westerners getting for their taxes? The federal government had neither removed the Indian menace nor pried Spain's grip off the Mississippi. Westerners, like most Americans most of the time ever since, wanted government to do more and cost less.

Law-abiding westerners trembled. James Flexner, Washington's biographer, writes: "During the Whiskey Rebellion, the little town of Pittsburgh—some two hundred houses—was in active fear of being sacked by the wild men of the further forest." With reason. A wealthy friend of the president, John Neville, who first opposed the tax then agreed to help collect it, had his house burned. Soldiers arrived, a man was killed, the soldiers were routed. Soon stills whose owners paid the tax were being perforated with bullets, and government agents were being tarred and feathered, and even seared with hot irons, which was somewhat severe, even for tax collectors.

But rough justice was no rougher than the insurgents, who were stiff-necked Scotch-Irish Presbyterians. America would see their likes again in Andrew Jackson and Woodrow Wilson.

Excisemen had been familiar afflictions back in Scotland and Ulster. Stanley Elkins and Eric McKitrick, in their magisterial *The Age of Federalism,* write with nice delicacy that "excisemen, not of very high character anyway, had come to serve as acceptable objects for social aggression."

A Scotch-Irish congressman, James Jackson, who understood the ravenousness of government, warned the House of Representatives, "The time will come when a shirt shall not be washed without an excise." Excise taxes frequently are fixed upon the enjoyments of the portion of the people least nimble at finagling exemptions. The tax on whiskey spared the effete eastern upper crust that went on sipping untaxed wines.

It is ever thus. Today cigarettes are not only anathematized by government, they may soon be burdened by a whopping excise tax increase. This is evidence that the middle and upper classes have decided smoking is déclassé, and is proof that smoking is increasingly a habit of the lower orders.

In 1794 one rattled resident of Pittsburgh—where the *Gazette* was reporting the nastiness of the French Revolution and some rebels were bandying the word "guillotine"—warned that the rebels would become a devouring torrent: "There can be no equality of contest, between the rage of a forest and the abundance, indolence, and opulence of the city." But resistance evaporated when Washington himself marched in with 13,000 militiamen.

Back then, when gun control meant felling a wild turkey at 200 yards, militias embodied popular sovereignty. The militias that pacified Western Pennsylvania put a stop, for a while, to loose talk about the local nullification of national laws, and to murmurings about secession. Pennsylvania would not know such excitement until the first week of July sixty-nine years later, when armed men again revisited the issues of federal sovereignty, at Gettysburg.

July 3, 1994

Huck in a Ford Explorer

It has changed how the landscape is experienced and how cities are shaped. In it uncounted millions of marriages have been proposed and relationships consummated. From courtship to crime to consumption, from the American economy to the American spirit, almost nothing would be as it is were it not for the handiest thing that ever happened for the hot pursuit of happiness. So let us now praise the automobile, born, sort of, 100 years ago.

The auto industry's centennial is being celebrated because in 1896 the Duryea brothers of Springfield, Massachusetts, sold thirteen cars. Critics, called "carmudgeons," who are legion and mostly liberals, ask, "What's to celebrate?"

Yes, cars emit exhaust, and 1899 produced America's first recorded traffic fatality, the first of—so far—2.8 million deaths from traffic-related injuries. But horses were lethal, and stifle your nostalgia for those suffocating summers when windows were sealed, but noses were not, against billowing dust of finely ground manure produced by horses such as those that deposited 60,000 gallons of urine on New York's streets every day.

The mass production of automobiles on moving assembly lines, emulating the disassembly of cattle by meat packing companies, increased productivity and wages, enabling workers to buy what they made. Before cars became consumer goods, people rarely went into debt intentionally. To facilitate purchases, automobile companies developed "installment buying," and credit unions flourished facilitating it. This destigmatized indebtedness, which government embraced with gusto, and increased Americans' reluctance to defer gratifications.

Automobile and oil companies pioneered franchising for dealers of their products. Credit cards were developed by oil companies to make credit portable for mobile Americans. The democratized possession of machines capable of inflicting personal injuries and property damage enormously stimulated the insurance industry. Supermarkets prospered because automobile owners could shop once a week. The automobile created vast wealth by increasing the value of land now accessible to people who worked in, but preferred not to live in, cities.

Today, when most commutes are not from suburb to city but from one suburb to another, automobiles are blamed for suburbs, which are blamed for urban decline and desecration of the countryside. Granted, suburbs sometimes are named, as novelist Peter De Vries said, for what their developers destroyed ("Forest View," "Rolling Acres"), but the American hankering for suburbs predates the automobile. By 1848, 118 commuter trains poured into Boston; in 1888, Richmond acquired the first of another maker of suburbs, the electric trolley.

The "getaway car" made criminals mobile, and gave us movie car chases. But liberals blame the automobile for myriad crimes, including Wal-Marts, "the mallification of America," and the breakdown of "community." Actually, automobiles were conquerors of rural loneliness, especially that of women, early in this century, when farm families lived an average of five miles from market, six miles from school, fourteen miles from a hospital.

Automobiles were indispensable for the establishment in the 1950s of the teenage nation-within-the-nation. Before James Dean totaled his Porsche and himself at age twenty-four, he was the archetypical teenager, a rebel without a cause but not without a car. From millions of dashboards poured a generation's anthems—rock 'n' roll. Automobiles solved what Frederick Lewis Allen called "the difficulty of finding a suitable locale for misconduct." Hitherto young swains had been confined to front porch swings, with the girls' parents and siblings underfoot. Now they could drive away and, more to the point, park.

GM's "ladder of consumption"—Chevrolet, Pontiac, Oldsmobile, Buick, Cadillac—gave America an ersatz class structure, but one easy to climb. Sure, fifties cars—from their protuberant, not to say nubile, front bumpers to their tailfins—looked, as a wit said, "like chorus girls coming and fighter planes going." And perhaps the "planned obsolescence" of annual model changes was not entirely, as Detroit insisted, "healthy dissatisfaction." Perhaps the television program *My Mother the Car* indicated that the tendency to anthropomorphize cars had gone a tad far.

Who cares. Forget the vulgarities, celebrate the virtues of automobility. Around 1970, Mississippi's appalling Senator James Eastland, musing about America's mistakes, regretted "giving niggers driver's licenses and letting 'em go north." He knew: An open road produces an open society.

The automobile has been an emancipating device, celebrated in our literature, from *The Great Gatsby* to *On the Road.* Were Huck to light out for the territories today, he would go in a Ford Explorer.

"Mason City. To get there you follow Highway 58, going northeast out of the city, and it is a good highway, and new." So begins *All the King's Men.* In the land of the automobile, every man's a king.

June 16, 1996

The Problem with Cats: Their Catness

Today's topic is nature, and what should be done to correct it. Cats, in their unregenerate catness, are behaving badly, so perhaps governments should do something.

Modernity's great project is the conquest of nature—enlarging the sphere of human choice by shrinking the realm of necessity. Thus, properly modern people were thrilled recently when science—fertility drugs, a donated egg—enabled a sixty-three-year-old, postmenopausal woman to give birth. So seventeen years from now there can be a seventeen-year-old with an eighty-year-old mother. Fresh from this progress in amending nature's cycles and life's seasons, let us get on with the reform of cats.

Concerning them, the crisis, which is international, is grounded in an intractable fact: They are killers. Feral, meaning homeless or free-roaming cats, kill many millions of birds and mice and other things. But so do domestic cats, if there really are such things. (A cat's domesticity seems to end when its paws touch grass.) Even well-fed cats are predators, apparently for the pure pleasure of the craftsmanship involved.

"The Charge Is Murder: But How Guilty Is Puss?" asks an eight-column headline in London's very serious *Sunday Telegraph.* Actually, the newspaper says the charge, leveled by defenders of cats' victims, is "mass slaughter," and cats are abundantly guilty. Britain's 8 million cats—up from 4.5 million in just seven years—are said to kill 210 million birds and wee animals a year, and to maim 42 million more, spending an average of thirty minutes playing with or torturing (depending on whether you side with the cat or the caught) their victims.

Yes, cats are natural-born killers. The wonder is that Caesar and Napoleon disliked them. Cat fanciers say despots prefer dogs because cats, not being docile, cannot be tyrannized. Furthermore, cats are killing machines who once saved civilization by protecting Egypt's granaries from rats. So there.

But that was then. This is now. In Australia, where there are as many cats as Australians (20 million), defenders of our feathered friends are out gunning for feral cats, and in some places the law forbids the acquisition of new cats and requires domestic cats to be kept indoors at night. In America the (supposedly) domestic cat is the most numerous pet (60 million—30 percent of households have them), and there may be 40 million feral cats. Extrapolation from a study in Wisconsin, where cats are estimated to kill 40 million birds a year, suggests that, nationwide, rural cats kill a billion small mammals and perhaps as many birds a year. And urban cats are busy, too.

Furthermore, cats are not only on the dishing-out end of nature, red in tooth and claw. Feral cats—California has an estimated 3.5 million—often lead lives that spread diseases and are nasty, brutish, and short. Groups that have sprung up to care for colonies of feral cats—colonies often containing twenty cats—are at daggers drawn with defenders of other wildlife.

Defenders of cats say that domestic cats out for predacious prowls are just doing what comes naturally, and feral cats fill the ecological niche once occupied by forest cats. The cats' critics say cats are dangerously depleting ground-nesting birds and the prey of owls, weasels, foxes, and other animals. Furthermore, predators that once might have preyed on cats, such as wolves, are now too few. Requiring bells on cats won't work because belled cats learn to stalk silently. Critics say there should be leash laws and mandatory vaccinations, spaying and neutering.

Look for attempts to break cats to the saddle of society. There is precedent. Back in the premodern era, around 1950, the Illinois legislature passed a bill to restrict the freedom of cats. Governor Adlai Stevenson vetoed it: "I cannot agree that it should be the declared public policy of Illinois that a cat visiting a neighbor's yard or crossing the highway is a public nuisance. It is in the nature of cats to do a certain amount of unescorted roaming. The problem of cat versus bird is as old as time. If we attempt to resolve it by legislation, who knows but what we may be called upon to take sides in the age-old problems of dog versus cat, bird versus bird, or even bird versus worm. In my opinion the State of Illinois and its local governing bodies already have enough to do without trying to control feline delinquency."

The probird faction deplores such defeatism. The libertarian cat lobby applauds.

July 13, 1997

Counting Sheep

Well, hello, Dolly. What are we to make of you, now that we have made you? And what are we to make of us?

In Scotland, a sheep named Dolly has been manufactured—literally, made by hand. Dolly is the result of the first cloning of an adult mammal. If one is now enough for multiplication, does this mean that there are no longer any endangered species? Or does it mean that humans are uniquely endangered?

Dolly is genetically identical to the one parent—if that is the right word—from which it was cloned. The word "parent" is problematic.

It does not quite fit the sheep which was merely an incubator for the embryo engineered elsewhere and then inserted into her. So the word "parent" here denotes, if anything, another adult sheep, the one that was the sole source of Dolly's genetic material. But that parent is sort of the sibling of its identical twin offspring, Dolly. Golly.

Such ambiguities will trouble only unusually thoughtful sheep. However, the featherless bipeds called human beings have the kind of consciousness that causes them to wonder about themselves: Given what we are, how ought we behave?

Now, what if the great given—a human being is the product of the union of a man and a woman—is no longer a given? The news from Scotland could have immense consequences for mankind's moral life—for thinking about "ought" propositions.

The biotechnology of cloning turns out to be remarkably simple, meaning it is accessible to scientists with training that is not especially recondite. And apparently there is no practical impediment to cloning the human animal. If freedom is the silence of the law, Americans are free to try it. And the bioethical code adopted by European nations, forbidding genetic experiments that would alter human generations, will inhibit only the conscientious.

The news from Scotland gives the slogan "our bodies, our choices" an interesting new dimension. And a society that couches every issue in the language of individual rights (as in the right of "choice" concerning "reproductive freedom") may have difficulties, now that narcissism and megalomania, two recurring human attributes, have a new avenue of expression: Make me my heir.

This subject is an invitation to playful imagining that soon turns serious. Imagine five Michael Jordans playing five other Michael Jordans. But, then, what makes him him is not just his genetic material but his competitive character, his fierce integrity. How much of character is genetically

361

influenced or determined? The nature vs. nurture argument continues. As the twig is bent: Would a cloned Jordan be Jordan without whatever it was about his family, and about North Carolina, that helped young Michael become the man?

And what about the soul? Is there such a thing? Is there a ghost in the machine, or only a machine? Are they right who say, "I do not have a body, I *am* a body"?

Mankind, a.k.a. *Homo Technologicus*, is making progress, in the form of sheep and other animals with immense potential for agricultural, medicinal, and other scientific advancements. But at what moral hazard? Twenty-five years ago Professor Leon Kass of the University of Chicago said much that now urgently needs resaying.

In his essay "Making Babies: The New Biology and the 'Old' Morality" Kass noted that technological corollaries to the pill—babies without sex—involve not just new ways of beginning life but new ways of understanding and valuing life. Connections with parents, siblings, and ancestors are integral to being human, although not to being a sheep. Can individuality, identity, and dignity be severed from genetic distinctiveness, and from belief in a person's open future?

Suppose a cloned Michael Jordan, age eight, preferred the violin to basketball? Is it imaginable? If so, would it be tolerable to the cloner? Imagine the emotional distress of a cloned person with foreknowledge of powerful genetic predispositions, psychological or biological.

Cloning, like eugenics generally, would produce, as C. S. Lewis wrote, "one dominant age . . . which resists all previous ages most successfully and dominates all subsequent ages most irresistibly." This is not the "conquest of nature," it is (to take the title of Lewis's book) the abolition of man, because humanity is supposed to be an endless chain, not a series of mirrors.

When Hiroshima occasioned anxious talk about the dangers of physics, Einstein replied that the world was more apt to be destroyed by bad politics than bad physics. Dolly raises the stakes of biology, but also of philosophy.

February 27, 1997

Disney Sounds Retreat

HAYMARKET, VIRGINIA—In a churchyard here a gravestone reads:

STONEWALL JACKSON CAMPBELL
MAY 2, 1863–DECEMBER 10, 1911

The infant Campbell was named for the Virginian who earned his name on a battlefield a few minutes gallop from the churchyard, a soldier who on May 2, 1863, received a mortal wound at Chancellorsville, not far from here.

Problem is, much of American history was made not far from here, often by men who lived nearby: The church is hard by the intersection of the James Madison and John Marshall highways. Just over yonder lives Miss Beauregard, great-granddaughter of the Confederate general. And so it goes. You can hardly turn around out here without bumping into evocations of the nation's making.

This would be merely nice, not a problem, were it not for something that threatens to be the unmaking of this area. The Disney Company seems determined, almost irrationally so, to turn this area inside out and upside down by building, about a half mile from the churchyard and 3.5 miles from the Manassas field where Jackson fought, a huge commercial and residential real estate development, at the core of which will be an American history theme park.

Unfortunately, many faulty reasons have been indiscriminately adduced for opposing Disney's project, so the one sufficient reason may get lost in the melee. It is that Disney has decided to build something that would radically transform, beyond recognition, an area that is, arguably, America's most defining landscape.

America has various defining landscapes, not all of them bucolic. One is Manhattan's forever unfinished skyline, emblematic of our heroic materialism. But none is more drenched in the history of heroic idealism than Virginia's Piedmont region, a perishable window on the past, a place which, were Jefferson and Washington and Lee to revisit it, would be comfortably familiar to them.

Some of Disney's critics would, if they could, freeze this region in time. They cannot. Development will come to this place because it is a short drive from Washington and the government that will not stop growing. But Disney's megadevelopment, by its scale and nature, would change beyond recognition a historic region rich in sites that millions of Americans come to as pilgrims to shrines of our civil religion.

Some of Disney's critics get the vapors at the thought of what the theme park might do to the telling of America's story. But if Disney or anyone else wants to make a skit, or a hash, of history, well, the right to vulgarize is one of America's most vigorously exercised rights. Anyway, Disney would be hard-pressed to do worse than, say, Oliver Stone's movies—or, for that matter, than some historians do, including some of Disney's academic despisers.

Disney has armed its despisers by talking foolishly, as when Chairman Michael Eisner said, "I was dragged to Washington as a kid and it was the worst weekend of my life," or when a Disney "creative director" said the park would "make you feel what it was like to be a slave." (See your sister sold down the river, then get cotton candy?) However, again, the point is not what Disney wants to do, but where it wants to do it.

The administration of environmental, transportation, and other federal, state, and local regulations provides many opportunities for Disney's opponents to slow the project's progress and raise its costs. In any such battle of attrition, bet on the multibillion-dollar corporation that buys lawyers by the battalions. But why does Eisner seem bent on becoming the archetype of the Hollywood vulgarian, greasing with money (some of it to politicians) the slide of a great corporation into the role of coarse bully, stamping its bootprints on hallowed ground?

One of the roads that would have to become an enlarged congested highway to serve the park is Route 15 which runs north to Gettysburg. There one of the Berkeley boys now buried in the churchyard here was captured at the crest of Pickett's charge, at the wall on Cemetery Ridge now known as "the high-water mark of the Confederacy." From there Lee's army beat an honorable retreat.

It is astonishing that Disney, out of sheer stubbornness, is risking its reputation as a good corporate citizen, and is doing so to put here a project that could be put in many more suitable places. But it is not too late for Disney to learn a lesson from Lee, who is revered by the nation he tried to dismember, revered partly because he knew how and when to surrender.*

July 17, 1994

---

*General Eisner knew when to sound retreat. Disney will build elsewhere.

ESPN Dependency

Recently my wife, Mari, with whom I am well pleased, and who must be obeyed, took me by the arm, marched me out onto the front lawn of our house, and pointed to the roof, where one of the chimneys seemed to have grown an appendage that looked like a pizza pan with an umbilical cord. "Happy anniversary," she said.

She had bought for me one of those small satellite dishes that enable people who are so inclined to watch, among much else in the way of sports and other entertainment, 800 major-league baseball games in a season, and an alarmingly rich "college basketball package," and similar abundances of other sports. Thanks to this electronic cornucopia now spilling into my living room, we were able to see, that first golden evening with the dish, the football coach at Clemson do his weekly show on a Greenville, South Carolina, television station. Is this a great country, or what?

Never mind that neither Mari nor I have even the slightest interest in Clemson football. Well, she has this interest: As a graduate of the University of South Carolina, she looks upon Clemson the way a duchess looks upon a scullery maid—down—and she wishes for Clemson football nothing but sprained ankles, strained ligaments, and academically ineligible nose guards. Never mind. The larger point is that the blessing of technology made it possible for us to watch the coach explain why Clemson's student athletes had suffered so much at the hands of Florida State's student athletes, and so we watched.

We watched the coach's show on the present Mari gave to me on my most recent birthday, a "big screen" television set. That is "big" as in "the Grand Canyon is a big ditch." On this huge television set the flared nostrils of Texas Rangers first baseman Will Clark look like railroad tunnels. When Clark has his game face on—which is to say, when his jowls look like Yasser Arafat's and his eyes turn toward the pitcher with the sort of baleful glint Benjamin Netanyahu's eyes have when turned toward Yasser Arafat—Clark's face fills the screen, which fills the room. It is not a sight for the fainthearted, but if that's the sort of thing you like, you'll like that sort of thing.

It will not be easy giving my enhanced television all the attention it deserves, but, heck, you gotta play hurt. So I probably have not only written my last book, I probably have read my last book. And I do not have the heart to tell Mari the truth, which is this: 500 channels are about 499 more than this viewer needs. Were someone to render my television set incapable of receiving anything but ESPN, it would be weeks—months, maybe—before I noticed.

Actually, there also is ESPN 2, for lesser events. And soon there will be a third offering, ESPNEWS, a sort of CNN for the sports-dependent— all-sports news, twenty-four hours a day. This, in spite of the fact that the whole world does not produce enough real news to fill a twenty-four-hour all-news channel, as CNN proves every day.

However, ESPN's puckish spirit is well displayed in promotional advertisements for the twenty-four-hour service. The screen is blank except for this: "4:21 A.M." The background music sounds like monks doing Gregorian chants. A hushed, earnest voice says: "In the middle of the night many of us search for answers to life's questions. Is there a God? Am I loved? Why was I created? Did the Yankees beat the Twins?"

Been there. Done that. Can't wait for ESPNEWS.

Until then, there already is the jewel in ESPN's crown—*SportsCenter.* It is, as everyone knows, the thinking person's *World News Tonight with Peter Jennings.*

Mari says the new dish will offer me lots of opportunities for something that there is, she clearly implies, lots of room for, namely improvement of my tastes and broadening of my interests. She mentions programs from Lincoln Center, and stuff like that.

Well, as a Nineties Man, I not only let my inner child frolic on a long leash, I am sensitive and caring as all get out. So from now on, when Mari is nearby, I will pretend to be fascinated by some of the 500 or so non-ESPN channels now at my fingertips—perhaps a twenty-four-hour professional bass fishing tournament channel, or a Tex-Mex vegetarian cooking channel. But my heart, like what remains of my mind, belongs to ESPN.

October 17, 1996

Strange Doings in the Living Room

CHEVY CHASE VILLAGE, MARYLAND—David Maseng Will, a prodigiously talented three-year-old, seemed, at first blush, blasé about the news. The news was that on Sunday night a stranger, a jolly, fat, oddly dressed man, would be coming down David's chimney with a sack full of toys, many of which would be strewn about beneath the tree in the living room, for David to enjoy, and for David to resist sharing with friends, as he resists sharing everything, other than germs.

David's response to this—one would have thought—astonishing news about the toy-strewing stranger was suitably wide-eyed, and yet he took it in stride, as additional evidence that people really do have more fun than anyone. Turns out, it is difficult to astonish a child, either because everything astonishes, or—which may be much the same thing—because nothing does.

For example, is it not just a bit peculiar that the adults at David's house, who make the rules and are supposed to make sense, and who get cranky if you bring into the house so much as a dead mouse, suddenly hauled a tree into the living room? The strangeness of that act was surpassed by the weirdness of the dispute about what to hang on it. Father wanted to hang twenty-eight glass balls bearing the emblems of major-league baseball teams. Mother didn't. Mother won. So the tree is decorated with angels and elves and trains and gingerbread men and other bric-a-brac that presumably add up to something, but they seem to the untutored eye to be so much flapdoodle. Of course nothing much adds up to children, for whom the flapdoodle quotient of daily experience is large.

Their lives consist largely of looking at, and maneuvering through, a forest of adults' knees, so the world is bound to seem strangely constituted. And given the fact that these tall people voluntarily give little people food, shelter, clothing, and television, it is understandable that the little people think the world is organized for their pleasure and that toy-laden people popping down chimneys is just part of the plan. Besides, once a child has experienced the central event on the child's calendar of bliss—Halloween—and learned that there is such a thing as a free lunch after all, and that it is 95 percent sugar, the sheer goodness of life becomes a given.

H. L. Mencken was disgusted because "the average American, whether young or old, simply lacks the mental stamina to face the concept of the irremediable." Maybe so, but Christmas, as the average American family practices it, is a splendid part of the cheerful adult conspiracy to keep children unaware, for a while, of the limits that life puts on desiring.

Presumably at his school, where he is in a class called Beehivers and is majoring in Lego blocks and minoring in advanced tricycle, David is acquiring a keen sense of reality—life is real, life is earnest, and all that. Already he seems to have a vocation, for working with words. Unlike the novelist Peter De Vries, who said he liked everything about writing except the paperwork, it is the paperwork that pleases David. At his mother's knee—she often works at home—he has become, by emulation, a worldly child of Washington. "What are you doing David?" asks his father as David pushes a pencil across a tablet. "Writing speeches for Bob Dole," replies David, matter-of-factly. Writing a list for Santa should be a snap.

Next year he will reach the list stage. Last year the ribbons and wrappings and boxes were as diverting as the gifts. This year he is content to let

Santa bring what he will, although David is showing an aptitude for becoming a proper American boy, fascinated by Power Rangers and other toys suggestive of mayhem.

It has been said that a teacher can never be adequately paid because a teacher gives the gift of truth, for which no material compensation is commensurate. No child can be given a Christmas present as precious as the pleasure a child gives to parents by taking pleasure from Christmas.

Charles Edison, the inventor's son, once described himself as "the result of one of my father's earlier experiments." David, who has a child's perfect sense of being the center of the universe, probably thinks exactly what a robust American Christmas encourages children to think—that they are the result that the universe exists to produce. Come to think about it, that is about right.

December 24, 1995

INDEX

Abe Lincoln in Illinois (Sherwood), 311
abolitionism, 87
abortion, 49–56, 60, 187, 255
    partial-birth, 52, 54–56
"abuse excuses," 149–50
academic freedom, 148
Adams, John, 81, 94, 100, 102, 104, 304
Adler, William M., 131–32
advertising, 229–31
affirmative action, 64, 80, 192–93
Affluent Society, The (Galbraith), 331
AFL-CIO, 262–63
African-Americans, 63, 64, 152–54, 197,
    212–13, 237, 280–81, 304, 338–39,
    354
African Queen, The, 25
Afrocentrism, 146–48
Agnew, Spiro, 78
Agrarian Movement, 93–95
Agricultural Adjustment Act, 91
agriculture, 261
AIDS, evolution of, 236–38
Aid to Families with Dependent Children
    (AFDC), 127–28, 129, 255
Alaska, 279, 286
Albers, Everett, 225
alcohol, 87, 135, 137
    price advertising of, 229–31
Alcoholics Anonymous, 77
Alexander, Jane, 226
Alexander, Lamar, 84–86, 250
Allen, Frederick Lewis, 358
Allende Gossens, Salvador, 292
"All Quiet on the (Post) Western Front"
    (Orwin), 192
All the King's Men (Warren), 359
American Bar Association, 121
American Civil Liberties Union (ACLU),
    116, 197, 198
American Conservative Union, 232
American Council of the Blind, 44

American Enterprise, 118, 133, 293
American Enterprise Institute, 86
American Heritage, 326
American Indian Religious Freedom Act,
    354
"American Pluralism and Identity" conver-
    sation kit, 31–33
Americans for Democratic Action, 232, 342
American Society of Anesthesiologists, 55
Americans with Disabilities Act (ADA),
    183–85
AmeriCorps, 176
Ames, Aldrich, 46
Anderson, Elijah, 153–54
Anderson, Eloise, 129–30
Anderson, Sherwood, 90, 157
Angola, 277
Anthony, Susan B., 351
anti-Semitism, 250, 277–79, 280–81
Apollo 13, 99
Apollo Project, 99
Arafat, Yasser, 298
Aristide, Jean–Bertrand, 284
Aristotle, 31, 146–47
Arizona, 98, 188
Arkansas, 131
Arkus-Duntov, Zora, 328–29
Ashes to Ashes (Kluger), 239–40
Astaire, Fred, 76
asteroids, 268
astronomy, 267–68
AT&T, 213–14, 263, 267
Athens (Ga.) *Banner-Herald*, 178
Atlanta Braves, 234
Atlantic Monthly, 153
Attica Prison, 217
Auschwitz, 252, 272, 276
automobiles, 357–59

baby boomers, 45–47
Baker, James, 273

Balfour, Arthur, 268
Balkan war, 274
ballistic missiles, 285–87
ballots, bilingual, 221–23
Baltimore, Md., 161–63, 234–35
Baltimore Orioles, 235
Baltimore Ravens, 235
Bank of the United States, 89, 212
Barbie, Klaus, 251
Barron's, 261, 292
Bartley, Robert, 213
Barton, Joe, 218
baseball, 73–74
basketball, 151–52
battered woman syndrome, 33–35
Baucus, Max, 232
Beach, Edward L., 288
Beacon restaurant, 339–41
Beats, 69–70, 336–37
Beckett, Samuel, 22
Before the Trumpet (Ward), 313
Belgium, 279
Belgrade, 273–75
Bell, Daniel, 65
Benet, Stephen Vincent, 99
Ben-Jochannan, Yosef A. A., 146
Bennett, Robert, 72–73
Bennett, William, 171, 250
Bergreen, Laurence, 332–35
Berlin, 279
Berlin Wall, 93
Bernstein, Leonard, 69
Bernstein, Richard, 141–42
Bickel, Alexander, 83
Bidwell, Mary, 78
Big Chill, The, 67
Bill of Rights, 60
bipartisanship, 257
Bismarck, Otto von, 253
Black, Hugo L., 59, 195
Blackboard Jungle, The, 69, 336
Black Canyon, 98
Black English, 139
Black Panthers, 332–33, 335
Blair, Tony, 256
Bleak House (Dickens), 22, 299
Bobbitt, Lorena, 73
Bonanza, 57
Bonfire of the Vanities, The (Wolfe), 153
Boorstin, Daniel J., 23, 330
Bork, Robert, 265
Bosnia, 73, 76, 78, 271–73, 274, 275–77, 280, 281, 282, 295, 316, 318
Boston, Mass., 179, 201, 358
Boston Braves, 234

Boyd, Fran, 232–33
Boys Town, 126
Bradley, Omar, 289, 315
Bradsher, Keith, 329
Brandeis, Louis, 320, 322
Bratton, William, 202–3
Braveheart, 95
Breyer, Stephen G., 182, 188, 197, 209
Brezhnev Doctrine, 294
Brinkley, Alan, 244
Brookline, Mass., 141
Brooklyn, N.Y., 51–52
Brown, John, 113
Brown, Ron, 121
Browning, Christopher, 278–79
Brown v. *Board of Education*, 189–91
Bryan, William Jennings, 103
Brzezinski, Zbigniew, 276
Buchanan, Pat, 84, 86, 212–13, 250–52, 264
Buckley, William F., Jr., 63, 250
Budapest, 294–95
budget, federal, 17, 74, 216–17, 252–53, 282
Bulgaria, 308
Bullock, Allan, 271
Bunker Hill Monument, 100
Bunting, Josiah, III, 183
Burke, Edmund, 21, 81, 83
Burns, Arthur, 319
Burns, Ken, 304–5
Bush, George, 143, 197, 272
    Inaugural Address of, 257
    in 1988 election, 249
    in 1992 election, 244
Bush, Vannevar, 286
Bushman, Richard, 25–26
busing, 57
Byrd, Richard, 78
Byrd, Robert, 264–67

Cahokia, Ill., 156
Calhoun, John C., 80–81, 94
Califano, Joseph, 61–62
California, 72, 100, 116, 129–30, 207, 244
California, University of (Berkeley), 60–61, 70, 77
California Bar Association, 121
California Civil Rights Initiative, 77
California State University (Chico), 39–41
California State University (Sacramento), 35–36
Cambodians, 278
campaign finance, 171–75, 331
campaigning, negative, 244–45, 266
Campbell, Carroll, 171

Canada, 95
capitalism, 81, 82, 102, 130
capital punishment, 54
Capitol Rotunda, 351–53
Capone, Al, 332–35
Capote, Truman, 337
Carey, Merrick, 283
Carnegie, Andrew, 80
Carr, Caleb, 283
Carter, Jimmy, 73, 243, 253
Casablanca, 25, 32
Casey, Bob, 55
Castro, Fidel, 57, 77
Catcher in the Rye, The (Salinger), 337
categorical representation, 37, 196–98, 199
Catholicism, 306–8
cats, 359–60
Central Intelligence Agency (CIA), 283, 297
Chafee, John, 352
Chaing Kai-shek, 297
Chambers, Whittaker, 324–25
Chambers brothers, 131–32
Champaign–Urbana, Ill., 353–55
Chaplin, Charlie, 322–23
Charles, Prince of Wales, 76
Chechnya, 273
Cheney, Dick, 171
Chesterton, G. K., 325
Chevy Chase Village, Md., 366–68
Chicago, Ill., 72, 73, 128, 151, 157, 158,
    201, 213, 234, 333–35
Chicago Transit Authority, 44
children, welfare and, 124–30
Chile, 292
China, People's Republic of, 264, 278, 283,
    286, 295–97, 319
Christian Coalition, 86
Christopher, Warren, 271, 282, 295–96
Chronicle of Higher Education, 38, 40, 225,
    226
Churchill, Randolph, 309
Churchill, Winston, 110
Cicero, 225
cities, 156–59
City Journal, 130
City Life (Rybczynski), 157–59
City Lights Books, 70
City University of New York, 139
civility, eclipse of, 25–27
civil liberties, 96–97
Civil Rights Act, 19
    Title VI of, 354
civil rights movement, 63, 71, 199–200
Civil War, U.S., 75, 100, 216, 311
Clark, Jim, 63

Clark, Russell, 190–91
Clark, Will, 365
Clemson University, 365
Cleopatra, 147, 148
Cleveland, Grover, 75, 76
Cleveland, Ohio, 159–61, 234, 235
Cleveland Browns, 233–35
Cleveland Indians, 76
Clinton, Bill, 41, 43, 73, 87, 144, 176, 206,
    243, 296, 298, 312
    abortion and, 52, 55
    AFDC and, 129, 255, 342
    Balkan war and, 274, 276–77
    ballistic missile defense and, 285–87
    budget and, 74, 250, 252–54, 342
    defense spending by, 269
    FDA and, 29–31
    Haiti and, 73, 284
    health care and, 72, 93, 255, 256
    as inconsequential, 250, 254–56
    in 1992 election, 243, 244, 255
    in 1996 election, 248
    1997 Inaugural Address of, 256–58
    North Korea and, 282, 285
    prison policy of, 206–7
    racial policies of, 194
    and reinventing government, 246
    sincerity of, 252–54
    Taiwan and, 295–97
Clinton, Hillary Rodham, 29, 73, 124–25,
    127, 199
cloning, 361–62
Cloud, Sunny, 29–30
CNN, 366
cocaine, 131–35
    crack, 131–32
Coconino county, Ariz., 194–95
Coles, Edward, 304
Colombia, 133
Colorado, 73, 188
Colorado River, 98
Colorado River Compact, 98
Columbia, S.C., 93–95
Columbia University, 128, 343–45
"Coming Russian Boom, The" (Layard and
    Parker), 293
Commack, N.Y., 52
Commerce Department, U.S., 91
communism, 279, 291–93, 323, 324–25
Community Building in Partnership, 162
"Compassion and the Globalization of the
    Spectacle of Suffering" (Orwin),
    299–301
compassionate corporation, 212–13
Confederacy, 81

Congress, U.S., 20, 43, 59, 245, 264, 298
    campaign finance regulated by, 172
    declining decorum in, 265–67
    defense spending by, 269–71
    health care and, 72, 247
    interstate commerce and, 208–10, 219
    during Johnson administration, 58–60
    1995 budget passed by, 74
    104th, 245–47
    supermajority of, 218–19
    Taiwan and, 295–96
    see also House of Representatives, U.S.;
        Senate, U.S.; *specific legislation*
Congressional Quarterly, 58, 232
Congress of Vienna, 269
Connie Mack Stadium, 337
Connolly, John, 319
Conscience of a Conservative, The (Gold-
    water), 82–83
conservatism:
    Buchanan and, 250–52
    campaign advertising and, 245–46
    capitalism and, 81, 82
    Constitution and, 102, 104
    Croly and, 84–86
    cultural contradictions of, 100–112
    evolution of, 79–84
    and function of government, 21
    Goldwater Republicans and, 70–71
    liberals' defense spending and, 269
    in 1960s, 68, 71
    on 104th Congress, 245–47
    poverty and, 125
    religion and, 86–88
    republican government and, 102
    social inertia and, 18
    Southern, 58
    of Taft, 85
    tensions of, 102, 104
Conservatism in America (Rossiter), 79–84
Conservative Party, U.S., 63
Constitution, U.S., 101, 187–89, 220
    amending of, 19, 218–19
    Commerce Clause of, 208–9, 219
    Contracts Clause of, 219
    Takings Clause of, 219
    see also specific amendments
Constitutional Convention, 106
consumerism, 45–47, 330
Continental Congress, 100
Contract with America, 85, 246
Coolidge, Calvin, 311
Cooper, Diana, 240
Cooper, John Milton, 311–12
Copernicus, Nicolaus, 76, 78

Cornelius, Wayne, 154–56
Cornell University, 37, 140–41, 283, 295
corporal punishment, 204–5
Corporation for Public Broadcasting, 61,
    225–27
Corpus Christi, Tex., 51–52
Corvette, 328–29
courts, 122
    American social evolution and, 59
    civic importance of, 22
    see also Supreme Court, U.S.
Cowpens, USS, 287–89
Craig, Larry, 232–33
Crevecoeur, Hector St. John de, 135
crime, 62–63
Croatians, 278
Croly, Herbert, 84–86, 322
Crouch, Stanley, 67
Cuba, 57, 77
cultural diversity, 192–93
cultural relativism, 192
Cultural Revolution, 278
Curzon's Law, 295–97
Customs Service, U.S., 136
Czech Republic, 294–95

Dakota Badlands, 310
Dangerous Summer, The (Hemingway),
    78
Darwin, Charles, 78, 309, 320
Darwinism, 87
Daschle, Tom, 252
Davis, David Biron, 281
Dean, James, 358
Dean, John, 318
Death of Common Sense, The (Howard),
    119–20
Debs, Eugene V., 326
Defense Department, U.S., 326
defense spending, 269–71, 282
De Gaulle, Charles, 253, 293
Degrelle, Leon, 279, 281
Delaware, 52, 53, 204
Deliverance Evangelistic Church, 338
de Man, Paul, 280
Democracy's Discontent (Sandel), 89–91
Democratic Party, U.S., 42, 55, 83, 244
    abortion and, 55
    affirmative action and, 64
    budget and, 252–54
    campaign funding of, 172
    in Johnson-era Congress, 58
    Legal Services Corporation and, 60
    mail voting and, 224
    in Minnesota, 342

in 1976 election, 243
in 1995 budget negotiations, 74–75
regulatory state and, 121
Southern, 58
Denny, Reginald, 150
Depression, Great, 91, 199
Desert Storm, 290
Detroit, Mich., 128, 131–32
De Vries, Peter, 185, 358, 367
Dewey, John, 343
Dewey, Thomas, 257
Diagnostic and Statistical Manual of Mental Disorders (DSM–IV), 184
Diana, Princess of Wales, 76, 77
Dickens, Charles, 22, 299
Dictatorship of Virtue (Bernstein), 141–42
Dictionary of National Biography, 77
Diggins, John, 143, 144
DiIulio, John, 338
Disney Company, 363–64
Disraeli, Benjamin, 307–8
Dissent, 70
Dodge City, Kans., 157
Dole, Bob, 247–49, 250, 297, 367
dollars, metal, 43–44
Dorchester, Mass., 167–69
Dos Passos, John, 84
Douglas, William O., 59–60
Drexler, Melissa, 49–51
Drucker, Peter, 320, 323, 327
Drug Enforcement Administration, 133–36
drugs, 66–67, 69, 236–37
    interdiction of, 132–38
    legalization of, 138
    screening tests for, FDA regulation of, 29–31
Du Bois, W.E.B., 148
Dukakis, Michael, 249
Dulles Airport, 228–29
du Pont, Pete, 92
Durant, Will and Ariel, 270
Durkheim, Emil, 128
Düsseldorf, 75–76
Dylan, Bob, 336

Earl, Harley, 329
Earls, Waymon and Sharon, 177–79
Easter Uprising, 308
Eastland, James, 358
Eberstadt, Nicholas, 128
economic dynamism, 212–14
economics, 259–60
    morality of, 89–91
Economist, 237

Eddington, Arthur Stanley, 196
Edison, Charles, 368
education, 138–40, 142–44, 163–65
    higher, 35–41, 88, 140–42, 181–83
Education Department, U.S., 354
Einstein, Albert, 362
Eisenhower, Dwight D., 82, 99, 247, 315, 326
Eisner, Michael, 364
elections, 247, 257, 318
    of 1938, 58, 243–45
    of 1964, 58, 172, 243
    of 1966, 243
    of 1968, 70, 243, 318
    of 1972, 172, 243
    of 1976, 243
    of 1978, 340
    of 1980, 243
    of 1982, 87
    of 1984, 243, 244
    of 1988, 243
    of 1992, 173, 243, 255
    of 1994, 22, 172, 173, 243–45, 255, 295
    of 1996, 77, 247–49, 250, 252, 254–56, 341
Elementary and Secondary Education Act, 19, 62
Eliot, T. S., 336
Elkins, Stanley, 356
Elshtain, Jean Bethke, 245
Emerson, Ralph Waldo, 113–14
Emory and Henry College, 77
Encyclopedia of the Holocaust, 251
energy crisis, 69, 347–48
English Football Association, 279
Enola Gay, 42
Entebbe, 299
entitlement, disappointment and, 258–60
Environmental Protection Agency, U.S., 319
Epstein, Joseph, 48
equal protection, 117–19, 181–82, 185, 188, 197
Eric the Red, 17
Erie Canal, 135
ESPN, 365–66
ethnic cleansing, 272, 273
Eton, 306
"extreme fighting," 123–24

Fair Labor Standards Act, 176, 177
families, 29–31, 64–65
family values, consumerism and, 45–47

Farrakhan, Louis, 339
fascism, 279–81
Faulkner, Shannon, 75
FDR Memorial Commission, 313
Federalist, 110
Feingold, Russ, 53
Feinstein, Dianne, 245
"Feminist Jurisprudence: Equal Rights or
    Neo-Paternalism?" (Weiss and
    Young), 34
Ferris, Timothy, 267–68
Finn, Chester, 84–86
First Amendment, 59, 111, 115, 171–75,
    178, 179–81, 229–31, 331
First-Class Temperament, A (Ward), 313
Fish, Stanley, 146
Fitzgerald, Ella, 167
Fitzhugh, William, 80–81
Flexner, James, 356
Fliegel, Seymour, 163–65
Foch, Ferdinand, 273–74
Fogel, Robert, 86–88
Foley, Tom, 244, 246, 257
Food and Drug Administration, 29–31
football, 233–35
Forbes, Steve, 171, 174
Ford, Gerald, speeches of, 253
Ford, Henry, 158, 329
Fourteenth Amendment, 178, 197
"Fourth Great Awakening and the Political
    Realignment of the 1990s, The"
    (Fogel), 86
Francis Boyer Lecture, 100–112
Franco, Francisco, 274, 291–92, 294
Frankenstein (Shelley), 350
Frankfurter, Felix, 106, 122, 313
Freeman, Douglas Southall, 68
Freud, Sigmund, 47, 320
Frey, Darcy, 151–52
Fried, Charles, 20
Friedman, Milton, 81
Friends, 27–29
Frost, Robert, 336

Galbraith, John Kenneth, 331
gambling, 240–42
Garcia, Jerry, 65–66, 76
Garment, Leonard, 227
Garvey, Marcus, 148
GATT, 214
Gay and Lesbian Commission, 75
Gelderman, Carol, 253
General Motors, 326–27, 329, 358
genocide, 251, 275–79, 316–18
George IV, King of England, 77

Georgia, 197, 237
Georgia, Republic of, 294
Germany, 76, 277–79
Gerson, Mark, 165–67
Gettinger, Stephen, 58–59
Gingrich, Newt, 59, 72, 99, 197–98,
    246–47, 249, 250–51, 264, 276
Ginsberg, Allen, 70, 336–37
Ginsburg, Ruth Bader, 182, 188, 197
Giuliani, Rudolph, 96, 164, 200–201, 202
Gladstone, William, 264–65, 305–10
Glendening, Parris, 206–7
Glendon, Mary Ann, 121–22
GLIB, 180–81
Glikes, Erwin A., 343–45
global free trade, 214–16
Golan Heights, 298
Golden Gate Bridge, 99
Goldhagen, Daniel Jonah, 277–79
Goldman, Ron, 75
Goldsmith, James, 214–16
Goldwater, Barry, 57, 58–59, 60, 70–71, 72,
    82–83, 85, 172, 243, 244, 297, 345
Gompers, Samuel, 264
Gone with the Wind (Mitchell), 68, 311
Good Life and Its Discontents, The
    (Samuelson), 259–60
Goodman, Robert, 241
Gordon, John Steele, 216–17, 326, 327
government, 101, 106, 110–11, 121, 219,
    245
    decentralization of, 91–93
    functions of, 18, 19, 21, 96, 114, 225,
        227, 257
    limits of, 18, 107, 110, 112
    moral agenda for, 96–97
    supply-side, 231–33
Gramm, Phil, 127, 250
Gramm-Rudman Law, 217
Grams, Rod, 342
Grapes of Wrath, The (Steinbeck), 68
Grateful Dead, 65–66
Great Awakening, 87
Great Society, 69, 80, 109, 225, 243, 255,
    259
Great Society, The, 61
Griswold v. *Connecticut,* 59
Grover, Francis, 76
Grubin, David, 311
Guevara, Che, 57
Gulf War, 282, 288, 290, 296
Gun-Free School Zones Act, 208

Hackney, Sheldon, 31, 226
Haiti, 73, 284

Halberstam, David, 329
Hamilton, Alexander, 80, 157, 212, 216
Hamilton's Blessing (Gordon), 216–17
Hand, Learned, 185, 187
Harborplace, 161, 235
Harding, Tonya, 73
Harding, Warren G., 311
Harlem, 163–65
Harpers Ferry, W.Va., 113
Hart, Eva, 78
Hart, Jeffrey, 336
Hartford Convention, 95
Harvard University, 75, 114, 241, 314
Hatch, Orrin, 122
Havel, Vaclav, 294
Hawaii, 77, 185, 240, 286
Hawthorne, Nathaniel, 207–8
Hayden, Tom, 335
Haymarket, Va., 363–64
Hays Office, 25
health care, 72, 247, 255, 256
Hemmings, Sally, 304
heroin, 133, 135
Hess, Cynthia (Chesty Love), 73
Hidden Persuaders, The (Packard), 330
Hiroshima, 42
Hispanics, 197, 237
Hiss, Alger, 77, 318, 319, 324–25
History of Warfare, A (Keegan), 285
Hitler, Adolf, 76, 251, 271, 272, 278,
    279–80, 317, 344
Hitler and Stalin (Bullock), 271
Hitler's Willing Executioners (Goldhagen),
    277–79
HIV, 75, 236–37
Hoffman, Dustin, 328
Hollings, Fritz, 340
Holmes, Oliver Wendell, 313
Holocaust, 251–52, 277–79
Holocaust Memorial Museum, 277, 280
homelessness, 117–18
Home Rule in Ireland, 308
homosexuals, 86, 185–89, 236–37
Honduras, 268
Hong Kong, 215
Hoop Dreams, 151
Hoover, Herbert, 98, 311
Hoover Dam, 98–99
Hosansky, David, 232
House of Representatives, U.S., 55, 58
    supermajority of, 219–21
Housing and Urban Development Depart-
    ment, U.S., 62
Houston, Tex., 228
Houston Oilers, 234–35

Howard, Michael, 270, 283
Howard, Philip, 119–20
Howard University, 63–64, 109, 281
"Howl" (Ginsberg), 70, 336
How We Die (Nuland), 236–37
Huffington, Michael, 245
Human Rights Commission, Illinois, 354
Humphrey, Hubert, 342
Hungary, 294
Hurley, John J. "Wacko," 180
Hussein, Saddam, 298, 316, 318
Huxley, T. H., 309

IBM, 213
Idaho, 188, 232
illegitimacy, 64, 126, 128–30, 160–61
Illiniwek, Chief of Oglala Sioux, 353–55
Illinois, University of, 353
illiteracy, 138–40
I'll Take My Stand, 93
Image, The (Boorstin), 23
immigrants, English literacy and, 222–23
immigration, 57, 154–56
imprisonment, 204–5
income, religiosity and, 86–88
India, 283, 297
Indianapolis, Ind., 234
Indianapolis Colts, 234
industrialism, 100–101
Information Age, 93
Intel Corporation, 93
Interstate Commerce Commission, 107
Interstate Highway System, 99, 348
In the Classroom (Gerson), 166
Iraq, 277, 282, 286, 288–89, 290, 296, 298
Ireland, 114, 308
Israel, 76, 282, 297–99
Italy, 75, 279

Jackson, Andrew, 172, 212
Jackson, James, 356
Jackson, Jesse, 198, 342
Jacoby, Jeff, 78
Jacoby, Russell, 38–39
Japan, 42, 156, 205, 212–13, 283
Jefferson, Thomas, 58, 80, 100, 106, 157,
    162–63, 212, 258, 284, 303–5, 355
Jenkins, Holman, Jr., 213
Jenkins, Roy, 305–10
Jersey City, N.J., 165–67
Jerusalem, 298
Jessup, Md., 206–7
Jewell, Richard, 77
Jews, 271, 277–79, 280–81, 298–99, 317,
    354

John Birch Society, 57
John Paul II, Pope, 77
Johnson, Jane, 56
Johnson, Lyndon Baines, 17, 57, 58, 59, 61, 63, 84–85, 243
  Great Society of, 69, 80, 109, 225, 243, 255, 259
  Howard University speech of, 63, 64, 109
Jones, Arnita, 226
Jones, Paula, 73
Joplin, Janis, 67
Jordan, 289, 299
Jordan, Michael, 76, 361–62
Jordan River, 298–99
journalism, 22–23, 344
Jungle, The (Sinclair), 107
Justice Department, U.S., 194, 197–98, 206–7

Kagan, Donald, 270
Kahan, Dan M., 204–5
Kanigel, Robert, 320–23
Kansas, 112, 113
Kansas City, Kan., 189–91
Kansas-Nebraska Act, 112
Kass, Leon, 362
Keegan, John, 285
Kefauver Committee, 241
Kelly, John F., 44
Kemp, Jack, 171
Kempthorne, Dirk, 232
Kempton, Murray, 252
Kennedy, Anthony M., 182, 188, 197
Kennedy, Edward, 341
Kennedy, John F., 82, 127, 257, 312
  assassination of, 68–69
  poverty and, 61, 259
Kennedy, John F., Jr., 77
Kennedy, Rose, 76
Kerouac, Jack, 336–37
Kerrey, Bob, 252
Keynes, John Maynard, 62, 90
Khmer Rouge, 278
King, Martin Luther, Jr., 37, 148, 340
King, Rodney, 73
Kissinger, Henry, 269, 294, 319
Kleiman, Mark, 137–38
Kluger, Richard, 239–40
Korean War, 289–90, 296, 315
Kozyrev, Andrei, 294
Kristol, Irving, 57, 65
KTOZ-AM, 175–77
Kunis, Richard, 96
Kurds, 277, 316, 318

Kuwait, 282, 288, 296, 298
Kyl, Jon, 219

labor, organized, 262–64
Labor Department, U.S., 176–77
Lafayette Park, 118
La Guardia, Fiorello, 163
Laird, Mel, 59
Land of Opportunity (Adler), 131–32
Lands' End, 46
Lanier, Bob, 235
Largent, Steve, 179
Last Shot, The (Frey), 151–52
Las Vegas, Nev., 98
Lautenberg, Frank, 53
law, proliferation of, 119–20
Laws of Our Fathers, The (Turow), 169
lawyers, 121–22
Layard, Richard, 293
Leatherman, Courtney, 40
Lebed, Alexander, 292–93
Lee, Robert E., 364
Leeson, Nicholas, 76
Lee Teng-hui, 295–96
Lefkowitz, Mary, 146–48
left, in 1930s vs. 1960s, 71
Legal Services Corporation (LSC), 60
Lenin, V. I., 316–18, 322
Leo, John, 55
Letters from an American Farmer (Crevecoeur), 135
Leuchtenburg, William E., 209
Lewis, C. S., 362
Lewis, John L., 263
Lewis, Sinclair, 90
Leyba, Ramon, 115–16
liberalism, 18, 37, 58, 125, 175, 269, 307, 326, 327, 328
  campaign finance reform and, 174–75, 331
  Croly and, 85
  and function of government, 21
  intellectual aspects of, 19, 82
  legislation vs. litigation by, 60
  New York City as capital of, 95–97
  of Nixon administration, 319
  race and, 199–200
  tradition of, 80, 81, 109
  of Wellstone, 341–43
Liberia, 277
Life, 336
Liggett Group Inc., 240
Lincoln, Abraham, 64, 75, 81, 112, 311
Lincoln High School, 151–52
Lincoln Memorial, 349

Lindsay, John, 63
Lingua Franca, 145
Linn, Thomas, 291
Lippmann, Walter, 81, 322
Liuzzo, Viola, 63
London, 135–36
London School of Economics, 315
London Times Literary Supplement, 78
Lonely Crowd, The (Riesman), 330
Lopez, Alfonso, 208–10
Los Angeles, Calif., 73, 75, 98, 126, 128, 201, 236
Los Angeles County, Calif., 223
Los Angeles Times, 43, 120
Louisiana Purchase, 89, 304
Loury, Glenn, 165
Love Letters to Adolf Hitler, 75–76
Lowell, A. Lawrence, 114
Lowell, Mass., 89
Lytle, Andrew, 93, 95

Maastricht Treaty, 272
Macaulay, Thomas, 124
McCain, John, 123–24, 228
McCloy, John J., 276
Mac Donald, Heather, 138–40
McDonald's, 328–29
McDougall, Walter A., 315
McGinnis, John, 219
McGovern, George, 172
Machiavelli, Niccolì, 284
Mack, Connie, 265
McKinley, William, 20, 311
McKitrick, Eric, 356
McNamara, Robert, 57
Madison, James, 105–6, 264, 355
Madrid, 273–75
Mailer, Norman, 70
majority rule, principle of, 220
"Making Babies" (Kass), 362
Malaysia, 73, 283
Manhattan Center for Science and Math, 163
Manhattan Institute, 125, 130
Manhattan Project, 99
Man in the Grey Flannel Suit, The, 330
Mansa Musa, 226
Mantle, Mickey, 76
Marines, 289–91
Markham, Beryl, 249
Marrow, Joanne, 35–36
Marshall, George Catlett, 314–16
Marshall, John, 80, 105, 106
Marshall Plan, 315–16
Martin Luther King Memorial Lecture, 146

Marx, Karl, 214–15, 320, 323
Marxism, 18, 280
Maryland, 206, 233–35
Massachusetts, 241
Mather, Cotton, 229
Mead, Lake, 98
Meat Inspection Act, 107
"Medicalizing Character" (Zuriff), 183
Medicare, 19, 62, 74
Meese, Ed, 178
Meet Me in St. Louis, 32
Mein Kampf (Hitler), 317
Meir, Golda, 299
Memphis, Tenn., 158
Mencken, H. L., 367
Menendez brothers, 73, 149–50
meteors, 267
methamphetamine, 134–35
Mexican-Americans, 126
Mexico, 137, 205, 250, 298
Miami, Fla., 155, 157
Michelangelo, 77
Michelman, Kate, 55
military power, commerce vs., 284–85
Milky Way, 77
Miller, George, 75
Million Man March, 75
Milwaukee, Wis., 234
Milwaukee Brewers, 234
Minnesota, 141, 342
Mirabeau, Comte de, 255
Mississippi, 75, 192, 196
Mississippi University for Women, 181
Missouri, 190
Mitchell, George, 246, 257
Mitchell, Margaret, 68
Mockler, Bill, 132–34
Modell, Art, 233–35
Modern Language Association, 139
Modern Times, 322–23
Mondale, Walter, 109, 342
Montana, 232
Montgomery, Ala., 63, 196
morality of politics and economics, 89–91
Moral Judgment (Wilson), 149
Morgan, J. P., Jr., 113–14
Morris, James, 25–26
Mother Jones, 55
"motor voter" law, 224
Mott, Lucretia, 351
Mount McKinley, 349
Mount Vernon Ladies Association, 43
Moynihan, Daniel Patrick, 18, 20, 61–62, 64–65, 127–29, 135, 163, 247, 252, 255, 271–72, 274, 275, 319

Muhammad, Khalid, 280–81
multiculturalism, 138–42, 143, 192–93, 280, 354
Munich Pact, 294
Muslims, 272, 275, 279, 316
Mussolini, Alessandra, 279, 322
Mussolini, Benito, 272, 280, 322
My Mother the Car, 358

Napoleon I, Emperor of France, 22, 290
Nashville, Tenn., 234–35
National Airport, 227–29
National Association for the Advancement of Colored People (NAACP), 198–99
National Conference of Teachers of English, 139
national debt, 216–17
National Endowment for the Arts, 43, 61, 74, 225–27
National Endowment for the Humanities, 31–33, 61, 225–27
National Interest, 299
National Journal, 231, 232
National Organization for Women, 164
National Review, 305–10, 332–35
National Sheep Industry Improvement Center, 231–33
National Wool Act, 231
Nation of Islam, 338
Nation Under Lawyers, A (Glendon), 121–22
Native Americans, 194–95, 353–55
Navajo county, Ariz., 194–95
naval warfare, 287–89
Nazis, 251, 281
NBC, 27–29
Nebraska, 100
"Negro Family, The" (Moynihan), 62, 64–65
Nelson, Horatio, 293
Netanyahu, Benjamin, 297–99
Netanyahu, Jonathan, 299
Neville, John, 356
Newcomb, Simon, 286
New Deal, 18–20, 22, 101, 108, 201, 208, 209, 255, 313
New Hampshire, 204, 241
Newman, John Henry, 306, 307
New Promise of American Life, The (Alexander and Finn, eds.), 84–86
New Republic, 56, 67, 183, 186, 199, 226, 251–52, 254, 274, 276–77, 322
Newsweek, 46, 72, 259
Newton, Huey, 332–35
New York, 75, 217

New York, N.Y., 95–97, 119–20, 128, 158, 159, 200–202, 236, 223, 261
New York Civil Liberties Union, 164
New Yorker, 267–68
New York Review of Books, The, 114
New York State Education Department, 37
New York Times, 47–48, 51–52, 57, 65–66, 72, 77, 210–11, 227, 320–23, 328–29, 337
New York Yankees, 78
NFL, 233–35
Nicholas II, Tsar of Russia, 317
1950s, 69
1960s, 65–71
1965, events of, 56–65
1980s, as decade of greed, 265
1990s, events of, 72–78, 243–45
Nineteenth Amendment, 352
Nixon, Alice, 320
Nixon, Julie, 319
Nixon, Richard M., 58, 73, 296, 318
  presidential elections of, 243
  resentment and tenacity of, 318–20
Nock, Albert Jay, 80
North, Oliver, 172
North American Free Trade Agreement (NAFTA), 264
North Atlantic Treaty Organization (NATO), 272–73, 274, 276, 282, 293–95
North Carolina, 75, 196
North Dakota, 225
Northern Ireland, 73
North Korea, 73, 282, 283, 284–85, 286, 296
Northwestern Wildcats, 76
Not Out of Africa (Lefkowitz), 147
nuclear proliferation, 281–83, 285
Nuland, Sherwin, 236–37

Oakland, Calif., 234, 333
Oakland Raiders, 234
Oates, Joyce Carol, 304
O'Brien, Conor Cruise, 303–4
Occupational Safety and Health Administration, 119, 319
O'Connor, Sandra Day, 182, 188, 196, 197
Oglala Sioux, 353
O'Grady, Scott, 27, 276
Oklahoma, 75, 188
Oklahoma City, Okla., 76, 113–15
Onassis, Jacqueline Kennedy, 73
One Best Way, The (Kanigel), 320–23
One By One from the Inside Out (Loury), 165

110 Rules of Civility and Decent Behavior in Company and Conversation, 26
O'Neill, Thomas P. "Tip," 72
On the Origins of War (Kagan), 270
On the Road (Kerouac), 330, 337, 359
Ordinary Men (Browning), 278
Oregon, 223–24
Organization Man, The (Whyte), 330
organized labor, 262–64
Orlando, Fla., 234
Orwin, Clifford, 192–93, 299–301
O'Shea, Katherine Page, 308
Ottoman Empire, 272
Ottoman Turks, 280
Owen, Kelly, 43
Owens, Major, 75
Oxford University, 306
Oxus River, 285

Packard, Vance, 330–31
Pakistan, 296
Palestine Mandate, 299
Palestinians, 298
Panama Canal, 258
Panetta, Leon, 42
Paris, 157
Parke-Davis, 135
Parker, John, 293
Parnell, Charles, 308
partial-birth abortions, 54–56
    ban on, 52–53
Pataki, George, 201
Patek Philippe, 45–46
Patrick, Deval, 194, 222
Patton, George, 315
Pearson, Hugh, 332–35
Peel, Robert, 308
Penn State, 76
Pennsylvania, 355–57
Pennsylvania, University of, 37, 140
Percy, Walker, 50, 81, 144
perimeter rule, 227–29
Perjury (Weinstein), 324–25
Perot, Ross, 171, 256
Pershing, John Joseph, 314
Philadelphia, Pa., 128, 235, 337–39
Philadelphia Athletics, 337–38
Philadelphia Eagles, 235
Philadelphia Phillies, 337–38
Phillips, Kim, 241
Phoenix, Ariz., 115–17, 234, 235
Phoenix Cardinals, 234–35
Phoenix Preparatory Academy, 115–16
Piggly Wiggly, 158
Pinochet Ugarte, Augusto, 291–92

Pipes, Richard, 294, 317
Pittsburgh, Pa., 98, 235
Pittsburgh *Gazette,* 356
Pittsburgh Steelers, 235
Planned Parenthood League, 59
Plato, 147
Plumb, J. H., 240
Poland, 278, 294
political correctness, 37–41
politics, 31, 37, 64, 199
    limits of, 18–19
    morality of, 89–91
polygamy, 188
pornography, 35, 95–97, 174–75
Porter, John, 222
Portes, Alejandro, 155
Postal Service, U.S., 78
Pottawatomie, Kans., 113
poverty, 125–26, 129–30, 162, 259
Powell, Colin, 75
Prague, 294–95
Pressler, Margaret Webb, 46
prison policy, 206–7
"Professionalization of Reform, The" (Moynihan), 61
Progressive movement, 84–85
progressivism, 322
Prohibition, 230, 332, 334
Promise of American Life, The (Croly), 84–86
Proposition 13, 244
protectionism, 86, 90
Public Interest, 56–65, 100–112, 138, 155, 183, 192, 342
Public Papers of the Presidents of the United States, 253
Public Philosophy, The (Lippmann), 81
public toilets, 119–20
Puritans, 241

Quantico Marine Corps Base, 289
Quayle, J. Danforth, 171
Quincy, Mass., 100

Rabin, Yitzhak, 76
racial gerrymandering, 194–95, 196, 198–99
racial minorities, 236–37
Racine, Wis., 51–54
railroads, 100
Ramos, Dante, 226
Ramparts, 335
Rand, Ayn, 81
RAND Corporation, 133
Randolph, John, 304

rape, 34, 272, 275
Rappaport, Michael, 219
Rauch, Jonathan, 186–87, 231
Rayburn, Sam, 59
Reagan, Ronald, 46, 60, 83, 246, 249, 250, 253, 256
    in 1964 election, 243, 245
    in 1984 election, 244
    tax code indexing of, 62
    tax cuts and reforms of, 217
Reassessing The Sixties, 67–71
Reeb, James, 63
Reese, Jimmie, 74
Reeves, Richard, 312
Rehnquist, William H., 180–81, 182, 188, 197, 208–9
R. E. Lee (Freeman), 68
religion, conservatism and, 86–88
religious freedoms, 75
rent seeking, 227–29
representation, 110–11
reproductive freedom, 52–54
Republican Party, U.S., 243, 244, 282
    abortion and, 55–56
    budget and, 74–75, 252–54
    campaign funding of, 172
    on federal functions, 225, 227
    intellectual pedigree of, 112
    John Birch Society and, 57
    in Johnson-era Congress, 58
    on mail voting, 224
    regulatory state and, 122
    Southern, 58
    Voting Rights Act and, 197
"Rethinking Columbus," 140
revolution, 17–18
Rhode Island, 229–31
Rhode Island Liquor Stores Association, 231
Ribbentrop, Joachim von, 271
Richmond, Va., 358
Ridgway, Matthew B., 315
rights, parental childrearing, 178–79
Ringle, Ken, 42
Ripken, Cal, 76
River Runs Through It, A, 47
Rivers, Eugene F., 3rd, 167–69, 338–39
Robespierre, Maximilien de, 255, 317
rock and roll, 69
Rock Around the Clock, 336
Rockefeller, Nelson, 70
Rocky Mountain News, 75
Rodman, Dennis, 25, 27
Rodman, Peter, 294–95
Roe v. *Wade*, 50, 55, 60

Rogers, Craig, 35–36
Rogers, Ginger, 76
Roll Call, 246–47, 265
Rolling Stones, 57
Rome, 284–85
Roosevelt, Alice, 311, 320
Roosevelt, Eleanor, 312
Roosevelt, Franklin D., 20, 84–85, 108, 110, 286, 311, 312–14
    1938 congressional elections and, 58, 244
    see also New Deal
Roosevelt, Theodore, 20, 81, 172, 258, 273, 274, 320
    "new nationalism" of, 84
    transformation of presidency by, 310–12
Root, Elihu, 121
Rosen, Jeffrey, 183, 199
Rosenberg, Philip, 236–37
Rossiter, Clinton, 79–84
Rothschild, Michael, 92–93
Rouse, Jim, 161–62
Rousseau, Jean Jacques, 301
Russell, Cheryl, 46
Russia, 273, 279, 283, 286, 291–95
Russian Revolution, 317
Russians, 287
Rustin, Bayard, 152
Ruth, Babe, 74
Rwanda, 73, 78, 277
Rybczynski, Witold, 157–59

Sacramento, Calif., 35
Saigon, fall of, 80
St. Anselm's College, 139
St. Louis, Mo., 234
St. Louis Rams, 234
St. Luke High School, 165–67
St. Patrick's Day parade, Boston, 179
Salk, Jonas, 76
same-sex marriages, 185–87
Sampras, Pete, 350
Samuelson, Robert, 259–60
San Bernardino Valley College, 36–37
Sandburg, Carl, 311
Sandel, Michael, 89–91
San Diego County, 134
Sandifer, Robert, 73
Sandtown-Winchester, 161–63
San Francisco, Calif., 65–66, 236
San Juan Hill, 310
Santa Ana, Calif., 117–19
Santorum, Rick, 53, 265, 340
San Ysidro, Calif., 136–38

Sarajevo, 272, 274, 275, 282
Saudi Arabia, 282
Savio, Mario, 335
Scalia, Antonin, 182, 188–89, 197
Schindler's List, 73
Schlesinger, Arthur, 144, 342
Schlesinger, James, 319
Schmitt, Gary, 284
school uniforms, 115–17
Science, 236
Seale, Bobby, 335
Sea Power, 283
Seattle, Wash., 234
Seattle Mariners, 234
Seattle Pilots, 234
secessionism, 86
secret ballots, 224–25
Selma, Ala., 63, 196
Senate, U.S., 58, 228
    Judiciary Committee of, 122
    partial–birth abortion ban in, 53, 55
    welfare bill in, 252–53
separation of powers, 219
Serbia, 272–73, 274–77, 280, 295
Serbs, 273, 279, 280, 282
Service Employees International Union, 263
Seventeen, 47
sex, sexuality, 27–29, 47–48, 69, 237–38
sexual harassment, 34, 35–37
Shakur, Tupac, 78
Shane, 32
Shapiro, Martin, 175
Shelley, Mary, 350
Shelley, Percy Bysshe, 22
Sherwood, Robert E., 311
"Should Immigrants Assimilate?" (Portes & Min Zhou), 155
Shriver, Sargent, 17
Shultz, George, 319
Silber, John, 221–23
Simpson, Nicole, 75
Simpson, O. J., 73, 75, 149–50, 199–200
Sinatra, Frank, 57
Sinclair, Upton, 107
Singapore, 76, 215, 292
single-sex education, 164, 181–83
Sistine Chapel, 77, 349
60 Minutes, 130
Skaggs, David, 219–21
slavery, 80, 87, 112, 281, 304
Sloan, Alfred P., 327
"Slow Pearl Harbors and the Pleasures of Self-Deception" (Wohlstetter), 287
Smith, Adam, 323

Smith, Ben, 337–39
Smith, Bradley A., 172–75
Smith College, 347, 349
Smith-Corona, 76
Smithsonian Institution, 41–43, 141
smoking, 237–40
Social Gospel movement, 87
socialism, 291–92, 294
Social Security, 238–39
Social Text, 144–46
Sokal, Alan, 144–46
Sound of Music, The, 57
Souter, David H., 179, 182, 188, 197
South Africa, 73
South Carolina, 339–41
South Carolina, University of, 365
South China Sea, 283, 296
Southeastern Legal Foundation, 177–78
Southern California, 98
Southern League, 94–95
Southern Patriot, 95
South Korea, 215, 296
Soviet Union, 95, 282, 286–87, 316, 319, 324–25
Spain, 156, 279, 292, 294
Spanish Civil War, 274
Spartanburg, S.C., 339–41
Specter, Arlen, 56
speech, freedom of, 97, 148, 175
Speed, Joshua Fry, 75
speed limit, national, 347–48
Spokane, Wash., 244
Springfield, Mass., 357
Springfield, Mo., 176–77
Srebrenica, 76, 277, 316
Sri Lanka, 277
Stahl, Lesley, 130
Stalin, Joseph, 271, 289, 316
Stalinism, 274
Stanton, Elizabeth Cady, 351
states' rights, 80
Status Seekers, The (Packard), 330
Steinbeck, John, 68
Stevens, John Paul, 182, 188, 197, 230
Stevenson, Adlai, 83, 326, 347, 360
Stilwell, Joseph, 315
Stone, Oliver, 114
Strawson, Galen, 78
"street," "decent" vs., 152–54
"suburban comparability," 190–91
Sullivan, Andrew, 187
Sunday Telegraph (London), 359
Supreme Court, Calif., 117–18
Supreme Court, Colo., 188

Supreme Court, U.S., 91–92, 106–7,
181–83, 187–91
abortion and, 49–50, 187, 255
Brown v. *Board of Education* decision
of, 189–91
campaign finance and, 172–73
and congressional regulation of commerce, 208–10, 219
congressional rulemaking and, 220–21
in FDR administration, 58, 208–9, 244
First Amendment and, 59, 172–74, 178,
179–81, 229–31
Griswold v. *Connecticut* decision of, 59
on liquor price advertising, 229–31
on parental child–rearing rights, 178–79
Roe v. *Wade* decision of, 49–50, 52, 60
on sexual harassment, 34
"suburban comparability" and, 190–91
on Voting Rights Act, 197–98
surplus revenues, 62
Sweeney, John Joseph, 262–64
Syria, 298

Taft, Robert, 81, 85
Taft, William Howard, 85, 103
Taiwan, 215, 283, 292, 295–97
Taiwan Relations Act, 296
Talbott, Strobe, 298
Tampa Bay Buccaneers, 234
Tarbell, Ida, 322
Tariff of Abominations, 86
taxation, 87–88, 355–57
supermajority required for, 218–19, 221
Taylor, Frederick Winslow, 320–23
teenagers, 47–48, 115–16
television, 27–29, 299–301
television journalism, 23
temperance movement, 87
Tenner, Edward, 350
Tennyson, Alfred, Lord, 309, 330
Tenth Amendment, 91–92
Texas, 192, 208
Texas, University of, 192
Thatcher, Margaret, 256
thin gruel, 21, 89, 301
Thirteenth Amendment, 75
Thomas, Clarence, 129, 130, 182, 188,
190–91, 197, 209, 230, 329
Thomas, Dylan, 336
Thomas, Lewis, 351
Thomas, Russell, 151–52
Thompson, Loren, 283
Thompson, Tommy, 130
Thurmond, Strom, 339–41
Titanic, 78, 350

tobacco companies, 238–40
Toccoa, Ga., 177–79
Tocqueville, Alexis de, 21, 103, 105, 158,
323
Tomlin, Lily, 23
Topeka, Kan., 189–91
totalitarianism, 316
Tran, Kim, 38
Treblinka, 251–52
Trilling, Lionel, 19
Truman, Harry S., 62, 135, 289–91
Tufts University, 37–39
Turow, Scott, 169
Twenty-first Amendment, 230

Ukrainians, 278
unemployment, 17, 57
Union Pacific, 100
United Automobile Workers, 326
United Auto Workers, 263
United Kingdom, 287
United Nations, 271–72, 282, 297, 318
arms embargo of, 272, 275
United Steelworkers, 263
Unknown Lenin, The (Pipes, ed.), 316
UNProFor, 271, 273
U.S. News & World Report, 55
Utah, 188, 240

Valley Forge, Pa., 241
Van Buren, Martin, 172
Van Riper, Paul K., 290
Vatican City, 77
Venice, 284–85
Vienna, Congress of, 269
Viereck, Peter, 82
Vietnam War, 57, 61, 69, 80, 217
Virginia Military Institute (VMI), 181–83,
314
Virginia Quarterly Review, 311
Virtually Normal (Sullivan), 187
volunteerism, 176–77
Von Nester, Wolfgang and Lisa, 65–66
voting, 63, 223–25
Voting Rights Act, 63, 194–95, 196–98,
222

Waitt, Don, 44
Waldheim, Kurt, 251
Walker, Lenore, 33
Wallace, George, 70–71
Wan, Carol, 38
Ward, Geoffrey, 311, 313
war on poverty, 17, 61
Warren, Earl, 59

Warren Court, 59–60
Warsaw, 294–95
Washington, D.C., 157, 235, 241
Washington, George, 26, 140, 241, 304, 356
Washington Post, 42, 44, 46, 51, 65, 78, 257, 258, 267, 296
Washington Redskins, 235
Waste Makers, The (Packard), 330
Watergate, 80, 243, 318–19
Watts, J. C., 198
Watts riots, 63, 80
wealth, distribution of, 210–12, 259–60, 342
Webster, Daniel, 107
Weicher, John C., 342
Weinstein, Allen, 324–25
Weisberg, Jacob, 251–52
Weiss, Michael, 34
welfare, 252–53, 255
    children and, 124–30
    reform of, 127–29, 246, 342
Well Baby Book, The, 56
Wellesley College, 146
Wellington, Duke of, 247
Wells, H. G., 334
Wellstone, Paul, 254, 341–43
Wesley, John, 136
West Bank, 298–99
West Side Story (Bernstein), 69
"What Do Alternative Sanctions Mean?" (Kahan), 204–5
When the Going Was Good! (Hart), 336
Whiskey Rebellion, 115, 355
White, Michael, 160–61
White, William Allen, 20
"White Negro, The" (Mailer), 70
Whitney, Eli, 140
"Why Johnny Can't Read" (Mac Donald), 138
Why Things Bite Back (Tenner), 350
Wickard v. *Filburn*, 91
Will, David Maseng, 366–68
Will, Mari, 365–66, 367
Will, Victoria, 29
Williams, Damian, 150
Williams, Roger, 352
Wilson, Charles E. "Engine Charlie," 325–28

Wilson, Clyde, 94
Wilson, James Q., 18–19, 32–33, 109, 125–27, 133, 149–50
Wilson, Pete, 56, 130
Wilson, Woodrow, 57, 84–85, 100–102, 106, 271
Wilson Quarterly, 25, 253
Wimbledon, 349–50
Windows 95, 76
Windsor family, 73
Winesburg, Ohio (Anderson), 157
Winslow, Ariz., 268
Wisconsin, 129
Wisconsin, University of, 114
With My Trousers Rolled (Epstein), 48
WJMP, 74
Wohlstetter, Albert, 286
Wohlstetter, Roberta, 286–87
Wolf, Naomi, 56
Wolfe, Tom, 153
women, 236–37
    battered, 33–35
    education of, 181–83
World War II, 259
Wright, Jim, 228

Yad Vashem memorial, 251
Yale Alumni News, 135
Yale Law Journal, 172
Yale University Press, 316
Yamada, Louise, 261–62
Yeats, William Butler, 114
Yeltsin, Boris, 274, 291–92, 294
YM, 47–48
Yom Kippur War, 68, 347
Young, Cathy, 34
Young Women's Leadership School, 164–65
Yucatán, 268
Yugoslavia, 95, 272, 318

Zhirinovsky, Vladimir, 279
Zhou, Min, 155
Zimmerman, Deborah, 51–54
Zinsmeister, Karl, 118
Zuniga, Krystal, 51–52
Zuriff, G. E., 183–85
Zyuganov, Gennady, 291

PERMISSIONS

Most of the selections in this book were previously published as Mr. Will's columns in the *Washington Post* and *Newsweek,* respectively. The works which appeared in the *Washington Post* are reprinted by permission. Copyright © The Washington Post Company, 1994, 1995, 1996, 1997.

"An Epithet No More" is reprinted by permission of the publisher from *Conservatism in America* by Clinton Rossiter, Cambridge, Mass.: Harvard University Press, Copyright © 1982 by the Presidents and Fellows of Harvard College.

"Eventful 1965" (as "Looking Back to 1965") and "The Cultural Contradictions of Conservatism" first appeared in *The Public Interest.* "Eventful 1965" is reprinted with permission of *The Public Interest,* number 121, fall 1995, pp. 3–15. Copyright © 1995 by National Affairs, Inc. "The Cultural Contradictions of Conservatism" is reprinted with permission of *The Public Interest,* number 123, spring 1996, pp. 40–57. Copyright © 1996 by National Affairs, Inc.

"Our Towns" and "Frederick Taylor: Busy, Busy, Busy" (as "A Faster Mousetrap") are reprinted from *The New York Times Book Review.* Copyright © 1995, 1997 by The New York Times Company. Reprinted by permission.

"The Passionate Life of William Gladstone" (as "Gladstone, Bagged") and "Al Capone and Huey Newton: Two Styles of Upward—For a While—Mobility" (as "Styles of Criminality") are reprinted from *National Review.* Copyright © 1994, 1997 by National Review, Inc. Reprinted by permission.

Grateful acknowledgment is made for permission to reprint excerpts from the following works:

Excerpts from the *DSM-IV* are reprinted with permission from the Diagnostic and Statistical Manual of Mental Disorders, Fourth Edition. Copyright © 1994 American Psychiatric Association.

"Summertime" by George Gershwin, DuBose & Dorothy Heyward, and Ira Gershwin. Copyright © 1935 (Renewed 1962) George Gershwin Music, Ira Gershwin Music and DuBose and Dorothy Heyward Memorial Fund. All Rights administered by WB Music Corp. All Rights Reserved. Used by permission. Warner Bros. Publications U.S. Inc., Miami, FL., 33014

The first four lines of "Howl" from *Collected Poems 1947-1980* by Allen Ginsberg. Copyright © 1955 by Allen Ginsberg. Reprinted by permission of HarperCollins Publishers, Inc.

"Can't Help Lovin' Dat Man" written by Jerome Kern and Oscar Hammerstein II. Copyright © 1927 PolyGram International Publishing, Inc. (Copyright Renewed) Used by permission. All Rights Reserved.

The new "Generations" press campaign was created for Patek Philippe by the London Advertising Agency, Leagas Delaney.

Louis MacNeice; two lines taken from "Valediction" as it appears in *The Collected Poems of Louis MacNeice,* published by Faber and Faber. Reprinted with permission of David Higham Associates Limited.

Excerpt from *The Bonfire of the Vanities* by Tom Wolfe. Copyright © 1987 by Tom Wolfe. Reprinted by permission of Farrar, Straus, & Giroux, Inc.

Collected Works of W. B. Yeats, Volume 1: The Poems, and edited by Richard J. Finneran. Copyright © 1940 by Georgie Yeats; copyright renewed 1968 by Bertha Georgie Yeats, Michael Butler Yeats and Anne Yeats. Reprinted with the permission of Simon & Schuster.

"Happy Days are Here Again!" by Jack Yellen and Milton Ager. Copyright © 1929 (Renewed) Warner Bros. Inc. All Rights Reserved. Used by permission. Warner Bros. Publications U.S. Inc., Miami, FL., 33014

Leon Degrelle photo used on page 281 used with permission of AP/Wide World Photos.